Education Reform and the Concept of Good Teaching

In an effort to address the problems confronting the American education system, the Obama administration has proposed structural and systematic reforms under the heading of *Race to the Top*. These initiatives introduce new statistics and accountability systems to gauge what constitutes "good" teaching, both from an administrative standpoint and the perspective of teacher training programs. This volume offers a direct critique of this approach, concluding that it does not respond adequately to the issues of education reform but rather raises new problems and actively stymies progress.

The author argues that at the heart of the confusion lies a misguided and rationalistic view of teaching and learning. He draws on the philosophical strategies of Ludwig Wittgenstein to break down the guiding assumptions of *Race to the Top*, allowing both the positive and the negative aspects of the policies to be heard. The author then proposes a different view of teaching and learning which considers how to effectively address the problems *Race to the Top* seeks to confront.

Derek Gottlieb is a research fellow at the University of Basel in Switzerland. He holds PhDs in English Literature and in Education. He has published on teacher training and educational evaluation; his next book will explore philosophical skepticism and the nature of exemplarity in the context of Shakespearean comedy.

Routledge International Studies in the Philosophy of Education

1 **Education and Work in Great Britain, Germany and Italy**
   Edited by Annette Jobert, Catherine Marry, Helen Rainbird and Lucie Tanguy

2 **Education, Autonomy and Democratic Citizenship**
   Philosophy in a Changing World
   Edited by David Bridges

3 **The Philosophy of Human Learning**
   Christopher Winch

4 **Education, Knowledge and Truth**
   Beyond the Postmodern Impasse
   Edited by David Carr

5 **Virtue Ethics and Moral Education**
   Edited by David Carr and Jan Steutel

6 **Durkheim and Modern Education**
   Edited by Geoffrey Walford and W. S. F. Pickering

7 **The Aims of Education**
   Edited by Roger Marples

8 **Education in Morality**
   J. Mark Halstead and Terence H. McLaughlin

9 **Lyotard**
   Just Education
   Edited by Pradeep A. Dhillon and Paul Standish

10 **Derrida & Education**
   Edited by Gert J. J. Biesta and Denise Egéa-Kuehne

11 **Education, Work and Social Capital**
   Towards a New Conception of Vocational Education
   Christopher Winch

12 **Philosophical Discussion in Moral Education**
   The Community of Ethical Inquiry
   Tim Sprod

13 **Methods in the Philosophy of Education**
   Frieda Heyting, Dieter Lenzen and John White

14 **Life, Work and Learning**
   Practice in Postmoderniity
   David Beckett and Paul Hager

15 **Education, Autonomy and Critical Thinking**
   Christopher Winch

16 **Anarchism and Education**
   A Philosophical Perspective
   Judith Suissa

17 **Cultural Diversity, Liberal Pluralism and Schools**
Isaiah Berlin and Education
Neil Burtonwood

18 **Levinas and Education**
At the Intersection of Faith and Reason
Edited by Denise Egéa-Kuehne

19 **Moral Responsibility, Authenticity, and Education**
Ishtiyaque Haji and Stefaan E. Cuypers

20 **Education, Science and Truth**
Rasoul Nejadmehr

21 **Philosophy of Education in the Era of Globalization**
Edited by Yvonne Raley and Gerhard Preyer

22 **Habermas, Critical Theory and Education**
Edited by Mark Murphy and Ted Fleming

23 **The New Significance of Learning**
Imagination's Heartwork
Pádraig Hogan

24 **Beauty and Education**
Joe Winston

25 **Education, Professionalization and Social Representations**
On the Transformation of Social Knowledge
Edited by Mohamed Chaib, Berth Danermark and Staffan Selander

26 **Education, Professionalism and the Quest for Accountability**
Hitting the Target but Missing the Point
Jane Green

27 **Geometry as Objective Science in Elementary School Classrooms**
Mathematics in the Flesh
Wolff-Michael Roth

28 **The Global Reception of John Dewey's Thought**
Multiple Refractions Through Time and Space
Edited by Rosa Bruno-Jofré and Jürgen Schriewer

29 **Social Reconstruction Learning**
Dualism, Dewey and Philosophy in Schools
Jennifer Bleazby

30 **Higher Education in Liquid Modernity**
Marvin Oxenham

31 **Education and the Common Good**
Essays in Honor of Robin Barrow
Edited by John Gingell

32 **Systems of Reason and the Politics of Schooling**
School Reform and Sciences of Education in the Tradition of Thomas S. Popkewitz
Edited by Miguel A. Pereyra and Barry M. Franklin

33 **Education, Justice and the Human Good**
Fairness and Equality in the Education System
Kirsten Meyer

34 **Education Reform and the Concept of Good Teaching**
Derek Gottlieb

Education Reform and the Concept of Good Teaching

Derek Gottlieb

LONDON AND NEW YORK

First published 2015 by Routledge

2 Park Square, Milton Park, Abingdon, Oxon OX14 4RN
711 Third Avenue, New York, NY 10017, USA

First issued in paperback 2016

Routledge is an imprint of the Taylor & Francis Group, an informa business

Copyright © 2015 Taylor & Francis

The right of Derek Gottlieb to be identified as author of this work has been asserted by him in accordance with sections 77 and 78 of the Copyright, Designs and Patents Act 1988.

All rights reserved. No part of this book may be reprinted or reproduced or utilised in any form or by any electronic, mechanical, or other means, now known or hereafter invented, including photocopying and recording, or in any information storage or retrieval system, without permission in writing from the publishers.

Product or corporate names may be trademarks or registered trademarks, and are used only for identification and explanation without intent to infringe.

Library of Congress Cataloging-in-Publication Data
Gottlieb, Derek.
  Education reform and the concept of good teaching / Derek Gottlieb.
    pages cm — (Routledge international studies in the philosophy of education ; 34)
  Includes bibliographical references and index.
  1. Effective teaching—United States. 2. Teacher effectiveness—United States. 3. Educational change—United States. 4. Educational accountability—United States. I. Title.
  LB1025.3.G686 2014
  371.102—dc23
  2014009452

  ISBN-13: 978-1-138-77624-1 (hbk)
  ISBN-13: 978-1-138-65783-0 (pbk)

Typeset in Sabon
by IBT Global.

To, for, and in the names of my many teachers

Contents

	Introduction	xi
1	Duncan's Speeches on Race to the Top and the Assumptions of the Reform Movement	1
2	Teacher Knowledge, Teacher Practice	58
3	Best Practices and Artificial Intelligence	84
4	Teacher Practices and Accounts of Rule-Following	100
5	A Phenomenological Account of Skill Development	125
6	Achievement Data and Matters of Inference in Teacher Evaluation	142
7	The Non-Formalizable and Teacher Evaluation	175
8	Schwab's Deliberation and the Responsiblities of Teacher Evaluation	196
	Conclusion: Courage, Conviction, Evaluation	220
	Index	229

Introduction

In the early part of 2012, a number of media and governmental outlets trumpeted a new round of reform-minded educational initiatives in the American landscape. On January 24th, President Obama heralded the importance of good teachers to a classroom's future economic prospects in the State of the Union address. On February 16th, Secretary of Education Arne Duncan appeared on *The Daily Show* to promote the RESPECT initiative that his department had introduced earlier the same day. In two separate columns, both appearing prior to the State of the Union address, *New York Times* columnist Nicholas Kristof took up the ongoing discussion of education reform in the same terms, even gesturing to the same stakes, as both Obama and Duncan (Kristof, 2012a, 2012b). In these columns, Kristof succinctly sketches the outline of the discussion, cites new research in the field (Chetty, Friedman, & Rockoff, 2011), and implores his readers to recognize the importance of good teaching. But what exactly *counts as* good teaching, as these various figures use the term? Combing through their tropes and studying the evidence they cite will help to understand the views of good teaching under discussion here.

The amalgam of source material referenced above also bears mention. In venturing into an examination of the nature and consequences of identifying something like "good teaching," one reaches, of necessity, beyond a subject-matter conceived in strictly academic or scholarly terms. The relevant distinction appears in the difference between the Chetty article mentioned above and the nature of the venues in which it is cited.

The Chetty article is academic in nature. It seeks to explore the linkages between high-performing teachers (defined here as the top tier of achievement-score lifters) and the socioeconomic outcomes of the students in those teachers' classes. Characteristic of such approaches is the appropriately strict and explicit definition of terms, the limited scope of the study (so as to achieve clarity on a matter quite specific), and most importantly a heightened consciousness of both of the foregoing points, which is visible in the researchers' warnings about "evaluating the policy implications of our findings" (Chetty et al., 2011, p. 5), given that the conditions under which their data was generated would change substantially should such findings be used to drive policy. In other words, the researchers have drawn a strong correlation between "effective teaching," as they define it, and improved financial and social outcomes for the students of that teaching, as they likewise explicitly define it; they strongly caution that this ought not to be confused with having established a causal relationship between such generally undefined terms as "good teaching" and "a better future."

The 2012 State of the Union address, the official press release, and the *Daily Show* interview concerning the RESPECT program, as well as the two Kristof articles, however, are examples of more or less political speech. This usage of academics' work starkly reinforces the fact that while education may be an object of scholarly attention, it is never *merely* academic. It is a matter of practice, both in the conduct of teaching and learning itself and in the sphere of political and social maneuvering, as well. As an area of investigation, then, it would be overly parochial to confine one's field of vision to studies like Chetty's. The Chetty article demonstrates precisely what it seeks to demonstrate, and no more. The authors are explicit on the boundaries of their findings. The fact that commentators and policymakers draw conclusions beyond these boundaries and refer, explicitly or implicitly, to research like this in support of those conclusions represents the profound and consequential interdependence of these discursive fields. The application of findings drawn in severely controlled contexts to the wider world of educational policy, as though these findings really did represent a kind of uncontestable fact about "good teaching" far beyond the scope that the researchers themselves claim for their conclusions, makes readily visible the apparent or assumed continuity of the concept of "good teaching" that both discursive fields address, as well as the stark distinction in the terms of the two forms of address. This sharp distinction, in turn, reveals a certain blurriness surrounding the *concept* of "good teaching" that each field seeks to understand.

For this reason—that political and public discourse inherently bears upon an academic or scholarly research agenda and vice versa—the references to media outlets like *The Daily Show*, *The New York Times*, and others are not only warranted, but necessary. In the academic field of education, one's findings will be put to practical use in the public domain, and so the nature of that political or public praxis remains itself within the field of education as an object of study, particularly where the conceptual stability of "good teaching" is at stake. The two Kristof articles, taken together, highlight the problems inherent in establishing the conceptual stability of good teaching most clearly, and therefore provide the most auspicious starting point for the discussion.

The first opinion piece, which appeared on January 12th, makes the following statements about the importance of good teachers: "A great teacher is worth hundreds of thousands of dollars to each year's students, just in the extra income they will earn. . . . Conversely, a very poor teacher has the same effect as a pupil missing 40 percent of the school year. We don't allow that kind of truancy, so it's not clear why we should put up with such poor teaching" (Kristof, 2012b). Later in the same piece, Kristof says, "Our faltering education system may be the most important long-term threat to America's economy and national well-being, so it's frustrating that the presidential campaign is mostly ignoring the issue." And finally: "This latest study should elevate the issue on the national agenda, because it not only underscores the importance of education but also illuminates how we might improve schools. An essential answer: more good teachers. Or, to put it another way, fewer bad teachers. The obvious policy solution is more pay for good teachers, more dismissals for weak teachers."

In order to expose the concept of "good teaching" at work in Kristof's piece, I would like to draw out clearly the terms in which Kristof characterizes the importance of good teaching and the urgency of developing policy initiatives that address the needs that he emphasizes. Firstly, Kristof posits an overarching axiological statement in declaring that our "faltering" educational system is crucial precisely to the degree that "America's economy and national well-being" are at stake. This statement functions in his argument as an indicator of urgency. Nothing less than our national economic health—and therefore our sovereignty and global influence—hangs in the balance.

The second piece of Kristof's picture has to do with the particular relation he imagines between our "faltering" public education system and our "economic and national well-being." On the one hand, it is easy to see how one might pass over this assumption without comment: the specific Chetty et al. study he cites seems to promise that better teaching causes more money in student lifetime earnings; more future money causes higher future GDP; higher future GDP equals better future "economic and national well-being." That the relation is more complex than this simplistic rendering ought to be obvious, but, perhaps due to the deeply-ingrained urgency of the crisis narrative visible in the above paragraph, the simplistic relation is almost always taken as truth.

Without developing a full-fledged argument against the view of education and hence teaching on display here, it is at least worth complicating the issue by noting that the two assumptions on which Kristof's argument hangs are not as certainly correct as it can sometimes seem. For example, that our education system is "faltering," or failing, or decrepit, is simply taken for granted rather than argued for. When it is argued for in popular media, the pattern of argumentation tends to draw upon both individual scenes of horrific conditions or awful teaching and large-scale data on graduation rates or test scores. Steven Brill's influential 2009 *New Yorker* piece on attempts to reform the nature of teacher tenure provides a perfect example of this (Brill, 2009). In pointing with the methodology of thick description to singular examples of the most awful conditions in the public schools nationally—which almost always occur in high-minority, high-poverty, inner-city schools—one can easily find horrific instances of obvious failure. Then, in pointing to national and international data on high school and college completion rates, as well as international measures of achievement, one invites extrapolation of the horrific conditions to the general state of public schools, and one sees systemic failure, a "faltering" *national* education system. The generalization from horrific individual cases, backed with data comparing our graduation rates and test scores with other countries' measures of the same, is not necessarily supported by the data. In questioning the assumption that our educational system is "faltering," I wish first of all to underscore how deeply ingrained the rhetoric of crisis is within the educational debate. Mainly, however, I wish to question the assumption of systemic failure, which would then call for systemic solutions.

The second assumption has it that a strong education system—strong, that is, in terms of the particular metrics Kristof cites—will cause more or less directly national prosperity and global dominance. But as Diane Ravitch has convincingly argued (Ravitch, 2010, 2013), this has never yet been the case: national dominance and economic well-being have never required the sort of educational system Kristof has in mind, and so it is at best unclear whether undertaking the reforms Kristof advocates will have the effects he wants.

In the 1960s, during the height of the space- and arms-races, the Kennedy administration lavished the fields of math and science with monetary and rhetorical attention, in the same crisis terms (Berliner & Biddle, 1997, pp. 144–148). Crisis rhetoric aside, the United States convincingly won those races. But in 1983, *A Nation at Risk* came out, famously declaring that "if an unfriendly foreign power had attempted to impose on America the mediocre educational performance that exists today, we might well have viewed it as an act of war" (Gardner, 1983), which certainly indicated that our education system was still mired in some sort of crisis. The Soviet Union collapsed during the years 1989–1991, and the United States moved into a position of unipolar dominance. In the 1990s, fueled by superlative levels of financial and technological innovation centered around Silicon Valley, the United States economy experienced a decade-long, unprecedented level of expansion.

Conspicuously absent from reflections upon winning the Cold War and experiencing an economic windfall were accolades for the American education system; in fact, given the pervasive continuity of the crisis narrative, one might well conclude that the United States accomplished these feats in direct spite of its education system's obvious flaws. The crisis narrative has remained untroubled by the United States' global dominance over the past half-century. But today, with a global economy struggling to recover from a recession, politicians and policy-makers once again point to the United States education system as a cause of our economic problems, and thus the economic downturn becomes another fact that indicates the dire need for educational reform.

Against Kristof's assumptions that shape the contour of the debate, the foregoing discussion reveals that one of two things must hold: either the metrics that we take to indicate the systematic failure of our education system in fact indicate no such thing, or else quality education has far less to do with "economic and national well-being" than we assume. The fact that the crisis narrative seems to function as a foundational truth immune to facts could indicate either.[1] But in either case, what Kristof proposes we do in order to simultaneously address the metrics that indicate systemic educational failure and our "economic and national well-being" appears suddenly problematic: the metrics and what they appear to indicate are not so tightly conjoined as Kristof thinks.

Kristof's problematic assumptions about the state of the education system and its relation to national health—and particularly the indicators he takes to make these two visible—leads directly to a certain view of "good teaching" and indeed to the practice of teaching generally. Kristof's proposal for correcting the flaws he glimpses in American education, which is also Obama's and Duncan's, is "more good teachers. Or, to put it another way, fewer bad teachers." Because he treats the problem in simple cost-benefit terms, the fact that good teachers are correlated with certain economic gains for their students indicates to him a glaringly self-evident consequence: "The obvious policy solution is more pay for good teachers, more dismissals for weak teachers." Obama's State of the Union address makes a nearly identical point:

> We know a good teacher can increase the lifetime income of a classroom by over $250,000. . . . Teachers matter. So instead of bashing them, or defending the status quo, let's offer schools a deal. Give them the resources to keep good teachers on the job, and reward the best ones. And in return, grant schools flexibility: to teach with creativity and passion; to stop teaching to the test and to replace teachers who just aren't helping kids learn (Obama, 2012).

Both Kristof and Obama cite the Chetty study in attributing the economic gains to "good teachers," and in doing so they each tacitly smuggle in the study's rigorous, explicit definition of "good teaching," which has only to do with the amount of improvement students demonstrate in reading and math achievement scores, and which has nothing at all to do with anything else one might take to be the duty of public schools.[2] Importantly, however, neither Kristof nor Obama make explicit reference to this particular definition, instead using the concept of "good teaching" in an ordinary, everyday, non-technical sense—one that is taken to be immediately available to the wide public that constitutes their audience. The State of the Union drives this point home as Obama appeals to the everyday familiarity of the experience of having a good teacher: "Every person in this chamber can point to a teacher who changed the trajectory of their lives" (Obama, 2012). The operative assumption, then, is that there is no difference between Chetty's technical definition of "good teaching" and the kind of "good teaching" that is so generally present and pervasive that Obama can rely upon the experience of *"every person* in this chamber" (emphasis added) in order to make his point.

In turning to Kristof's second article, it will be important to bear in mind the two senses of "good teaching" that occur in the State of the Union: on the one hand, there is the "good teaching" so familiar that the President can assume that "every person in this chamber" has the memory of such an experience; while on the other hand, there is a kind of "good teaching" that is knowable (only) by means of looking at gains in student achievement scores. The assumption, once more, is that the kind of good teaching—one that reflects an explicit and technical definition, and one that reflects an experience of everyday school life—are more or less the same. In fairness to Kristof, as well, Obama is the one who directly conflates the senses of "good teaching." Nothing in Kristof's first article refers to any ordinary, non-technical sense of teacher quality, remaining wedded, as it is, to the Chetty article's definition. However, in Kristof's second article, the columnist does indeed risk conflating the two senses, and in particularly egregious ways. This egregiousness itself, and the fact that he cannot see the way he runs together different senses of teacher quality, indicates the level of difficulty at hand.

Kristof pens his second article on January 22nd, as a rejoinder to reader feedback on his first article. He says, "Skeptics of school reform wrote me to say: sure, a great teacher can make a difference in the right setting, but not with troubled, surly kids in a high-poverty environment. If you think that, or if you scoff at the statistics, then listen to Neal" (Kristof, 2012a). Kristof proceeds to respond to these skeptics by retelling the personal narrative of a "troubled, surly" student who experienced the life-altering effects of good teaching; the aim is to show that good teaching is both important and effective even or especially in such cases and so locating and rewarding it ought to be of the highest priority.

Olly Neal has the traits that Kristof requires in order to answer his critics. In terms of his temperament, Neal describes himself as "not a nice kid," as being "the only one who made [Mrs. Grady] cry." He "had a reputation." Neal was also poor, on which basis Kristof's critics objected to the commentator's championing of the reform agenda in question. As Kristof says, "Olly Neal was a poor black kid with an attitude. He was one of 13 brothers and sisters in a house with no electricity, and his father was a farmer with a second-grade education. Neal attended a small school for black children—this was in the segregated South—and was always mouthing off. He remembers reducing his English teacher, Mildred Grady, to tears."

Kristof here retells the story of a child with neither socio-economic status, nor "attitude," nor even race—"this was the segregated south"—on his side; and yet, it is Neal's story of having his life changed by a "great teacher" that for Kristof indicates that good teachers do indeed make an important difference in all cases, and thus we ought to adopt the reform agenda he lauded in the previous article.

Introduction xvii

In 1957, "the fall of his senior year" of high school, Olly Neal "cut Mrs. Blakely's class" and "wandered in the library, set up by Grady, the teacher he had tormented." A book with a "risqué cover" "caught his eye," but he "didn't want word to get out to any of his classmates that he was reading a novel." "So I stole it," as Neal himself says. Upon returning to the library sometime later, he was surprised to find another book by the same author, and he stole that, too. "Four times this happened." As Kristof says, "His trajectory changed, and he later graduated to harder novels, including those by Albert Camus, and he turned to newspapers and magazines as well. He went to college and later to law school. In 1991, Neal was appointed the first black district prosecuting attorney in Arkansas. A few years later, he became a judge, and then an appellate court judge."

At a reunion some years later, "Grady stunned Neal" by revealing that she had known he was stealing books and that she had in fact been restocking the shelves with the author that he liked—"all in hopes of turning around a rude adolescent who had made her cry. She paid for the books out of her own pocket." Kristof then asks, "How can one measure Grady's impact? Not only in Neal, but in the lives of those around him. His daughter, Karama, earned a doctorate in genetics, taught bioethics at Emory University, and now runs a community development program in Arkansas."

For Kristof, the "implication is that we need rigorous teacher evaluations, more pay for good teachers and more training and weeding-out of poor teachers." This is exactly the conclusion for which Kristof argued in his first article. Grady's impact, in Kristof's retelling, is difficult to measure—not only did she turn Neal's life around, but that intervention paved the way for Neal's daughter's success as well, a success which is, in turn, benefiting communities across the state. Grady is the model, here, of a great teacher, one worth retaining and rewarding.

It is precisely at this point that I would like to examine the way that Kristof arrives at the "implication" he derives from this particular example. Grady, first of all, is without doubt an example of an extraordinary teacher who achieved or enabled profound educational results even in a troubled, impoverished student. There remains a question, however, as to whether this particular example does indeed support the need for those "rigorous teacher evaluations," in defense of which Kristof offers the narrative in the first place. This question might be settled by asking whether the proposed methods of evaluating teachers would capture and convey Mrs. Grady's quality as easily as Neal's autobiographical narrative does.

In asking this question, I assume that by "rigorous teacher evaluations," Kristof means teacher evaluations that are based on or otherwise tied to the teacher's ability to lift a student's scores on achievement tests. I trust that my assumption about Kristof's notion of rigor is safe because of the words Kristof himself has used. Neal's story is offered, after all, as a response to those who "scoff at the statistics,"—the statistics being the ones he quoted in his previous article, presumably. The "good teaching" he has in mind, then, is specifically the "good teaching" visible by means of Chetty's definition. At issue in this exercise is the relative similarity of that definition to the everyday-familiar one that Obama has used, and that Kristof's narrative also invites readers to recognize. For Mrs. Grady is surely an example of our ordinary sense of great teaching—this everydayness stands out in the fact that no recourse to advanced metrics is required in order for Kristof to make her excellence visible. But is Mrs. Grady an example of both?

Let us imagine that the Olly Neal story occurred under the regimen of the "rigorous teacher evaluation" Kristof demands. Would the rigorous evaluation agree with our judgment that Mrs. Grady is an excellent teacher? Would Mrs. Grady's excellence register by means of the metrics?

This is actually a very simple matter, and the answer is "no." One glaring fact leaps out before all the others: Olly Neal "cut Mrs. Blakely's class" in order to venture into Mrs. Grady's library in the first place. Mrs. Grady *had been* his teacher, but was no longer officially responsible for his education at the time of the manifestation of her teacher quality. Under no circumstances whatever would any reading score gains have accrued to Mrs. Grady. Mrs. Grady's life-changing intervention on Olly Neal's behalf would not show up in any "rigorous" attempt to trace his achievement score gains back to their source.

In the second place, however, it is absolutely unclear that Neal would have been assessed to begin with, such that any score gains would have existed at all. Neal was a high school senior; Federal law calls for yearly assessment between grades three and eight, and one assessment during high school. No state of which I am aware assesses seniors—as such assessments occur during the spring semester.

In the third place, it is not out of bounds to draw into question the likely size of any score gain. We know that Neal stole the first book "in the fall of his senior year," sometime after which, he absconded with books two through four. College applications are due in the late winter or early spring. When Kristof claims that Neal's "trajectory changed" and that "he went to college and later to law school," the columnist invites one to believe that prior to the first book-stealing, college and law school were not on Neal's agenda. That may be the case. But one's acceptance into college depends upon the demonstration of aptitude and accomplishment in a variety of realms and over the course of one's high school career. It is implausible to suppose, in other words, that Neal was *without* visible aptitude or academic skill prior to Mrs. Grady's intervention, even if he was a tough kid to handle in class. This is not to minimize Grady's impact on Neal's direction in life. It is rather to call into question the assumption that Neal would have performed poorly on standardized assessments of reading in previous years, such than any assessment following Mrs. Grady's intervention would have revealed substantial achievement *growth*, upon which Kristof's "rigorous teacher evaluations" would depend.

It is straightforwardly impossible that the "rigorous teacher evaluations" for which Kristof advocates would recognize Mrs. Grady's excellence in this case. It is unlikely that a student of Neal's age would be assessed at all; and even if assessed, given the facts of the case, it is not immediately obvious that Neal's change of trajectory would register in terms of any boom in his reading scores; but, most concretely, even granting the assessment *and* the score explosion, it is inescapable that Mrs. Grady herself would miss out on the credit. It was *her* intervention, but she was not the one nominally responsible for teaching Neal how to read. Mrs. Grady is an example of excellence, but it is a kind of excellence that Chetty's definition of "good teaching" excludes.

It seems reasonable to conclude on this basis that the kind of rigorous evaluations designed to identify teacher quality will, in at least some cases, fail to pick up the sort of excellence in teaching that is already visible to the naked eye, as it were. The suggestion is that the public and policy discourse conflates two different concepts of "good teaching," erroneously treating them as identical to one another. Though Kristof holds up Mrs. Grady as the reason we need "rigorous teacher evaluation" in order to reward the good and weed out the bad, the very methods he defends would *fail to identify* Mrs. Grady's quality. And yet, it is simultaneously obvious that Mrs. Grady is an exceptional teacher. Two divergent senses of "good teaching" are thus in conflict here.

Mrs. Grady's story appeals to an everyday sense of "good teaching," precisely the sense to which Obama gestures in the State of the Union address, as he asks the assembly to recall that "every person in this chamber" can remember an experience with such a teacher. The "rigorous evaluations" to which Kristof gestures, meanwhile, access a *technical* view of "good teaching," one that fails to map cleanly onto the ordinary sense of the term. The assumption in applying advanced metrics to achievement data is that the potential discrepancy between the two senses can be eliminated with the proper application of statistical methodology. But it is no such matter.

Let us go further and charitably extend the idea of "rigor" in rigorous evaluations to cover something like on-hand observational measures. For the sake of this argument, let us also allow that Grady was Neal's teacher at the time of her intervention.

Kristof himself does not discuss the classroom-observation aspect of teacher evaluation, but it, too, belongs to the Obama administration's reform agenda, and it is factored into determinations of which states qualify for NCLB waivers and for Race to the Top funding (DOE, 2011). The pairing of achievement data metrics with advanced observational data is highlighted, in fact, in the press, as well: "Spurred by the requirements of the Obama administration's Race to the Top competition, Tennessee is one of more than a dozen states overhauling their evaluation systems to increase the number of classroom observations and to put more emphasis on standardized test scores" (Anderson, 2012). The sense of rigor in such evaluations derives from their standardized nature. Observers look for specific characteristics and behaviors—best practices, one might say—in a given teacher's planning and instruction. Tennessee offers a case in point, as detailed in the aforementioned *New York Times* article:

> Each observation focuses on one or two of four areas: instruction, professionalism, classroom environment and planning. Afterward, the observer scores the teacher according to the state's detailed and computerized system. Instruction, for example, has 12 subcategories, including "motivating students" and "presenting instructional content." Motivating students, in turn, has subcategories like "regularly reinforces and rewards effort." In all, there are 116 subcategories. (Anderson, 2012)

This particular description emphasizes the level of detail in the observation rubric, which, while aimed at ensuring its rigor, simultaneously makes it unwieldy. But the "unwieldy" criticism misses the point in our case. Mrs. Grady's decision to allow Neal to steal a book, the educative act that Kristof highlights as indicative of her excellence, was both laudable and situation-specific. No observation rubric can be imagined to include "permitting students to steal library books." It was the right decision for that child in that place at that time, but it is simply not generalizable to all teachers in all circumstances for all children. Obviously, only generalizable traits can appear on an observation rubric, as one implicitly expects any teacher whatsoever to demonstrate or perform the trait in question. The on-site evaluation process would therefore likewise miss Mrs. Grady's excellence.

In his second column, Kristof narrates the history of one great teacher's impact on an otherwise lost student. The teacher's greatness shows up clearly in Kristof's recounting, which he offers as a means of defending the main contention of his first article: we should pay good teachers more money and we should weed out the weak ones. Insofar as Kristof specifies methods of identifying good teachers, thus establishing a basis on which to decide whom to weed and whom to reward, the methods fail to accurately identify good teaching *even in the case Kristof cites* in defense of employing "rigorous teacher evaluation" to "improve national competitiveness, improving the ranks of teachers." He labors under the misapprehension that the technical definition of "good teaching" is, if not identical to, then a reliable proxy for, the everyday sense of "good teaching" that we in fact wish to reward. The case of Olly Neal and Mrs. Grady profoundly undermines the compatibility of the two concepts at work in this discussion.

Whether or not to reward and punish on the basis of teacher quality remains beyond the scope of my concern here. Rather, I am struck by the slipperiness of the concept of good teaching, the ways in which something so obvious that a simple narrative can effectively reveal it proves so onerous that it eludes or evades 116-point evaluation rubrics and the very best efforts of the field of Economics and Educational Measurement. The classroom-evaluation methods examine specific behaviors and practices on the one hand, and outcome measures on the other. If these means remain insufficient to demonstrate or secure the conceptual recognition of "good teaching" we wish to reward, on what basis is "good teaching" so immediately and *actually* visible in Mrs. Grady's story? If not communicable in terms of specific practices or measurable outcomes, how else could our ordinary concept of "good teaching" become visible in the present, as opposed to the past? If the proposed methods of identifying excellent teachers are as insufficient as they appear, how deeply has the conceptual confusion penetrated the popular and political discourse on the subject? How might an alternative approach arise, and what might it look like?

Mrs. Grady's example is so near to us that we need neither rubrics nor metrics to reveal its quality; yet it remains for all that beyond the very reach of our best rubrics and metrics. Perhaps our trouble in coping with teacher evaluation lies not within good teaching's mysteriousness, but rather in its profound familiarity. This study will seek to explore the constructions of "good teaching" throughout the policies of the Obama administration, across the platforms of press releases, policy speeches, and state policies themselves; and it will likewise trace the contours of the discourse on "good teaching" as it appears in commentary in national news media of all varieties. In exploring the shape of the conceptual distortion revealed in this Introduction, I will also develop and offer an alternative theoretical framework by means of which questions pertaining to teacher quality can safely—without, that is, requiring divergent concepts of good teaching or technical definitions—be posed.

Mrs. Grady did the right thing in Olly Neal's case, and it had a tremendous and lifelong effect. Teachers like her are worth retaining and rewarding. Our methods of identifying good teachers ought to be able to pick out Mrs. Grady's quality. I take her, then, as the test of any approach to questions of teacher evaluation: if it cannot capture Mrs. Grady's excellence, it cannot function as an indicator of teacher quality. Call it the Mrs. Grady test.

NOTES

1. By "immune to facts," I do not mean to imply that the crisis narrative is unsupported by any facts. I mean that no evidence of successful teaching or learning is capable of overturning the systematic nature of the narrative of systematic failure. In the interview with Jon Stewart, Arne Duncan said that, "We're trying to put a huge amount of resources behind those places to take to scale what is working. I would say for every challenge we face in education, the answers are out there. It's happening. The challenge is, it's not happening at scale. We have to take these pockets of excellence, these islands of excellence, and make them systems of excellence" (Stewart, 2012). Good teaching is an *island* of excellence. But horrific school conditions are imagined to be *everywhere*. It comes down to distinguishing what one takes to

be the exception from what one takes to be the rule. That is hardly the only problematic issue with this particular soundbite, but more on that later.
2. Ravitch, for instance, notes that in addition to the laudable goals Kristof cites, schools also have a duty to inculcate citizenship practices in children, and to "endow every individual with the intellectual and ethical power to pursue his or her own interests," neither of which is captured in Chetty's metrics (Ravitch, 2013, p. 237).

REFERENCES

Anderson, J. (2012). States Try to Fix Quirks in Teacher Evaluations. *New York Times*, p. A1. New York.

Berliner, D. C., & Biddle, B. J. (1997). *The Manufactured Crisis: Myths, Fraud, and the Attack on America's Public Schools*. White Plains, NY: Longman Publishers USA.

Brill, S. (2009) The Rubber Room. *The New Yorker, 85*(26), 30.

Chetty, R., Friedman, J. N., & Rockoff, J. E. (2011). The Long-Term Impacts of Teachers: Teacher Value-Added and Student Outcomes in Adulthood. *NBER Working Paper No. 17699*.

DOE. (2011). Obama Administration Sets High Bar for Flexibility from No Child Left Behind in Order to Advance Equity and Support Reform. Retrieved from http://www.ed.gov/news/press-releases/obama-administration-sets-high-bar-flexibility-no-child-left-behind-order-advanc

Gardner, D. P. (1983). A Nation At Risk. Retrieved from http://www2.ed.gov/pubs/NatAtRisk/index.html

Kristof, N. (2012a). How Mrs. Grady Transformed Olly Neal. *New York Times*, p. SR13. New York.

Kristof, N. (2012b). The Value of Teachers. *New York Times*, p. A27. New York.

Obama, B. (2012). State of the Union Address. whitehouse.gov. Retrieved from http://www.whitehouse.gov/the-press-office/2012/01/24/remarks-president-state-union-address

Ravitch, D. (2010). *The Death and Life of the Great American School System*. New York: Basic Books.

Ravitch, D. (2013). *Reign of Error: The Hoax of the Privatization Movement and the Danger to America's Public Schools*. New York: Knopf.

Stewart, J. (2012). February 16. *The Daily Show*. thedailyshow.com.

1 Duncan's Speeches on Race to the Top and the Assumptions of the Reform Movement

1.1 INTRODUCTION

Since the overarching strategy of this investigation rests on a few assumptions, and since this strategy is at least somewhat different from other similarly-oriented studies, it would behoove me to be as open and transparent about these assumptions, and as explicit about the strategy, as possible, distinguishing each of these from a few similar projects.

Emerging from the Introduction, the primary assumptions I make with respect to education policy are (a) that any individual policies or initiatives, such as those enumerated in Race to the Top agenda and the state laws designed to win the proffered federal money, are addressed to perceived shortcomings in one or more aspects of the operation of the national education system, (b) that the (national) public must at least tacitly consent to or agree with the broad-strokes view of education—its responsibilities, its effects, its conduct and processes, its shortcomings, and so on—that the policy-makers expound in order for any given policy to win out and receive implementation, and (c) that therefore to consider educational initiatives themselves, the public speeches employed to convince various audiences and stakeholders of their worthiness, the research programs that such initiatives and policies call upon for evidentiary support, and the public press that comments upon them will reveal the conceptual shape of "teaching" and "learning," the twin components of education. As the Introduction has already suggested, the suspicion guiding my exploration is that the conceptual shape of "teaching" and "learning" will fail, when examined closely, to be self-consistent. Such inconsistencies will, however, because of (a) and (b), nevertheless reveal important aspects of what we want or expect from our education system; getting clear about what that is will be a first step toward aligning policy with these expectations and desires.

But a second and equally important assumption bears mention as well: despite the citation of my "suspicion" in the previous paragraph, I take it for granted that policy-makers, educational researchers, and newspaper columnists alike are all genuinely dedicated to the improvement of the American educational system. That is, I simply assume that any failures of self-consistency in the concepts of "teaching" and "learning" on display in the educational reforms discussed herein are as it were accidental rather than deliberate. Making this assumption is, I take it, not a simple act of naivety. In addition to the platitudinous observation that assuming the good intentions of others in matters of political conversation within a democracy is absolutely necessary to making genuine progress in any area of concern whatever, making this assumption also does justice to the difficulty of the subject matter under discussion here. In other words, while one *may* turn out to be right in accusing a political opponent of deliberate conceptual malfeasance, such an accusation may also serve to deflect or underplay the factors that have led an opponent to make the sort of conceptual mistake on display, which amounts both to a failure to take seriously the claims, concerns, and evidentiary standing offered by an interlocutor and also to a diminution of the field of conceptual play: it makes something like teaching and learning overly or excessively or inaccurately *simple*.

In making each of these assumptions, I owe a powerful debt to the work of Ludwig Wittgenstein and his later interpreters. In speaking of an analogous situation in the philosophy of language, Wittgenstein says, "One cannot guess how a word functions. One has to *look* at its use and learn from that. The difficulty, however, is to remove the prejudice that stands in the way of this learning. It is not a *stupid* prejudice" (Wittgenstein, Anscombe, & Hacker, 2009, §340). Taking the conceptual shapes of "education," "teaching," and "learning," to be revealed in their *use* in the various discursive areas discussed above is therefore a Wittgensteinian sort of approach.

In following out a suspicion that there are multiple and occasionally conflicting concepts of "teaching" and "learning" at work in the discourse around education reform, I likewise assume, with Wittgenstein, that failing to see these contradictions is neither the result of stupidity-born blindness nor self- (or money-)interested shenanigans. I assume instead that it is at least possible that such contradictions are simply difficult to see and easy to miss. It is striking, for example, to recall that a man as smart as Kristof can wield the Mrs. Grady narrative in support of the need for the evaluation protocols demanded by Race to the Top, and that he offers this narrative in direct spite of the seemingly obvious fact that such protocols would not have identified Mrs. Grady's quality at all. While this admittedly might be either stupidity or malfeasance at work, I think (and assume) that it is much more likely that the confusion results from the difficulty of the conceptual terrain involved.

When I speak of my investigation differing from other similarly-oriented projects, I have in mind two recent works in particular: Jal Mehta's critique, in his book *The Allure of Order*, of an (historically-rooted) American love affair with instrumental rationality, of which the recent accountability movement in education is a manifestation, and Diane Ravitch's latest refutation of the many claims put forth by advocates of education reform, which she offers in her 2013 book, *Reign of Error*. Both scholars in their individual treatises are importantly and profoundly correct when it comes to their central theses. Tracing the points of my divergence from these scholars' very astute critiques will help to concretize and reinforce my own methodological assumptions as I have detailed them in the previous paragraphs; and although, as divergences, these will mark areas of my disagreement with these authors, that fact ought not to be understood as ingratitude for the compelling arguments that they both make.

A major point of divergence between the exploration contained here and Ravitch's recent work has precisely to do with my guiding assumption that educational reformers, and indeed all policy-makers, are offering proposals with the ultimate good of the American education system at heart. Ravitch is exceedingly skeptical on this point, as her subtitle "The Hoax of the Privatization Movement and the Danger to America's Public Schools" is sufficient to indicate. Early on, she allows that

> Some in the reform movement, believing that American education is obsolete and failing, think they are promoting a necessary but painful redesign of the nation's ailing schools. Some sincerely believe they are helping poor black and brown children escape from failing public schools. Some think they are on the side of modernization and innovation. But others see an opportunity to make money in a large, risk-free, government-funded sector or an opportunity for personal advancement and power. (Ravitch, 2013, p. 20)

Ravitch proceeds to eviscerate reformers' arguments for the expansion of charter schools, the restructuring of teacher tenure, the role of student achievement tests in accountability, and so on. She conducts her argument always with an eye to the ways in which the reformers' agenda is geared toward offering technological solutions to such seemingly intractable problems as poverty, solutions that—like test design, teacher training protocols, etc.—come with a certain price tag. She may well be correct to see moneyed interests pushing very particular educational innovations that would funnel federal or foundation cash their way, and given her particular history with education reform, she is in a unique position to know.

But her focus on discrediting the several claims offered by reformers leads her to miss the salience of the conceptual problem indicated in my Introduction. Specifically, Ravitch holds a view on which poverty is the major driver of educational inequality in America, and accordingly holds that there will be no solution to the educational problems reformers wish to correct absent the addressing of this particular issue on its own terms. Mocking the tone of reformers' calls to find out "what works" in education, Ravitch says, "We know what works. What works are the very opportunities that advantaged families provide for their children" (Ravitch, 2013, p. 6). She puts it even more straightforwardly elsewhere: "Only by eliminating opportunity gaps can we eliminate achievement gaps" (Ravitch, 2013, p. 8).

The problem that Ravitch encounters is that by "what works" she means to indicate the things that work to "spark [students'] creativity, and to fulfill their potential" (Ravitch, 2013, p. 8), as well as to "enhance their chances for a good life, and strengthen our society" (Ravitch, 2013, p. 6). But this is not what the reformers mean by "what works," at least not directly. In anticipating a later argument in my own project, the reformers quite generally, as in the Chetty study cited in the Introduction, operationalize these otherwise vague notions in order to study them empirically: the "good life" that Ravitch wishes students to attain is therefore quantified in terms of measures of neighborhood quality, annual income, rates of teenage pregnancy, and other concrete factors. Once (technically) defined, it becomes possible, through regression modeling, to partition out the effects of students' socioeconomic status on this aggregate definition of a "good life." Where differences then exist between, say, the level of the "good life" experienced by students who had classes with a teacher of "excellent" as opposed to "mediocre" quality (as measured in any variety of ways), it becomes possible for reformers to argue that teacher quality makes a difference over and above the effects of poverty, and indeed, as we shall see, that improving the quality of teachers can *overcome* the effects on students of economic inequality.

To reformers of Chetty's ilk, Ravitch's insistence on claiming that economic inequality is the primary factor behind the achievement gap, despite their statistical evidence to the contrary, must seem like a simple refusal of the facts, its own form of deliberate blindness. But at issue—and consistently ignored in the discussion—is the relative similarity of these two versions of the "good life." Because both Ravitch and the reformers use the language of "what works," and because both parties have in mind something that seems unobjectionably like the "good life," it becomes all too easy to suppose that the two sides are engaged in an argument about the same *object*, an argument that can and ought to be settled with facts. Indeed, one might interpret the exasperated tone with which the more polemical members of each side of the debate engage the other as an expression of this supposition. If I am correct, however, in perceiving a divergence in something that is, at bottom, conceptual, then no recitation of facts will suffice to settle the matter. Ravitch's book accomplishes a great deal, and I will rely on aspects of its findings in my own work, but its working assumptions and the way it addresses the reformers differ from my own.

Jal Mehta's *The Allure of Order*, meanwhile, locates a different sort of problem lurking behind the accountability movement, one that he grounds in a particularly American "school of rationalization" (Mehta, 2013, p. 249). In this incisive observation, Mehta joins a wide and interdisciplinary subfield that attends to the problematic faith in processes of rationalization in several aspects of American political life. Tom Medvetz's sociological history of the rise and conduct of think tanks in American media and politics provides one example of this subfield (Medvetz, 2012), and a more pointed look at the limitations—to put it charitably—of recruiting the "best and brightest" to apply the methods of rationalization to the political and military problems of the Vietnam War is on offer in Edwin Martini's recent historical work (Martini, 2012). At bottom, Mehta's critique in the realm of education reform centers on the drawbacks in making policy on the belief that something like education is amenable to the sort of managerial or centralized planning implied in the instrumentalism of this "school of rationalization." Mehta puts it nicely, with italics in the original: "The core of the educational problem is that *we have been trying to solve a problem of professional practice by bureaucratic means*" (Mehta, 2013, p. 270).

Mehta thus locates the barriers facing meaningful educational improvement in an excessive and sometimes blind adherence to rationalization in the (organizational) conduct of schooling, which is quite close to one of the findings of my own study. The divergences between Mehta's work and my own pertain to the solutions offered. For Mehta, the shortcomings of the "school of rationalization" imply that bureaucratic, managerial control of teacher practice is doomed to fail, and so "developing consistent expertise among frontline practitioners"—teachers—presents itself as a promising alternative direction (Mehta, 2013, p. 271). The development of expertise that he pictures, however, bears a troubling resemblance to the rationalization in opposition to which it is offered:

> This would entail developing a much larger stock of practical knowledge about how to teach, creating effective training regimens to inculcate that knowledge, and building ongoing organizational processes to ensure that knowledge is consistently applied. (Mehta, 2013, p. 271)

Most succinctly, when Mehta envisions the development of teacher expertise, he imagines this development proceeding both (1) by centralized means, as the result of objective research into "what works" or "best practices," which process would seem to reinvest in the "school of rationalization" that the proposals are meant to overcome, and also (2) on a rationalist model of expert practice, in which practitioners *have* expertise in the form of some "stock" of "practical knowledge," which can be "larger" or smaller, and which can be "consistently applied" across contexts.

Mehta does not discuss the work of Lee Shulman or Deborah Ball, whose research on Pedagogical Content Knowledge (PCK), ongoing since the 1980s, is the very embodiment of his proposals, which serves the subject of a later chapter of this investigation, and for which he might well advocate. Putting the points of agreement between our work as straightforwardly as possible, I take Mehta's critique of the "school of rationalization" to be timely, accurately aimed, and well done; my arguments will join in this critique. However, in light of the view of skillful practice I will offer later on, it becomes difficult to see how Mehta's solution succeeds in escaping the rationalism he condemns: his view of expert teacher practice, which shapes his proposals for the salutary reorganization of the educational system, is itself rationalist in nature. While Mehta rightly rejects the possibility of rationalizing the conduct of education through accountability or organizational measures, he nevertheless accepts and propagates a view on which educational practice lends itself to just this type of rationalization.

Mehta's acceptance of such a view, like Kristof's mistake in the Introduction, speaks to the strength of rationalism's grip on the American (and more broadly Western) intellectual imagination. Since my overarching purpose pertains to showing the way, or what is required, to bring educational policy into alignment with our aims and expectations for an education system, a critique (in the Kantian sense) of this rationalism will not, at least initially, seek to refute it directly, but will rather seek to loosen its grip through a deflationary process. Once more, this is a strategy derived from Wittgenstein, who compactly puts it this way: "the best that I can propose is that we yield to the temptation to use this picture, but then investigate what the *application* of this picture looks like" (Wittgenstein et al., 2009, §374). Taking up Wittgenstein's proposal, the following sections of this study will explicate the "picture" of education embodied in the Obama administration's Race to the Top program, compare that picture with the stated ends and goals toward which such a program aims, question whether such a picture thus applied is in principle capable of delivering on the claims it makes, and, where the program is found wanting, suggest alternatives.

1.2 ACHIEVEMENT DATA AND THE COMMON CORE STANDARDS

I wish initially to make explicit the conceptual form of teacher quality as it appears in official policy, which includes for these purposes the Department of Education's Race to the Top application process and Secretary of Education Arne Duncan's speeches and interviews in regard to this initiative. I will save for a later subsection the substance and evaluation of various states' applications for these funds, since they will represent, as Wittgenstein says, "the *application* of this picture." Rather, my goal in this section is better characterized as drawing out and making visible the concepts of teacher quality that emerge in this discourse.

In approaching the material in question, I will trace the development of these ideas through their myriad forms, spending considerable time on both Duncan's cycle of four policy speeches delivered during the summer of 2009 and on the notions contained therein as they later translate to state teacher-evaluation policies undertaken in attempts to win Race to the Top funding. Revealing the shape of the concept(s) of teaching and teacher quality as they circulate within the policies of the Obama administration will require examining what policy-makers understand the principal challenges facing education to be, how these challenges have become visible or pressing, and what might be done in order to overcome or ameliorate these difficulties. Each of these questions will shed light on the kind of *thing* (process, practice, behavioral syndrome, cause) that the Obama administration takes teaching and learning most fundamentally to be.

In June and July of 2009, Arne Duncan embarked on a Listening and Learning Tour, during which he delivered four addresses to various groups. These speeches outlined and advocated for the major reforms proposed under the eventual aegis of Race to the Top. On June 8th, Duncan spoke to the attendees of the Institute of Education Sciences's fourth annual research conference on the importance of achievement data to education research (Duncan, 2009b); on June 14th, he addressed the 2009 Governors Education Symposium on the topic and function of what would later come to be known as the Common Core standards (Duncan, 2009c); on June 22nd, he delivered a speech on school turnaround initiatives and methods to the National Alliance for Public Charter Schools Conference (Duncan, 2009e); and on July 2nd, he challenged the National Education Association (NEA) to embrace specific reforms around improving the quality of the teaching profession (Duncan, 2009a). On July 24th, Duncan preceded Obama to the podium and announced the advent of the Race to the Top program itself, in which address he briefly summarized the major points from each of the aforementioned speeches (Duncan, 2009f). I note the placement of Race to the Top's announcement in the timeline because I wish to include in the picture of teaching and learning applied by the Obama administration a later speech of Duncan's, as well, one geared toward teacher preparation and offered at Columbia Teacher's College on October 22nd, 2009 (Duncan, 2009d).

The particular utility and importance of reforming standards emphasized in Duncan's first two speeches comes out most clearly, in fact, in his official announcement of the advent of Race to the Top: "For starters," Duncan notes, "we expect that winners of the Race to the Top grants will work to reverse the pervasive dumbing down of academic standards and assessments that has taken place in many states" (Duncan, 2009f). In directly contrasting the Race to the Top initiative with a "pervasive dumbing down of academic standards and assessments," Duncan references the problems that emerged in the education legislation of the Bush administration, the No Child Left Behind Act (NCLB). Early in Duncan's first speech, geared to the value of data in the reform movement, he makes his ambivalence toward NCLB explicit: "There's a lot I don't like about *No Child Left Behind (NCLB)*, but I will always give it credit for exposing our nation's dreadful achievement gaps" (Duncan, 2009b).

Indeed, whatever distance from his predecessors that Duncan wishes to achieve, some striking similarities exist between NCLB and Race to the Top: both programs involve making a certain infusion of federal money earmarked for education in general contingent upon individual states (autonomously) adopting policies designed to meet specific requirements established by the federal government. In order to receive the money promised under the original Elementary and Secondary Education Act (ESEA), its later incarnation as NCLB, and the Race to the Top program alike, states must bring their nominally autonomous education systems into alignment with federal guidelines, including undertaking the adoption of certain accountability protocols.

But the very name of Race to the Top reflects a dramatic turn away from NCLB accountability methods. NCLB requires the annual assessment of all students in grades 3–8 and once again in high school in order to evaluate whether or not students have made adequate yearly progress (AYP) toward achieving proficiency in the domains of reading, math, and—beginning in 2007–2008—science. Implemented in the 2001–2002 school year, the law required that states develop a plan to move 100 percent of its students to proficiency in each of those domains by 2014. However, because the education of children is not a federal power specified in the Constitution and thus devolves to the states, as per the 10th Amendment, each state was empowered to define proficiency for itself. Some states seemed to avail themselves of the opportunity to ensure their continued federal funding by defining proficiency at a minimal level: this is the practice that Duncan labels "the pervasive dumbing down of academic standards."

In his data speech, Duncan in fact points to this very problem: the gap between the definition of proficiency utilized by the Nation's Report Card—the NAEP—and that which certain states use for compliance purposes can be "staggering" (Duncan, 2009b). The tendency to deliberately define down the concept of proficiency, as unintentionally incentivized by NCLB, came to be derisively termed the "race to the bottom." Duncan decries this practice as a form of manifest dishonesty: "When states lower standards, they are lying to children and they are lying to parents" (Duncan, 2009b).

In drawing a distinction in this regard between NCLB and Race to the Top, Duncan makes it known that the particular programs and accountability protocols incentivized by Race to the Top are designed to shore up or restore the validity of the concept of "student achievement," which, in his view, has become unmoored from reality, and become so completely unmoored, in fact, that abiding by a given state's definition of "proficient" can count as an example of "lying." Another way of putting the above is to say that Race to the Top seeks to solve, as a first priority, a *skeptical* problem, which is to suggest that it will actively attempt to reestablish a connection between the concept of proficiency and the objective reality from which it has become untethered. Increasing the profile of student achievement data and reforming state standards and assessments will be used, then, both to reduce or eliminate state-to-state variation and to ensure that the concept of proficiency recovers its meaningful, objective content.

The bifurcated structure of the sort of skepticism to which Race to the Top responds must be emphasized: Duncan gives voice, on the one hand, to a fear that "proficiency" lacks objective content per se, that it is insufficiently attached to the real world; on the other hand, he also voices the related fear that the profusion of available definitions of proficiency, namely, those established by each of the fifty states under NCLB, reflects deliberate chicanery, a willful conceptual manipulation that rises to the level of "lying." Locating an objective, meaningful definition of "proficiency" and finding a means of encouraging each state to adopt this definition would foreclose upon both horns of the skeptical threat at once: the inability to trust a *word* and the inability to trust *another* (person or state).

In his address to the Governors Education Symposium, Duncan specifically tackles the need to stem the tide of conceptual variation between states, and the proposed fix that he offers reveals the shape of his particular response to the possibility of doubting the probity of each state's definition of proficiency. In the speech, Duncan lauds Governor Jim Hunt for the latter's leadership in promoting what would become the Common Core standards, noting that that Hunt was "call[ing] for common national standards when it wasn't politically popular" (Duncan, 2009c). Two sentences later, Duncan praises Governor Roy Romer as well for his role in the development of common standards, saying "we wouldn't have 46 states and three territories agreeing to adopt high common standards if it weren't for his hard work" (Duncan, 2009c). In calling for a *common* core of standards, standards that are not only adopted by all states but also "internationally benchmarked" and "college-and-career-ready" (Duncan, 2009c), Duncan puts to rest simultaneously the troubling specters of state-to-state differences in, for example, the concept of "proficiency" and also concerns around the "essential knowledge and skills our kids need" (Duncan, 2009c).

Put another way, in appealing to transcendent standards, Duncan solves the skeptical difficulty inherent in trusting state and local officials to define standards and set appropriate curriculum by eliminating the need for trust entirely. In light of correct and common standards, combined with rigorously-aligned assessments, we stand to achieve an unprecedented measure of *certainty* that American schools are teaching students what they need to know, both in terms of content and in terms of achievement level, where the level is determined by comparison with the international community and the content is determined by the (projected) demands of the future job market and institutions of higher education. Duncan is quite explicit on this point: "The standards must be tied to the end point of making sure students are ready to succeed in college or in the workplace" (Duncan, 2009c).

I take pains to enumerate Race to the Top's proposals as particular responses to problems with the status quo—problems that arise in the form of skepticism—in order to make evident the weight that certain aspects of Race to the Top's proposals will have to bear in order to succeed in their appointed task of overcoming or refuting this skepticism. Duncan's call to reform state standards, to make them both more rigorous and also common to all states, is aimed at defeating skepticism with respect to the questions of both whether American children are learning *what* they require and whether they are learning this content at the proper level or degree. That Duncan and the reform movement in general understands the Common Core standards, along with improved assessments, as the preferred form of response to the aforementioned skepticism unearths some underlying assumptions not only about the function of education, but also and importantly about how the relative success of an educational endeavor is expected to become visible or accessible.

In addition to revealing the relatively unobjectionable supposition that education—teaching and learning—can be conceived as preparation for one's future adulthood, including the responsibilities of maintaining employment, Duncan's appeal to a criterion of "college and career readiness" comes with built-in assumptions about the relation between "college readiness" and "career readiness"—that they are identical—and about the form in which each might be made evident or predicted. It also implies that because federal policy under NCLB actively encouraged state-level bureaucracy to play fast and loose with the meaning of "proficiency," administrators and teachers were more or less actively discouraged from attending to the demands of "college and career"; Race to the Top seeks a sort of realignment in this regard. I point out this latter implication because it comprises part of the sense that in Race to the Top's turn away from NCLB, a real educational revolution is on offer, which is to say that in order to see "college and career readiness" as a *new* criterion at work in the educational world, one will have to accept the notion that teachers working with students in the classroom have either been relatively ignorant as to what will prepare kids for college and careers, or have succumbed to incentives *not* to care about college and career as a goal, or have been uninterested in working toward such a goal, period.

Since "college and career readiness" will play such an important criterial role in terms of both the concept of educational success and the curricular content by which such success is to occur, and since it is offered as a new and corrective element to previous policy mistakes, the nature of this criterion bears investigation: what does it consist in, and how will it be used to measure "student achievement"?

Although he never defines it explicitly, Duncan's speech to the Governors Education Symposium lays out, through the indicators of our national failure in this regard, what he means by "college and career readiness":

> Today, our standards are too low and the results on international tests show it. Worse yet, we see the signals in the international economy as more and more engineers, doctors, and science and math Ph.D.s come from abroad. You must resist the temptation to make these standards too easy. Our children deserve to graduate from high school prepared for college and the jobs of the future. Your standards must be rigorous and they also must be tightly focused on the most important things students need to know. (Duncan, 2009c)

An influx of foreign "engineers, doctors, and science and math Ph.D.s," combined with "the results on international tests," serve as evidence of both the inadequate level of our standards and the sprawl of curricular content areas to which standards are currently applied. At the end of a passage raising the specter of high-level math- and science-related professionals from abroad taking the jobs that (implicitly) ought to be occupied by Americans, Duncan calls for standards that are both "rigorous" and "tightly focused on the most important things students need to know." This conjunction communicates the sense that the content areas under discussion here, as well as the levels of achievement by which success or failure will be apparent, are those that would equip a person for a high-level math- or science-related career.

The international tests to which Duncan refers, and which he in fact mentions by name in his data-oriented speech (Duncan, 2009b) are tests of math, science and reading. Although the problems inherent in comparing such results internationally are well-documented (Ercikan & Koh, 2005; Ercikan & McCreith, 2002; Sireci, 1997), these results nevertheless influence the policies and popular discourse not only of the United States, but of other countries as well, even ones with which we are often unfavorably compared (Brügelmann, 2011; Fehr, 2010). The "limiting" effect in Duncan's call to "limit standards to the essential knowledge and skills our kids need so teacher can focus in depth on the most important things kids should know" involves by necessity narrowing what it is that we expect teachers to accomplish. "College and career readiness," insofar as it surfaces in minimally concrete form in Duncan's speech, is thus revealed by certain proxy measures: standardized test scores, most evidently; and also the percentage of our "engineers, doctors, and math and science Ph.D.s" that emerge from our own education system.

Putting aside for the moment the obvious objection that engineering, medicine, and science do not comprise the totality of available career fields, there remains the problem, for Duncan, of designing state assessments that will adequately speak to his concrete objective to prepare students for college and career. As Duncan himself makes clear, the current reliance on "multiple choice tests" is insufficient to this task:

> We need tests that measure whether students are mastering complex materials and can apply their knowledge in ways that show that they are ready for college and careers. We need tests that go beyond multiple choice, and we know that these kinds of tests are expensive to develop. (Duncan, 2009c)

The implication in this passage is that *because* multiple choice exams cannot adequately "measure whether students are mastering complex material" such that students would be "ready for college and careers," they do not have good construct validity. Although they purport to reveal something important about student learning, they do not adequately represent what we really mean by *"student learning,"* which, Duncan suggests, is visible in the concrete terms of students' readiness for college and careers.

But given the careers that Duncan chooses to highlight and the international tests to which he refers, "college and career readiness" will be established in terms of improved scores in math, particularly, but also in reading. Should college and career readiness consist in certain levels of math and reading scores, and should all teachers be evaluated according to their contributions to students' readiness for college and careers, it follows that teacher quality will be accessible in terms of students' growth in measures of math, reading, and science.

It is particularly important to showcase the apparently inevitable recourse to achievement data in grounding the concept of "learning" for which "good teaching" is responsible precisely because in each of the speeches under consideration here, Duncan makes a special point of acknowledging that the "complex, nuanced work of teaching can never be reduced to a simple multiple choice test," while stating in the same breath that "to remove student achievement entirely from evaluation is illogical and indefensible" (Duncan, 2009a). The fallibility of student achievement measures, and the way such measures can be disingenuously manipulated, give rise to the very skepticism against which Race to the Top's proposals are meant to defend. This fallibility in achievement measurement, after all, is on full display in the way in which NCLB unwittingly encouraged states to make "proficiency" into an empty signifier, unmoored from any real-world application. Duncan's words point to a problem with the form of assessing students' academic success, but his policies seem geared mainly toward ameliorating a problem with the criteria according to which students are assessed. While Duncan's "college and career readiness" criterion is intended as a correction to the previous error, it appears at least possible that preparation for college and career will be made knowable in relation to the same unstable metrics that are available in student achievement data. The relative success of both teaching and learning will be visibile in measures of student achievement derived according to something very similar to NCLB's assessment protocols.

Duncan confirms this possibility, along with some caveats, in the speech he delivers to the Institute of Education Sciences on the very topic of "robust data." Data, Duncan says in an echo of the speech's title, "gives us the roadmap to reform. It tells us where we are, where we need to go, and who is most at risk" (Duncan, 2009b). In the notion that the data Duncan imagines indicates a present level of achievement and picks out individuals or groups "most at risk," the data that Duncan envisions certainly seem to consist in various measures of student achievement. He identifies some of these metrics by name in his address: high school graduation rates, TIMSS and PISA results, state assessments, the NAEP, the proportion of college students requiring remedial courses, and preschool enrollment figures.

The idea that data can reveal "where we need to go" is another matter, as it is not directly entailed in any of the measures noted above. While one could claim that a 75 percent graduation rate shows us the distance we have left to cover in achieving a rate of 100 percent, the data on graduation rates does not in itself show that a 100 percent rate is "where we need to go." But when Duncan calls for a "longitudinal study of teachers and an international survey of adult competencies" (Duncan, 2009b), he does suggest a form of data collection that would produce something plausibly approaching "college and career readiness." A survey of adult competencies, when identified with particular levels of socioeconomic status or earning power, which are in turn tethered to such and such a score on state or international assessments, would then produce at once "the essential things that our kids need to learn" and the requisite levels of achievement on state or international assessments.

Of course, once such an operation—pegging international or state assessment scores to varying indicators of socioeconomic standing—has been conducted, the "survey of international adult competencies" would simply drop out, since socioeconomic outcomes could be directly linked to achievement levels on assessments that already measure the domains of reading, math, and science. Indeed, as I will take up in a later section, the Chetty study I cited in the introduction (Chetty, Friedman, & Rockoff, 2011) and that Obama references in his 2012 State of the Union Address makes just such a move, tying socioeconomic achievement metrics to student test scores without the interloping of any particular "competencies." For the criterion of "college and career readiness" and its relation to data, the upshot is that "the essential things kids need to learn" will be the very domains already assessed on state and international exams; the task of knowing whether or not a given child is ready for college or career will be undertaken through the analysis of the results of these exams. Duncan is positively utopian in his aspirations for the predictive power on offer here: "Hopefully, one day we can look a child in the eye at the age of eight or nine or 10 and say, 'You are on track to be accepted and to succeed in a competitive university and, if you keep working hard, you will absolutely get there'" (Duncan, 2009b).

In terms of the purposes of reforming state standards through the rigorous use of "robust data," then, one must conclude that the primary aim pertains to combatting the conceptual degradation of "proficiency" witnessed under the NCLB regime. While Duncan touts "college and career" as the determining factor of both content and achievement levels, it becomes relatively clear that pegging particular achievement levels in the already-assessed domains of reading, math, and science to various socioeconomic outcomes will be sufficient to define readiness for college and career. The analysis of data, here, would translate desirable adult outcomes into the language, as it were, of student achievement on state or international exams. Arriving by means of such analysis at a secure connection between student assessments and adult outcomes, and encouraging states through the promise of federal funding to encode the results of this data analysis in their educational standards, would thus achieve precisely the kind of result that Race to the Top seeks: an (a) empirically anchored concept of "proficiency" that (b) is ratified by all 50 states.

Given the sort of skeptical fear that drives the particular reforms on display in Race to the Top, one that questions whether we really know what "proficiency" means and that wonders whether we can trust state or local officials when they declare their students "proficient," the use of data and financial incentives to derive a standard of proficiency to which all states will adhere proposes to solve the problem of skepticism by refutation: we *can* know what proficiency means, and we *can* know whether this or that reporting agency is equivocating with the concept.

1.3 ACHIEVEMENT DATA AND TEACHER PRACTICE

A similarly bifurcated skepticism pervades the reform discourse on teaching at large throughout Duncan's 2009 speeches, and these skeptical worries are similarly answered by student achievement data. Put as briefly as possible, a lack of official differentiation in the arena of teacher quality exposes the threatening possibility that no one can recognize good or bad teaching, or put another way, that no one *knows* what good teaching is, looks like, or consists in. The related fear is that teachers themselves lack a measure of requisite practical knowledge, both with respect to what their own students need and with respect to the best methods with which to teach them.

In this realm, as with the skepticism around content standards considered earlier, the use of student achievement data is aimed at solving a problem of knowledge, a problem that, once solved, would shut down both aspects of skeptical doubt just enumerated. Unlike the case of the content standards, however, Duncan's speeches acknowledge at various points the limitations of using student achievement data with respect to teachers. At such points, he indicates a region of epistemology that student achievement data can neither access nor eliminate, which will have important ramifications for the concept of "teaching" to which Race to the Top responds.

Duncan quite explicitly declares that data, as he envisions it, can answer multiple calls simultaneously. In his opening address before the Institute of Education Sciences, he asserts that that education reform "starts with robust data systems that track student achievement and teacher effectiveness" (Duncan, 2009b). The data that Duncan has in mind will thus serve at least these two interlocking purposes: measuring student progress and measuring teacher quality. Although in the same speech, he frames this relation as a hypothesis—"we will also ask whether the data around student achievement is linked to teacher effectiveness"—he nevertheless continues:

"We need to do a much better job of tracking students from pre–K through college. Teachers need this data to better target instruction to students. Principals need to know which teachers are producing the biggest gains and which may need more help" (Duncan, 2009b).

The data that Duncan envisions will thus also allow teachers more analytical insight into their students' particular needs, and allow principals a more incisive view into the particular strengths and weaknesses of teachers who "may need more help," which straightforwardly implies that "teacher effectiveness" is *obviously* connected to "student achievement." He sums up his vision for data like so:

> We can one day do a better job of understanding what makes great teachers tick, why they succeed, why they stay in the classroom and how others can be like them. Hopefully, we can track good programs to higher test scores to higher graduation rates. (Duncan, 2009b)

The ultimate goal of these proposed uses of data emerges in two forms. Duncan says, "hopefully, someday, we can track children from preschool to high school and from high school to college and college to career. We must track high growth children in classrooms to their great teachers and great teachers to their schools of education."

In this speech alone, the "robust data systems" Duncan envisions will be used by teachers (for instructional purposes), principals (for teacher evaluation purposes), local- and state-level administrators (for parental reporting and the evaluation of teacher training programs) and academic researchers (for the purposes of "understanding what makes great teachers tick," among other things). The data in question must then *simultaneously* reveal (a) student achievement levels, including specific areas for improvement, such that teachers can tailor instruction accordingly; (b) teacher quality, which is explicitly visible in the phenomenon of "high-growth children"; (c) teacher-preparation quality, which is recursively defined in terms of producing the teachers who produce the "high growth children"; and (d) the probable trajectory of a third- or fourth-grader's life. Duncan appropriately calls for *robust* data systems; given the number of tasks to which the data will be assigned, "robust" is the operative term.

The obvious question to raise at this point, which has also arisen in the consideration of the defining criterion of "college and career readiness," concerns the *nature* of this robust data. While Duncan never says explicitly what will count as data in his vision, it is difficult to miss the implication that the data will consist of the student achievement scores inherent in seeking out "high growth children." That Duncan takes such a variety of educational aspects to be visible in student achievement data—and that he takes knowledge about teachers and teaching as one such aspect—reveals important assumptions regarding the conceptual shape of teaching and learning, which it remains my project to draw out.

In particular, where student achievement data's relation to teaching is concerned, Duncan exhibits a great deal of revelatory ambivalence, which he most succinctly formulates in this very speech: "Data may not tell the whole truth, but it certainly doesn't lie." This formulation is revelatory both insofar as it acknowledges that there is something that data cannot do—namely, tell the whole truth—and also inasmuch as it reinforces the sense in which Race to the Top responds most directly to the possibility of being lied to. That is to say, Duncan reveals that achieving *certainty* is more important than achieving a perspicuous view of what one wishes to be certain *about*. Whether distinguishing "telling the whole truth" from "not lying" is possible at all will be an open question.

A scant few moments apart in this speech, Duncan posits two striking positions that echo the above formulation. First he asserts that "we will also ask *whether* the data around student achievement is linked to teacher effectiveness" (emphasis added); a minute later, he objects to what he sees as union obstructionism to involving student achievement data when he says that "to somehow suggest that we should not link student achievement and teacher effectiveness is like suggesting we judge a sports team without looking at the box score" (Duncan, 2009b). On the one hand, as we have seen, he does not take it for granted that student achievement data is inherently yoked to teacher effectiveness. On the other hand, he dismisses the possibility that student achievement is wholly *unrelated* to the concept of teacher quality. He speaks further to this ambivalence in such statements as, "I absolutely respect the concerns of teachers that test scores should never be used solely to determine salaries" and "I also appreciate that growth models as they exist today are far less than perfect." But he rejects any iteration of the notion that, as he says, "since standardized tests are not perfect, eliminate testing until they are," calling such an idea "absolutely ridiculous." While acknowledging that these tests are "not perfect," Duncan still avers that "we need to monitor progress. We need to know what is and is not working and why" (Duncan, 2009b). He constructs the problem similarly in a later speech to the NEA:

> I understand that tests are far from perfect and that it is unfair to reduce the complex, nuanced work of teaching to a simple multiple choice exam. Test scores alone should never drive evaluation, compensation, or tenure decisions. That would never make sense. But to remove student achievement entirely from evaluation is illogical and indefensible. (Duncan, 2009a)

It is crucial to note the particular way Duncan rhetorically envisions and copes with this ambivalence. Firstly, his rhetoric constructs and responds to a questionable dilemma, an all-or-nothing situation, as though if testing is to count for *anything* then it must count for *everything*,[1] as though one's only two options were to judge a sports team by the box score alone or to foreswear judging a sports team at all. Secondly, by dismissing as "absolutely ridiculous" the notion that student achievement has nothing to say about the nature or success of teaching, he renders the opposite extreme the more palatable of the two, and he finishes off the argument by appealing to the urgent need to know *something* about teaching, however imperfect: "We need to monitor progress. We need to know what is and is not working and why." This is a clear example of what Stanley Cavell would call "one side tak[ing] undue credit from the denial of the other" (Cavell, 2013, p. 51).

The emergence of Duncan's ambivalence with respect to student achievement data thus marks two important developments: (1) the multifaceted functions that data is meant to serve will be unable to foreclose completely on the skeptical danger in defense of which it has been recruited—whether "the whole truth" can be revealed at all remains in question—and (2) this new skeptical worry is *dismissed* on the grounds of the need for urgent action rather than *defeated* by argumentation. However, the fact of the dismissal will lead Duncan and many others to treat student achievement data as though it *had* in fact solved the skeptical problem at which it was aimed, as though achievement data really did establish certainty in the areas of teaching practice and evaluation.

Treating the dismissal of the problem as a victory is precisely what enables his statement that student achievement data is called for by a need both to "monitor progress" and to discover "what is and is not working and why." Granting the sincerity of Duncan's concern about the imperfections of tests in their current forms, it may nevertheless be possible to ascertain a ballpark estimate of a child's academic progress in the assessed domain(s), as long as that measure is understood as a rough estimate. But it hardly therefore follows that such measures reveal much at all about "what is and is not working," since any findings as to what is and is not working are derived from measures of achievement that are *admittedly* blurry. Despite the differences, the purpose of loosely "monitoring progress" through ad-hoc means necessitated by imperfect assessments seamlessly metamorphoses into making "data-driven decisions," ones based on acknowledged imperfections, as a matter of policy. Despite the known limitations of the measures, the assumption that one can use those measures to reliably distinguish "what is and is not working" remains somehow intact.

The intransigence of this particular assumption is revealing, I will later contend, of a belief that any flaws in testing protocols are merely technical matters, which would hold that if teaching and learning are not perfectly accessible by recourse to achievement tests as they currently exist, this results from temporary and remediable flaws in the current assessments themselves. In short, "monitoring progress" and discovering "what is and is not working" are *in principle* achievable by the same means, namely by measuring students against Common Core standards using standardized tests, even if they are not yet so achievable *in fact*.

In focusing on the conceptual construal of "teaching" as a skillful activity in the policies under discussion, I wish to test the fit between the robustness of the data that Race to the Top utilizes in its policies and the kind of robustness necessary to the myriad tasks it is assigned, particularly as regards the evaluation and study of teachers. To return, then, to the matter at hand, it will be worth asking what would fundamentally need to be true of teaching in order for Duncan's view of achievement data to succeed in each of the tasks he envisions for it.

Of data's utility for teachers, Duncan says,

> They need to know how well their students are performing. They want to know exactly what they need to do to teach and how to teach. It makes their job easier and ultimately much more rewarding. They aren't guessing or talking in generalities anymore. They feel as if they're starting to crack the code. (Duncan, 2009b)

Data, in this passage, is something that allows teachers to know how their "students are performing." But it also, Duncan implies, allows them "to know exactly *what they need to do to teach and how to teach*" (emphasis added); student achievement data is thus taken to reveal something about the *practices* involved in good teaching. Duncan provides a clue to his working assumptions in referring to data's enabling insights in terms of "crack[ing] the code," which seem to allow teachers to avoid "guessing."

The code-cracking metaphor is hardly an idle figure of speech, but it is a complex one. In the first place, code-cracking implies the transmission of a message, which is not an uncommon way to characterize teaching, though it is a reductive and largely discredited one in both P-12 and higher education (Laurillar, 2002; Tishman, Jay, & Perkins, 1993; Trigwell, Prosser, & Waterhouse, 1999). In a transmission model, the teacher's task is to impart certain knowledge to the students, who then come into possession of said knowledge, and can thus be said to have *learned*. Given that this metaphor appears in a speech focusing on student achievement data, these achievement measures presumably reveal the *amount* of students' new knowledge, and thus the relative success of the "message's" "transmission." So, students who demonstrate the most growth on achievement measures have learned more and better than those whose scores indicate little growth. Recursively, the teachers of "high growth" students have done a superior job of transmitting the message. The higher rate of transmission, one might call it, is then attributed to the teacher's fluency in some sort of code.

The above construction has at least three ramifications for the conceptual shape of teaching. First of all, the very concept of teaching would have to be limited to the transmission model, wherein teachers are in possession of knowledge that students require, and wherein the job consists of transporting that knowledge to the students' brains. Secondly, knowing "how to teach" would consist in the possession of a particular "code" that would best enable the successful transmission of knowledge from teacher to student. Such know-how would therefore rest upon a knowledge *of* something abstract, something like a secret syntax. In other words, knowing-how would really be a specific kind of knowing-that, inasmuch as the "how" of good teaching is contained in the "that" of a universal code. Thirdly, the "code" that allows and constitutes skillful teaching would indeed have to universally shared among students. Duncan claims that data allows teachers to feel like "they're starting to crack *the* code" (emphasis added); without the universal applicability of the code to all students, there is no sense in talking about "the" code at all.

Duncan's view of data's role with respect to teacher practice thus reveals a particular view of the concept of teaching itself. Through delving into Duncan's preliminary remarks on the matter, the shape of this view of teaching has emerged in outline form, whose major contours involve an adherence to a transmission model of instruction, a concept of skillful classroom practice based upon the possession of an objectively-knowable code, and a vision of students as fundamentally identical (on the levels that matter, at any rate) to one another, such that methods that "work" to achieve test score gains in one place are assumed to "work" to the same or a similar degree in any other.

The latter point deserves expansion, as it opens onto another salient assumption about the nature of high-quality teacher practice in particular—one that surfaces in another speech in the metaphor of "taking what works to scale." Duncan uses the particular phrases "take to scale" and "scale up" often in his thinking about quality schooling. It appears in the 2012 interview on *The Daily Show* (Stewart, 2012), in which he says that while there "are pockets of excellence" in the American school system, the task is to "take them to scale. . . . It's happening. It's just not happening at scale." In his speech on turning around troubled schools, he praises charter school organizations, to whom he delivers the speech, for "getting to scale" (Duncan, 2009e). In the same speech, he says, referring to the great schools he has visited, "The hard part is to replicate those conditions everywhere, and you need to challenge yourselves and challenge each other to turn one success into a hundred and a hundred into 200." In remarks to a group of Oregon educators in 2011, Duncan lauds the good work they do as specifically worthy of replication, saying, "The CLASS Project is a tremendous example of the successful work that should be taken to scale, because students benefit when teachers work together to share best practices and learn from one another" (Craig, 2011).

This trope is not Duncan's own: the scaling metaphor and the assumptions that undergird it simply pervade the reform-movement milieu from which Race to the Top's innovations spring. In the speech on turning around the lowest-performing schools, for example (Duncan, 2009e), Duncan touts certain charter networks and alternative certification routes, among them Uncommon Schools and Teach For America. The former organization was co-founded by Doug Lemov, whose recent book on teaching technique has been oft-heralded (Lemov, 2010); and the latter organization uses Lemov's methodology in developing new recruits in a very compressed span of time. Says Lemov of the primary issue in teacher training: "The really good question is, can you get people to improve really fast and at scale?" (Green, 2010). The metaphor has likewise made the rounds in education reform discourse quite generally over the past two decades (Elmore, 1996; Goggin, O'M Bowman, Lester, & O'Toole, 1990), and receives extensive airtime in Ford Foundation-financed studies on educational innovations (Glennan, Bodilly, Galegher, & Kerr, 2004). Other examples are simply legion and do not require citation here. Rather, two things stand out immediately in the uses of this scale-up or take-to-scale trope.

First is the scaling metaphor's native land, so to speak, the regions of language from which it comes to education policy discourse. To "scale up" or to "take" a given process "to scale" comes from two contexts: the world of business and the world of computer science. In the business context, scaling refers to the process of adding volume to an existing system as a means of or accruing income geometrically while incurring costs arithmetically; in the computer-science context, scaling has to do with generalizing a particular program or node's function in a limited context to a larger domain. In the business context, the cost of adding volume to an existing system is lower than the cost of building a new system of production from the ground up, but the price of the widget remains the same, resulting in greater profits without the commensurate effort or money required in reinventing the wheel, so to speak.

In the education reform movement that Duncan champions and codifies in Race to the Top, the notion of scalability retains its basic conceptual shape as it slides over from the economics and business context. Instead of adding *volume* to an existing system, scalability in education reform most often refers to integrating "successful" methodological innovations into existing methods of conducting the American school. In this sense, scaling proposes to locate instances of particular educational success and transfer the structures of practice and administration responsible for that success to other parts of the system, thus substantially lifting the central tendency metrics of the system as a whole without having to spend inordinate amounts of energy or money on discovering "what works" in each particular and unique setting.

When Duncan says to the charter school assembly, "The hard part is to replicate those [successful] conditions everywhere, and you need to challenge yourselves and challenge each other to turn one success into a hundred and a hundred into 200" (Duncan, 2009e), this is what he has in mind: implementing the innovative conditions that caused success in these particular instances much more generally, so that "one success" turns into "a hundred and hundred into 200." As the title of the Elmore article, with its focus on "good educational practices," reveals—a fact further echoed in

Duncan's mention of "best practices" in his remarks to the Oregon teachers highlights (Craig, 2011)—the idea of scalability comes with a built-in sense of the means of its own attainment, which will bear further exploration and critique in later chapters. For the time being, it will suffice to sketch the picture of good teaching that Duncan's comments paint.

In order for good teaching, in particular, to be amenable to something like scaling, certain things must be true of teaching. In the first place, teaching must be conceived at a fundamental level as a more or less integrated—but ultimately atomizable—set of behaviors or beliefs. When Duncan wishes to take innovations "to scale," either in the realm of teaching practice or school administration, the working assumption is that a successful innovation in one context will have a similar effect in another, and the basis of that assumption lies in the conception of teaching and learning as *fundamentally* a collection of isolated objects (behaviors or techniques) linked to specific outcomes. Unless the *contents* of "successful" education can be transferred elsewhere in the "system," there is no sense in talking about scaling.

In the second place, in order for the above assumption itself to function as it does, educational *quality* must be wholly separate or separable from its context of actualization or demonstration and contained within the structures responsible for success. In other words, since the successful innovations themselves are constituted in certain structures of administration or the behavioral practices of teachers, their "successfulness" is conceived as an internal feature of these structures of practice or administration. Insofar as scaling successful educational endeavors involves spreading success throughout the system by means of inculcating particular "good" or "best" practices, that which makes the practices "good" or "best" must be internal to the structures themselves. After all, scaling theoretically involves spreading the success of the innovative techniques to the far reaches of the education system by means of propagating the behavioral or structural contents of that innovation. Unless the contents of *successful* education can be transferred elsewhere in the "system," there is no sense in talking about scaling.

The frequency of the scaling metaphor's appearance reinforces its conceptual potency as it proliferates in policy and public rhetoric. The upshot of the conceptual analysis of scaling in education reveals a version of the educative process in which (1) the practice of teaching is comprised of isolated behaviors that (2) are causally related to "successful" outcomes at both the level of the individual student and the level of the school, and whose (3) fundamental quality is a predicate of the behaviors themselves as they manifest in (4) any classroom whatsoever without much respect to context, if any.[2]

The sort of good teaching amenable to scaling is, then, precisely the sort depicted in the subtitle of Doug Lemov's book: *Teach Like a Champion: The 49 Techniques that Put Students on the Path to College*. On Lemov's view, teaching is divisible into 49 (or *n*) "techniques," which, taken together, have an implied causal relation to the end goal of college-preparedness, and this relation *itself* determines the quality that inheres in the techniques. Good teaching therefore consists in the performance of the proper techniques in classroom settings, specific techniques whose "properness" has been defined by the behaviors' correlation with achievement score growth, as Elizabeth Green explicitly notes (Green, 2010).

The way in which Lemov's work links "college and career" preparation to the notion of "good teaching" through the use of student achievement data provides a succinct recapitulation of my investigation thus far. I noted at the opening of this subsection that the particular skepticism Race to the Top seeks to overcome with respect to teachers pertains, in part, to a fear that no one, including teachers, really *knows* what good teaching is and the particular practical methods that comprise it. The solution to this skepticism that Race to the Top's proposals offer involves the use of student achievement data in just the way that Lemov exemplifies, that is, to connect particular practical techniques to eventual "college and career"-related outcomes. The exploration of the assumptions about teaching practice that such a solution would require has revealed that Race to the Top has in view a very specific picture of what it is to practice a skill, one that holds that *knowing how* to do anything at all means knowing isolable techniques and knowing the proper situations in which to demonstrate them.

It will be important at this point to recall Duncan's ambivalence about the relation between teaching and student achievement data. Achievement data would infallibly reveal the sum total of good teaching, both in terms of its purposes and its practices, as long as two assumptions held: (1) growth in math, reading, and science assessments either directly entailed or reliably proxied for all of the goals that we as a society set for our education system, and (2) teaching as a skillful endeavor really did operate on the rationalist view above, wherein know-how is encapsulated in the knowledge of a "code" or a list of "best practices" along with a set of rules or maxims that governed their application in the classroom context.

Duncan's allowances of the limitations inherent to using student achievement data give reason to doubt both assumptions, insofar as the assumptions are imagined to (re)produce excellent teaching practice. The second assumption, however, must be dealt with independently from considerations specifically pertaining to achievement data or any other specific means of deriving *best* practices in order to test whether the dangers to teacher practice and preparation posed by adopting Duncan's proposals are simply a matter of looking in the *wrong places* for "best practices." That will be the subject of the next few chapters.

In the meantime, there remains the related skeptical worry pertaining to teachers that Race to the Top seeks to address through the use of student achievement data, and this skepticism manifests itself in the form of doubting or denying that present techniques of evaluating teachers are sufficiently capable of perceiving or recognizing teacher quality.

1.4 STUDENT ACHIEVEMENT DATA AND TEACHER EVALUATION

Skepticism around the relative ability to officially ascertain teacher quality comes out in two particularly demonstrative facts that Duncan cites in his speeches during the summer of 2009: the failure of ground-level administrators to distinguish among individual teachers, and the failure of state- or national-level officials to place individual teachers on a meaningful quality spectrum relative to one another. Since one of Race to the Top's primary strategies for improving the American education system involves improving the aggregate quality of classroom teachers, one method of which, as addressed above, has to do with using student achievement data to determine the *content* teachers ought to be teaching and the specific *practices* that teachers ought to employ, another aspect of the effort to improve the quality of teachers will of necessity entail knowing which teachers are succeeding, which are not, and why.

As Duncan says, laying out the threat of failure in this regard, "When great teachers are unrecognized and unrewarded, when struggling teachers are unsupported, and when failing teachers are unaddressed the teaching profession is damaged" (Duncan, 2009a). The dual implication, expressed across the range of his speeches, is (1) that we "have to fix our method of evaluating teachers, which is basically broken" (Duncan, 2009c), and (2) that incorporating student achievement data into teacher evaluations can solve this problem. He is absolutely clear on the relation between the inadequacies of current teacher evaluation protocols and the refusal to consider student achievement data, noting in close proximity that "a recent report by the New Teacher Project shows that 99 percent of teachers are all rated the same," and that "most teacher rating systems don't take student achievement into account" (Duncan, 2009c). The 99 percent statistic and Duncan's use thereof hints that achievement data will make local evaluation of individual teachers much more rigorous.

But it will also solve a perceived problem that exists at the state and national level, one that he observes in the following fact:

> In California, they have 300,000 teachers. If you took the top 10 percent, they have 30,000 of the best teachers in the world. If you took the bottom 10 percent, they have 30,000 teachers that should probably find another profession, yet no one in California can tell you which teacher is in which category. Something is wrong with that picture. (Duncan, 2009b)

> The development of an absolute way of measuring teacher quality—which in its assumptions is akin to the efforts to achieve absolute notions of "what works" in the practice of teaching and an absolute sense of "the essential things kids need to know"—will enable rigorous comparisons among 300,000 teachers distributed across an entire state.

It is significant that Duncan voices this latter iteration of his skeptical worry in terms of the *inability* implicit in his "no one in California *can* tell you which teacher is in which category" (Duncan 2009b) locution. Such an inability is likewise implicit in his connection of the fact that 99 percent of teachers are all rated the same with the fact that some states prohibit the inclusion of student achievement data in processes of teacher evaluation. Failures to distinguish among teachers in terms of their quality are thereby attributed to the same cause across the administrative levels of the local, the state, and the nation: refusing to take student achievement into account has made it impossible to *know* "which teacher is in which category"; student achievement data removes this impossibility at long last, and thereby makes such knowledge possible.

I raise the leveling of differences among local, state, and national contexts through the ascription of a shared epistemological inability in terms of teacher quality for two reasons. In the first place, while it is certainly fair to say that the ability to compare 300,000 teachers distributed across an entire state to each other would be a first in human history—one that has been neither possible nor required in any other professional domain, including plumbing, law, medicine, or accounting, for instance—and while it thus makes sense to say that the development of a universal measure of teacher quality according to which to compare hordes of teachers would count as developing a brand new human capacity, it is far less clear that the 99 percent statistic unambiguously indicates a straightforward epistemological *inability* in terms of knowing teacher quality at all, even at the local level. That is, many factors other than ignorance could account for the fact that 99 percent of teachers are rated the same, including prominently the lack of financial incentive to record qualitative differences, thanks to the seniority and tenure rules written into the collective bargaining agreements.

While these are also issues that Duncan wishes to address with Race to the Top proposals, it is at least possible that administrators, parents, and students can readily perceive distinctions among the teachers in a given building, but that there is currently neither a compelling mechanism nor any incentive to rank teachers officially from best to worst. In fact, as I will shortly draw out, Duncan's own ability to perceive quality at the level of both teachers and individual schools makes it significantly unlikely that the epistemological limitation visible in the inability to draw distinctions among 300,000 teachers generalizes to an epistemological limitation as regards educational quality *as such*.

In the second place, the proposal of student achievement data as a solution to the skeptical danger so constructed entails conceptual consequences for the view of teaching addressed in Race to the Top policy. These are the very conceptual consequences that were spelled out in the previous subsection: in order for teaching to be the sort of thing fundamentally knowable in terms of student achievement data, such that comparing 300,000 teachers to one another despite the contextual differences of subject specialty, grade level, classroom composition, et (endlessly) cetera, teaching's *aims* would have to reducible to a single, unified criterion, such as college and career readiness; this aim itself would need to be measurable and expressible according to the same student achievement data; and teacher *practice* would need to be rigorously linked to this aim and likewise visible and expressible in terms of the same student achievement data.

In Duncan's claim that, while the top 30,000 teachers in California are among the world's best, the bottom 30,000 "should probably find another profession," he indicates the profound stakes in wielding student achievement data as a solution to skepticism about the ability to achieve certainty in terms of teacher quality: the 30,000th teacher from the bottom of the list *ought* to lose his or her job; the 30,001st should not. That is a very fine distinction to make, and Duncan rhetorically places his faith in achievement data to make it.

The use of student achievement data in the process of evaluating teachers must, for Duncan, come with real consequences if such evaluations will encourage great teachers to stay, help new teachers to improve, and identify teachers who "should probably find another profession." It is for this reason that in several of these addresses, he faults state laws for preventing the inclusion of achievement data in teacher evaluation. In addition to amending this aspect of state codes, Duncan calls for restructuring the collective bargaining agreements (CBAs) that teachers' unions have struck with school districts, agreements that enshrine tenure protection and that tie compensation to seniority rather than quality. Changing these rules would create the conditions for an influx of great teachers, as measured according to achievement scores, into classrooms all over America.

Teachers requiring replacement will leave the classroom for a variety of reasons, but two in particular urge Duncan's attention: the mass retirement of baby boomers and attrition or termination. Improving the quality of the teaching corps generally thus requires two specific efforts, one geared toward ensuring that the quality of new teachers entering the profession be superior, aggregately, to those leaving it, and one geared toward giving local education agencies in particular greater freedom to make decisions with regard to personnel—in terms of both termination and compensation—to the effect of removing poor teachers, retaining good ones, and recruiting promising ones. That comprises the main thrust of Duncan's speech to the NEA.

In the second half of this speech, he lays the responsibility for the current failings of the public schools at the feet of the profession itself, in the form of the teacher unions:

> And I'm telling you as well that, when inflexible seniority and rigid tenure rules that we designed put adults ahead of children, then we are not only putting kids at risk, we're also putting the entire education system at risk. We're inviting the attack of parents and the public, and that is not good for any of us.

I believe that teacher unions are at a crossroads. These policies were created over the past century to protect the rights of teachers, but they have produced an industrial factory model of education that treats all teachers like interchangeable widgets. (Duncan, 2009a)

A 2005 report on the effect of existing CBAs on urban districts' hiring policies, conducted by the New Teacher Project, sums up the situation in words that Duncan echoes in his 2009 speech:

At the core of these transfer and excess rules is a single principle: every incumbent teacher is guaranteed a job in a school, frequently in seniority order, even if no school wants to hire him or her . . . by adopting factory model protections, these efforts codified an important set of assumptions that structures the work and culture of urban schools to this day. These early contracts determined that job protections and teacher movements would occur according to seniority and required that all teachers be treated as if they were interchangeable in every other respect. (Levin, Mulhern, & Schunck, 2005)

The "factory model," in which teachers are "interchangeable widgets," reflects Duncan's dissatisfaction with the failures of contemporary evaluation methodologies to distinguish among teachers in terms of quality at all. Thanks to the union-negotiated CBAs, nothing pertaining to teacher quality separates one teacher from another; instead, seniority remains the only distinguishing feature. Amending state laws regarding the use of achievement data in teacher evaluation, combined with the greater flexibility afforded to local school administrators as a result of restructuring tenure and compensation rules in CBAs, would allow states and districts to take decisive personnel action based upon an unprecedented level of certainty about teacher quality, a certainty achieved in overcoming the epistemological limits that have prevented both state-level officials and building-level administrators from officially recognizing teacher quality.

Given the consequences attached to the use of student achievement data in determining teacher quality, it will be important to recall once more Duncan's vocal ambivalence with respect to such data's ability "to tell the whole truth," an ambivalence also visible in his hesitation to reduce the "complex" and "nuanced work of teaching to a single test score." As I said in the previous subsection, this ambivalence points in the direction of a region of the concept of teaching that is inaccessible to student achievement, or one that student achievement data cannot make visible. Is this conceptual region therefore *simply* inaccessible to knowledge? Duncan's descriptions of his own visits to schools and his personal experiences with teachers suggest that it is not.

In his speech on turning around the bottom five percent of schools, Duncan addresses both quantitative and qualitative means of recognizing the caliber of a school. He specifies the relevant criteria of quality at work in his vision:

> Sherman Elementary saw a five-point jump in the percentage of students meeting standards in the first year. Harvard reduced absences by five days per student in the first year. And Orr High School saw a 15-point jump in attendance in its first year. (Duncan, 2009e)

The percentage of students meeting standards and attendance rates constitute quantitative evidence of school improvement for Duncan, and those are certainly and obviously accessible in terms of data. But he ventures outside of the strictly or obviously measurable, as well, in this speech, citing anecdotes of Chicago parents who

> talk about their kids 'looking forward to school for the first time,' coming home and 'talking about their teachers.' They say it's 'a totally different atmosphere' even though it's the same schools with the same kids and the same socioeconomic conditions. (Duncan, 2009e)

The use of anecdotal evidence itself, such as the citation of "a totally different atmosphere," is remarkable in this speech because it helps to concretize that which Duncan resolutely avoided making explicit in other speeches, namely, the aspects of teacher and school quality that lie alongside or outside the achievement data. Examining the type of evidence he cites and the way that he expects it to function in other contexts reveals important aspects of his approach to educational quality in general, both at the level of the school and at the level of the teacher.

Duncan returns to the use of atmospheric comments as he refers to specific indicators of good schools, both in traditional public schools and in charters:

> We know what success looks like. I see it the moment I enter a school. It's clean, orderly, the staff is positive and welcoming, and the kids and the classroom are the focus. I see award-winning school work on the walls. I see discipline and enthusiasm in the children. I see parents engaged and teachers collaborating on instruction. (Duncan, 2009e)

Absent from these indicators is any mention of the achievement data that has played such a prominent role so far. In this instance, Duncan discusses "what success looks like." In terms of school-wide building characteristics, he points to cleanliness, orderliness, and the presence of "award-winning school work" hanging on the walls; in terms of student affect, he points to "discipline" and "enthusiasm"; in terms of the adults in the building, he cites a "positive and welcoming" atmosphere, an atmosphere where "kids and the classroom are the focus," and one that seems to encourage parent engagement and teacher collaboration.

What stands out immediately in this description is Duncan's assertion that he can see success "the moment [he] enter[s] a school." The immediate visibility of success inherent in the claim that "we know what success looks like" signifies the ordinary, everyday experience of judging schools, whether by laypeople, experts, or politicians. This, then, is an example of the intrusion of what I have earlier called the "ordinary concept" of good teaching in Duncan's discourse, which otherwise speaks of good teaching according to the "technical sense" visible in achievement data.

The conceptual development here, in which Duncan explicitly references an immediately apparent aspect of educational quality, will serve as an important bookmark to which to return on occasion. In his call for "robust data systems," Duncan's approach presents a view of learning—of school and teacher quality—that is fundamentally *mysterious* or at any rate occult, such that the use of achievement data to sort good teachers from bad teachers, and high-performing from low-performing schools, is required. The technical concept is *necessary*, on this view, precisely because it is assumed, thanks to an interpretation of the 99 percent statistic as expressing an epistemological inability, for instance, that we do not know with any clarity or rigor what good teaching is or what it looks like. But Duncan's "we know what success looks like" directly contravenes this assumption.

To frame the issue in slightly different terms, the skeptical problem to which the use of student achievement data presents a solution is one on which we *do not know* whether this or that practice is an example of good teaching, whether this or that skill is what a child ought to be learning, whether this or that school is failing. Duncan paints the refusal to take student achievement data into account in talking about educational quality as an absurdity, but in assembling the conceptual machinery whereby instructional techniques, teacher quality, college and career readiness, and curricular content are all simultaneously revealed in student achievement data, he engages in another sort of absurd refusal, namely, a denial of the very perceptual ability according to which the excellence of a given educative endeavor stands out clearly "the moment [he] enter[s] a school." This is roughly what Stanley Cavell has in mind in discussing Wittgenstein's view of skepticism's temptations, in which Wittgenstein "discovers the threat or temptation of skepticism in such a way that efforts to solve it continue its work of denial" (Cavell, 1990, p. 21).

Duncan's citation to the immediately available aspects of school quality might function as recitations of the criteria by which excellent educational practice is ordinarily knowable; this would be the conceptual region whose existence prompts his ambivalence about the use of student achievement data. In his own account of his childhood, which he recalls to his audience during his speech to the NEA, he develops such criteria further and confirms that these are indeed inaccessible to the achievement data that undergird his hopes for the improvement of the American education system.

Duncan raises this ordinary conceptual terrain through narrating relevant memories of his own boyhood, in which his mother "began an after-school, inner-city tutoring program." He highlights his "community's chaos" and the experience of "early, violent deaths" due to the violence of the neighborhood, but he notes that,

> from the group of friends I grew up studying with and playing ball with, from one street corner at 46th and Greenwood, emerged literally a brain surgeon, a Hollywood movie star, one of my top administrators at the Chicago Public Schools, and one of IBM's international corporate leaders. (Duncan, 2009a)

Like the Olly Neal narrative in Kristof's second article, Duncan's recollection here is meant to militate against the sort of claim Ravitch makes in *Reign of Error*, which has it that solving poverty is a necessary first step to solving achievement-gap issues. Duncan attests here to the fact that great teaching can entail its life-changing effects in despite of socio-economic disadvantage. Duncan attributes this outlying success to the influence of a meaningful adult involvement in his life:

> How did this happen? Because these children, despite tremendous poverty, despite staggering neighborhood violence, despite challenges at home, had my mother and others in their lives who gave them real opportunities, real support and guidance over the years, and had the highest expectations for them.

Duncan's rhetoric thus far accomplishes two things with respect to his explicit agenda: in the first place, it offers a preliminary depiction of an ordinary sense of good teaching, and in the second place it emphasizes the potential impact of such teaching in terms of "college and career." The distinction between the sense of "good teaching" that appears in his narrative and the highly technical sense visible only according to student achievement data comes out in a few particular spots.

In the first and most obvious indication of difference, the concept of teacher quality visible in the above narrative only becomes knowable— *tellable*—in extreme hindsight, after Duncan and his childhood friends have already achieved career success. Would such success have been predictable by virtue of math and reading scores (and is becoming a "Hollywood movie star" contingent thereupon at all)? The assumption that Duncan makes in his use of this particular anecdote as a means of indicating the need for increased data use in teacher evaluation protocols is that it would. In the second place, though, Duncan alludes to the way the teacher figure in this narrative offered "support and guidance *over the years*," a fact that distinguishes the concept of "teaching" involved here from that accessible in terms of the technical sense visible in student achievement data. Duncan must assume that the technical sense of teaching implicitly includes the kind of "teacher quality" that exceeds the scope of measures upon which his technical definition rests, since what he points to—the over-the-years involvement of great teachers—can in no way be inferred from students' score growth from one year to the next.

That a teacher would function *as* a teacher in both an administratively official capacity (i.e. one in which the student appears on the class list assigned to the teacher) and, in ensuing years, in an unofficial capacity, offering longer-term "support and guidance" of precisely the kind Duncan depicts in the instance of his mother, certainly is a common feature of elementary, middle, and high school experience alike. Duncan is quite right to recognize that the concept of "teacher quality" pertains to this domain as well. This very region of the concept of "good teaching," however, exceeds the technical definition, which cannot measure this sort of impact. While some correlation may exist between the two definitions, it certainly cannot be assumed.

Duncan attributes tremendous lifelong effects to his mother's program; it is therefore clear that her quality as an educator is epistemologically available *now that* Duncan and his cohort have achieved adult success. The problem for teacher evaluation is to know such quality *in the present*, while students' adulthood successes are still a long way off; this is what the use of student achievement data promises. But Duncan's mother ran an "after-school" tutoring program which generated (or was responsible for) no achievement data whatsoever. In an exact replay of the problems cropping up in Kristof's citation of Olly Neal's story, the quality of Duncan's mother would not be visible, and also, more nefariously, the classroom teachers on whose rolls Duncan and his friends appeared would have received, unearned, the credit for any score gains. This reveals both the obvious yet easily forgotten point that a multitude of adults are involved in a given child's learning of a particular skill or subject at any given moment, which complicates the appeal of achievement data; and also that a wholesale turn to teacher-quality metrics based on such data depends upon making the assumption that those familiar with his mother's program were in a sense *ignorant* of whether or not she was good at what she did.[3]

It seems ridiculous even to suggest that her quality would have been somehow invisible to anyone locally familiar. Rather, Duncan appears to display an instance in which a teacher's quality would have *required* no data, in which a teacher's quality would have been *immediately visible*, much as when Duncan knows a successful school "the moment [he] enter[s] the school."

He introduces, in short, an overt reference to the ordinary or everyday concept of teacher quality, one which is emphatically not a subset of the technical variety. The use of student achievement data is intended explicitly to shore up a problem constructed as an epistemological weakness with respect to knowing teacher quality, but Duncan's remarks regarding an immediately visible notion of teacher quality enervates the temptation to consider the problem of addressing teacher quality *as* one stemming from an epistemological inability; and his citations of the sorts of teaching that his policies seek to encourage would appear—at least initially—to be less than commensurate with the technical view of teaching visible according to student achievement data. The suggestion, when these two facts are taken together, is that Duncan's response to a problem constructed along skeptical lines would in fact make the desired state of affairs less, rather than more, likely to emerge from his policies.

1.5 THE ORDINARY, THE TECHNICAL, AND THE IMPORTANCE OF MULTIPLE MEASURES

The implicit premise undergirding the appeal of and to student achievement data in matters of teacher evaluation particularly, but a premise that also extends to data's appeal in the criterion of college and career preparedness and matters of teaching practice, is that the sort of teaching and learning that it makes visible or knowable is more or less identical to the sort of teaching and learning that shows up in the narrative form of Duncan's recollections, Obama's 2012 State of the Union address, and Kristof's Olly Neal invocation. Duncan's many acknowledgements that teaching is irreducible to "a simple multiple choice exam" (Duncan, 2009a) or that, as in the interview with Jon Stewart, "multiple measures" are required in evaluating teachers (Stewart, 2012), evince an awareness that bringing these two pictures of good teaching into alignment with one another will require some extra effort and due consideration. The nature and derivation of these multiple measures and the sort of due consideration involved bears exploring here, as does the bottom-level requirement that Duncan and his policies take the problem of relating these concepts to one another seriously.

It is by no means clear that he is as militant in policing the distinction between these two concepts as he would need to be in order to effectively carry out the task of rigorously relating them to one another. In characterizing the ordinary sense of good teaching—that sense available immediately and through narrative recollection—Duncan specifies some of the content of the concept:

> All of us remember an educator or coach who changed our life. It stays with us forever. It sustains us, guides us, and inspires us. They're the ones who commit those everyday acts of kindness and love and never ask for anything in return. They counsel troubled teens, take phone calls at night, and reach into their pockets for lunch money for children who are too ashamed to ask. (Duncan, 2009a)

By inviting the audience to communally and individually "remember and educator or coach who changed our life," Duncan underlines an experience so ordinary that he can assume that his entire audience shares it. He fleshes out the content that constitutes the teacher quality he depicts in pointing to "those everyday acts of kindness and love," such as "counsel[ing] troubled teens, tak[ing] phone calls at night," and so on. None of this content shows up in lesson plans; none of it would be more than implicit in achievement data. The concept of teacher quality on display here clearly and self-evidently differs from the technical definition—the very content *indicative* of each concept per se fails to evince even the slightest overlap. Nothing at all warrants the assumption that the sort of teachers Duncan depicts in the concrete example of his mother and in the reverie he conjures in the above quotation would *also and necessarily* be the sort of teachers to consistently lift student test scores.

In a speech on teacher education programs given in October of the same year (Duncan, 2009d), the Secretary once again invokes the ordinary concept of good teaching, and he offers new conceptual content as well. But on this occasion, he immediately runs together the ordinary sense with the technical, as though the two *were in fact* commensurate with one another, as though to speak of one was also and simply to speak of the other.

> Now there is a reason why so many of us remember a favorite teacher forever. A great teacher can literally change the course of a student's life. They light a lifelong curiosity, a desire to participate in democracy, and instill a thirst for knowledge. It's no surprise that studies repeatedly document that the single biggest influence on student academic growth is the quality of the teacher standing in front of the classroom—not socioeconomic status, not family background, but the quality of the teacher at the head of the class. (Duncan, 2009d)

The sense of urgency that runs throughout Duncan's speeches has its basis in his recognition of the importance of teachers. In an ordinary sense, he names the reasons and the ways in which great teachers *are* important: "They light a lifelong curiosity, a desire to participate in democracy, and instill a thirst for knowledge." But in the very next sentence, the teacher importance to which he refers has nothing to do with "light[ing] a lifelong curiosity" or any of the other salutary effects that he attributes to great teachers in the previous sentence. He says, "studies repeatedly document that the single biggest influence on student academic growth is the quality of the teacher standing in front of the classroom." Suddenly, Duncan speaks of "student academic growth" rather than "curiosity-lighting" or "knowledge-thirst."

When he claims in the latter sentence that teacher quality represents "the single biggest influence on student academic growth," he entirely departs from the realm in which quality appears in any sort of "lighting" or "instilling" or "inspiring." The teacher quality he refers to in the latter sentence is revealed in the amount of variance in student math or reading scores accounted for by variance in "teacher quality," however that variable is (technically) defined. So the two concepts of teacher quality are precisely as (dis)similar as inspiring a lifelong love of learning in a student on the one hand, and accounting for variance in a math or reading score from one given year to the next, on the other.

In a subtle and perhaps unintentional move, he thus abruptly conflates the great teacher "so many of us remember" with a teacher who "influences student academic growth." He, himself, has been adamant that these are different constructs, and with good reason. But his own example above indicates the ease with which the dramatic distinction between these concepts simply vanishes in the course of discussing teacher quality.

This ease of conflation or confusion comes out in another spot, as well. Earlier in this very speech, referring to administrative encouragement for professional development, Duncan says, "I am a big believer in this program, but let's also be honest: school systems pay teachers billions of dollars more each year for earning PD [professional development] credentials that do very little to improve the quality of teaching" (Duncan, 2009a). Duncan appears to refer to factual knowledge here, something established as true or accurate; and not only that, but also something somewhat obvious, as his "let's be honest" appeal indicates: additional credentials—teacher certification and advanced degrees—"do very little to improve the quality of teaching."

When claiming that professional development or additional credentials have little effect on "the quality of teaching," he invokes one or both of two lines of research that trace the effects, respectively, of teachers holding graduate degrees and of teacher certification status on student outcomes *as measured by growth in student test scores*. A typical finding in the latter instance tells the story like so: "Finally, consistent with previous work, there is little or no evidence that a master's degree raises the quality of teaching. All estimates are small (or negative) and statistically insignificant" (Rivkin, Hanushek, & Kain, 2005), and it is a point echoed in myriad other places both prior and subsequent to Duncan's speech (Chingos & Peterson, 2011). Meanwhile, in terms of credentialing or certification, an oft-cited study concludes, "Our results suggest that the emphasis on certification status may be misplaced. We find little difference in the average academic achievement impacts of certified, uncertified and alternatively certified teachers" (Kane, Rockoff, & Staiger, 2008). When these authors speak of "academic achievement" in such academic studies, they explicitly point to math and reading achievement scores alone.

When Duncan claims, then, that professional development seems to "do very little to improve the quality of teaching," the teaching he has in mind is the form of teaching defined *only* in terms of the insufficient data he is elsewhere careful to bracket with caveats about the need for "multiple measures" of quality. No such multiple measures appear in the accepted truth about teacher credentialing that he claims in this example. It will be notable that when other proxies for the broad concept of learning are employed in academic research—equally incomplete proxies, one must add—different conclusions result. A recent study that considers the impact of teacher credentials on student learning as revealed in student GPA, for example, which takes data from Swedish compulsory schools, finds that certification does indeed have a significant effect on "student learning" (Andersson, Johansson, & Waldenström, 2011). Whether or not credentialing has an impact on "teacher quality" seems to depend—as common sense would predict—on what is taken to constitute or reveal "student achievement" as itself an indirect indicator of "teacher quality."

Despite Duncan's attempts to maintain the integrity of an ordinary concept of good teaching, and to bear in mind its distinction from the technical definition thereof, the technical definition seems to usurp the place of the ordinary sense of the term when Duncan's back is proverbially turned. When Duncan calls for the inclusion of achievement data in teacher evaluations, citing also the caveat that teaching and learning can never be reduced to such a measure, he explicitly wishes to use a technical sense of "teacher quality" to achieve a fuller view of the *ordinary* concept of good teaching; instead, the technical sense comes to function interchangeably with the ordinary sense, and thus threatens to supplant it entirely.

In pointing to or evoking the life-changing capacity of teachers, Duncan appeals to another criterion of success than that which appears merely in achievement data, something more akin to the face value of "college and career readiness." He raises the aforementioned narrative examples of excellent teaching in order to highlight the *concrete* importance of good teachers to the future lives of their students. In referencing the "everyday acts of kindness and love," for example, he indicates that the *quality* of the acts are bound up genitively with the contextualized acts themselves, rendering this quality immediately apparent to the situated observer. No mediating, abstract knowledge-producing protocol seems required to understand the acts in question as acts *of kindness*, for example, and no arguments seem necessary to link "acts of kindness" with the concept of good teaching. The real-world outcomes that serve as the ultimate aim of teaching in his rhetoric remain tied to the immediately visible quality of the teachers whose stories he tells. The immanence and commonality of the kind of teacher quality he has in mind in moments like these distinguishes the everyday concept of "good teaching" from the technical variety outlined earlier.

The distinction between the ordinary concept of good teaching and the technical sort remains important to this discussion precisely because Duncan himself insists upon it. That is, the driving impetus to pursue these concepts *as* distinct follows from Duncan's own words on the matter that appear in this very speech: the "complex, nuanced work of teaching can never be reduced to a simple multiple choice test" (Duncan, 2009a). Duncan's use of the term *reduction* in the foregoing sentence emphasizes that the "complex, nuanced" work of teaching *exceeds* the scope of existing achievement measures. If it is indeed the case that good teaching cannot be "reduced" to achievement metrics, then neither can it be *simply* extrapolated from achievement data. Duncan avers, in essence, that good teaching is more than lifting achievement scores. This *more than* manifests itself in the both the example of his mother—an extracurricular tutorial figure over several years in the life of neighborhood children—and in his appeal to the audience to recall the transformative, life-changing teachers in their own life.

Putting into evaluative practice Duncan's acknowledgement about the excessive (to achievement data) region of the concept good teaching would require an explicit means of bringing the immediately-visible aspects of teacher quality into conversation with the technical aspects revealed according to achievement data. In order for the use of student achievement data to produce the sort of improvement in the teaching corps that Race to the Top seeks to effect, it must work together with the ordinary concept. Duncan likewise acknowledges this fact in citing as an example a pilot performance-pay system he implemented in Chicago, a program that based teacher compensation on teaching *quality*, as that quality was revealed across several measures.

Such performance-pay systems would provide one way of slowing attrition rates among high-quality teachers and also of incentivizing all teachers to reach the level of excellence: "Many schools give nothing at all to the teachers who go the extra mile and make all the difference in students' lives. Excellence matters and we should honor it—fairly, transparently, and on terms teachers can embrace" (Duncan, 2009a). "Excellence," as he speaks of it here, is clearly bound up with "go[ing] the extra mile" and "mak[ing] all the difference in students' lives": this is the ordinary sense of excellent teaching. In the interest of demonstrating the fair, transparent and cooperative nature of such endeavor, he describes the program he developed in Chicago with the aid of "24 of the best" teachers in the system: "It was based on classroom observation, whole school performance, and individual classroom performance, measured in part by growth in student learning" (Duncan, 2009a). "Classroom performance, measured in part by growth in student learning" straightforwardly refers to student achievement gains. "Whole-school performance" is also measurable in terms of such achievement data. "Classroom observations," therefore, provide the context in which an evaluator might be able to officially record the ordinary sense of good teaching that Duncan's policies explicitly seek: only a few minutes later in the same speech, he makes the explicit statement to which I have already referred, and to which the invocation of "classroom observations" responds: "I understand that tests are far from perfect and that it is unfair to reduce the complex, nuanced work of teaching to a simple multiple choice exam. Test scores alone should never drive evaluation, compensation, or tenure decisions" (Duncan, 2009a).

As technically defined—in its technical sense—good teaching appears in the student achievement growth to which Duncan refers here. But Duncan also notes that this technical sense is not enough. He clearly alludes to the insufficiency of the *means* of ascertaining the technical sense of good teaching to reveal something durable about the everyday or ordinary sense of good teaching, and in doing so he zeroes in on the ordinary sense.

Rewarding and terminating on the basis of the ordinary sense of good teaching, therefore, remains the centerpiece and goal of his strategy. In noting that achievement score growth alone reveals merely the technical sense, such that the exemplary model of a functional evaluation procedure to which he points employs both achievement data *and* "classroom observation," the observation piece clearly and self-evidently plays the role of rounding out the evaluation such that the ordinary sense of good teaching would emerge into view above and beyond the technical sense. Classroom observations' value therefore lies in bridging the conceptual gap between the explicitly inadequate technical sense revealed in test scores and the everyday concept of good teaching that remains Duncan's ideal. This task of in-person observations is positively central to the ability of a given evaluation protocol to access and address what it is that we really want from such a system. In order for classroom observations to bridge the conceptual gap between the technical and the ordinary senses of good teaching, they must obviously remain free to detect good teaching over and above the technical definition.

Nothing in the scholarly literature indicates that this is the case. In fact, insofar as classroom observation has been assessed for its value, the value has been determined in terms of observations' ability *to detect the technical sense of good teaching alone*. Thomas Kane and others conclude happily for the sake of classroom observations that, when "well-executed," observations appear highly correlated with what achievement results reveal: "We find that evaluations based on well-executed classroom observations do identify effective teachers and teaching practices. Teachers' scores on the classroom observation components of Cincinnati's evaluation system *reliably predict the achievement gains made by their students in both math and reading*" (Kane, Taylor, Tyler, & Wooten, 2011, emphasis added). Where the role that Duncan's rhetoric assigns to classroom observations has explicitly to do with augmenting a view of teaching revealed in math and reading achievement scores, the studies that Kane conducts measure—and celebrate—precisely observations' ability to *conform* to that which math and reading growth already reveal. Kane and his colleagues are hardly alone in this tendency.

Glaringly, despite the fact that some scholars voice a hesitancy around the value-added metrics by which Kane and company assess teacher effectiveness, this criterion of quality continues to function as the standard against which classroom observations are judged. I quote a recent study's discussion of the matter at length to expose the shape of the thinking that undergirds it:

> We have chosen to define educational effectiveness narrowly as the value a teacher adds to gains in student learning as measured by standardized

test scores. We share some of the skepticism surrounding value-added scores, yet we acknowledge that they reflect something that policy makers and much of the public truly value, and we believe that at least in aggregate they measure what they claim to measure. Nonetheless, we also believe it is important to use other methods for measuring student learning. Regardless of how student learning is defined, in the present climate of Race to the Top and other accountability initiatives, the search for effective teachers has become widespread, urgent, and high stakes, and it is our hope that an observational measure that reliably identifies the best teachers will help administrators find and support them, and in so doing advance the cause of education in a meaningful way. (Strong, Gargani, & Hacifazlioğlu, 2011)

Strong and colleagues reveal many of the problems of conceptual conflation running throughout this discourse. Despite their "skepticism," Strong et al. assert that these value-added metrics "reflect something that policy makers and much of the public truly value." This statement is accurate, insofar as the public and policy makers value a technical sense of "student learning" that can be attributed to "good teaching." But Duncan has already indicated that, while valuable in terms of "monitoring" or knowing "what's happening," such metrics are not by themselves sufficient to the concept of good teaching that he and his policies ostensibly pursue. Additionally, though, Strong et al. make a few other interesting statements bearing mention, notably that "in aggregate," value-added metrics "measure what they claim to measure." They offer this statement as a means of defending their choice to define teacher effectiveness "narrowly," in value-added terms; and the "hope" expressed in their study is that "an observational measure that reliably identifies the best teachers will help administrators find and support them."

They certainly cannot be wrong in asserting that value-added methods "measure what they claim to measure." Strong et al., state precisely what this construct consists of in the preceding sentence: "the value a teacher adds to gains in student learning as measured by standardized test scores." When the researchers then refer to "an observational measure that reliably identifies the best teachers," they clearly conflate the highly technical sense of good teaching that they detailed a moment earlier with an ordinary sense of what "the best teachers" means; or, in what amounts to the same thing, they assume that these two concepts are identical. Value-added metrics, to which these studies of classroom observations are pegged, do measure exactly what they claim to measure. The problem, from a conceptual standpoint, is that what they claim to measure is explicitly, per Duncan's many examples, not exactly what we talk about when we talk about "the best teachers."

Strong et al., in contrast to Kane and his colleagues, find it easy to declare classroom observers "inaccurate" in terms of an ability to identify "the best teachers." Inaccuracy is clearly expressed in terms of deviation from measures of effectiveness ascertained by value-added methods:

> In every case, judges achieved relatively high levels of agreement but were absolutely inaccurate, leading us to question whether educators can identify effective teachers when they see them. This in turn has motivated us to undertake development of an observational measure that can predict teacher effectiveness. (Strong et al., 2011)

While I am struck by the potential significance of the "high levels of agreement" among the judges, I will leave that discussion for a later chapter. For now, I merely suggest that judges' "agreement," coupled with their "inaccuracy" (deviation from achievement score data), might indicate precisely the presence of the conceptual bridge that Duncan's policies require.

While the Strong group arrives at the opposite conclusion from Kane and colleagues, ultimately questioning "whether educators can identify effective teachers when they see them," in both studies, the success or failure of classroom observations is revealed in the observations' relative ability to *agree with* the kind of teacher effectiveness demonstrated in "the value a teacher adds to gains in student learning as measured by standardized test scores."

If the "classroom observations," which are offered as a necessary *complement* to student achievement measures, ostensibly to round out the assessment of teacher quality, do no more than seek out and check off the desirable behaviors whose desirability is a function of achievement score growth, then such observations offer no complement whatever. Such observations would merely proxy for the achievement score data whose inadequacy to the task of evaluating teachers has been roundly proclaimed by all sides of the discussion.

Nevertheless, Duncan himself also references the immediately visible quality that seems to require no such behavioral prescription, which means that in the concept of teacher quality undergirding the Race to the Top, there remains—rhetorically, at least—something like a version of "good teaching" that is knowable without any recourse to data whatsoever. But if it is indeed the case, as Duncan himself avers, that some kind of educational quality is immediately apparent, classroom observations of the sort I have just described would *systematically preclude* the possibility of recognizing this quality as such: this is the sense in which the temptations to *solve* the problems of skepticism in fact continue skepticism's "work of denial," as Cavell has said. So long as observations' relative validity rests upon agreement with that which is revealed in the achievement data, there is no sense in speaking of a multiplicity of measures at all.[4] The concept of teacher quality that would result from the combination of value-added metrics and classroom observations so conceived would remain firmly tethered to the technical definition thereof. For all the rhetorical feints in other directions, it really would be test scores all the way down.

1.6 THE ORDINARY, THE TECHNICAL, AND MATTERS OF TEACHER PRACTICE

In praising the professionalism of teachers and in criticizing the broken evaluation systems according to which they are judged, Duncan has decried the way in which these evaluation protocols handle teachers: Duncan says that this "industrial factory model of education . . . *treats* all teachers like interchangeable widgets" (emphasis added); the implication is precisely that teachers are obviously *not* interchangeable widgets.

I raise this issue not to dispute the point, but rather to refer back to an earlier part of the discussion in the interest of demonstrating its importance relative to the ordinary and technical concepts of teacher quality, and in particular, the way in which his denigration of the "factory model" seems on the surface to run directly counter to the "scaling up" trope that he uses so frequently. Put simply, the insistence above is that *quality teachers*, in Duncan's locution, are *not* interchangeable; *teacher quality*, through the process of behavioral scaling, on the other hand, somehow *is*. This confusion has ramifications for the ordinary/technical distinction.

It is an ordinary feature of everyday experience in any number of domains, be it sports or knitting or music: novices who enter a profession or any other skill domain get better at navigating that domain skillfully over a given period of time. At a certain point, they cease to improve at the same rate but do not necessarily noticeably decline. We then say that they have "reached their potential." The potential, and the eventually-attained skillfulness, are *theirs*, such that it makes sense to talk about *them* being good at a given thing, *their* quality in the skill domain. A person is a good knitter, a good tennis player, a good violinist. According to Duncan's assumptions, as well, there are likewise *good teachers*.

If quality teachers are not interchangeable, then such quality must *inhere* in individual teachers. A certain level of quality therefore must simply be a more or less permanent predicate of any given teacher. The feature of relative permanence and stability in terms of quality therefore also goes along with the ordinary sense of good teaching. Such permanence or stability need not be absolute—teaching as a practice can be taught and learned like any other skillful practice, and one's skills can fade in the realm of teaching as they can fade in any other domain—but the notion that teaching *is* a holistic endeavor in the first place, and one whose quality does not fluctuate to extremes in the second place, undergirds Duncan's declaration that "quality teachers" are not "interchangeable widgets."

In the earlier discussion of the scaling-up trope, I pointed out that in order to be amenable to scaling, teaching must consist in what Elizabeth Green calls "a series of bite-sized moves" (Green, 2010) or isolated "techniques" (Lemov, 2010). In order for *quality teachers* to be non-interchangeable, however, such that the teachers themselves are being distinguished from one another in an evaluation process, the having of these particular techniques or moves needs to manifest itself all at once, not in piecemeal fashion. The picture wherein good teaching consists of a set of techniques that correlate with the lifting of test scores (the technical view) does not self-evidently match up with a picture of good teaching as a holistic, self-consistent and relatively constant quality.

On a view according to which quality teachers are not interchangeable widgets, a view on which a certain level of teacher quality is a stable feature of this or that teacher, the incentivizing of teachers to stay or the expulsion of teachers on the basis of quality makes perfect sense. The very notion of rewarding good teachers requires that the quality of the teacher be assumed to persist into the future. It is in fact this very (ordinary) notion of teacher quality that Duncan has in mind when he advocates changing the tenure protections included in many CBAs:

> We created tenure rules to make sure that a struggling teacher gets a fair opportunity to improve, and that's a good goal. But when an ineffective teacher gets a chance to improve and doesn't—and when the tenure system keeps that teacher in the classroom anyway—then the system is protecting jobs rather than children. (Duncan, 2009a)

Teacher quality is conceived in the above quotation in terms of its development over time, such that a given teacher ought to receive "a fair opportunity to improve," after which opportunity, the teacher is considered beyond the possibility of meaningful improvement. Following this temporal window for improvement, a teacher's true quality will be manifest. The teacher will then either be of high quality and deserving of reward, or of low quality and thus deserving of replacement. The stability of teacher quality after an early period of growth is thus built into the ordinary sense of good teaching. If an ineffective teacher, as Duncan says, "gets a chance to improve and doesn't," the teacher is considered *stably* or *constantly* or *perpetually* ineffective. When one *knows* something about a teacher's quality, then, one knows something *lasting*, something that *endures*.

But the use of student achievement data to measure teacher quality or effectiveness has resulted in a sort of teacher quality that bears none of this stability, which in part justifies its distinction *as* a technical notion of teacher quality. The results of a number of studies, as summarized in an Economic Policy Institute briefing paper, reveal these two conceptual assumptions about the nature of teacher quality to be fundamentally in contradiction with one another. The passage deserves quotation in full:

> VAM [value-added methodology] estimates have proven to be unstable across statistical models, years, and classes that teachers teach. One study found that across five large urban districts, among teachers who were ranked in the top 20% of effectiveness in the first year, fewer than a third were in that top group the next year, and another third moved

all the way down to the bottom 40%. Another found that teachers' effectiveness ratings in one year could only predict from 4% to 16% of the variation in such ratings in the following year. Thus, a teacher who appears to be very ineffective in one year might have a dramatically different result the following year. The same dramatic fluctuations were found for teachers ranked at the bottom in the first year of analysis. This runs counter to most people's notions that the true quality of a teacher is likely to change very little over time and raises questions about whether what is measured is largely a "teacher effect" or the effect of a wide variety of other factors. (Baker et al., 2010)

The conceptual contradiction is revealed in the statement that the above evidence of instability in measures of teacher effectiveness "runs counter to most people's notions that the true quality of a teacher is likely to change very little over time." Faced with these results, one must either conclude that value-added measures of teacher effectiveness—teacher quality according to the technical concept—reveal something *accurate* about the quality of a teacher, but something also *fundamentally unstable*, such that it would make no sense at all to terminate or reward a teacher on such a basis, since such a teacher might very well be excellent or awful in a subsequent year; or else that, as the above researchers conclude, and in fact as Duncan himself reiterates again and again, the technical concept of teacher quality cannot proxy satisfactorily for the ordinary sense thereof.

A further possibility, of course, would be that this technical *concept* really is a reasonably accurate proxy for the ordinary concept, and that data-driven measures of quality in an individual teacher will be (normally) distributed around a "true" quality value *over the years* of annual measurement. But as a minimally-adequate sample size of years to draw conclusions about a teacher's true value (n=30) would span the majority of a teacher's career, it is difficult to see how these measurements improve upon our ordinary experiences with teacher quality. In particular, if part of the value of using student achievement data lies in allowing us to say something *now* about a teacher's quality, rather than waiting to recall "teacherly" excellence on the model of Duncan's mother or Mrs. Grady, then student achievement data offers no panacea in this regard.

References to hesitancy with respect to relying on student achievement data for access to teacher quality appears in several academic studies and also in Duncan's speeches, which indicates a certain inchoate wariness around the possibility of conceptual conflation or corruption, at least in terms of the ability to distinguish among teachers on the basis of quality. However, in Duncan's rhetoric, at least, this wariness fails to prevent the very conflation that undermines his well-intentioned project: to reward the good teachers, support the struggling, and replace the poor.

Not to be forgotten, though, remains the fact that Duncan's rhetoric has also highlighted the ordinary aspects of teacher quality that have the characteristic of being *immediately perceptible*, such that the potential for apprehending good teaching in its ordinary sense and in the present remains a genuine possibility. The role of classroom observations, as we have seen, provides the structural possibility of augmenting the inadequate sense of teacher quality revealed in student achievement growth alone. We have likewise seen in academic studies the destructive tendency to understand the relative success of classroom observations in direct proportion to their ability to confirm the findings of achievement-data analysis. For all that, classroom observations and other local means of witnessing great teaching in its immediately-accessible aspect retain their utility as potentially fruitful additions to the otherwise insufficient reduction of teacher quality to student achievement measures.

The conditions under which such observations could play this role in ascertaining the ordinary concept of teacher quality have already been enumerated, at least in terms of minimal necessity. The primary requirement involved remains the relative ability to extend beyond the view of teacher quality afforded by achievement data. That academic studies tend to evaluate classroom observations with respect to value-added judgments of teacher quality does not augur for the likelihood that state policies enacted with an eye to winning Race to the Top funding will give sufficient attention to this distinction, but an exploration of the policies of such states certainly remains warranted.

1.7 STATES' POLICIES REGARDING DATA AND CLASSROOM OBSERVATIONS

The National Council on Teacher Quality (NCTQ), a "non-partisan research and policy organization" (NCTQ, 2010) which focuses on the project of ensuring that "every child has an effective teacher," provides a comprehensive overview of the steps taken by individual states to address Race to the Top's reforms in the years between 2009 and 2011. While legitimately non-partisan as regards a Democrat-Republican axis, the NCTQ represents full-throated support for Duncan's reforms. Its advisory board includes a veritable who's-who of proponents that Duncan himself, and the popular media, cite relentlessly and hold up as models of the reform movement. The advisory board includes, for example, once-touted and now-former heads of large school districts who became famous for taking major steps toward precisely the kinds of reforms that Race to the Top encourages: Michelle Rhee and Joel Klein, the former appearing alongside Duncan at a recent panel on education reform (Winerip, 2012) and the latter the subject of a *New Yorker* exposé into the challenges of tackling teacher tenure rules (Brill, 2009). The advisory board also includes one prominent curriculum theorist in E. D. Hirsch, Jr., most famous for his advocacy of a core-knowledge curriculum and his authorship of the *Dictionary of*

Cultural Literacy. It likewise includes the founders of several prominent charter school organizations and alternative routes to the teaching profession, among them KIPP schools and Teach For America, examples Duncan regularly holds up as innovations deserving of replication; and experts in measurement and economics (NCTQ, 2010).

The NCTQ's research, then, not only provides factual insight into the particular policy developments resulting from the implementation of Race to the Top, but also rhetorical support for such policies as well. The particular outlook on education reform that NCTQ reveals mirrors Duncan's own approach right down to the studies that each cites, the examples of "dysfunction" that crop up in the discussion, and so on. For this reason, NCTQ's view on states' reform "progress" provides a good proxy for Duncan's view, as well.

I turn to an examination of states' policies for the specific purpose, once more, of tracing the role that achievement data and classroom observations, among other measures, play in teacher evaluations with respect both to each other and to the conceptual terrain of teacher quality in general. The task of teacher evaluations generally, as Duncan's rhetoric has constructed it, is to identify good teachers and distinguish them from poor ones. Whether or not existing and emerging policies exhibit a concern for the relative ability of the technical sense of good teaching to shed light on or speak to the ordinary sense comprises the subject of my investigation at this point. The technical sense, as we have seen, has value explicitly only insofar as it proxies for the ordinary; the danger that continues to stalk Duncan's rhetoric lies in the proxy's usurpation of the ordinary sense, its shift from a partial indicator of what the reforms pursue to the very thing itself.

The NCTQ report opens with a statement of the problem, which reiterates Duncan's position in the four speeches during the summer of 2009, albeit in much more succinct fashion:

> The move to rethink how to evaluate a teacher's performance and explicitly tie assessments of teacher performance to student achievement marks an important shift in thinking about teacher quality. The demand for "highly qualified" teachers is slowly but surely being replaced by a call for highly effective teachers
>
> The change is significant because policymaking around improving teacher quality to date has focused almost exclusively on a teacher's qualifications—teacher credentials, majors, degrees and licensing. Those criteria would be all well and good if they were associated with positive gains in student learning. Unfortunately, by and large, they are not. (NCTQ, 2011)

In contrasting "highly effective" to "highly qualified" teachers, the report echoes Duncan's skepticism of the value of teaching credentials such as advanced degrees and certification. The skepticism originates, as we have seen, in the fact that such variables have not been shown to have a significant effect on student achievement growth, which remains the criterion of "effective" teaching. In support of its claim that qualifications bear little or no association to "positive gains in *student learning*" (emphasis added), the report cites the Kane et al. study that I have already spoken to (Kane et al., 2011). The linking of "student learning" to "achievement score gains" indicates once more that the concept of good teaching (and student learning) at work in this report is by and large a technical one.

The failures of traditional evaluations function as justification for the turn to including student achievement data in teacher evaluations: "Their [The New Teacher Project's] study across a set of twelve districts in four states found that less than one percent of teachers received unsatisfactory evaluation ratings" (NCTQ, 2011). As in Duncan's example, the need for more robust systems of evaluation becomes visible in the fact that "99 percent of teachers are all rated the same" (Duncan, 2009c). The use of achievement data as a solution to this problem—an objective means of identifying and reporting teacher quality—assumes an epistemological inability to distinguish good from bad teaching, even at the ground level. However, as we have already seen, *what* is knowable according to the value-added metrics alone does not conceptually match the teaching we wish to know something *about*.

In discussing the teacher evaluation practices and policies across several states, the report singles out a few for special praise, linking them explicitly to Race to the Top policies:

> Several RTT winners are clearly at the forefront of efforts to develop and implement performance-based teacher evaluations. Delaware, Florida, Rhode Island, Tennessee, and D.C. Public Schools, for example, all require annual evaluations of all teachers and require that annual evaluations include objective evidence of student learning—not as an option, but as the *preponderant criterion* for assessing teacher effectiveness. (NCTQ, 2011)

The report characterizes these teacher evaluations as "performance-based," where teacher performance is visible in terms of test scores. "Evidence of student learning" functions as an (emphasized-in-the-original) "preponderant criterion." The centrality of growth on achievement scores to the concept of "student learning" that represents the effect of "good teaching" cannot be overstated here. Tennessee, New York, and D.C. have all adopted weighted formulas for rating teachers, which establish aprioristically how much of a judgment of any teacher's quality will be directly produced by achievement data. Tennessee's system places particularly significant weight on these measures: "A total of 50 percent of a teacher's annual evaluation must be based on student achievement data, of which 35 percent must rely on student growth data from the Tennessee Value-Added Assessment System (TVAAS)" (NCTQ, 2011).

Teacher quality, on this view, is once more taken as a causal factor whose causal value becomes visible in the teacher's effect on "student learning," represented by achievement measures. But the NCTQ report, like Duncan, seems aware of the fallibility of achievement data to a certain extent, and also as in Duncan's case, holds up classroom observations as a potential corrective to the otherwise monocular attention to test scores in determining teacher quality.

For example, the NCTQ report includes a subsection called, "States Shouldn't Lose Sight of Classroom Observations." The report goes so far as to cite the absence of stringent and rigorous classroom observation as a major weakness of the older evaluation systems: "The criticism of many current evaluation systems is not just their failure to take student learning into account, but their failure to include high-quality classroom observations" (NCTQ, 2011). High-quality classroom observations once again appear as an *additional* element to be attended to, over and above "student learning," however that is defined. In other words, observations are understood to reveal something *other* than what analysis of "student learning" will reveal. The *distinction* between student achievement measures and classroom observations emerges even more strongly in the same paragraph:

> While there is a great deal of attention focused on linking value-added and student growth results to teacher evaluation, it is equally important to gather evidence observing behavior—what teachers do and what students are learning in the classroom—during classroom observation. (NCTQ, 2011)

Student growth measures are explicitly taken to reveal something different from what classroom observations can reveal. The "evidence observing behavior" that an evaluator might gather in a classroom setting according to some particular methodology will help to augment or round out the picture of a teacher's quality available through an achievement-data lens. The specific methodology, as well as what the method observes in collecting its own kind of data, will be important: there is evidently a distinction between a "high-quality classroom observation" and the inadequate sort of observations conducted under the current regimens.

The language of *behavior* becomes particularly important at this point. The above passage already notes that the aim of such observation is to "gather evidence observing behavior." A further clarification of this suggestion reveals other commitments in this area:

> A strong observation rubric should focus almost exclusively on teacher practices and student behaviors that can be observed in the classroom. While other criteria are not without merit, they may call for too much subjectivity and guesswork on the part of the evaluator. (NCTQ, 2011)

What arises for evaluation is described here in terms of "practices" and "behaviors"—and those of the sort that do not "call for too much subjectivity and guesswork." In other words, evaluators will be using a "rubric" that will identify specific and isolated behaviors for evaluators to locate and check off. That is, evaluators will look for teachers and students to demonstrate *certain* behaviors or practices that the evaluator can witness; the demonstration of these behaviors will reveal an aspect of "teacher quality" that has been explicitly conceived as differing from achievement data.

That good teaching can appear in the form of "behaviors" implies that the *presence* of these behaviors also *makes present* good teaching itself. Teaching, then, really is "a series of bite-sized moves," in Elizabeth Green's words. A further implication is that, if "high-quality" observations will use a rubric in order to pick out specific teaching behaviors as both relevant to the practice of teaching and amenable to qualitative judgment, then some connection or link between each such behavior and a sense of "good teaching" must exist. What makes a certain behavior desirable in a teacher's practice, such that it can *make present* good teaching itself? What qualifies it as something for an observer to seek out?

By this point, the root source of the behaviors that evaluators are tasked with recognizing will be wholly unsurprising: the value of any given behavior or practice is determined by its correlation with lifting achievement scores. Says the report:

> New research is encouraging on this front. Well-designed and executed classroom observations can be effective at identifying the effectiveness of teachers, particularly teachers at the top and bottom ends of the distribution. Recent research also finds that good evaluations impact teacher effectiveness–that is, evaluations don't have to be just summative report cards. If done well, they can indeed be formative tools that drive teacher improvement. (NCTQ, 2011)

In substantiating the claim that "well-designed and executed classroom observations can be effective at identifying the effectiveness of teachers," as well as the claim that such "evaluations impact teacher effectiveness," the report cites the Kane study I mentioned earlier, which asks about the visibility of the isolated behaviors associated with test score growth (Kane et al., 2011). The NCTQ also echoes Duncan's assertion that this data will not only reveal teacher quality, but allow practicing teachers specific help in terms of improving the quality of their teaching.

While the NCTQ report explicitly articulates the need to "gather evidence observing behavior" with the aim of *supplementing* achievement data in the evaluation of teachers, the very behaviors for which observations would look will be defined *according to* the achievement growth in question. Classroom observations, as the NCTQ imagines them, therefore cannot function as a conceptual bridge between a technical and an ordinary concept of good teaching, since the observations themselves are restricted to the hunt for indicators of the technical sense of teacher quality. While cloaking themselves in the desire to add something to achievement data metrics, classroom observations in states winning Race to the Top funding, such as Tennessee (Anderson, 2012), remain hermetically sealed within the realm of achievement data, the technical view. In a bait-and-switch maneuver, classroom observations function to further strengthen the self-sufficiency of the technical sense of good teaching.

Such self-sufficiency is also revealed in the burgeoning primacy of "effective" teaching in the rhetoric of the discussion here, a phenomenon that emerges even in Duncan's speeches from 2009. Effective teaching refers only to a technical sense of good teaching, one in which teaching appears merely in terms of its (presumed) causal relation to its salient effect, "student learning," as revealed in test scores. The ordinary sense of good teaching—the kind of teacher quality *immediately accessible* in a way that Duncan recognizes in his various speeches—has simply disappeared from the discussion.

The completeness of this disappearance becomes even more clear in considering a Brookings Institution report that the NCTQ cites on the relation of value-added metrics to other means of evaluating teachers, and also in the NCTQ report's discourse on the precision of measures. The Brookings Institution report (Glazerman et al., 2011) attempts to answer criticisms of value-added measures as they are applied to teacher evaluations. It declares, among other statements, that

> We have previously issued a report that describes some of the imperfections in value-added measures while documenting that: a) they provide one of the best presently available signals of the future ability of teachers to raise student test scores; b) the technical issues surrounding the use of value-added measures arise in one form or another with respect to any evaluation of complex human behavior; and c) value-added measures are on par with performance measures in other fields in terms of their predictive validity. (Glazerman et al., 2011)

None of the points offered here is capable of responding to the conceptual problems that have emerged in this chapter, but the first two, in particular, deserve some discussion. Point (a) is particularly glaring: the value of a VA measure lies in the fact that it is one of the "best presently available signals of the future ability of teachers to raise student test scores." Two problems arise, one minor and one significant. In the first (minor) place, the fact that there is no better predictor available is so totally obvious that it hardly deserves mention, but it also simply misses the objection to which it would respond: simply because there is none *better* in this regard does not render such existing methods of prediction conceptually *valid* for use in teacher evaluations in the first place.

In the second and substantially more important place, the *function* of measuring teacher effects on "student learning" has heretofore had ostensibly to do with providing some sort of insight into the ordinary sense of teacher quality, of which the technical sense is an admitted reduction. But this locution, wherein the defense of the appropriateness of value-added metrics appears in terms of their predictive power *of themselves*, eliminates the ordinary sense from the discussion altogether. The authors can assert that value-added metrics are useful to teacher evaluations because they remain the best predictor of "the future ability of teachers to raise student test scores." The technical view has completely occluded any other concept of teacher quality that might arise.

I wish to pull out and bookmark point (b) from the above report as well, which avers that the "technical issues" in value-added methodologies appear in "any evaluation of complex human behavior" (and of which point (c) is essentially a rephrasing). I agree that the sorts of problematic issues to which these scholars refer also crop up in gauging or evaluating any other skillful endeavor, but I hold that the assumption that these are merely "technical issues," amenable to technical solutions that are, by implication, just a little ways over the horizon, is the result of a misconception, which I will explore in some detail in the coming chapters.

The Brookings Institution report, and the language in which the problem is conceived, indicates that the scholars at work on developing teacher evaluations have very little awareness of the conceptual problem they face. The technical definition of teacher quality to which their studies speak is emphatically and explicitly not the sense of teacher quality to which Duncan's anecdotes and audience exhortations appeal. The gap between the two remains unaccounted for, and worse: the very existence of the conceptual chasm goes unacknowledged in such studies. In conflating the technical sense of effective teaching with the ordinary sense of good teaching, the Brookings Institution demonstrates this fact perfectly:

> This assumption [that true performance is relatively stable] is buttressed, in the case of value-added measures, by the fact that value-added measures from one period predict student achievement in future periods. It is also buttressed by anecdotal evidence that some teachers are simply more effective than other teachers and, as a result, parents work to get their children into these teachers' classrooms. (Glazerman et al., 2011)

In attesting to its conclusion about teacher quality's stability with both statistical reliability metrics *and* "anecdotal evidence," the report would have it that the "teacher quality" that is revealed by each type of evidence is the same. This is not obviously the case.

The "anecdotal evidence" cited here, in which parents desire certain teachers for their children, is certainly a common feature of school life. But it is an unwarranted assumption that parents are basing their "work" at getting their children into certain classrooms on any sort of "effectiveness" criterion in the technical sense that these scholars measure. After all, value-added rankings are only publicly available in a few places nationwide, and this sort of parental lobbying has been going on since time immemorial. Parents certainly want their children to have the best teachers, but as data of the kind that the Brookings report uses has not heretofore been available, and as such data is supposed to make visible a heretofore *invisible* quality, it is completely unclear that parents have been trying to "get their children into *these teachers'* classrooms" (emphasis added).

The simple disappearance of the ordinary concept of good teaching that we have seen attend the operationalization of "teacher quality" in psychometric discussions and policy papers also becomes glaringly apparent considering the NCTQ's justification for using admittedly imperfect value-added methodologies in determination of teacher quality in relation to Duncan's words on the capacities of student achievement data. In 2009, Duncan says, as I have quoted much earlier, "I absolutely respect the concerns of teachers that test scores should never be used solely to determine salaries" and "I also appreciate that growth models as they exist today are far less than perfect" (Duncan, 2009b). In this speech, the imperfection of growth models appears to speak to problems in accurately measuring student learning; that "standardized tests are not perfect" refers to the tests' imperfect ability to measure something about *students*. Because it is an inadequate measure of *student learning*, Duncan implies, "test scores should never be used solely to determine [teacher] salaries."

In the 2011 NCTQ report, however, the authors reiterate the rhetorical structure of Duncan's argument almost point by point, but in a profound shift, the focus on the imperfections of "growth models" now speak directly to "teacher effectiveness" rather than to student learning. In other words, the ability of "standardized tests" to ascertain precisely what is important in "student learning" is suddenly and entirely taken for granted. In the NCTQ report, the authors echo nearly verbatim Duncan's insistence that imperfect measures ought not to prevent us from using student achievement data at all, they repeat Duncan's citation pertaining to the fact that "99 percent of teachers are all rated the same," and then they say,

> Student growth and value-added methodologies are still emerging. However, examining student achievement as a metric for assessing teacher effectiveness, even if measurement is imperfect, represents a big step forward. Indeed, we set the whole enterprise up for failure if we attach unrealistic expectations to the exact precision of every measure—and doom ourselves to the alternative of doing very little to measure and examine teacher performance. At the same time, the reality of measurement and limits to teacher control over student outcomes do argue for measured caution in developing teacher effectiveness policies. (NCTQ, 2011)

The authors of this report argue, in a false-dilemma strategy reminiscent of Duncan, that the *only* alternative to basing teacher evaluations on students' standardized tests is to forego evaluation entirely.

When Duncan sounded a note of caution in his 2009 rhetoric about measures' imperfection, it occurred in a context of questioning whether scores in math and reading were perfect representations of *student learning*; here, that achievement data authentically capture student learning is merely assumed. Now the question appears to be whether teacher *effectiveness*, itself the technical definition, can be perfectly hitched onto this narrowed sense of "student learning." If so, it is implied, "teacher effectiveness policies" would require none of the "measured caution" the report calls for, because policy would then be operating from a position of certainty in terms of meaningful teacher quality, despite any objections based on the oft-acknowledged fallibility of one-shot assessments of student achievement. The validity of the assessments themselves in expressing *everything* relevant to "teacher quality" is beyond question. The "teacher quality" under discussion, then, is the technical view. The ordinary sense is no longer even on the table.

The calls for caution in treating the metrics as indicators of the concepts we would use them to measure do not seem to translate into policy or practice. Delaware's teacher evaluation rules perhaps demonstrate this fact better than any other argument. The NCTQ report summarizes beautifully:

> Delaware's DPAS II system formula is organized around five key evaluation components or topics: 1) planning and preparation, 2) classroom environment, 3) instruction, 4) professional responsibilities and 5) student improvement. Teachers are rated highly effective, effective, needs improvement or ineffective in each individual area. A summative rating depends on the number of effective or not effective ratings teachers receive in each of the individual component areas. All other components aside, if a teacher does not meet or exceed student growth requirements in Delaware, the teacher cannot be rated any higher than needs improvement overall, regardless of ratings in the other four components. (NCTQ, 2011)

Despite the fact that student achievement data reflects only math and reading performance (and only that in a limited sense itself), the test score is king.

It is curious, also, that the state's policies plan for the contingency in which a teacher could fail to meet growth goals while earning high marks in every other category, since the teacher behaviors according to which a teacher would be assessed in "classroom environment" and "instruction" are directly and intentionally pegged to "student improvement." Even, it is implied, in cases where student growth is subpar *despite a teacher's demonstrating the behaviors correlated with student score growth*, the test results would be unmerciful: that teacher "needs improvement," though *what* a teacher might do to improve in this case is entirely mysterious.

In the NCTQ report, as in Duncan's own rhetoric from 2009, there is concerted effort on the part of reformers to acknowledge the limitations of student achievement data in terms of attaining the ultimate ends for which their use is proposed. Duncan frames examining teachers through the lens of achievement data in terms of "reducing" a "complex" and "nuanced" practice, and he straightforwardly says that such measures ought not to determine compensation or personnel decision. Likewise, the NCTQ urges "measured caution" in using student achievement data to evaluate teachers. In both cases, however, the proposals of "high-quality" classroom observations, which are offered as a complement to the otherwise inadequate tool of student achievement data, turn out to be grounded on the same achievement measures that they are meant to flesh out.

Race to the Top pays lip service to the complexity of teaching and learning, but when it comes to the project of knowing—knowing *what* to teach, knowing *how* to teach, and knowing *quality* in both teaching and learning—there is simply nothing outside the test.

1.8 SUMMARY AND SEGUE:

The methodological assumptions undergirding this project bear mentioning once more as I move to summarize the results of the investigation thus far and seek to extend it in the direction of the upcoming sections. The most basic assumption I make pertains to the relevance of Duncan's speeches on his proposed reforms, the studies and lines of research that he cites, and the translations of this research and rhetoric into policy. At bottom, I assume that such speeches, studies, and policies pertaining to teacher quality reveal the conceptual shape of what we take teaching *to be*.

In this respect, my investigation has uncovered two distinct and eminently distinguishable concepts of "teacher quality" at work in policy speeches, research, and policies themselves. On the one hand lies what I have been calling the "ordinary" conception of good teaching, so named in accordance with its particular content and its contexts of evocation. Content-wise, the "ordinary" concept of good teaching is associated with references to such educative actions and results as a "thirst for knowledge," the "inspiring" of students, "everyday acts of kindness and love," the "counsel[ing] of teens," the "tak[ing of] phone calls at night," the "lighting of a lifelong curiosity," and the ability to "literally change the course of a student's life." Prevalent features of the ordinary concept include the types of long-lasting and real-world impacts of the sort Duncan mentions above, and to which his "college and career ready" criterion is intended to speak; a certain stability over time, such that teachers can themselves be good or bad; a persisting and influential relationship with students, as in the case of his mother's guidance "over the years"; and a sort of immediate accessibility or visibility of the kind Duncan avers he can spot "the minute I enter a school." The ordinary sense of good teaching, in short, is the one we have in mind when Duncan encourages us to think of a "favorite teacher" that we remember "forever."

The ordinary concept of good teaching tends to emerge in the context of policy speeches, and is wholly absent from academic studies and state policies. The absence from the latter two contexts is fairly unsurprising, since what makes the ordinary concept ordinary in the first place has to do with its independence from rigid definitions of the sort that academic studies and state legislation tend to require. The ordinary concept, however, is not therefore necessarily insufficient to the purposes of studies and policies; rather, as evidenced by Duncan's effortless conjuring of the ordinary concept through appeals to the teachers that "all of us remember" (Duncan, 2009a) or that "so many of us remember" (Duncan, 2009d), as well as his platitudinous statements about the "complex, nuanced work of teaching" (Duncan, 2009a), the ordinary concept simply requires no such crystalline definition and fails to stand up to attempts at such definition, though it is explicitly the one that occasions the urgency underwriting the Race to the Top Program.

On the other hand, my investigation has also unearthed a concept of "teacher quality" that positively requires and rests upon explicit definition, a concept that I have termed, for this very reason, the "technical concept" of teacher quality. The technical concept of good teaching, as I indicated above, differs from the ordinary primarily insofar as it rests upon explicit characteristics or features laid out aprioristically. It is in every instance defined according to its causal relation to "student learning," which itself is a technical term, distinct from the sorts of "thirst for knowledge" or "lifelong curiosity" criteria that serve to characterize the perceived effect of the ordinary concept of good teaching on students. "Student learning" in its own technical sense is revealed in students' score growth on math, reading, and science assessments. Good teaching in its technical sense is then revealed according to its effectiveness in lifting test scores. For this reason, the technical concept of good teaching also goes by the name of "effective teaching" in the literature.

Due to its inherently close—indeed, tautological—relation to student achievement data, the technical sense of good teaching evinces certain stark differences with the ordinary concept. These differences include what one might call the *mediate* nature of teacher quality, where teacher quality is assumed to be opaque or hidden and thus in need of an abstract theoretical means of becoming visible; the associations with highly specific teacher behaviors, as evidenced in observation protocols under development at the state level and in academic attempts at linking classroom observations to indicators of "effective teaching"; and also, importantly, the present-tense availability of actionable evidence of teacher quality. This last contrast refers to the notable fact that citations of ordinary-concept "great teachers" of the type explored in this study tend to refer backward from present adulthood, implying that while an ordinary sense of great teaching may be immediately accessible or knowable, it is somehow not relatable or transferable in plausible narrative form until the students involved have become adults.

Despite this delineation of the ordinary and technical concepts of teacher quality in terms of their differences from one another, perhaps the most important result to emerge from the investigation so far involves the degree of conceptual interpenetration and usurpation that have emerged in the speeches, studies, and policies explored above. In particular, I have formatively outlined the ways in which the technical concept borrows liberally from—to the point of entirely supplanting, in some cases—the ordinary concept.

In particular, where the self-evident need for greater attention to teacher quality derives its urgency and importance from the ordinary concept of teacher quality, as Duncan's speeches repeatedly demonstrate, the methods involved in ascertaining teacher quality and addressing matters pertaining thereto all refer to the technical concept at bottom. Despite the regular recitation of the caveat that "it is unfair to reduce the complex, nuanced work of teaching to a simple multiple choice exam" (Duncan, 2009a), even the classroom observations offered in a complementary role are rooted in the exam data itself: a need with its basis in the ordinary concept is supposedly answered by means of the technical concept.

But other borrowings proliferate as well, as we have seen: the enduring nature of teacher quality, for instance, is a feature of the ordinary concept; such stability of teacher quality, as critics of value-added methodologies have pointed out (Baker et al., 2010), is not at all in evidence in analyses of teaching according to the technical sense. Yet when policies and speeches seek to identify and reward good teachers, whose goodness is a stable and enduring trait, they propose to do so by technical means. This conflation emerges once again in the dissonance between Duncan's deploring of the "factory model" of education while discussing innovations in terms of "scaling up," in which quality is supposed to be both intrinsic to a teacher (ordinary sense) and yet also to consist in specific and isolated behaviors (technical sense).

Nevertheless, as we have seen, for all the conceptual interpenetration and usurpation, the ordinary sense of teacher quality really is distinct from the technical sense, and really has functioned as the teleological goal toward which reform initiatives look(ed) and around which the American public has rallied. The ordinary sense of great teaching certainly has an effect on students—life-changing impacts are repeatedly attributed to it, and first-person testimonials to this effect pervade the discourse—and certainly part of that effect would show up in terms of student learning, even the "student learning" represented in the narrow terms of year-to-year math or reading score growth. But at the outset of Race to the Top's proposals, it was rhetorically understood that the technical sense of teacher quality required actual supplementation in order to bridge the gap between its own sense and the ordinary sense which represented the actual goal, the actual source of urgency. Classroom observations, as we have likewise seen, were to bear most of this burden.

In tracking the way in which the technical sense of good teaching has come to stand in for the ordinary, a very specific (and technical) notion of what good teaching *is* has come into view, and it is this "good teaching" to which evaluators are instructed to attend by means of classroom observation rubrics. Simply put, this view of good teaching considers teaching to be a series of isolated behaviors whose relative quality is determined according to established correlations with achievement score growth. Such observations also attend to student engagement behaviors, which are likewise correlated with score growth and demonstrate whether a teacher is having an "appropriate impact" (NCTQ, 2011). Because score growth remains the bottom-line determinant of what an observer ought (or is able) to observe, when the originally-imagined role of classroom observation pertained specifically to a domain of what teaching is that exceeded the technical sense, it is clear that the types of observations currently being implemented across the country cannot fulfill that role. Instead, what "good teaching" is taken to be is straightforwardly restricted to this behavioristic view.

But, in the spirit of that most basic assumption undergirding this investigation, it remains the case that classroom observations were originally tasked with speaking to a wider domain, over and above the technical sense. If classroom observations once seemed appropriate to this role, and if they were searching for the ordinary sense of teacher quality, it would stand to reason that a conception of teaching that restricts itself to the piecemeal demonstration of particular behaviors will not suffice. Another account of "good teaching" is needed—and perhaps it may also address the reasons underlying Glazerman, et al.'s assertion that "technical issues" always crop up in "evaluation of complex human behavior."

It is now time to ask the questions that will signal the transition to the remainder of this investigation: if classroom observations were assigned a bridging role between the technical sense and the ordinary sense of good teaching, what aspects of good teaching do we imagine inherently and necessarily to escape evaluation in terms of achievement data, such that observations could function as a conceptual bridge in the first place? If it is the case that the ordinary sense of good teaching exceeds definition of the kind that the technical sense of good teaching requires, how might classroom observations come to seize upon this excessive dimension at all? The ordinary sense of good teaching has been described by Duncan and others in terms of a certain immediate availability; well, *what* do we take to be immediately available, and how—in what terms—might one vouch for or attest to its quality?

We have seen that the ordinary sense of good teaching needs no explicit definitions of the sort that the technical sense requires, and the ordinary sense may in fact even resist attempts at definition; would an ordinary sense of teacher quality be meaningfully reportable on a yearly basis in the absence of such definitions? Can one do something well without first explicitly defining what "well" means? What, in the domain of education, are the relations among knowing, doing, and evaluating?

NOTES

1. I owe the structure of this formulation to Cavell's work on intentionality and postmodernism.
2. When I say "without much respect to context," I mean to indicate that while certain factors like the grade level of the students certainly factor into consideration—one does not use "proven reading techniques" designed for fourth graders on high school students—certain contextual factors often predictively associated with achievement outcomes, as, for particular example, because it pops up in Duncan's speech, socioeconomic status, are believed to be irrelevant.
3. Citing the effects of an after-school tutoring program entails further complications for the technical view of good teaching, as well: the students receiving such help are very likely to be children of parents highly invested in their kids' education—invested not only in showing up with cameras at sporting events or in political lobbying for higher standards and better teachers, as Duncan very recently recommends (Duncan, 2014), but also invested in actively seeking out and paying for such additional academic help. The teachers of such students will unwarrantedly appear to be more effective teachers than teachers of identical true quality who happen to teach kids who do not receive such outside help. Looking only to the data is in effect to blind oneself to this equivalence.
4. Though I emphasize classroom observations, this is but one among the "multiple measures" with which Duncan proposes to augment raw test-score analysis; they all fall prey, though, to the same basic flaw: that their worth is determined by agreement with achievement data. In Amanda Ripley's journalistic work on other measures involved teacher evaluations, she notes that Ronald Ferguson's student surveys were remarkably effective as teacher quality measures. "The responses did indeed help predict which classes would have the most test-score improvement at the end of the year" (Ripley, 2012).

REFERENCES

Anderson, J. (2012). States Try to Fix Quirks in Teacher Evaluations. *New York Times*, p. A1. New York.

Andersson, C., Johansson, P., & Waldenström, N. (2011). Do You Want Your Child to Have a Certified Teacher? *Economics of Education Review, 30*(1), 65–78. doi:10.1016/j.econedurev.2010.07.003

Baker, E. L., Barton, P. E., Darling-Hammond, L., Haertel, E., Ladd, H. F., Linn, R. L., . . . Shepard, L. A. (2010). Problems with the Use of Student Test Scores to Evaluate Teachers. *EPI Briefing Paper #278*.

Brill, S. (2009) The Rubber Room. *The New Yorker, 85*(26), 30.

Brügelmann, H. (2011). Pisa macht die Schulen nich besser. *Die Zeit*. Retrieved from http://www.zeit.de/2011/03/C-Pisa-Kritik

Cavell, S. (1990). *Conditions Handsome and Unhandsome*. Chicago: University of Chicago Press.

Cavell, S. (2013). *This New Yet Unapproachable America: Lectures After Emerson After Wittgenstein* (p. 144). University of Chicago Press. Retrieved from http://books.google.com/books?id=qmWUMQEACAAJ&pgis=1

Chetty, R., Friedman, J. N., & Rockoff, J. E. (2011). The Long-Term Impacts of Teachers: Teacher Value-Added and Student Outcomes in Adulthood. *NBER Working Paper No. 17699*.

Chingos, M. M., & Peterson, P. E. (2011). It's Easier to Pick a Good Teacher Than to Train One: Familiar and New Results on the Correlates of Teacher Effectiveness. *Economics of Education Review, 30*(3), 449–465. doi:10.1016/j.econedurev.2010.12.010

Craig, A. (2011). US Secretary of Education Arne Duncan Meets with CLASS Project to Hear Progress Report. Retrieved from http://chalkboardproject.org/press-room/us-secretary-of-education-arne-duncan-meets-with-class-project-educators-to-hear-progress-report-on-24-4-million-federal-investment-in-oregon-teachers-and-students/

Duncan, A. (2009a). Partners in Reform. U.S. Department of Education. Retrieved from http://www2.ed.gov/news/speeches/2009/07/07022009.html

Duncan, A. (2009b). Robust Data Gives Us the Roadmap to Reform. U.S. Department of Education. Retrieved from http://www2.ed.gov/news/speeches/2009/06/06082009.html

Duncan, A. (2009c). States Will Lead the Way Toward Reform. U.S. Department of Education. Retrieved from http://www.ed.gov/news/speeches/states-will-lead-way-toward-reform

Duncan, A. (2009d). Teacher Preparation: Reforming the Uncertain Profession. U.S. Department of Education. Retrieved from http://www.ed.gov/news/speeches/teacher-preparation-reforming-uncertain-profession

Duncan, A. (2009e). Turning Around the Bottom Five Percent. U.S. Department of Education. Retrieved from http://www.ed.gov/news/speeches/turning-around-bottom-five-percent

Duncan, A. (2009f, May 1). The Race to the Top Begins. U.S. Department of Education. Retrieved from http://www2.ed.gov/news/speeches/2009/07/07242009.html

Duncan, A. (2014). Parent Voices for World-Class Education. U.S. Department of Education. Retrieved from http://www.ed.gov/news/speeches/remarks-us-secretary-education-arne-duncan-national-assessment-governing-board-educati

Elmore, R. F. (1996). Getting to Scale with Good Educational Practices. *Harvard Educational Review, 66*(1), 1–26.

Ercikan, K., & Koh, K. (2005). Examining the Construct Comparability of the English and French Versions of TIMSS. *International Journal of Testing, 5*(1), 23–35. doi:10.1207/s15327574ijt0501_3

Ercikan, K., & McCreith, T. (2002). Effects of Adaptations on Comparability of Test Items and Test Scores. In In D. F. Robitaille & A. E. Beaton (Eds.), *Secondary Analysis of the TIMSS Data*. (pp. 391–405). Springer Netherlands. doi:10.1007/0-306-47642-8_24

Fehr, M. (2010). Schweizer Berufsbildung—wirksam gegen die Krise. *Neue Zurcher Zeitung*. Zurich. Retrieved from http://www.nzz.ch/nachrichten/startseite/schweizer_berufsbildung__wirksam_gegen_die_krise_1.5865921.html

Glazerman, S., Goldhaber, D., Loeb, S., Raudenbush, S., Staiger, D., Whitehurst, G. J., . . . Quality, B. C. T. G. on T. (2011). *Passing Muster: Evaluating Teacher Evaluation Systems*. Brookings Institution. Retrieved from http://www.brookings.edu/reports/2011/0426_evaluating_teachers.aspx

Glennan, T. K., Bodily, S. J., Galegher, J. R., & Kerr, K. A. (2004). Expanding the Reach of Education Reforms. Santa Monica, CA: RAND Corporation.

Goggin, M. L., O'M Bowman, A., Lester, J. P., & O'Toole, L. J. J. (1990). *Implementing Theory and Practice Toward a Third Generation*. Glenview, Il: Scott, Foresman/Little, Brown.

Green, E. (2010). Building a Better Teacher. *New York Times Magazine*. New York: New York Times.

Kane, T. J., Rockoff, J. E., & Staiger, D. O. (2008). What does certification tell us about teacher effectiveness? Evidence from New York City. *Economics of Education Review, 27*(6), 615–631. doi:10.1016/j.econedurev.2007.05.005

Kane, T. J., Taylor, E. S., Tyler, J. H., & Wooten, A. L. (2011). Identifying Effective Classroom Practices Using Student Achievement Data. *Journal of Human Resources, 46*(3), 587–613.

Laurillar, D. (2002). Rethinking Teaching for the Knowledge Society. *EDUCAUSE Review, 37*(1), 16–25.

Lemov, D. (2010). *Teach Like a Champion*. San Francisco: John Wiley & Sons.

Levin, J., Mulhern, J., & Schunck, J. (2005). Unintended Consequences: The Case for Reforming the Staffing Rules in Urban Teacher Union Contracts. *ERIC Clearinghouse*. New Teacher Project. Retrieved from http://www.eric.ed.gov/PDFS/ED515654.pdf

Martini, E. (2012). *Agent Orange: History, Science, and the Politics of Uncertainty*. Amherst: University of Massachusetts Press.

Medvetz, T. (2012). *Think Tanks in America*. Chicago: University of Chicago Press.

Mehta, J. (2013). *The Allure of Order*. Oxford: Oxford University Press.

NCTQ. (2010). Advisory Board. Retrieved from http://www.nctq.org/p/about/advisory.jsp

NCTQ. (2011). *State of the States: Trends and Early Lessons on Teacher Evaluation and Effectiveness Policies*. National Council on Teacher Quality.

Ravitch, D. (2013). *Reign of Error: The Hoax of the Privatization Movement and the Danger to America's Public Schools*. New York: Knopf.

Ripley, A. (2012, October). Why Kids Should Grade Teachers. *Atlantic*. Retrieved from http://www.theatlantic.com/magazine/archive/2012/10/why-kids-should-grade-teachers/309088/

Rivkin, S. G., Hanushek, E. A., & Kain, J. F. (2005). Teachers, Schools, and Academic Achievement. *Econometrica, 73*(2), 417–458. doi:10.1111/j.1468-0262.2005.00584.x

Sireci, S. G. (1997). Problems and Issues in Linking Assessments Across Languages. *Educational Measurement: Issues and Practice, 16*(1), 12–19. doi:10.1111/j.1745-3992.1997.tb00581.x

Stewart, J. (2012). February 16. *The Daily Show*. thedailyshow.com.

Strong, M., Gargani, J., & Hacifazlioğlu, Ö. (2011). Do We Know a Successful Teacher When We See One? Experiments in the Identification of Effective Teachers. *Journal of Teacher Education, 62*(4), 367–382. doi:10.1177/0022487110390221

Tishman, S., Jay, E., & Perkins, D. N. (1993). Teaching Thinking Dispositions: From Transmission to Enculturation. *Theory into Practice, 32*(3), 147–153.

Trigwell, K., Prosser, M., & Waterhouse, F. (1999). Relations between Teachers' Approaches to Teaching and Students' Approaches to Learning. *Higher Education, 37*(1), 57–70. doi:10.1023/a:1003548313194

Winerip, M. (2012). Amid a Federal Education Inquiry, an Unsettling Sight. *New York Times*, p. A10. New York.

Wittgenstein, L., Anscombe, G. E. M., & Hacker, P. M. S. (2009). *Philosophical Investigations* (4th ed.). Malden, MA: Wiley-Blackwell.

2 Teacher Knowledge, Teacher Practice

2.1 TEACHING AS A FUNCTION OF LEARNING

We have seen in Chapter 1 that the technical sense of good teaching derives from a highly technical sense of learning, namely one representable in the form of student achievement data. The features of this sense of learning that indicate its "technical" nature go beyond the simple fact that the domains of student skill that the relevant assessments measure are limited to reading and math, to the exclusion of history, art, geography, and the like. As other scholars, like Rothstein (Rothstein, 2008), have pointed out, these are important subject-matter exclusions. As such, they represent a certain kind of restriction of the domain of learning to which teaching as an endeavor addresses itself: a restriction of *what* ought to be taught and learned. But beyond a domain restriction in terms of content, the paramount importance of student achievement data in answering questions about learning and teaching (such that achievement data can and ought to be the "predominant criterion" for teacher evaluation) evinces a *conceptual* restriction of learning, and therefore of teaching, as well. In other words, the reliance upon student achievement data limits *what counts* as the learning of anything at all in ways that we have already seen, to the effect that the types of learning characterized by developing a student's "lifelong curiosity" and "thirst for knowledge" are either nowhere in evidence or assumed to simply go along with rising scores on reading and math assessments.

The conceptual restriction of learning leads directly to a certain restricted view of the concept of good teaching, which I have also called the technical sense thereof. In his speech at Columbia Teachers College in the autumn of 2009, Arne Duncan makes it clear that the technical sense of good teaching is what his reforms aim to develop. Touting the virtues of exemplary teacher-training programs, Duncan says, "And these programs have a shared vision of what constitutes good teaching and best practices—including a single-minded focus on improving student learning and using data to inform instruction" (Duncan, 2009b). By combining the notion of "using data to inform instruction" with these programs' "single-minded focus on improving student learning," Duncan leaves little doubt as to the type of learning he has in mind: the technical variety, revealed according to achievement score data. But here, he makes an additional claim connected to teaching: these programs, characterized by the monomaniacal pursuit of "student improvement" by means of "using data to inform instruction," "share a vision *of what constitutes good teaching and best practices.*" The vision of teaching for which Duncan advocates here is thus directly related to the technical sense of learning that I traced in Chapter 1.

This particular view of what good teaching and best practices amounts to is dangerous to the project of improving the quality of the teaching profession in two different ways. Chapter 1 has already highlighted the way in which attempting to improve educational quality in an ordinary sense by addressing technical indicators of educational quality leads one astray as a matter of policy, which is to say that working to develop a technical sense of good teaching specifically fails to attend to the aspects of good teaching involved in instilling a lifelong curiosity or taking late-night phone calls.

But in the second place, this technical sense of good teaching rests upon and reinforces an erroneous picture of skillful practice quite generally. The assumptions that undergird Duncan's view—as well as the views of many scholars in the academic field of teacher education—bear a striking resemblance to assumptions made in early (and failed) attempts at Artificial Intelligence (AI). Put briefly, these views assume that knowledge of how to do something consists in the having of certain rules or maxims by means of which to navigate a world of bare facts in order to achieve a particular end.

The "consists in" in the previous sentence ought to be understood as implying both that *what happens* during good teaching *is* the application of transcendent and articulable-in-principle rules to a situation comprised of articulable facts, and also—and therefore—that the facts and rules themselves *are* a transferable form of good teaching. According to this view, to study good teachers and to develop novices in the profession toward competence is to extract the rules and the salient facts from particular situations and then to give those to the neophyte so that the novice can implement them in another, analogous situation.

This picture is dangerous precisely because it is not obviously wrong, especially inasmuch as the "learning" connected to this view of teaching is itself distorted. But even a more robust view of student learning and good teaching allows for the place of conceiving skillful activity in terms of facts and rules. Thus, when Duncan lauds colleges of education that attend to a view of "good teaching and best practices" by focusing on what the data reveals, he is not incorrect, strictly speaking. New teachers, like new tennis players, must start off by consciously and deliberately following certain maxims or rules.

Whether or not the practice of excellent *veteran* teachers also consists in rule-following behaviors on the same model is what I wish to draw into question. If the "best practices" view of teacher quality only characterizes actual teacher practice up to a certain and limited degree of competence, then it follows that seeking to replicate or pass on excellent teaching practice by means of seeking out the maxims and rules imagined to underlie the practices of visibly extraordinary teachers will not suffice.

I have already spent some time discussing Arne Duncan's vision for the use of data in guiding teacher decision-making, as well as in reforming teacher-training programs, and I have made preliminary remarks on what the above reveals in terms of Duncan's ontology of teaching. In returning to those remarks now, I wish to make two arguments. In the first place, Duncan's valorization of student achievement data as the final arbiter and definitional touchstone of "learning" tempts policy in a misguided, behavioristic direction. A behavioristic view would hold that "best practices"—here defined as isolated behavioral techniques on display in a teacher's classroom—constitute good teaching such that the focus of teacher development ought to attend to the extraction of techniques that "work" and their inculcation in pre-service, underperforming, or maturing teachers.

Absent from such a behavioristic view is any consideration of how these isolated techniques ought to be combined into a total practice, or which situations call for which specific behaviors. Such a behaviorism presumably takes those aspects to be already implicit in the act of teaching itself, in which case the specific techniques are to be understood simply as the best version of what already happens. I think it worth mentioning that I doubt that Duncan would directly espouse raw behaviorism in the form of an argument that teacher training ought to consist of installing fixed responses to broadly-defined situations in pre-service teachers; but I do think, as the example of Delaware's teacher evaluation protocols at the end of Chapter 1 made clear, that Race to the Top policies lead in that direction.

The second argument that I wish to make addresses one of the ways in which such raw behaviorism is finessed, and this argument will lead on to my larger critique. This second argument pertains to an ongoing project to codify the types and content of the knowledge that excellent teachers use in practice. On this second model, conceived and developed by Lee Shulman, Heather Hill, Pam Grossman, and Deborah Ball, primarily (Ball, Thames, & Phelps, 2008; Grossman, 1990; H. Hill & Ball, 2009; H. C. Hill, Kapitula, & Umland, 2011; H. C. Hill, Rowan, & Ball, 2005; Loewenberg Ball & Forzani, 2009; L. S. Shulman, 2007; L. Shulman, 1986, 1987, 2005), teacher knowledge runs deeper, so to speak, than mere behavioral response; their research project explicitly takes up questions around *how* teachers know what to do in particular situations, that is, how teachers decide upon a specific course of action in a specific context.

I will argue, however, that as conceived by Shulman in particular and later implemented by Grossman, Hill and others, the notion of teacher knowledge remains inadequately constructed. What Ball and Hill, following Shulman, have meticulously developed is, on my view, a much finer—and therefore superior—way of understanding skillful teacher practice, one consisting of rationalist rule-governed behavior. Call this the mentalistic view. In seeking to critique the limitations of such a picture, I hope to distinguish two very different views of what "following a rule" in the performance of learned, skilled behavior amounts to, and to lay out the ways in which the picture of good teaching on display in Duncan's rhetoric shares salient and problematic assumptions with both Lemov's behaviorism and the rationalism of Shulman, Ball, and Hill's Pedagogical Knowledge for Teaching project.

2.2 TEACHING, DATA, AND GETTING TO SCALE: A THEORY OF PRACTICE AT WORK

To recapitulate some points from Chapter 1 in a new light, I will return to some of what Duncan has to say about the relation of data to teaching and expand upon a discussion of the literature of scaling. Duncan views the utility of data for the practice of teaching in the following terms:

> [Teachers] need to know how well their students are performing. They want to know exactly what they need to do to teach and how to teach. It makes their job easier and ultimately much more rewarding. They aren't guessing or talking in generalities anymore. They feel as if they're starting to crack the code. (Duncan, 2009a)

In Chapter 1, I indicated that the "code" trope both implies a transmission model of education, which comes with well-known and much-discussed limitations, and also constructs the practice of teaching as somehow representable in terms of that data, as though "what they need to do to teach" and "how to teach" were directly visible in achievement measures. The nature of this connection has to do with a certain propositional knowledge: such and such behavior or belief is effective; such and such behavior is ineffective. Duncan further cements the role that such knowledge is imagined to play in successful teaching by referencing the dual purpose that achievement data serves: revealing the relative quality of teacher practice and revealing the individual components of said practice with respect to their successfulness. This comes out in his insistence that "we need to monitor progress. We need to know what is and is not working and why" (Duncan, 2009a). Student achievement data serves both to "monitor progress" but also indicates "what is and is not working."

In Chapter 1, I sought to bring out the conceptual problems involved in thinking of the "working" of teaching purely in terms of its effect on student achievement data. In Chapter 2, now, I wish to highlight the way in which Duncan conceives of teaching as a "what"—or a collection of "whats"—that either "is" or "is not working." Since achievement data reveals the "working" of teaching, Duncan takes it to simultaneously reveal the "what" of teaching that either does or does not work.

The implication in suggesting this connection is that differences in teacher quality between two teachers will be attributable to differences between the teaching *practices* of those two teachers, where such practice is thought in terms of "what." Thomas Kane, whose role in the development of value-added measures I mentioned in Chapter 1, is quite explicit on this point. In an interview with the *New York Times*' Joe Nocera, Kane claims that seeking out and studying the teachers with the highest impacts on student achievement data is geared toward "identifying the practices associated with student achievement" (Nocera, 2012). This attempt at the identification of practices is likewise visible in the studies supporting Race to the Top's teacher-evaluation policies that I discussed in Chapter 1, particularly in the way scholars set out to calibrate the role of classroom observations in terms of specific behaviors (Glazerman et al., 2011; Kane, Taylor, Tyler, & Wooten, 2011).

"Practices" therefore ought to be understood in this context as collections of isolated techniques, including (or not) the maxims or rules that guide their implementation. Examining the practices of each teacher (or groups of teachers) will reveal differences in habits and behaviors, or, one level further down, differences in mental states (beliefs and desires) that give rise to such differential practices. Thus, when teachers want to "know what to do to teach and how to teach," achievement score data and its correlated behaviors can point to an answer by revealing the "what" of the matter—the behaviors or the mental states underlying them—in which knowing "*how* to teach" is taken to consist.

According to such a view, in which skillful practice can be dissected into its component parts, whether imagined as expressed behaviors or as the internally-located rules and maxims underlying the appearance of a holistic practice, the development of good teachers involves giving the pre-service or underperforming teachers in question something quite tangible: rules to apply in feature-defined situations or broadly-sketched behaviors to exhibit in any situation whatever.

The project of teacher development as a whole, as it appears in Duncan's rhetoric and Kane's many studies, thus sets itself the task of (a) identifying the teachers associated with "high growth students," (b) videotaping or otherwise observing the practices of those teachers, and (c) distilling the practices of those teachers into their component parts for later transmission to new or underperforming practitioners. The ultimate aim of such an undertaking is, as I quoted Duncan saying in Chapter 1, "to replicate those [successful] conditions everywhere" (Duncan, 2009c). By defining successful teaching in terms of the ability to influence achievement scores, and then by distilling the practices of teachers associated with exceptional score gains into the smaller parts that comprise them, Duncan and other reformers hope to render successful teacher practice into a form that can be "replicated" and thus applied in any classroom whatsoever. The assumption underlying such an endeavor is that such replication of teacher practice so distilled will also as a consequence replicate the achievement score gains according to which success is defined.

As I noted in the introduction to this section, there are several assumptions at work in this line of reasoning, and I wish to take issue with them in turn. Since I have already dealt in Chapter 1 with the conceptual problem of defining teacher quality in terms of influencing achievement score gains, I will set aside for the time being the assumption about the commensurability of the ordinary and technical goals at which Duncan's rhetoric and his policies aim.

First among the problematic assumptions undergirding the view of teaching as a skillful endeavor that Duncan and Kane espouse is the possibility that skillful practice is comprised of isolated techniques or "bite-sized moves" in the first place, which falls under the behavioristic assumption I discussed earlier. Second among these assumptions is the notion that while teacher practices might not be defined according recognizably identical *behaviors*, they might rather be defined according to the recognizably identical *rules or maxims* that guide situationally-appropriate behaviors or responses, which I have associated with the mentalistic assumption.

I highlight here, and then leave for the time being, the bottom-line assumption of which both the behaviorist and the mentalist visions are derivative: the notion that skillful practice in a given domain *must be* a product of isolable and identifiable component parts, whether these parts are taken to be pure behaviors or mental states. Without such an assumption, attempts to "replicate" skillful practice by extracting particular techniques, behaviors, or rules from successful teachers for the purpose of transferring them to new or underperforming teachers would be incoherent. In suggesting that neither an approach according to the behavioristic assumption nor one according to the mentalistic assumption can satisfactorily do the job of replicating excellent practice, I also draw into question this larger, overriding assumption about the composite nature of skillful practice in general.

2.2.1 The Behavioristic Assumption in Practice

One way for which a scholar or policy-maker to approach the question of replicating high-quality teaching under the conditions enumerated above would be the discomposing of data-substantiated, high-quality teaching practice into the recurring behaviors within that practice, the behaviors out of which, one might say, the practice in question is made. Doug Lemov, as I briefly mentioned in Chapter 1, has undertaken just such an approach to the problem of developing teacher quality. The resulting 49 techniques are meant to stand in as highly general behaviors that constitute, or at least form the core of, the excellent teaching practices from which they were distilled.

As one review of his work succinctly notes, "The techniques described in Lemov's study convey the replicable behaviours, mannerisms, classroom management techniques, time management skills, lesson delivery styles, and preparation methods of teachers whose students excel on state benchmark assessments" (Hollabaugh, 2011). The emphasis in the above review lies on the replicability of the specific behaviors in question, the piecemeal nature of teaching practice. Another scholar attends to the claim of generality entered on behalf of these techniques: Lemov's view makes no distinction among the various kinds of classrooms one finds in the world: "Mr. Lemov, Mr. Pianta, and others take the position that many of the core elements of effective teaching transcend the subjects taught" (Keller, 2010). This distinction serves to highlight the broad assumption underwriting Lemov's approach, namely that the "core elements of effective teaching" are taken to be behavioristic in nature (Hollabaugh even terms it a variety of "Skinner-style behaviourism"), and thus are, as Elizabeth Green says, meant "to be adaptable to anyone" (Green, 2010).

The particular view of skillful practice underlying Lemov's project comes out most clearly in his discussion of direction-giving, a discussion that Green highlights as an outstanding advance in teacher training protocol. At the heart of Lemov's "What To Do" technique is an attempt to solve problems of unfocused, undesired, or contrary student behavior. Lemov notes quite correctly that such undesirable behavior is not always the result of some sort of oppositional attitude on the part of the student but lies rather in simple misunderstanding, the result of insufficient clarity on the part of the direction-giver. This is not to imply that all oppositional behavior stems from such misunderstanding, but Lemov avers that "a larger portion [of noncompliance] than many teachers ever suppose" can be attributed to clarity problems in direction-giving. The solution, according to Lemov, is more clarity:

> When you tell a student to pay attention, ask yourself if she knows how to pay attention. Has anyone ever taught her? Does she know your specific expectations for paying attention (having her eyes on the speaker, say)? Has anyone ever helped her learn to avoid and control distractions and distractedness? The command "pay attention" provides no useful guidance because it fails to teach. (Lemov, 2010, p. 178)

In the previous chapter, I cast the rhetoric around the school reform movement that Race to the Top embodies as a particular sort of response to a *skeptical* problem. Lemov's depictions of the "What to Do" technique mirror his overall project of offering teachers the various behaviors that constitute the complex skill of excellent teaching. In the above passage, Lemov specifically offers his direction-giving technique as a solution for the problematic situation in which a teacher does not or cannot *know* whether oppositional behavior is produced by a failure of understanding. The proffered solution is effectively to remove the possibility of doubt.

Lemov describes the "What to Do" technique of direction giving like so: "To be effective, directions should be specific, concrete, sequential, and observable" (Lemov, 2010, p. 179). He helpfully continues to use the "pay attention" situation as he explains these four sub-features of effective direction-giving technique. I will focus on the first two of these four in order to draw out the shortcomings and insufficiencies of Lemov's view. Lemov says,

> Effective directions are specific. . . . Instead of advising a student to pay attention, for example, I might advise him to put his pencil on his desk or keep his eyes on me. This provides useful guidance that he can take action on and pay attention to doing. (Lemov, 2010, p. 179)

The skeptical doubt to which Lemov's technique responds is a powerful one, and well-founded. Any objections to Lemov's solution ought at least to acknowledge this fact. The teaching profession remains, as Arne Duncan points out in a variety of speeches, insufficiently diverse in many ways; it remains principally the domain of white, middle-class women. Insofar as the students in a given classroom differ widely from the teacher and from each other in terms of race, socioeconomic status, and a general style of upbringing (among unreckonable further qualities), a given teacher cannot simply assume that his or her students all share the sort of lifeway in which the directive to "pay attention" has meaning for the teacher. "Pay attention" could well imply different reactions on the parts of different students, and to the extent that these reactions diverge from the teacher's expectations for attention-paying, all such divergent reactions will be treated as non-compliance with the direction. In responding to all such non-compliance as misbehavior, possibly the result of an oppositional disposition or disrespect, for example, the teacher risks alienating students, with potentially significant and negative educational effects.

But two particular problems remain in Lemov's account, problems directly related to framing both practical conduct and the difficulties that such conduct addresses as hinging upon absent or insufficient knowledge. Lemov's "What to Do" technique is designed to produce the proper response in students; the purpose of giving directions that are "specific, concrete, sequential, and observable" will make demonstrating the requested behaviors easy for students, and it will eliminate doubt as to whether or not any non-compliance is attributable to misunderstanding: it cannot be. One problem that Lemov faces has to do with the presumed equivalence of "producing the proper response" and demonstrating a "complex skill." The other problem pertains to the generality or transcendence of this method of giving directions.

In the first case, while Lemov derides the teacher who simply utters the command to "pay attention" for "provid[ing] no useful guidance" because such a command "fails to teach," it remains unclear whether or not any teaching of the sort Lemov imagines is present in his solution, either. While certainly his sequential and concrete instructions allow and enable students to demonstrate the requested behaviors, advising a student to "put his pencil down" and "keep his eyes on me" is not in itself equivalent to teaching a child the meaning of "pay attention." Another way of drawing out this issue is to say that Lemov is never clear on whether or not the hypothetical teacher is using these directions to teach such complex skills directly or whether that teacher is using much simpler commands as a means of circumventing the need for common understanding of "pay attention" en route to a further goal.

In the former case, the question will be whether or not the addition of smaller behaviors, such as stillness and a focused gaze to the front of the room, are *themselves* the attention-paying that the teacher wishes to teach. Raising it as a question turns Lemov's solution on itself. It is a phenomenological fact that students can fake attentiveness—students can both genuinely and artificially attend to a teacher's lesson. But conceiving of attentiveness merely in terms of the isolated behaviors that attend it denies this distinction. That is to say, if there exists such a thing as fake attentiveness, then there must be a way to distinguish it from genuine attentiveness; and if isolated behaviors are all that attentiveness *is*, there is no possibility of drawing this distinction, a distinction that we can—if not flawlessly or consistently—nevertheless draw. The distinction itself shows that there is something more to paying attention, something that listing component behaviors will miss.

In the latter case, meanwhile, it is simply disingenuous to claim that students are demonstrating any complex skill at all, such as the attention-paying that Lemov's directions are designed to elicit. If Lemov's teacher wishes to transition from one part of a lesson to another, and if such a transition requires something like stillness in the classroom, then saying "pay attention" has the same purpose and effect as saying "pencils down, eyes on me": both result in the stillness of the classroom. But the fact that still pencils or focused gazes go along with paying attention does not, in this case, imply that they are the same thing. In point of fact, the teacher who in such a circumstance says "pencils down, eyes on me" is explicitly *not* asking for attentiveness as such, nor is there any *teaching* (of attentiveness) involved. There is behavioral guidance, to be sure, and there are multiple "simple" tasks required, but there is no effort to combine them *into* anything else, unless that is supposed to happen implicitly. And of course the point of Lemov's direction-giving protocol is precisely that reliance upon implicit expectations is untrustworthy; explicitness is offered as the solution. If that turns out also to depend on implicit expectations, such a fact would badly undercut its claims to superiority.

The above seems perhaps like an obstinate point to raise, as though I have to refuse commonsense understanding in order to make the claim that separating a request for what Lemov calls a "complex skill" like paying attention (i.e. one that is "rarely equated with a single specific action" [Lemov, 2010, p. 179]) into a request for those single specific actions does not add up, somehow, to the whole of "paying attention." After all, to most observers, a roomful of students with pencils down and eyes up front looks to all the world like a roomful of students paying attention. But it is worth recalling that it is specifically such a situation that Lemov intends to solve by means of such specificity—one in which a commonsense understanding of a "complex skill" like paying attention does not suffice for both parties in the direction-giving parley. In fact, part of the claim and allure of such behaviorism in general is that no commonsense understanding is required; by specifying particular behaviors, one circumvents the problem entirely.

In raising the obstinate point, I address precisely the issue of whether or not successfully requesting that a child demonstrate the component behaviors that one associates with paying attention constitutes asking the child to pay attention. The teacher receives the specific behavioral responses that he or she associates with paying attention—the putting down of the pencil and the upfront-ness of the eyes—but these behavioral responses, one might say, are not the same as "paying attention." Paying attention involves listening, as well, for one example; it involves focusing one's mind on a particular topic, place, or person. It is certainly and obviously true that wandering eyes and scribbling pencils can indicate the absence of attention-paying, but this is not always so, and it is further not the case that stilled pencils and attentive eyes comprise attention-paying. In asking for the performance of a "complex skill" in terms of a series of "single specific action[s]," Lemov's teacher indeed receives the single specific actions, but not necessarily any performance of the complex skill characterized by those actions. If all that the teacher desires are the specific behaviors—if he or she wants only quiet children—such methods of direction-giving are perfectly sufficient. If he or she wishes the students to perform some complex skill, the behavioristic account seems to leave out something essential.

To make the claim stronger and more general, I would like to say that on display in Lemov's discussion of "What to Do" is the bottom-line assumption undergirding Lemov's entire project: that the "complex skill" of teaching itself is merely a collection of many, many "single specific action[s]," and that encouraging people to perform each of those single, specific actions (grouped together under each of the "49 techniques") constitutes teacher education.

Lemov holds the assumption, which was just underlined, that "complex skills," "rarely equated with a single specific action," can nevertheless be analyzed by means of decomposing them into such single, specific actions as would render them performable by a rank novice. The assumption, framed another way, is that the complexity of complex skills is a matter of mere (if presumably enormous) quantity of behaviors. Given the 49 techniques of Lemov's book, any college graduate, let us say, could perform the behaviors associated with the excellent teacher practice—and with "high growth students"—from which the behaviors have been extracted. The result will be, on Lemov's view, the replication of excellent practice.

But there yet remains the further problem of transcendence or generality to raise about Lemov's behaviorism, one that appears in these techniques' claim to be, in Green's words, "adaptable to anyone." Lemov seems to assume that performing combinations of behaviors in a particular sequence constitutes the performing of a given holistic skill, as we have seen. Lemov likewise seems to assume that teachers can and ought to frame directions such that they are comprised of actions that "any student knows how to do" (Lemov, 2010, p. 179). To return to the example of the practice of direction-giving, it is true that breaking down something like "pay attention" into specific, concrete, sequential and observable behaviors" will likely eliminate any misunderstandings about how to accomplish the behaviors the teacher will equate with the "complex skill." The implication is that one should always frame directions in this way, and if the only danger in terms of inappropriate direction-giving were noncompliance of one form or another, that would surely be the case. Another way of putting the previous statement would be: the "What to Do" technique works flawlessly in an artificially limited domain, one in which non-compliance represents the only negative response to or consequence of direction-giving.

In actual classrooms, however, there are other negative responses for teachers to consider. For example, while breaking down complex skills into their simple components works excellently in precisely the problem situation in which students do not understand what the exhortation to "pay attention" entails, it makes students who *do* share the form of life in which paying attention follows as a matter of course from the exhortation to "pay attention" feel condescended to, which has precisely the alienating effect that the technique was meant to preclude. In other words, if the technique of providing simplified, concrete, and sequential behaviors is meant to *overcome* any gap in understanding between teacher and student, using the technique also *requires* that gap as a starting point, as something to solve. The condescension that, say, well-heeled middle-schoolers would feel upon a teacher's attempt to explain attention-paying as though they did not already know what it means is the very creation of this gap, the denial of the shared-ness of a shared (in this case) understanding of attentiveness. Once more I am reminded of Cavell's thought that some attempts to solve a problem of skepticism merely continue its work of denial.

Perhaps one would respond to this objection by saying that a teacher has to know the level of specificity required by his or her students and tailor instructions accordingly. Two avenues of response open up on this rejoinder. First, the 49 techniques are meant to transcend any relevant differences; they are supposed to be themselves the core elements of skillful practice. To claim that their application depends upon further knowledge is to undercut precisely that which is supposed to constitute their value. It also reveals the threat of a regress, in which actionable knowledge of a technique requires further knowledge about something else, which may well lead on to other necessary knowledge, infinitely. I will return to that idea later on in greater depth.

In the second place, however, even assuming that the teacher has such knowledge of the specificity required and that such knowledge really is the end of the road, most if not all teachers address a variety of students in any single class, such that providing instructions perfectly tailored to one group necessarily occurs at a suboptimal level for another. If teachers address a variety of students and wish to alienate a minimum number through either confusion or condescension, then teachers require a 50th technique, one for simultaneously appealing to several learning styles and modalities. This consideration points to still further additional knowledge required for the successful implementation of teaching techniques so formulated, and thus, in the direction of the same regress.

The above considerations, brief though they are, highlight the fact that even the simple technique of giving directions in a way that students can successfully follow with a minimum of negative response turns out to be much more complicated than it initially appears. Lemov's 49 techniques address only, one might say, the bare behaviors he has correlated with achievement score growth; it is obviously not enough to describe those behaviors, tell new teachers to perform them, and then expect excellence in teaching. Given these bare behaviors that Lemov has identified, practitioners still require rules for their successful implementation, such that the novice avoids, for the purposes of my chosen example, the error of talking down to some of his or her students in direction-giving without speaking in a mystery code to others.

Teaching, on Lemov's view, consists in the combination of specific behavioral techniques. Performing these behaviors constitutes high quality teaching practice. I wish to say, in segueing to the next section, that the argument I have to make about skillful practice includes a place for something like Lemov's view: the behavioristic picture of teacher practice, I would add, is self-evidently correct as far as it goes. The bone of contention, here and throughout, has to do with how far such a view of teaching can take one toward the ordinary concept of "good teaching" outlined in Chapter 1.

Another route to discovering both the appropriate plaudits and cautions with respect to the type of behaviorism Lemov espouses is to point once more to the (skeptical) problem that Lemov's "What to Do" technique is meant to solve. If inadequate knowledge, or the possibility of being mistaken as to the cause of student non-compliance, represents the danger that clear and simple directions will foreclose, then it is perfectly obvious that the "What to Do" technique is sufficient to this task. But pointing out that other dangers specifically pertaining to inadequate knowledge—of the level of background understanding possessed by this particular group of students, for example—would go unaddressed by *simply* enacting the technique suggests that further or deeper knowledge is required for the successful implementation of any of these techniques.

The breadth and generality of Lemov's techniques is thus the source both of its appeal and of its impracticality. In seeking to be "adaptable to anyone," it requires something more for its own implementation. In discussing many of the techniques, Lemov seems to assume a sort of background understanding of what schools and classrooms are like in general, their organization and their purpose, the typical problems that arise, and so on. But as no teacher operates in classrooms in general, and as each one faces some particular set of circumstances, choosing the right technique for the present moment in the present situation seems to appeal to a faculty of judgment, which lies beyond a baldly behavioristic account.

I point this out not to pick at details in Lemov's approach, but to shine a light on problems in his assumptions about the nature of skillful practice themselves, problems revealed in the combined propositions that Lemov's techniques are (a) derived from excellent teaching practice and (b) insufficient *in themselves* to perfectly replicate that practice. The "What to Do" technique has it that complex skills are simply composites of simple behaviors; great teaching might be such a complex skill. The "What to Do" technique is specifically designed to make misunderstandings impossible by cutting out the necessity of a background understanding of a given skill set, but following the directive to "put your pencil down" *also* relies on certain, albeit different, background understanding (down on the floor? *Pointed* down?), and thus a teacher must be sensitive to the correct level of direction-giving in any given circumstance in order to use the technique properly. The "What to Do" technique does not solve the problem of background understanding in the way it appears to; background understanding is still involved, even at a simple and highly concrete level.

Taken together, the twin facts that Lemov has found these techniques in several disparate cases of excellent teaching practice and that these common techniques cannot by themselves reproduce excellent teaching practice without more help suggests that Lemov is incorrect in conceiving of teaching, or complex skills more generally, as mere composites of Green's "bite-sized moves." These twin facts suggest that any particular techniques shared by some set of excellent teachers are not *essential* to—the core essence of—excellent teaching itself. Something further will be necessary.

2.2.2 The Mentalistic Assumption in Practice

The family of research programs reliant upon Lee Shulman's Pedagogical Content Knowledge (PCK) project seeks to improve upon a Lemov-style behaviorism in a few different ways. In the first place, researchers readily recognize that knowing or being able to perform any particular technique is insufficient to ensure excellent practice. Deborah Ball and colleagues point out that "the teacher need not only understand *that* something is so; the teacher must further understand *why* something is so" (Ball et al., 2008, p. 391), a proposition that mirrors Shulman's own declaration: "The teacher is not only a master of procedure but also of content and rationale, and capable of explaining why something is done" (L. Shulman, 1986, p. 13). A Pedagogical Content Knowledge approach proposes to supplement an account of quality teaching that depends upon mere "procedure" with its "rationale."

Additionally, the Pedagogical Content Knowledge view takes seriously the possibility that any essential techniques or knowledge of how to teach may be inextricably tied to the subject being taught. In fact, Pedagogical Content Knowledge has generated, in the work of Ball and Hill especially, but also elsewhere, a sub-field dedicated to Mathematical Knowledge for Teaching (MKT) (Carpenter, Fennema, Peterson, & Carey, 1988; H. Hill & Ball, 2009; H. C. Hill et al., 2005; Marks, 1990). Researchers are likewise teasing out the implications of Shulman's framework in the realms of science education (Magnusson, Krajcik, & Borko, 1999; Van Driel, Verloop, & de Vos, 1998) and in pedagogical uses of classroom technology (Mishra & Koehler, 2006).

To make the contrast explicit, Lemov's view holds that applying specific techniques will have consistently positive educational effects; good teaching, on this view, consists in the demonstrations of these particular behaviors. On the other hand, the assumptions of Shulman's approach recognize that teacher knowledge of specific behaviors can only account for a very narrow range of teacher quality. Shulman likewise appreciates the fact that a teacher's knowledge of a course's subject matter is a poor predictor of that teacher's ability to in fact teach the content involved. Knowing *how to teach* is therefore reducible neither to the specific and simple techniques employed by all excellent teachers as such nor to any teacher's level of content mastery. As Heather Hill and others aver, "Shulman and colleagues' work expanded ideas about how knowledge might matter to teaching, suggesting that it is not only knowledge of content but also knowledge of how to teach content that influences teachers' effectiveness" (H. C. Hill et al., 2005).

Indeed, the framework for understanding and inculcating skillful teaching practice that Shulman originally proposed in the 1980s has had demonstrative predictive value, at least as far as the technical sense of good teaching is concerned: the measures Ball and Hill, among others, have developed for "MKT" have proven to be one of very few useful teacher-characteristic predictors of student outcomes in terms of achievement on standardized tests of mathematics (H. Hill & Ball, 2009; Kane, Rockoff, & Staiger, 2008). In other words, if Lemov's extraction of specific behaviors from the practices of excellent teachers represents a certain kind of step in the direction of replicating excellent teaching elsewhere, the concept of "teacher knowledge" toward which Shulman and his acolytes labor represents a more refined step in the same direction, insofar as it addresses Lemov's issue pertaining to the knowledge of when and in what circumstances to exercise a given technique and insofar as the statistical methodologies of determining teacher effectiveness validate this approach. Shulman's assumptions about the relation of knowledge to teaching practice, in sum, have led to certain advances in terms of identifying teacher characteristics associated with influencing achievement score growth.

Whether or not these assumptions about the relation of knowledge to teaching practice are entirely accurate or sufficient to developing great teachers in an ordinary sense remains the primary concern here. I have suggested that Lemov may go astray in conceiving the excellent teaching he witnesses as a composite of isolated behaviors; if Shulman and his exegetes likewise go astray, the false steps will have to do with conceiving of the excellent teacher practice he witnesses as a series of enacted decisions following from certain principles, maxims, or beliefs.

Shulman opens an oft-cited article, "Knowledge and Teaching" (1987) with a narrative account of the practice of an excellent English teacher, whom he pseudonymously calls "Nancy." Shulman's account notes that "the observer was well impressed with the depth of [her] understanding of that novel and her skill as a pedagogue, as [the observer] documented how Nancy helped a group of California high school juniors grasp the many facets of that masterpiece" (L. Shulman, 1987, p. 1). While an interview with Nancy leads the interviewer to conclude that she has a theoretical framework underlying her skillful teaching, the observer claims that this framework is not implemented as a rigid set of guidelines: "Thus Nancy's pattern of instruction, her style of teaching, is not uniform or predictable in some simple sense. She flexibly responds to the difficulty and character of the subject matter, the capacities of the students (which can change even over the span of a single course), and her educational purposes" (L. Shulman, 1987, p. 3). From Nancy's example, Shulman hopes to elicit the skillfulness of practice. His goal, like Duncan's and Lemov's, is to see "teaching like Nancy's . . . become typical."

What "typical" means for Shulman appears slightly different from what it means for either Duncan or Lemov. First and foremost, no particular behavior or technique seems to characterize Nancy's practice, and so simply extracting and repeating behaviors will be insufficient to replicating her excellence. Rather, as the description of Nancy's practice has it, instead of a behavioral "pattern of instruction" that one might expect to be "uniform or predictable in some simple sense," one instead finds that Nancy "flexibly responds to the difficulty and character of the subject matter, the capacities of the students (which can change even over the span of a single course), and her educational purposes." The *flexible responsiveness* to her particular situation defies accounting in terms of isolable, repeatable behavioral techniques. Nothing so outwardly stable undergirds Nancy's practice. What requires replication is not *behavioral*, then.

But Shulman's research questions make clear an assumption that *something* stable must ground the excellence of Nancy's practice, and this stability exists in the form of certain kinds of knowledge. Asks Shulman: "What does Nancy believe, understand, and know how to do that permits her to teach as she does?" (L. Shulman, 1987, p. 3). In its stability and causal relationship to excellent teacher practice, Shulman's picture of teacher knowledge resembles the assumptions in Lemov's work.

When Shulman avers that, "One of the more important tasks for the research community is to work with practitioners to develop codified representations of the practical pedagogical wisdom of able teachers" (L. Shulman, 1987, p. 11), his project likewise dovetails with Lemov's: both researchers take any instance of excellent practice to be caused by something underlying and stable, and both take it for granted that transferring this underlying, stable element to pre-service or underperforming teachers will have the effect of transferring excellent practice itself. In a much later talk, Shulman proposes that teacher training programs must "converge" on the "small set of 'signature pedagogies' that characterize all teacher education" (L. Shulman, 2005, p. 7). While he and Lemov would mean different things by "signature pedagogies," the notion that excellent teacher practice is an expression or effect of some core set of elements remains the same. Lemov's model depends upon the repetition of behavioral technique; Shulman's allows that "Nancy's" practice is not "uniform or predictable" in the way that Lemov's view would have it, but he nonetheless assumes that her flexible responsiveness must mask a uniformity beneath the surface.

Shulman's view, then, holds the following assumptions: skillful practice has specific, identifiable causes; these causes consist in what skillful practitioners "believe, understand, and know how to do"; and the task of the research community is to develop codified representations of the same. Such codified representations will thus enable the propagation of the causal conditions of excellent or skillful practice, and thus skillful practice itself. Among the elements that must be codified for Shulman's view to work is what he calls "the wisdom of practice" and "strategic understanding," both of which elements refer to "professional judgment" (L. Shulman, 1986, p. 13).

The very notion of codifying a "wisdom of practice" or "strategic judgment" raises a problematic philosophical history around attempts at conceiving of practical knowledge as a subspecies of theoretical knowledge, of attempting to formulate a theory of practice. This is, in fact, the crux of the matter in Race to the Top policies quite generally, where the ability to articulate, according to abstract and theoretical tools, *how* one knows something skillful is imagined to access necessary and sufficient conditions for the performance of the skillful behavior in question. All knowledge, including, in Shulman's case, knowledge-how, is conceived as a species of knowledge-that. This is the salience of the form of Shulman's question: "*what does* Nancy . . . know how to do that permits her to teach as she does?"—that know-how is conceived as the propositional answer to a question in the form of "what." Nancy's skillful teaching is thus conceived as the result of a chain of causation which bottoms out in abstract, theoretical knowledge amenable to the form of a proposition. Shulman's account of "strategic knowledge" and the "wisdom of practice" help us to see the problems in conceiving of skillful behavior in this mentalistic—that is, mentally-grounded—way.[1]

Shulman's definition of the "wisdom of practice" brings out his assumptions about the nature of skillful activity: "Wisdom of practice" consists of "the maxims that guide (or provide reflective rationalizations for) the practices of able teachers" (L. Shulman, 1987, p. 11). The practices of able teachers—not merely beginners, but *able* teachers—are held, on this view, to be more or less explicitly guided by maxims. Skilled practitioners thus know maxims or rules, and knowing these rules accounts for the skillfulness of the practice. Knowing *how* to teach consists in knowing the "what" of propositional rules. If this is in fact the case, then certainly the rendering explicit—the codifying—of these maxims, so that they can be transferred to new or underperforming teachers, will enable the replication of excellent teaching that Race to the Top and academic scholars alike strive to attain.

Shulman is very aware of the danger of *reducing* excellent teaching to a collection of maxims; the role of the "wisdom of practice" is supposed to offer a means of avoiding such a reduction: "The great danger, occurs, however, when a general teaching principle is distorted into a prescription, when maxim becomes mandate" (L. Shulman, 1987, p. 11). Shulman's maxims themselves must be brought together in particular ways in particular situations: neither isolated teaching behaviors nor a set of maxims roughly guiding their application will be sufficient to generate excellence in teaching. The bringing of judgment to bear—Shulman's "strategic knowledge" or "strategic understanding" (L. Shulman, 1986, p. 13)—is his means of accounting for the demonstration of the proper action in its proper place.

The intervention of "strategic knowledge" becomes necessary because, unlike Lemov, Shulman recognizes that in certain situations, the "rules or maxims" that comprise the "wisdom of practice" may come into conflict. Either the rules themselves do not provide adequate guidance, or else the situation seems to bear features that call for the following of different or even contradictory rules. On this point, he is explicit: "When strategic understanding is brought to bear in the examination of rules and cases, professional judgment, the hallmark of any learned profession, is called into play. What distinguishes mere craft from profession is the indeterminacy of rules when applied to particular cases" (L. Shulman, 1986, p. 13).

But Shulman's development of the notion of "strategic knowledge," prevents it from playing the bridging or mediating role between the theoretical and the practical realms for which it is designed. Shulman describes the nature of strategic knowledge by emphasizing its nature as *knowledge*, as I quoted earlier: "The professional holds knowledge not only of how—the capacity for skilled performance—but also of what and why. The teacher is not only a master of procedure but also of content and rationale, and capable of explaining why something is done" (L. Shulman, 1986, p. 13). The emphasis throughout the section in which this quotation appears is on the role of reflection, both in making decisions—"reason[ing] about both ends and means, and then [acting] while reflecting upon one's actions"—and in "communicating the reasons for professional decisions and actions to others" (ibid). I note here only the fact that excellent teacher practice is assumed to follow a deliberative reasoning process identical to the one involved in providing post-hoc explanations.

In short, in discussing the concept of the "strategic knowledge," Shulman conflates the guiding function of maxims with their rationalization-providing function. The difficulty is that the "strategic understanding"—postulated to mediate between a general maxim and a concrete circumstance—is imagined to be available itself, both before and after the fact, to a practitioner internally and to an interlocutor alike, in the form of a proposition, a concrete reason. It is unclear how this process of internal or external appeal differs in kind from appealing to any other proposition, a maxim or a rule or a principle. There is no obvious candidate for what makes the product of reflection the articulation of a "judgment" *as opposed to* a "maxim."

Indeed, while in acknowledging that the conflicting nature of maxims or rules make judgment necessary, Shulman's solution to the indeterminacy in these situations appears in terms of "knowledge of what and why," or principles for action according to which such indeterminacy is to be settled. In other words, Shulman's "strategic understanding," amenable as it is to "explanation" and "knowledge of what and why," is conceived as a codifiable and *higher* order of rules and maxims. But given that these are also rules and maxims, and that in lived situations, rules and maxims come into conflict, how is the practitioner to navigate among the conflicts among these *higher* principles? Presumably, on this model, with further, higher principles.

This is the infinite regress to which attempts to formulate practical know-how in terms of mentalistic or behavioristic principles that can be theoretically known are famously prone. Tyson Lewis critiques modes of understanding teacher practice in terms of mentalistic accounts along similar lines (Lewis & Garcia, forthcoming). This logical regress implies that if judgment of this kind—judgment involved both in practice and in the explanation or justification of any given practice—is invoked to explain the bringing-together of the general maxim and specific situation, such a model of judgment will be insufficient, at least in terms of the *practical action* under discussion here. The insufficiency is evident in the fact that any judgment amenable to propositional reasoning remains open to a further "why" question. At some point in any practical reasoning process, like a parent explaining things to a three-year-old, one answer or another will simply end the colloquy—one answer or another will be the final one before a practitioner takes action. But whatever it is that *makes* this or that proposition, this or that answer, the end point for this chain of reasoning cannot *itself* be a proposition, an interpretation, or a judgment of the type imagines: if it were, it too would be open to "why," and would thus be no resting point at all. A practitioner's action, even in the model above, might have reasons and reasoning associated with it, but no reason or chain of reasoning will be *sufficient* to cause any particular action.

This is not to argue against the role of deliberate reflection in teaching, nor to discount the importance of a teacher's ability or responsibility to explain why something is done, nor even to deny that teachers pull back and deliberately weigh options when confronted with any particular dilemma or unfamiliar situation; it is rather and merely to question the *place* and *function* of this ability, to caution against inflating the undeniable presence of reflective reasoning in *some* instances and at *some* points of teacher practice into a general model of all skillful practical behavior as such.

The raising of the regress argument on my part is meant to accomplish two things. In the first place, on a point I will continue to reiterate, Shulman's allusions to content-specific teacher knowledge and to the possibility that "flexibility" or "grounded unpredictability" might manifest consistently high-quality teacher practice *do indeed* move one closer to the goal of replicating skillful practice that Duncan, Lemov, and Shulman all share. In this sense, Shulman's conceptions of "strategic knowledge" and the "wisdom of practice" represent notable improvements on the abstract behavioral account that Lemov offers. In the second place, though, the threat of the regress implies that the pursuit of finer-grained content- or maxim-specifications is literally infinite, and so attempting to replicate the excellent skillful practice that in fact exists by these means alone are bound to fail.

This bound-to-fail contention ought to be heard in two ways: failure to replicate excellent practice by these means is inevitable in light of the regress threat because (a) bottoming-out in some sort of foundational domain or fact or rule or principle seems implausible by the very nature of an infinite regress, and (b) this impossibility of bottoming-out, in combination with the *actual existence* of excellent practice, implies that excellent skillful practice is not comprised of following maxims and rules in the way that either the behavioristic or the mentalistic account assumes. Whatever would be generated according to either a Shulman or a Lemov model would not be, therefore, identical to the kind of practice from which it is derived. To speak of the replication of excellent teacher practice on this assumption, then, ceases to make sense.

On that note, I return to the first problem I located in Shulman's arguments around "strategic knowledge" and "the wisdom of practice": that an ability to offer post-hoc rationalizations or explanations of why something is done seems to indicate to Shulman that such rationalizations or explanations also provide the aprioristic guiding function he attributes to the "rules and maxims" of practical wisdom. The regress argument provides one form of demonstrating the implausibility of this assumption: the failure to reach the bottom in attempts to dissect skillful practice into the rules and maxims that apparently guide it, and then into rules for navigating among conflicting rules and maxims, and so on, suggests that perhaps skillful practice does not start with something like the most general or abstract facts and rules, and thus that rules and maxims may not "guide" practice, even reflectively, in the way that Shulman imagines.

But the phenomenology of various skillful endeavors also casts doubt on Shulman's conflation of post-hoc and aprioristic reasoning. When we teach our toddlers to tie their shoes, we say "the rabbit goes around the tree." When approaching the counter of a café in a foreign country, we consciously deliberate about how best to order coffee—in terms of politeness, grammatical correctness, and so on. Beginners, in other words, absolutely depend upon conscious and deliberate cogitation in order to demonstrate any given skill. It is by no means equally clear that we as adults or we as native speakers of our native tongues, ordering coffee in our native lands, *also* rely upon this sort of conscious reasoning. If anyone approached me on the street and demanded to know how I tied my shoes just now, or why I said, "Just a black coffee, please" instead of any other phrase that would have procured the object of my desire, I would be able to, and indeed would, explain how or why I did thus and so. But this does not indicate that the reasons I provide to an interlocutor I must *also* have provided to myself in advance of tying my shoe or ordering coffee, such that this reasoning can be said to have *caused* my particular practical behavior.

The fact that one follows rules and maxims as a beginner is nevertheless taken as evidence that such a process occurs throughout one's skill development, even if unconsciously. But in ordering coffee in Madison, Wisconsin, say, I no more employ particular rules than I think to myself, "the rabbit goes around the tree" as I tie my shoe.[2] Neither my ability to *do* it, nor an ability to offer an explanation of *how* I did it in terms of particular facts and rules, is sufficient to indicate that the terms of the explanation amount to the causal conditions of the performance itself. Such after-the-fact explanations do not necessarily support the assumption that whenever one does something skillfully, the skillful performance is a behavioral manifestation of interlocking maxims and rules. Shulman's attempt to codify the wisdom of practice with the ultimate aim of replicating the skillfulness of this practice, however, makes just such an assumption.

I suggest that while such codification of rules and maxims—like Lemov's behavioral techniques—does indeed have value in the realm of teacher training, its utility has limits, and a certain cognizance of the limits of this approach is quite necessary to the development of the excellent teachers that Duncan, Lemov, and Shulman all desire. Seen in this light, Lemov and Shulman's assumption that some self-consistent and transcendent knowledge of behavioristic or mentalistic rules underlies any particular skilled performance does indeed make progress in the direction of excellent teacher practice.

But if one entertains the notion that excellent teachers are not themselves, generally speaking, being guided at every moment by rules and maxims, then attending to their practice only with an eye to *extracting* rules and maxims will prove inadequate to the replication of their practice. Without considering what happens as we move from explicitly following rules, like a non-native speaker ordering coffee, to some other form of skilled practice, as in adult-level shoe-tying, we risk misplacing the end goal of teacher training in general. If something *different* from explicit rule-following behavior comprises excellence in a given skill domain, then the progress one can make in the direction of excellence by means of identifying, codifying, and transferring rules will eventually run out and some entirely new approach will have to take over.

While conceding that extracting rules and maxims has value, and that implementing them makes progress toward excellence, I would like to assert—a point I will substantiate in a later chapter—that this represents an example of what Hubert Dreyfus calls the fallacy of the successful first step.

2.2.3 Another Sense of Scaling in Duncan's Rhetoric

In Chapter 1, I noted the prevalence of the metaphor of scaling in Duncan's discussion of improving the teaching corps and the quality of schools in general, nation-wide. I likewise noted that the scaling metaphor comes from two different contexts of origin, a business or economics context and a computer-science context. In the previous chapter, I focused primarily on the salience of "scaling-up" in the business sense. In returning to the notion of "scaling-up" educational successes in light of the discussion of the scholarly or academic hunt for the *knowledge* or behaviors necessary to the skillful practice of excellent teachers, I would like to consider attempts at taking educational reforms to scale in its computer-science-derived sense.

In the business sense, as I discussed, scaling-up means adding volume to an existing system; in the computer-science sense, scaling-up has a somewhat similar meaning, but its particular valence has primarily to do with *generalizing* the mechanisms by which a given program achieves results in a certain delimited domain to other domains, and expecting the achievement of similar results. This sense of scaling makes two assumptions from a given fact: from the fact of demonstrable and obvious success in a given place, a scale-up approach assumes, correctly (because we are speaking here of programming), that the success is directly attributable to the coding involved—that is, to the symbolic representations of facts and to the rules programmed for manipulating them. The scale-up approach then further assumes that generalizing from this success is a matter of *adding* further symbolic representations to account for additional features in an expanded or altogether different domain and necessarily also *adding* rules for navigating among this expanded set of features. Thus, generalizing from a limited success is imagined to follow from grasping the rules and representations active in the limited domain and expanding upon them as needed for transference to another, wider application.

Duncan's comments on scaling, offered on a variety of occasions, reveal the similarities between his view of the problem of educational success and the computer-science sense of scaling. In his interview on *The Daily Show*, Duncan demonstrates the similarity most clearly: he acknowledges that while there "are pockets of excellence" in the American school system, the task is to "take them to scale. . . . It's happening. It's just not happening at scale" (Stewart, 2012). The "pockets of excellence" he sees imply to him that the answers to the questions of how to teach exist and all that is now required is some sort of means for making those answers generally available or widely practiced. Coming from the discussions of Lemov and Shulman, it will be obvious that "how to teach" is assumed to exist in the form of information, in a set of "codified representations" analogous to those involved in coding or programming. Duncan's enthusiasm in this interview, the energy driven by a sense of frustration, also drives home the impression that he feels that the large step—discovering the essential rules and facts that underlie "how to teach"—has already been taken. Generalizing ought to be the *denouement*, and thus the frustration with the "pockets of excellence" and the fact that it is "not happening at scale."

Speaking in Oregon, as I also already mentioned in Chapter 1, Duncan says, "The CLASS Project is a tremendous example of the successful work that should be taken to scale, because students benefit when teachers work together to share best practices and learn from one another" (Craig, 2011). Here, too, Duncan emphasizes the ease of generalization, once given the existence of local success. Noting that the CLASS Project represents an example of "successful work that should be taken to scale," Duncan hints that the *isolation* of the project's success has to do with insufficient information-transfer among either schools, administrators, or teachers: "[S]tudents benefit when teachers work together to share best practices." The concept of "best practices," by this point, is freely understood to consist in specific, isolated structures of behavior applied by rule.

"Sharing" best practices would consist in simply offering the behaviors in question much the way Lemov does, and accounting for the local conditions in making minor additions and modifications. In the way that any necessary adaptations or modifications are assumed to be negligible in generalizing from one particular context to another, such that the "best practices" maintain the spotlight, this comment of Duncan's likewise bolsters the similarity between the sense of scaling he has in mind and that derived from a computer-science context. Duncan's sense that achieving success in a local context represents the *largest* step toward achieving widespread application—generalization problems being, on this view, matters of ineffective communication, or entrenched bureaucratic opposition, or the like—is echoed in the literature on scaling-up educational innovations.

One group, attempting to bring innovations in science education to scale and proposing ways to deal with the vast varieties of contexts in which the innovation will be applied, notes the general pattern of efforts to take such innovations to scale: "The stages involved in 'going to scale'—designing an educational innovation, assessing its efficacy, testing its effectiveness, and, finally, implementing it on a large scale—are under development as well" (Lee & Luykx, 2005). In the stages cited by the authors, three of the four have to do with creating something that works in a local situation and demonstrating *that* it works. "Implementing it on a large scale," on their view, is not one of Lemov's "complex skills," as it does not appear to require any further specification. It is itself, then, taken to be simple and singular.

Another group expresses similar frustrations with the problems of getting to scale. Noting that "pockets of good educational practice can be found almost *anywhere*," the authors remark that "Nevertheless, good educational practice cannot be found *everywhere*. The incidence of usage of available knowledge, and the rate of spread of effective practices, is grievously low" (Healy & DeStefano, 1997, p. 2). Having spied successful practice in pockets, and relying on the assumption that such successful practice rests upon explicit knowledge or information, the frustration with the slow spread of best practices is natural. The "usage of available knowledge" is once again taken to be a simple matter.

In noting the frustrations with attempts to take education reform to scale, and in thinking of "scaling" in its computer-science valence, it will perhaps be helpful to make a broad analogy between the ways in which skillful teacher practice is assumed to work—i.e., as a matter of atomizable behaviors or techniques whose implementation is governed by rules or maxims—and attempts at generating skillful or intelligent behavior where no such *assumptions* are necessary. The project of Artificial Intelligence needs *assume* no underlying rules-and-facts ontology to computer programs; such programs *absolutely* run on symbolic features linked by rules.

In spending considerable time drawing out this analogy, I hope to suggest that the problems of scaling local successes in both education and symbolic Artificial Intelligence are related to one another insofar as both take the discovering of applied rules and facts that lead to success in a limited domain to be the difficult part of the task, and the generalization of those same to some larger domain to be the simple part.

Similarly, I wish to assert that failures of symbolic AI to demonstrate any sort of skillful flexibility of the kind Shulman attributes to "Nancy" likewise threatens the assumption that our own skillful practice *actually* stems from the sorts of "rules and maxims" that Shulman takes to underlie the practices of accomplished teachers. That the many attempts to generate intelligent or skillful behavior according to the same assumptions on which the studies of Shulman and Lemov rest—as well as the whole of the educational reform movement typified by Race to the Top policies—have met with only the most limited types of success ought to call those very assumptions into question. The demonstrable and repeated failures of symbolic AI to achieve its projected goals ought to caution the education reform movement away from conceiving of the generalization problem as a simple one, and should also encourage us to revisit our assumptions about what skillful practice is made of. In this new light, the concept of "best practices," I intend to argue, thus carries us a much smaller distance toward our goal of developing excellent educational practice than we often assume.

NOTES

1. Deborah Ball has more recently discussed the importance of "training" as a means of directly acknowledging the limitations of "propositional knowledge and beliefs" discussed here (Loewenberg Ball & Forzani, 2009, p. 503). She is quite right to note that such propositional knowledge is not enough, and her turn to practical "training" is laudatory. However, if an appeal to training gets her out of the problems of relying on propositional knowledge alone, she circles around to demand that training be *standardized* for the good of teacher education, period. The standardization of such training experiences—according either to behaviors, or outcomes, or contexts—would make training dependent upon the very "propositional knowledge and beliefs" that practical training was originally invoked to circumvent. The Pedagogical Content Knowledge project has not yet found a suitable way of bringing their ground-level assumptions about the *nature* of practice to the practical demands of teaching.
2. There are, of course, thinkers who would certainly contend that this is *exactly* what happens; my claim is that in order to make such an argument, they must appeal to *logical* grounds, since parties on both sides of this issue agree that nothing *conscious* or empirically available is going on which could support their claim.

REFERENCES

Ball, D. L., Thames, M. H., & Phelps, G. (2008). Content Knowledge for Teaching: What Makes It Special? *Journal of Teacher Education, 59*(5), 389–407. doi:10.1177/0022487108324554

Carpenter, T. P., Fennema, E., Peterson, P. L., & Carey, D. A. (1988). Teachers' Pedagogical Content Knowledge of Students' Problem Solving in Elementary Arithmetic. *Journal for Research in Mathematics Education*, 385–401.

Craig, A. (2011). US Secretary of Education Arne Duncan Meets with CLASS Project to Hear Progress Report. Retrieved from http://chalkboardproject.org/press-room/us-secretary-of-education-arne-duncan-meets-with-class-project-educators-to-hear-progress-report-on-24-4-million-federal-investment-in-oregon-teachers-and-students/

Duncan, A. (2009a). Robust Data Gives Us the Roadmap to Reform. U.S. Department of Education. Retrieved from http://www2.ed.gov/news/speeches/2009/06/06082009.html

Duncan, A. (2009b). Teacher Preparation: Reforming the Uncertain Profession. U.S. Department of Education. Retrieved from http://www.ed.gov/news/speeches/teacher-preparation-reforming-uncertain-profession

Duncan, A. (2009c). Turning Around the Bottom Five Percent. U.S. Department of Education. Retrieved from http://www.ed.gov/news/speeches/turning-around-bottom-five-percent

Glazerman, S., Goldhaber, D., Loeb, S., Raudenbush, S., Staiger, D., Whitehurst, G. J., . . . Quality, B. C. T. G. on T. (2011). Passing Muster: Evaluating Teacher

Evaluation Systems. Brookings Institute. Retrieved from http://www.brookings.edu/reports/2011/0426_evaluating_teachers.aspx

Green, E. (2010, March 7). Building a Better Teacher. *New York Times Magazine*, p. MM30. New York: New York Times.

Grossman, P. L. (1990). *The making of a teacher: Teacher knowledge and teacher education*. New York: Teachers College Press.

Healey, F. H., & DeStefano, J. (1997). Education reform support: A framework for scaling up school reform. *Policy Paper Series (Research Triangle Park, NC: Research Triangle Institute*.

Hill, H., & Ball, D. L. (2009). The Curious—and Crucial—Case of Mathematical Knowledge for Teaching. *The Phi Delta Kappan*, 91(2), 68–71. Retrieved from http://www.jstor.org/stable/40344904

Hill, H. C., Kapitula, L., & Umland, K. (2011). A Validity Argument Approach to Evaluating Teacher Value-Added Scores. *American Educational Research Journal*, 48(3), 794–831. doi:10.3102/0002831210387916

Hill, H. C., Rowan, B., & Ball, D. L. (2005). Effects of Teachers' Mathematical Knowledge for Teaching on Student Achievement. *American Educational Research Journal*, 42(2), 371–406.

Hollabaugh, J. (2011). Review: Teach Like A Champion. *International Journal of Instruction*, 4(1).

Kane, T. J., Rockoff, J. E., & Staiger, D. O. (2008). What does certification tell us about teacher effectiveness? Evidence from New York City. *Economics of Education Review*, 27(6), 615–631. doi:10.1016/j.econedurev.2007.05.005

Kane, T. J., Taylor, E. S., Tyler, J. H., & Wooten, A. L. (2011). Identifying Effective Classroom Practices Using Student Achievement Data. *Journal of Human Resources*, 46(3), 587–613.

Keller, B. (2010). Content Seen Lacking Specificity. *Education Week*, 30(11), S17–S19.

Lee, O., & Luykx, A. (2005). Dilemmas in Scaling Up Innovations in Elementary Science Instruction with Nonmainstream Students. *American Educational Research Journal*, 42(3), 411–438. Retrieved from http://www.jstor.org/stable/3700458

Lemov, D. (2010). *Teach Like a Champion*. San Francisco: John Wiley & Sons.

Lewis, T., & Garcia, J. (forthcoming). Getting a Grip on the Classroom. *Curriculum Inquiry*.

Loewenberg Ball, D., & Forzani, F. M. (2009). The Work of Teaching and the Challenge for Teacher Education. *Journal of Teacher Education*, 60(5), 497–511. doi:10.1177/0022487109348479

Magnusson, S., Krajcik, J., & Borko, H. (1999). Nature, Sources, and Development of Pedagogical Content Knowledge for Science Teaching. *Examining Pedagogical Content Knowledge: The Construct and Its Implications for Science Education*, 6, 95–132.

Marks, R. (1990). Pedagogical Content Knowledge: From a Mathematical Case to a Modified Conception. *Journal of Teacher Education*, 41(3), 3–11.

Mishra, P., & Koehler, M. J. (2006). Technological Pedagogical Content Knowledge: A Framework for Teacher Knowledge. *Teachers College Record*, 108(6), 1017–1054. doi:10.1111/j.1467-9620.2006.00684.x

Nocera, J. (2012). Gates Puts the Focus on Teaching. *New York Times*, p. A27. New York.

Rothstein, R. (2008). *Grading Education*. New York: Teachers College Press.

Shulman, L. (1986). Those Who Understand: Knowledge Growth in Teaching. *Harvard Educational Review*, 57, 1–22.

Shulman, L. (1987). Knowledge and Teaching: Foundations of the New Reform. *Educational Researcher*, 15(2), 4–14.

Shulman, L. (2005). Teacher Education Does Not Exist. *Stanford Educator*.
Shulman, L. S. (2007). Practical Wisdom in the Service of Professional Practice. *Educational Researcher*, 36(9), 560–563 CR—Copyright © 2007 American Educa. Retrieved from http://www.jstor.org/stable/30137941
Stewart, J. (2012). February 16. *The Daily Show*. thedailyshow.com.
Van Driel, J. H., Verloop, N., & de Vos, W. (1998). Developing science teachers' pedagogical content knowledge. *Journal of Research in Science Teaching*, 35(6), 673–695.

3 Best Practices and Artificial Intelligence

The primary assumption pertaining to the ontology of teacher practice, if I can call it that, shared by Lemov and Shulman alike has it that what an observer witnesses in any given teacher's practice is the apparent and contingent manifestation of an underlying guarantor or causal mechanism that generates the particular practical behaviors on display. This assumption, as I have said, is likewise shared by Duncan and the reformers he cites more generally: his use of the scaling trope, and that trope's employment in the academic literature, is sufficient to demonstrate this fact, especially in combination with his suggestion that student achievement data will reveal something important about "how to teach." In earlier chapters, I have framed Duncan's policies as responding to a skeptical fear, namely that an observer might be wrong in ascribing this or that level of quality to a given instance of teacher practice or student learning.

Lemov and Shulman's view of skillful teaching, however, also seeks to foreclose upon a skeptical fear, the fear that any instance of excellent teaching might occur by *accident*, as it were, hinging on something as mysterious and ineffable as mere chance. Identifying either the common (or essential) behavioral characteristics of good teaching or, as in Shulman's case, the sort of practical knowledge that grounds the "grounded unpredictability" of excellent and flexible teacher responsiveness, would provide a means of both assuring oneself that the teaching practice in question is in fact high-quality teaching *and* inculcating with certainty the qualitative essence of that practice in pre-service or underperforming teachers.

Such a response to skeptical doubts—the assumption about the nature of skillful practice itself—also enshrines a strong view of skilled behavior on which any actual instance or demonstration of skillful practice, however irregular or exceptional or "unpredictable," is in fact explained and caused by something external or transcendent to that instance of skilled practice, something that is itself stable, regular, or certain. Lemov thinks of this stability in terms of the identity of behavioral techniques across various examples of teacher practice. Shulman thinks of it in terms of the "codified representations" of teachers' practical wisdom. Arne Duncan's speeches imply that he would mostly agree with the basic assumption of each.

This basic assumption pertaining to the source and nature of consistently skillful or intelligent practical behavior as such has its roots in a particular view of the way that the mind is involved in guiding or initiating practices, a particularly rationalist view of skillful human activity. Such a view takes it that the essence of mind, going back to Plato, involves operating with signs or performing calculations, however these signs and calculations are derived from the world that our senses encounter or are given a priori in the capacity to reason. It is on the basis of this assumption that the digital computer, the universal machine, appears to be such a promising candidate for the replication of skillful practice, the demonstration of artificial intelligence: if the human mind most essentially processes information by means of symbol manipulation, then any machine that does *only* that—but rigorously, without error, and without tiring—ought to be able to mimic the operation of the mind *perfectly*.

Although there are notable differences between any computer and an actual person—computers don't have bodies, for instance, and have never been "raised" by parents within any particular culture—these differences will not be significant as long as all that "having a body" or "being raised within a culture" amount to are themselves formalized in the mind as symbolic representations. When Shulman claims that a primary goal of teacher researchers ought to be to "develop codified representations of the practical pedagogical wisdom of able teachers" (Shulman, 1987, p. 11), he also takes *practical skill* to be had by a teacher in codified form: the purpose of research, in this sense, is to make this code, currently hidden in a given teacher's mind, *transparent* and external. The assumption that skillful practice is based upon or caused by an underlying structure, ultimately consisting of formalized representations (of behavioral techniques, of rules and maxims, of facts and features), will go by the name of the "rationalist assumption," as Dreyfus terms it, for the purposes of this book. But philosophers have named it various other things, as well.

Kevin Cahill calls this assumption the "disengaged view" of practice; Hubert Dreyfus elsewhere terms it the "detached view" and also a form of "cognitivism"; Charles Taylor calls it the "intellectualist view." Cahill's succinct explanation of the "disengaged view" recalls the assumptions upon which Shulman, Lemov, and, Duncan's vision for data usage in guiding teacher practice, rest:

> Perhaps the main intellectual requirement that the disengaged picture makes on us is that we must envisage for ourselves a way to account for the rationality manifest in our various activities that is completely independent of those activities. In the particular case of following an arithmetic rule, the disengaged view requires us to be in possession of something that would satisfy the requirement that our understanding transcend all of our actual responses when we write out a numerical series. (Cahill, 2011, p. 116)

Lemov's search for the 49 techniques of great teachers, as well as Shulman's search for the maxims and rules—the knowledge—that comprise the "wisdom of practice," both assume, exactly as Cahill puts it, that "the rationality manifest in our various activities" results from something (the knowing *of* specific techniques, the knowing *of* rules and maxims) that "is completely independent of those activities," that "transcend[s] all of our actual responses" in lived situations. The value of the specific techniques that Lemov extracts, or the particular maxims and rules that Shulman locates, depends upon the view that the skillful practices from which researchers derive them are in fact rule- or maxim-guided activities, that the "complex skill" of teaching under observation is *in fact* the manifestation of "single specific actions," as Lemov has it, combined in practice according to particular (and transcendent) rules. Only if this is the case does a "best practices" approach to teacher development have the possibility of replicating the excellent practice for which purpose it is designed.

The dominance of a "best practices" approach to the problem, mentioned earlier, of propagating the "usage of available knowledge" (Healy & DeStefano, 1997, p. 2) in many practical fields, including the field of education, is such an obvious fact that it practically defies through sheer quantity the possibility of adequate documentation.[1] "Best practices" represent an outgrowth of a mode of problem-solving developed in the modern era by the RAND corporation but evincing the American propensity to such thinking that Jal Mehta documents in *The Allure of Order*. RAND codified, if you will, "the method of *systems analysis*. The very height of means-ends rationality, systems analysis is the interdisciplinary science of maximizing efficiency and economy given a particular objective and a set of 'system parameters'" (Medvetz, 2012, p. 71).

In Chapter 1, I detailed the *conceptual* problems inherent in applying such "means-ends rationality" to the project of education, wherein the *great* teaching immediately visible to Duncan upon his entering a school proves inadequately defined for the purposes of such "systems analysis." Quantified proxy measures of teacher quality, however—where "effective teaching" is defined according to the ability to influence achievement scores—does the trick.

Here in Chapter 3, I emphasize that in addition to the considerable problem presented by the fact that the "best practices" sought by researchers like Lemov and Thomas Kane are derived from an analysis conducted in terms of a distorted goal, there is also no reason to assume—and substantial reason to doubt—that spreading "best practices" even according to the ordinary sense of great teaching will be coextensive with the dissemination of skillful teaching practice.

This is not to claim (to reiterate an earlier point) that Shulman and Lemov's work and the "best practices" to which it is related are without value. It is very much to claim, however, that whatever such approaches can do in terms of teacher development dries up well in advance of the greatness that provides Race to the Top's justification. A good test of the limits of the assumptions about skillful behavior typified by Lemov and Shulman, as well as by the "best practices" regime, will be to examine the relative successes and setbacks of the projects of the AI research community, whose machines operate according to just such a features-and-rules model that the aforementioned scholars believe mirrors our own.

3.1 THE RATIONALIST ASSUMPTION OF AI AND THE PROJECTS INVOLVED

The critical perspective from which my analogy proceeds will rely to a substantial degree on the work of Hubert L. and Stuart E. Dreyfus, originally undertaken in a consulting capacity for the RAND corporation, as the think tank sought an evaluation of its AI projects (Selinger & Crease, 2002, p. 249). Because the brothers—Stuart an engineer and Hubert a philosopher—present for simplicity's sake much of their work from Hubert's point of view (Dreyfus & Dreyfus, 1986, p. 1), I will likewise do so, referring to "Dreyfus" in the singular even in cases where both are assumed to have done the authoring.

At the outset of venturing into a critique of AI and the "best practices" approach to teacher development, I wish to say plainly that in pointing out the shortcomings of the rationalist or intellectualist assumptions undergirding Race to the Top's teacher-quality policies along Dreyfusian lines, and in describing the ways in which Dreyfus's account of skill development proceeds from a different set of assumptions, I hope to claim (1) that ordinary-sense excellent teaching is simply not reproducible according to a best-practices approach, and that (2) Dreyfus's alternative account points us in helpful and fruitful directions. It must also be noted that, despite the fact that Dreyfus's criticism of AI's assumptions dates back to the 80s, 90s, and even earlier, new paradigms in the field retain the most salient assumptions that Dreyfus takes apart. The current head of Google's AI research division, Ray Kurzweil, recently published a book entitled, *How to Create a Mind* (Kurzweil, 2012); his proposal of a Pattern-Recognition Theory of Mind, along with Colin McGinn's exposure of the argument's shortcomings (McGinn, 2013), is sufficient to demonstrate that AI's fundamental assumptions regarding the mind and skilled behavior remain beset by the problems Dreyfus identifies.

Dreyfus's Introduction to the MIT edition of *What Computers Still Can't Do* provides the most straightforward account of the assumptions according to which the projects of symbolic Artificial Intelligence proceed. Says Dreyfus:

> GOFAI [Good Old-Fashioned AI] is based on the Cartesian idea that all understanding consists in forming and using appropriate symbolic representations. For Descartes, these representations were complex

descriptions built up out of primitive ideas or elements. Kant added the important idea that all concepts are rules for relating such elements, and Frege showed that rules could be formalized so that they could be manipulated without intuition or interpretation. Given the nature of computers as possible formal symbol processors, AI turned this rationalist vision into a research program and took up the search for the primitives and formal rules that captured everyday knowledge. (Dreyfus, 1992, p. xi)

Dreyfus expands a bit later:

> Rationalists such as Descartes and Leibniz thought of the mind as defined by its capacity to form representations of all domains of activity. These representations were taken to be theories of the domains in question, the idea being that representing the fixed, context-free features of a domain and the principles governing their interaction explains the domain's intelligibility. On this view all that we know—even our general know-how for getting around in the world and coping with things and people—must be mirrored in the mind in propositional form. (Dreyfus, 1992, p. xvii)

But one need not take Dreyfus's word for either the assumption that AI researchers themselves see either their own project or the human intelligent behavior it ought to surpass on this view. Allen Newell and Herb Simon, the pioneers, assert this assumption themselves:

> The principal body of evidence for the symbol-system hypothesis [of mental functioning] . . . is negative evidence: the absence of specific competing hypotheses as to how intelligent activity might be accomplished whether by man or by machine. (Newell & Simon, 1985, p. 50)

Because digital computers represent the rationalistic view *par excellence*, AI proponents from the 1950s onward have claimed that the universal machine would soon match and exceed the human capacity for intelligent behavior. These claims have gone persistently unfulfilled. Examining attempts and failures at achieving intelligence on these assumptions in the area of NL (Natural Language understanding) and the view of skillful behavior guiding its turn to the use of "micro-worlds" will help one to see the limitations of this picture.

According to Dreyfus, proceeding from the "symbol-system hypothesis" fails to account for—and thus has so far failed to replicate—certain aspects of what we freely recognize as intelligent behavior. Dreyfus terms this stumbling block the "commonsense knowledge problem":

> There are really at least three problems grouped under this rubric:

1. How everyday knowledge must be organized so that one can make inferences from it.
2. How skills or know-how can be represented as knowing-that.
3. How relevant knowledge can be brought to bear in particular situations. (Dreyfus, 1992, p. xxviii)

Doug Lenat, whose ongoing Cyc work represents a continuation of the GOFAI approach in the present day, acknowledges and attempts to account for the failures of NL projects in revealing ways:

> The problem of understanding natural language (NL) is another chicken-and-egg one. On the one hand, our real AI must be able to surf the web, read books, carry on conversations, tutor and be tutorable, and so on—things that human beings primarily do through natural language. On the other hand, as we saw above (with numerous examples involving resolving polysemy, anaphora, ambiguous prepositional phrase attachment, noun-noun phrases, interpreting metaphor and analogy, recognizing irony and sarcasm, and so on) understanding the next sentence one reads or hears might require almost any piece (out of many many millions) of prior presumed knowledge.
>
> One of the reasons this impediment is on my list is that AI researchers—NL researchers—have watered down the problem to the point where they "succeed" on every project, and yet natural language understanding of the sort we need is not here, nor is it, frankly, just around the corner yet. They talk about parsing an English sentence into logical form, for example, but then turn out to mean transforming it into something that structurally, syntactically fits the definition of "in logical form." As a caricature: add parentheses at the very start and end of the sentence, and declare success. (Lenat, 2008, p. 18)

All of the features that, on Dreyfus's view, plague the Artificial Intelligence field in general are on display in Lenat's comment. The first point to observe about Lenat's assessment is the language in which Lenat characterizes the difficulties in NL: the grasping of a sentence's sense from among the multifarious possibilities, given the ways in which the given speech structure might occur in practice, "might require almost any piece (out of many many millions) of prior presumed knowledge." Lenat conceives, then, of the problem of understanding something like the contextualized situation in terms of mentally accessing pieces of prior (propositional) knowledge. But the massive database of facts supposed to represent commonsense knowledge do not seem to result in an ability to flexibly and speedily arrive at something like correct understanding, which flies directly in the face of the way human beings seem to operate. This is a manifestation of Dreyfus's "relevance" problem, which Dreyfus describes thusly:

> Indeed, AI researchers have long recognized that the more a system knows about a particular state of affairs, the longer it takes to retrieve the relevant information, and this presents a general problem where scaling up is concerned. Conversely, the more a human being knows about a situation or individual, the easier it is to retrieve other relevant information. (Dreyfus, 1992, p. xxi)

The marked difference between the way a symbol-system and a person respond to "knowing more about a situation or a person" suggests a difference in the ways in which each entity arrives at a determination of the *relevant* aspects of a given state of affairs.

Additionally, however, Lenat mentions the temptation and proclivity to define down "success" in the NL field, a temptation that he laudably resists. This defining-down recalls both Duncan's complaints about the emptiness of state definitions of proficiency and also the danger inherent in confusing a technical sense of good teaching with an ordinary one. What makes the confusion around notions of "success" in the NL arena possible is similar to what I blame for confusing distinct concepts of educational quality: in seeking to "parse" the English sentence into its "logical form," AI researchers operate on the assumption that English sentences, *as they occur in ordinary practice*, have and indeed rely upon a transcendent logical form for their intelligibility, which is very much the rationalist assumption of skillful teacher practice shared among Lemov, Shulman, and Duncan.

Lenat's charge that breaking down or "parsing" an English sentence into logical form somehow distorts ordinary language suggests that when we use language with one another in ordinary, native-speaker situations, we do something other than internally applying logical rules to symbolic representations. The problem, as he and Dreyfus both note, has to do with the task of *scaling up*—of generalizing a particular success in one region of language-processing to the domain of language as a whole:

> Naturally, all programs are built on some primitives (predicates, frames, slots, rules, functions, scripts). But if you choose task-specific primitives, you'll win in the short run (building a program for that narrow domain) but lose in the long run (you'll find yourself painted into a corner when you try to scale the program up). (Lenat & Guha, 1990, p. 15)

On Lenat's view, the problems in scaling-up have to do with the use of task-specific primitives (like Ball and Hill's "Mathematical Knowledge for Teaching," one might note); Lenat's project is to develop symbolic representations of the *general* primitives underlying language use. Dreyfus, meanwhile, takes issue with the very assumption of the existence of such primitives. Another way of putting the distinction is that Lenat holds the requisite commonsense knowledge to be *in fact* unformalized, as yet. Dreyfus holds that the requisite commonsense knowledge is *in principle* non-formalizable. Dreyfus's response to Lenat and Feigenbaum's discussion of codifying human input in order to solve the relevancy project bears quotation in this regard. Lenat and Feigenbaum suggest that they, as researchers, ought to

> wait until our programs are finding many, far-flung analogies, but inefficiently, i.e. only through large searches. Then investigate what additional knowledge *people* bring to bear, to eliminate large parts of the search space in those cases. Codify the knowledge so extracted, and add it to the system. (Lenat & Feigenbaum, 1991, p. 221)

Dreyfus simply points out that "The assumption that people *are* storing context-free facts and using meta-rules to cut down the search space is precisely the dubious rationalist assumption in question. . . .

> ["]In the end, Lenat's faith that Cyc will succeed is based neither on arguments nor on actual successes but on the untested traditional assumption that human beings have a vast library of commonsense knowledge and somehow solve the scaling-up problem by applying further knowledge. (Dreyfus, 1992, p. xxii)

Notably, Dreyfus originally penned this critique of the Cyc project in 1992; in Lenat's 2008 paper he continues to claim progress in assembling this massive database of commonsense knowledge, as he has been doing since the early 1980s, but the resulting programs and database still seem unable to mimic the alacrity or flexibility (what Dreyfus calls an ability to "zero-in" on the relevant aspects of a situation) of a situated human being (Dreyfus, 1992, p. 30).

It is precisely the disjuncture between the digital processor's many superiorities to human abilities—most notably, as Dreyfus concedes, "their rigor, reliability and indefatigability," which allows "computers used as logic machines to do extremely well what human beings do only poorly" (Dreyfus & Dreyfus, 1986, p. 63)—and its striking inability to achieve humanlike intelligence or skillful understanding in terms of NL (and many other domains not considered here) that ought to indicate that the view of skillful behavior on which human beings refer to "codified representations" of facts or rules in any performance of skilled practice is at best incomplete. The problems encountered with scaling-up successes in skill domains such as NL seem to imply that, for us, something other than combining facts and rules is involved as we become generally proficient in various skill domains.

Dreyfus's analysis of the SHRDLU program's use of "micro-worlds" from the 1970s will provide a helpful segue back to the ways in which similar assumptions about skillful teaching practice permeate the policy, academic, and public discourse on teaching and learning in the age of Race to the Top.

SHRDLU, initiated by Terry Winograd, was a 1971 program in NL, which researchers at the time referred to as "a major advance" in that it employed the concept of a micro-world. Micro-worlds, as the name implies, are strictly limited domains, based upon "primitives" of the kind Lenat mentioned earlier. Dreyfus describes the micro-world like so:

> SHRDLU simulates a robot arm which can move a set of variously shaped blocks and allows a person to engage in a dialogue with the computer, asking questions, making statements, issuing commands, about this simple world of movable blocks. The program is an integrated system which makes use of syntax, semantics, and facts about blocks. (Dreyfus, 1992, p. 5)

And it worked, that is, it was able to carry out commands, identify objects, and report progress within this world. AI researchers saw this as a major improvement upon earlier attempts (like the famous ELIZA program) because, using the concept of primitives to derive success in a micro-world, it seemed a comparatively small and merely technical step to code the necessary primitives to all micro-worlds, and thus, to the whole. Dreyfus's analysis of SHRDLU's success, his description of the assumptions on which its ambitious scaling-up proceeded, and his explanation of the inevitability of its eventual failure will lead back to a discussion of Duncan, Lemov, and Shulman. I present three paragraphs culled from within Dreyfus's longer, original analysis:

> What characterizes the period of the early seventies, and makes SHRDLU seem an advance toward general intelligence, is the very concept of a micro-world—a domain which can be analyzed in isolation. This concept implies that although each area of discourse seems to open out into the rest of human activities its endless ramifications are only apparent and will soon converge on a self-contained set of facts and relations. (H. L. Dreyfus, 1992, p. 10)

> It is true that physical theories about the universe can be built up by studying relatively simple and isolated systems and then making the model gradually more complex and integrating it with other domains of phenomena. This is possible because all the phenomena are presumably the result of the lawlike relations of a set of basic elements, what Papert and Minsky call "structural primitives." (H. L. Dreyfus, 1992, p. 12)

> In our everyday life we are, indeed, involved in various "sub-worlds" such as the world of the theater, of business, or of mathematics, but each of these is a "mode" of our shared everyday world. That is, sub-worlds are not related like isolable physical systems to larger systems they *compose*; rather they are local elaborations of a whole which they *presuppose*.

If micro-worlds *were* sub-worlds one would not have to extend and combine them to reach the everyday world, because the everyday world would have to be included already. (Dreyfus, 1992, p. 14)

Of particular note with regard to Shulman, Lemov, and Duncan's thinking is Dreyfus's twin assertions that, on the one hand, "[each area of discourse's] endless ramifications are only apparent and will soon converge on a self-contained set of facts and relations," and on the other, that "sub-worlds are not related like isolable physical systems they *compose*; rather they are local elaborations of a whole which they *presuppose*." Lemov and Shulman regard what Shulman calls the "outrageous complexity" of teaching practice in terms of a very limited sense of complexity: despite the vast divergences among the actual practices of various teachers in various situations, these behavioral differences are, as Dreyfus says, "only apparent," masking a deeper sort of essential core.

Dreyfus's comments on the presupposed whole, meanwhile, draw into question researchers' assumptions about the problem of scaling: although severely restricting a given domain such that proceeding by means of given facts and rules may afford a passable simulacrum of skilled behavior, there is no reason to suppose that it will, ultimately, prove amenable to being "taken to scale," as Duncan has it, by the same facts-and-rules processing on which the initial success was predicated. It was, after all, in the very attempt to compose a larger whole from initial and promising successes in AI, by means of the same symbol-system hypothesis involved in the restricted domain, that each of the promising successes in AI failed to generalize. As Dreyfus has it, this failure is attributable to the fact that what we call intelligent or skillful human behavior in a given domain is, contra Lemov, *not* a composite of smaller (unintelligent?) behaviors governed by rules or maxims; rather, it is a kind of local elaboration of a holistic sense of a given skill, one intimately involved with and inseparable from what Dreyfus, following Heidegger, elsewhere calls one's "understanding of being."

The empirical experience of the field of AI research, based as it is upon the rationalist assumptions also underpinning Duncan, Lemov, and Shulman's working theories of teacher practice, provides no evidence at all that the teacher practices that Lemov and Shulman study, the "good teaching" that justifies Duncan's Race to the Top, will be replicable according to the rationalist assumption upon which their work and policies proceed.

3.2 AI'S SCALING PROBLEM AND THE DEVELOPMENT OF GOOD TEACHERS

The analogy I have suggested here between the pursuit of Artificial Intelligence along the lines suggested by what Dreyfus calls the "rationalist assumption" and the political and academic view of teaching ability is apt and germane in a few different ways.

In the first place, the analogy explains the predictive success of Ball and Hill's "Mathematical Knowledge for Teachers" measure that I noted in the previous chapter. Their measure can account for 11 percent of the variance in mathematics achievement scores (Hill, Rowan, & Ball, 2005), which is more variance than any other teacher characteristic explains. Noting that the measure itself reflects a narrowing of the teaching skill domain to (a) the teaching of mathematics (a single subject area) as measured by (b) standardized achievement tests (i.e. according to no "inspiring" or "instilling a thirst for knowledge" criteria), it stands to reason that the measure would be both *as successful as it is* and also *no more successful than it is* in accounting for variance in math scores.

Even though any claim to causation between the measures of "MKT" and student achievement results remains at most implicit in Ball and Hill's work, I might suggest that attempting to influence student math scores by means of developing individual teachers' "MKT" could indeed prove fruitful. As we have seen, understanding skillful behavior according to rationalist postulates has led to relatively successful replication under such particular and severe domain constraints. But this does not imply that "MKT" or any other subject-specific pedagogical content knowledge is somehow either necessary or sufficient to the practice of good teaching in its ordinary sense. The fact that "MKT" only accounts for 11 percent of the variance in test data even under these relatively ideal conditions points both to its utility and to that utility's limits.

In the second place, to speak of problems in scaling-up local success in a given school building to a wider context, Dreyfus's account of the failure of facts-and-rules approaches to achieve *generally* successful intelligent practice provides an alternate explanation for Healy and DeStefano's observed discrepancy between the fact that "good educational practice can be found almost *anywhere*" and the persistent, obstinate fact that it "cannot be found *everywhere*." Tellingly, as a reminder, Healy and DeStefano regard the failure to generalize in terms of a failure to communicate. It is simply assumed that *knowledge* of "effective practices" will work in one place as well as in another. But AI's failures in the realm of NL might instead cast serious doubt upon assumptions regarding the *general* value of locally obtained "primitives" and also, due to Dreyfus's relevance problem, of generally-applicable primitives in any given *local* situation. When Duncan frames the problem of scaling as merely one of teachers needing to "share best practices," where "sharing" is imagined merely as the communication of codified representations, he therefore trades on an assumption that has demonstrably failed another field.

As we have seen, developing a particular teacher's skillfulness according to a "best practices" model, whether this is understood according to Lemov's or to Shulman's framework, requires an *atomizable* view of skillful practice itself, such that linking pieces of practice (either knowledge or technique) together adds up to the skillful whole. In the previous chapter, I suggested that the logical problems with Lemov and Shulman's accounts might indicate that each is mistaken about *what* he is observing when he observes teacher practice. In this chapter, I will follow up on this suggestion to a degree.

Lemov revealingly—and accurately—draws an analogy between the teaching world and the art world in order to situate his emphasis on the "foundational skills" he associates with good teaching:

> Great art relies on the mastery and application of foundational skills, learned individually through diligent study. You learn to strike a chisel with a mallet. You refine the skill with time, learning at what angle to strike and how hard to drive the chisel. Years later, when and if your work makes it to a museum, observers will likely talk about what school of thought or theory it represents. They are far less likely to reflect on the degree to which proficiency with the chisel made the vision possible. But although lots of people conjure unique artistic visions, only those with an artisan's skill can make them real. Every artist is an artisan. And while not everyone who learns to drive a chisel will create a *David*, neither can anyone who fails to learn it do much more than make marks on rocks. (Lemov, 2010, p. 1)

The analogy Lemov draws is apt; his inference is not. Lemov makes the argument that foundational skill with a chisel is a necessary but not sufficient condition for Michaelangelo's *David*. Broadly speaking, he is surely correct. Presumably, a foundational skill with a brush would be similarly necessary (but not sufficient) to the painting of *Water Lilies*. But it is not self-evident that this "skill with a brush" is the same as the "skill with a brush" necessary (but not sufficient) to the painting of *Guernica*. And then there is Jackson Pollock to consider. These are all freely regarded as masterful artists and artworks.

I invoke three painters working in three different movements precisely to draw out the fact that Lemov's approach to teacher practice takes it for granted that all skillful teaching is identical at a certain level—analogous, ironically, to the presumably identical *artistic-ness* of "*unique* artistic visions (emphasis added)." "Mak[ing] them real," according to Lemov, requires an "artisan's skill." Were this the case, and were "artistic vision" not in fact unique at all, certainly the *same* skills would be requisite for working in the same medium. In fact, this is precisely what Lemov assumes:

> I had always thought Picasso was a king of abstraction, of a symbolism that made the ability to draw accurately and realistically irrelevant. His sketches, filling the margins of the pages, bore witness to his mastery of fundamentals and a habitual need to refine his skills. Even in the

stray moments of his schooling, he was constantly honing the building blocks of his technique. (Lemov, 2010, pp. 1–2)

Despite the fact that "the building blocks of his technique" are nowhere in evidence *themselves* in the masterpieces for which Picasso is known—those that "made the ability to draw accurately and realistically irrelevant,"— Lemov assumes that his margin-note sketches remain present in the masterpieces as necessary conditions, even if, somehow, beneath perceptibility or consciousness. Treating Picasso's "sketches" in the margins of his notebook as "building blocks"—rather than pedestrian doodling—mirrors in important ways Shulman's tendency to equate a teacher's post-hoc rationalization for a given decision as evidence of internal deliberation prior to that decision. We will return to this assumption in some detail in a later section. Irrespective of the appearance of the masterpieces themselves, Lemov assumes that all artistic masters possess the same skills.

But the particular skills brought to bear in particular masterpieces, such as the ones cited above, remain manifestly different from one another; in fact, the only thing that makes the techniques *skills* in this sense is the "unique artistic vision" entailed in the finished product itself. Only if the "vision" of art were reduced to some sort of explicit definition toward which each artist separately labors would Lemov's vision of the foundational role of isolated and abstract skills hold.

Here, once more, we encounter the value and the danger of the technical sense of "learning" in the direction of which the technical sense of "good teaching" aims. The value of a technical sense of teaching and learning lies in its ability to establish the identity of excellence such that all skill-development proceeds in just this direction. The danger lies here also: precisely this direction has been officially (and ordinarily) understood as *insufficient*, as Duncan's many insistences about the inability to "reduce the complex, nuanced work of teaching" to precisely this definition confirm and reiterate.

Lemov's view of the developing the skills to realize unique artistic visions— unique except for an identical if inchoate sense of artisticness—also suggests an analogy with Lenat's view of the NL field's failure to produce the *general* skills it seeks. His claim, recall, is that the field has "watered down the problem to the point where they 'succeed' on every project," which has not solved the larger problem the methods were meant to address: "the natural language understanding that we need is not here yet, nor, frankly, is it just around the corner." Whatever teacher-preparation success is achievable through the use of Lemov's technique-extraction methodology, I contend, is achievable because the "relevance problem" has been precluded a priori: the explicit and technical definition of "student learning" as the only relevant feature guiding the discovery and application of teacher skillfulness restricts the domain of teaching and learning to the extent necessary for a facts-and-rules approach to succeed in some passable form.

The notion that by having achieved success in a reduced domain, we have taken a considerable step toward achieving success in the larger domain is rendered dubious by the AI experience. A facts-and-rules approach that functions in a limited domain does not therefore provide the necessary or sufficient conditions for success in the domain as a whole, which is the ordinary sense of good teaching. In other words, while there is nothing at all wrong with the facts-and-rules approach in its limited application, something goes very wrong indeed when the limited domain is confused with the general whole of ordinary teaching, which, as Chapter 1 has demonstrated, it regularly is.

Returning to Lemov's analogy with art, I would like to suggest that his considerations of the "foundational skill" of chiseling, the physical familiarity with the practice, is indeed requisite to the production of the *David*. But working backward from the *David* to extract the chiseling skills involved will only work to reproduce the practice insofar as the *David*, or something very like it, absolutely defines the desired outcome. The *same* skills are not required—nor would they be particularly useful—to Rembrandt or Monet, who also produce *great art*.

If one so desired, one could pull back and attempt to locate the piecemeal physical skills that transcend these particular media, the skills that Michaelangelo shares with Rembrandt and Monet. But then, perhaps, one factors in ceramic artists, and must account for the physical skills of *that* medium as well, all under the rubric of discovering the necessary skills for the production of great art. At this point, or perhaps earlier, one realizes that whatever physical skills happen to transcend these media, and are in fact shared among all the artists involved, can account for very little indeed of the individual finished masterworks. Insofar as the reproduction of the transcendent elements of excellent teacher practice represents Lemov's goal, there is no reason to suppose that such an approach by itself will be able to reproduce anything close to the practice of any one of the particular teachers who are taken to apply the rules or principles or techniques.

The recognition of just such a weakness in a "best-practices" approach inspires Shulman's project in teacher development, where no such transcendence of *all* fields of content is sought, the notion being that, to continue Lemov's analogy, the skills necessary to sculpture are different than those necessary to painting, and so, in specifying the distinction, we can focus on the individual skills necessary to each *field*. This is the sense in which Shulman improves upon Lemov's model. By narrowing the domain further—not simply from ordinary-sense great teaching to technical-sense great teaching, but now also to technically great *math* teaching, for example—one improves the functioning of the facts-and-rules approach. But one need not stop there. By narrowing the domain further and further, the facts-and-rules approach will work progressively better.

But for every narrowing of the domain, which allows for progressively greater success, one reduces the generalizability of one's techniques. Conversely, attempting to find (and inculcate) more and more general facts and rules progressively reduces their applicability in any particular setting. The freezing of relevance through the defining of good teaching in its technical sense helps with this problem to a certain degree, but it also and simultaneously precludes any serious attempt on the part of colleges of education or other teacher-training programs to develop ordinary-sense great teachers. The next two chapters provide an account of why this is so and offer a formative view of skill development that would address the flaws exposed here.

In closing this chapter, it is worth mentioning again—so that it may be heard in light of the foregoing discussion—Duncan's assuredness about the role of data in teacher development:

> In the end, I don't think the ingredients of a good teacher preparation are much of a mystery anymore. Our best programs are coherent, up-to-date, research-based, and provide students with subject mastery.... [T]hese programs have a shared vision of what constitutes good teaching and best practices—including a single-minded focus on improving student learning and using data to inform instruction. (Duncan, 2009)

The "ingredients" of a good teacher preparation certainly are not mysterious any longer, but the *solving* of the mystery, my discussion suggests, has much more to do with "water[ing] down the problem" in order to make it amenable to a particular view of skillful practice than the discovery of a revolutionary approach to understanding teaching and learning. That "what constitutes good teaching and best practices" can be rendered in propositional form at all may be a consequence of the narrowed domain of teaching and learning, a narrowing achieved by defining "teaching" in terms of its effect on "student learning," and "student learning" as reflected in achievement score growth, none of which has anything explicitly to do with "inspiring" students or "instilling a thirst for knowledge," or any of the myriad other skills that comprise the "ordinary" sense of good teaching.

In turning to a critique of the rationalist assumption itself, a critique that AI's many failures have demonstrably warranted, I hope to show that transcendent facts and rules, in however general or limited of a domain, while sometimes *sufficient* to the reproduction of practical competence, are neither necessary *nor* sufficient to the reproduction or regularity of our shared practices, including and especially the excellent practices of great teachers, and that developing great teachers from novices will require relying on some other means of accounting for this regularity.

NOTES

1. A search of the University of Iowa Library's database turned up over 8,000 articles in journals ranging across the fields of medicine, law, business, microbiology, engineering, education, and many, many more.

REFERENCES

Cahill, K. (2011). *The Fate of Wonder: Wittgenstein's Critique of Metaphysics and Modernity*. New York: Columbia University Press.

Dreyfus, H. L. (1992). *What Computers Still Can't Do: A Critique of Artificial Reason*. Cambridge, MA: M.I.T. Press.

Dreyfus, H. L., & Dreyfus, S. (1986). *Mind Over Machine: The Power of Human Intuition and Expertise in the Era of the Computer*. New York: Free Press.

Duncan, A. (2009). Teacher Preparation: Reforming the Uncertain Profession. U.S. Department of Education. Retrieved from http://www.ed.gov/news/speeches/teacher-preparation-reforming-uncertain-profession

Healy, F. H., & DeStefano, J. (1997). Education Reform Support. U.S. Department of Education. Education Resources Information Center.

Hill, H. C., Rowan, B., & Ball, D. L. (2005). Effects of Teachers' Mathematical Knowledge for Teaching on Student Achievement. *American Educational Research Journal*, 42(2), 371–406.

Kurzweil, R. (2012). *How to Create a Mind: The Secret of Human Thought Revealed*. New York: Penguin.

Lemov, D. (2010). *Teach Like a Champion*. San Francisco: John Wiley & Sons.

Lenat, D. (2008). The Voice of the Turtle: Whatever Happened to AI? *AI Magazine*, 29(2), 11–23.

Lenat, D., & Feigenbaum, E. (1991). On the Thresholds of Knowledge. *Artificial Intelligence*, 47(1–3).

Lenat, D., & Guha, R. V. (1990). *Building Large Knowledge-Based Systems*. Reading, Mass: Addison-Wesley.

McGinn, C. (2013). Homunculism. *New York Review of Books*. Retrieved from http://www.nybooks.com/articles/archives/2013/mar/21/homunculism/?pagination=false

Medvetz, T. (2012). *Think Tanks in America*. Chicago: University of Chicago Press.

Newell, A., & Simon, H. (1985). Computer Science as Empirical Inquiry: Symbols and Search. In J. Haugeland (Ed.), *Mind Design*. Cambridge, Mass: MIT Press.

Selinger, E. M., & Crease, R. P. (2002). Dreyfus on Expertise: The Limits of Phenomenological Analysis. *Continental Philosophy Review*, 35(3), 245–279. doi:10.1023/a:1022643708111

Shulman, L. (1987). Knowledge and Teaching: Foundations of the New Reform. *Educational Researcher*, 15(2), 4–14.

4 Teacher Practices and Accounts of Rule-Following

Duncan's speeches announcing the aims of Race to the Top, and particularly the exhortations pertaining to the use of student achievement data to inform teacher practice and teacher development, take it that teaching skillfully, teaching well, is a matter of consistently performing the correct action in the correct circumstances. The research agenda he lays out before the Institute of Education Sciences, in which he proposes that uncertainty around the quality of a given teacher or a given school administrative structure or a given technique is to be settled by "the research and the facts" (Duncan, 2009a), operates, as we have seen, on the following assumptions about teaching practice: (a) the correctness of any given action can be derived from its effect on student learning as represented in achievement score growth on math and reading assessments; (b) such actions are atomizable, which means both that they can be fully described in isolation from any other action and also that the whole of teaching practice is made up of such actions, comprised thereof without remainder; and (c) variation in circumstances or context can likewise be formalized such that, when paired with a set of potentially-correct teacher actions, the optimal behavior will stand out (given the appropriate rules for behavior selection).

What I have called the particular ontology of teaching practice—of skillful practice in general—is thus at least partially generated according to the requirements of a systems-analysis approach, one in which both means and ends are formalized a priori and set into interaction with one another. In order for teaching practice to *be* so formalized, it *must* be "a series of [formalizable] bite-sized moves," as Green has it. While Lemov's approach takes the formalizable moves to be broad and behavioral, which lessens the requirement for the formalization of circumstances, the approach taken by Ball, Hill, and Shulman understands the "codifiable" aspects of teacher practice as something like *mental* behaviors or rules generated from internal interactions among still other formalized sets of facts (pertaining not only to practical behavior, but also to the particular subject matter being taught and to "students").

I have suggested in earlier chapters that it would be helpful and productive to see this ontology of teaching practice, the particular picture of teaching and learning on which education reform policy operates, as a response to certain skeptical fears that come out clearly in Duncan's rhetoric and especially in his interpretation of the New Teacher Project's 99 percent statistic. This skepticism wonders whether we *really* know what good teaching is; the fact that 99 percent of all teachers are rated "the same" is understood to indicate that we do not, that we fail when we attempt to draw meaningful distinctions when observing teacher practice. The drive to use student achievement data as a means of speaking to teacher quality is a more or less direct response to this worry: by formalizing what we *expect* teachers to do—namely, raise student test scores—we establish a method of differentiating good teachers from poor teachers. But the suggestion that overcoming the sort of "intellectual lack" around recognizing teacher quality, as Cavell characterizes this type of skepticism (Cavell, 1996, p. 68), will *also* overcome a *practical* lack implies a very peculiar view of the relation between knowledge and skilled practice. In Chapter 1, I was most concerned to point out that this formalization of teaching's *ends* is necessarily a reduction of our expectations of teaching in general, a criticism echoed by many others, particularly Ravitch and Rothstein (Ravitch, 2010, 2013; Rothstein, 2008) and even one acknowledged by Duncan.

In Chapters 2 and 3, I have mostly ignored the obvious point that, if derived from a distorted goal, then no characterization of teaching practice in whatever form will suffice for its larger purpose. Instead, I have argued that Shulman and Lemov's projects misunderstand the nature of practical skill generally, irrespective of the criterion of correctness to which the formalizable features of teaching practice are pegged. (For Lemov, it is indeed test scores; for Shulman, it is not—his characterization of "Nancy's" excellence relies on something much more akin to the "eye test.") The analogy between a "best practices" view of skillfulness in general with the failures of Artificial Intelligence projects to reproduce skillful behavior is meant to suggest a deeper sort of flaw in the picture.

Specifically, far from being simply mistaken about the particular *ends* at which teaching is supposed to point, the general ontology of skillful practice apparent in the education reform policies under discussion, as well in as Lemov and Shulman's research, is mistaken about the role and constitution of practical knowledge, which is to say, about the relation of knowledge to practice, about the *nature* of practical knowledge itself. The role of skepticism in this picture is evidenced in the drive to improve teaching through the formalization of practical rules and behavioral techniques: if one knows (with certainty) which actions are best in particular contexts, then the resulting performance of teaching will be optimal. Skepticism around the question of whether we adequately *know* how to teach generates the need, as Cahill has pointed out, for a kind of knowledge that transcends all particular instantiations of teacher practice. The AI analogy suggests that human beings, when performing with expert skill, are not using *knowledge* as imagined in this picture, that is, they are not applying formalizable techniques or codifiable rules to situations defined by facts and features. This is the point that Dreyfus raises: "human beings may not normally use commonsense *knowledge* at all. What commonsense *understanding* amounts to might well be *everyday know-how*" (Dreyfus & Dreyfus, 1986, p. 99).

The danger in attempting to conceive of teacher practice according to a facts-and-rules approach, the danger in attempts to formalize excellent practice in order to *guarantee* the excellent performance of teachers, is not merely that what one generates will diverge to some extent from a more or less mechanical version of the actual practices of actually excellent teachers, but rather that by committing to the particular view of skillfulness as an effect of formalizable knowledge, one will in fact preclude the development of expert skillfulness altogether. This is the lesson to draw from the failures of AI: formalization of means and ends in the realm of skillful performance is not simply to take the long (albeit certain and reproducible) way to excellence; it is to prevent *arriving* at excellence at all.

With this lesson in mind, the argument of Chapter 4 seeks to accomplish two goals: making an in-principle argument, rather than an argument by analogy, that the formal picture of knowledge as applied to practice, required by responsiveness to skeptical fears, cannot perform the tasks it is invoked to perform; and offering the emphatic reminder that failures of formalizable views of practical skill and knowledge are only visible *as failures* in comparison to actual models of skillful practice, which is as much as to say that raining on this particular possibility of developing, reproducing, or inculcating excellent teacher practice is by no means to deny the possibility of the development, reproduction, or inculcation of practical teacher excellence *as such*. The failure of a given model to explain, recognize, or reproduce practical excellence is not a denial of the phenomenon, nor a denial of its recognizability or reproducibility.

4.1 THE CHICKEN AND THE EGG

Several twentieth-century philosophers have taken on the task of revealing the logical and practical problems with transcendent structures of knowledge and determination in a variety of skillful public practices. My secondary argument in this chapter will militate against a persistent misunderstanding of, or a faulty inference from, the insights of such thinkers, particularly those of Jacques Derrida.

The AI failures to reproduce intelligent human behavior have done serious work toward disconfirming the rationalist view of skillful behavior in general: returning to Lenat's characterization of what he calls the "chicken-and-egg" problem helps to introduce the issues involved with applying the rationalist assumption to the practical public skill of using language. To present Lenat's description of the problem once more,

> The problem of understanding natural language (NL) is another chicken-and-egg one. On the one hand, our real AI must be able to surf the web, read books, carry on conversations, tutor and be tutorable, and so on—things that human beings primarily do through natural language. On the other hand, as we saw above (with numerous examples involving resolving polysemy, anaphora, ambiguous prepositional phrase attachment, noun-noun phrases, interpreting metaphor and analogy, recognizing irony and sarcasm, and so on) understanding the next sentence one reads or hears might require almost any piece (out of many many millions) of prior presumed knowledge. (Lenat, 2008)

The chicken-and-egg nature of this issue has to do with the problem that, in order for AI to know *what* is being learned, it must first know what the particular input words are instances *of*. To *what else* are they similar? Generating a structure of knowledge from "surfing the web" and so on requires that AI be able to group new facts together under various categories; but grouping new facts together in this way requires the very structure of knowledge that such facts are supposed to generate.

Dreyfus puts it in similar terms:

> To recognize any context one must have already selected from the indefinite number of possibly discriminable features the possibly relevant ones, but such a selection can be made only after the context has already been recognized as similar to an already analyzed one. (Dreyfus, 1992, p. 54)

The rationalist assumption itself requires a sort of transcendent structure upon which things like situation-specific relevance and similarity can be made to depend. Derrida's deconstructive project represents a successful attack on the notion that any such account is in principle capable of accounting for the regularity or the novelty in our use of language As Simon Glendinning puts it,

> According to Derrida, the problem is that, once one embarks on an analysis of language based on the radical distinction between linguistic systems and linguistic events, the conceptual resources at one's disposal cannot account for the possibility of the very phenomenon it is claiming to delimit. This is because the impossible condition of both the historical priority and the logical posteriority of speech ruins any attempt to provide an internally consistent account of the conditions of possibility for the phenomenon of language. (Glendinning, 1998, p. 113)

The phenomenon of language, here, as with the phenomenon of learning *via* language that Lenat discusses, demonstrably defies an accounting in terms of transcendent rules or primitives on the one hand and particular situations on the other. As in Cahill's passage from the previous chapter, the suspicion is that the *requirement* of a way of accounting for the "rationality of our practices" that transcends any particular instance is responsible for the conceptual distortion evident in the logical impossibility of a familiar, everyday practice.

It is worth pointing out once again that when Shulman asks after what Nancy "believe[s], understand[s], and know[s] how to do," he is in search of precisely the transcendent structure upon which the particular practice of her teaching is assumed to draw. The chicken-and-egg problem that Lenat encounters in engineering human-like learning and that Derrida discovers in traditional accounts of language suggest that what "permit[s] Nancy to teach as she does" will not appear in a form Shulman would recognize as a potential answer to his questions. Nevertheless, Nancy's teaching *is* excellent. If attempts to account for this excellence according to the requirements of the rationalist assumption fail, it is not a denial of that excellence, nor of our ability to recognize it; it is instead an indictment of the picture of knowledge and practice that guides Shulman's research project.

Wittgenstein's work, particularly in the *Blue Book* (Wittgenstein, 1969, henceforth BB) and the *Philosophical Investigations* (Wittgenstein, Anscombe, & Hacker, 2009, henceforth PI), takes seriously the possibility that the rationalist assumption might provide a means of explaining the regularity of our practices and our ability to develop others' skillfulness in any practical domain, and he attempts, as I said in the Introduction, to see "what the application of the picture looks like." For Wittgenstein, the favored examples pertain to learning the meaning of a word, continuing a numerical series, and following a mathematical rule (or signpost, or custom). All are examples of rule-following in general, the idea being that, in a tack similar to Derrida's, when one uses a given word in any specific situation, one is following a rule that more or less stipulates that this word is appropriate for this situation. All instances of performing a given practice in the way that others would, too, that is, regularly, will therefore count as *rule-following activities*. At stake in Wittgenstein's work are precisely the issues that have already been raised: can a rule be understood as transcending all instances of its application? And: does *following* a rule require the possession of such a transcendent or "codified representation" of the rule?

It is important to reiterate yet again that the *phenomenon* of rule-following is what Wittgenstein attempts to sort out. The rationalist account of rule-following likewise presupposes the existence of regularity in public and skillful practices. A failure of any account of this regularity is not tantamount to denying regularity as such. I am at pains to point this out, apparently endlessly, largely because of the way that the "antifoundationalism" of Derrida in particular, but also of Heidegger and Wittgenstein, has been understood as denying the very possibility of regularity or normativity wholesale.

Postmodern literary criticism, for example, has become a caricature of the sort of radical relativism that is imagined to proceed from Derrida's work. This caricature looks something either like, "Words have no meaning" or, "The meaning of any word is completely up to me," each of which flies in the face of obvious phenomenological fact. John McDowell notes the prevalence of this particular misunderstanding: "If one is wedded to the picture of rules as rails, one will be inclined to think that to reject it is to suggest that, say, in mathematics, anything goes: that we are free to make it up as we go along" (McDowell, 1981, pp. 150–151). The rejection of a view of skillful practice based on logical or causal necessity will imply to some a rejection of all normativity or regularity altogether.

The heart of Wittgenstein's antifoundationalism, which is also present to varying degrees in the work of Derrida and Heidegger, is not that foundations (of linguistic meaning, of rule-following practices) *do not exist*; it is that we have a flawed idea of what a foundation *is* (or *looks like*). Wittgenstein is very clear on the possibility of reaching what he calls "bedrock" (*PI* §217): "Proof and justification come to an end," he says (*PI* §204). "Explanations come to an end somewhere" (*PI* §1). On any particular occasion, any given response or any given action is in fact grounded: proofs, justifications, and explanations are offered to someone else (or to oneself) and are, at some point, counted as adequate. Whether this *grounding* is absolute and transcendent is precisely the issue at hand. If it is *not*, then those committed to the requirements of the rationalist assumption will not recognize the foundation of a particular action *as* a foundation, since actual foundations must be, on this (disengaged) view, exactly so transcendent and absolute. Wittgenstein notes this tendency as well: "The difficult thing here is not, to dig down to the ground; no, it is to recognize the ground that lies before us as the ground" (Wittgenstein, 1983, VI, 31).

In the *Blue Book*, Wittgenstein follows the rationalist assumption down a certain rabbit-hole in the direction of paradox and regress. Imagining a scenario in which he commands another to go out and fetch him a red flower, Wittgenstein asks, "How is he to know what sort of flower to bring, as I have only given him a *word*?" (*BB*, p. 3). In answer to this rhetorical question, Wittgenstein offers a rationalist response, supposing that "he went to look for a red flower carrying a red image in his mind" (*BB*, p. 3). The use of an "image" is incidental to the rationalist picture—this might also have been a definition of redness, a list of facts and features constituting "red" and so on. In all cases, though, it is a *something* that is possessed in the mind. This is roughly akin to the "practical knowledge of able teachers" that Shulman seeks out—the "codified representations" of content, students and practice alike that interact internally, through a process of "reflection," in order to arrive at a particular decision.

Wittgenstein acknowledges that this "carrying a red image in his mind," and "comparing it with the flowers to see which of them had the colour" is indeed a "way of searching" (*BB*, p. 3), but he notes that it "is not at all essential that the image we use should be a mental one."

> In fact the process may be this: I carry a chart co-ordinating names and coloured squares. When I hear the words "fetch me etc." I draw my finger across the chart from the word "red" to a certain square, and I go an look for a flower which has the same colour as the square. (*BB*, p. 3)

Wittgenstein makes two moves in order to problematize this version of using a mental process consisting of the possession of a certain stabilizer of meaning—the red patch, whether in the form of an image or a definition or a list of facts and features—as a means of accounting for the ability to follow a simple order. In the first place, he points out that "this is not the only way of searching and it isn't the usual way" (*BB*, p. 3), which is to say, in the latter half of the claim, that most people do not in fact carry color-coordination charts around with them in order to identify red flowers.

In the second place, he raises an issue for the general picture of mental interpretation implied by the structure he posits. He points out that in fact when we follow such orders, "[w]e go, look about us, walk up to a flower and pick it, without comparing it to anything" (*BB*, p. 3). This is obviously not an explanation of how we are to know which one is the red flower; it is merely to suggest that we neither use a physical chart in this ordinary case (as opposed to, say, the special case of selecting a fine shade of a color for repainting the bathroom) nor have the conscious experience of both holding an image of redness in our minds and also comparing it to the various flowers we confront in a field. Any notion that we *must* have some sort of mental possession, such as an image or a definition, and that this internal mental possession comes into contact with instances of flowers in the external world through a sort of matching process mythologized in the physical example by the drawing of a finger from the word "red" to the red patch, remains purely hypothetical: this picture itself is required by the rationalist assumption's radical separation of mind and world.

Furthermore, on the same page, Wittgenstein hints that this model does not hold up: "To see that the process of obeying an order can be of this kind"—i.e. one on which a person simply goes and picks a flower "without comparing it to anything"—"consider the order '*imagine*' a red patch.' You are not tempted in this case to think that *before* obeying you must have imagined a red patch to serve you as a pattern for the red patch which you were ordered to imagine" (*BB*, p. 3). Wittgenstein's "you are not tempted" locution serves two functions: it deflates, in the first place, the urge to take a rationalist view of rule-following as a *general* state of affairs, a *general* characterization of what obeying an order requires. "You are not tempted," in this case, operates as a phenomenological claim. To the extent to which one is actually not tempted to use the picture of imagining a red patch as an object of comparison in order to explain how one is able to follow an order to "imagine a red patch," the claim works.

But the example of the order to "*imagine* a red patch" also reveals the weaknesses of the rationalist account more generally. By moving the entire process into the realm of the mind—which is similar to invoking the physical chart to move the entire process into the realm of the physical world—Wittgenstein shows that in order to follow the command to imagine a red patch *correctly*, one would require a way of insuring the correctness of the mental image to be used for the purposes of comparison. In other words, if a mental image of redness is supposed to serve, in the rationalist account, as the guarantor that the person following orders will in fact return with a red flower, the only way of checking the accuracy of the *mental image* of redness is by the flower with which this person actually returns. In the case of the order to "*imagine* a red flower," meanwhile, there is no way to confirm the accuracy of the image at all—either by the person doing the ordering *or* by the person doing the imagining.

Something similar is shown by the case of using a physical chart to match "red" with a color patch, and then to an actual flower. Wittgenstein imagines that one makes use of this chart—as one would—by drawing a finger from the word "red" to the image of redness. But this is not a *mechanical* or fixed procedure, as fingers can be drawn in a plurality of directions. "Drawing a finger" in such and such a way depends upon a certain practical knowledge of how to use a chart—it is conceivable that one might draw one's finger diagonally upward from the word to a color patch just as easily as one would draw one's finger horizontally. (He makes precisely this point at *PI* §86, in fact.) What makes one way correct and another incorrect is not given in the simple fact of the chart's existence. Even the postulation of a transcendent system of definitions in this case would require a set of rules to govern their correct use. But the ability to follow rules in the obedience of an order was the very phenomenon that was supposed to be explained by invoking a chart; if this, too, depends upon further or deeper rules, then nothing at all is explained. Wittgenstein says it best in *PI* §84: "Can't we imagine a rule regulating the application of a rule; and a doubt which *it* removes—and so on?" This is the same sort of regress that troubles Shulman's attempt to solve the problem of the "indeterminacy of rules" by appealing to "strategic understanding."

But what remains, and what requires reiteration, is Wittgenstein's phenomenological observation that "this [chart] is not the only way of searching and it is not the usual way"; in characterizing "the usual way" as "we go, look about us, walk up to a flower and pick it, without comparing it with anything," he offers a description of rule-following in practice, that is, a description of obeying an order with conviction. The implication is that rule-following *according to the rationalist assumption* is impossible—because no rule is self-interpreting—but that rule-following as a practice is a quotidian feature of everyday life, one that the rationalist explanation simply gets wrong.

Wittgenstein thus characterizes the emergence of the regress in the first place as resulting from a "misunderstanding":

> That there is a misunderstanding here is shown by the mere fact that in this chain of reasoning we place one interpretation behind another, as if each one contented us at least for a moment, until we thought of yet another lying behind it. For what we thereby show is that there is a way of grasping a rule which is *not* an interpretation, but which, from case to case of application, is exhibited in what we call "following a rule" and "going against it". (*PI* §201b)

Robert Fogelin calls this arrival at a regress in the attempt to explain rule-following according to the rationalist assumption the "paradox of interpretation." Fogelin explains Wittgenstein's sense of "a misunderstanding here" by saying that "for Wittgenstein there is no 'paradox' of rule-following. The thought that it is paradoxical is the product of a misconception, namely, the misconception that rule-following is always grounded in (or implicitly contains) acts of interpretation" (Fogelin, 2009, p. 22). David Stern puts the misunderstanding in similar terms: as Stern has it, the quest for a final formalization that itself requires no interpretation is "both unnecessary and impossible. It [is] unnecessary because we do not need an unmoved mover in order to follow a rule; it [is] impossible because nothing could perform that task" (Stern, 1995, p. 116).

In Dreyfus's view, meanwhile, the rationalist assumption's dependence on an ability to represent to ourselves in formalized terms our own skillful activity will inevitably raise this insoluble paradox. It is the representational requirement created by the rationalist picture of the mind as wholly and originally separate from the world, such that a mediating component is in all cases necessary, that is to blame for the confusion. As Dreyfus says, expanding on a passage I have quoted earlier:

> In the end the very idea of a holistic information processing model in which the relevance of the facts depends on the context may involve a contradiction. To recognize any context one must have already selected from the indefinite number of possibly discriminable features the possibly relevant ones, but such a selection can be made only after the context has already been recognized as similar to an already analyzed one. The holist thus faces a vicious circle: relevance presupposes similarity and similarity presupposes relevance. The only way to avoid this loop is to be always-already-in-a-situation without representing it so that the problem of the priority of context and features does not arise. (Dreyfus, 1992, pp. 54–55)

If an information processing model ends up in an unworkable and inevitable paradox, Dreyfus points to the possibility of "being always-already-in-a-situation without representing it" as an alternative model. Wittgenstein's invocation of the importance of training in the processes of teaching and learning offers a means of understanding Dreyfus's locution.

4.2 EXAMPLES AND EXERCISES

Following Descartes, the rationalist view of understanding opens with an isolated, disembodied consciousness, from which perspective any recognition of filiation or similarity between self and others, as well as self and world, must be *produced or deduced* by means of something like the identification of certain features in common. Indeed and especially, the particular relation between self and world *embodied* in practical skillfulness is taken to depend upon this peculiar sort of knowledge. Stephen Mulhall characterizes Cavell and Wittgenstein's approach to this sort of rationalism as follows:

> The truth of the matter is rather that this fundamental relation to the world (the human creature's basis in the world as a whole) is not one of knowing; but, as the tenacity both of the sceptical [sic] impulse and of the impulse to oppose scepticism in epistemological terms makes clear, nothing is more human than the compulsion to characterize this relation in that way. (Mulhall, 1998, p. 106)

Dreyfus's reference to Heidegger's Dasein or being-*there* at the conclusion of the previous section also reflects a Heideggerian suspicion that epistemological questions regarding everyday practices of any kind "come too late" (Heidegger, 1977, p. 305): such questions always presuppose an existing, practical relation on the basis of which they can be asked at all: "Each one of us is what he pursues and cares for. In everyday terms, we understand ourselves and our existence by way of the activities we pursue and the things we take care of" (Heidegger & Hofstadter, 1982, p. 159). Mulhall's suggestion that our "fundamental relation to the world is not one of knowing" most succinctly homes in on the basic idea.

It will therefore follow that attempts to alter practical behavior in the world—attempts to teach others or train oneself—*might* proceed in some cases by means of conveying knowledge as conceived on a rationalist model, that is, in terms of formalized or representational facts and rules, but that such attempts *need* not proceed in this way, and further, that imagining that any such attempt to train oneself or others *must*, in order to ensure regularity, rely upon any general rule, maxim, or fact will leave out all that is *given* by being always-already-in-a-situation and will thus risk the sorts of inflexibility and unskillfulness that AI projects tend to demonstrate.

Wittgenstein's many scenes of teaching, particularly in the *Investigations*, emphasize both avenues of the above point. In §208, Wittgenstein asks:

> How do I explain the meaning of "regular", "uniform", "same" to anyone?—I'll explain these words to someone who, say, speaks only French by means of the corresponding French words. But if a person has not yet got the *concepts*, I'll teach him to use the words by means

of *examples* and *exercises*.—And when I do this, I do not communicate less to him than I know myself. (*PI* §208)

The insistence that, in giving another person "concepts" by means of examples and exercises, the teacher does "not communicate less to him" than he knows himself militates directly against the rationalist assumption's picture of practical skillfulness. This is clarified in §210–211, when Wittgenstein's "voice of temptation"[1] suggests that there *must* be an "essential thing" linking together the various examples, a "drift" that characterizes the teacher's "intention." This "essential thing" would be one among many possible interpretations that might arise in either party's mind.

But the "voice of correctness" then proceeds to give the voice of temptation what it wants: a scenario in which "every explanation I can give myself I give to him too." The effect of this move is to make clear that if what Fogelin will call a "secret key" is involved in performing these exercises or linking these examples, then it is *equally* involved for both student and teacher. Not merely the student, but also the teacher, would have to "guess the essential thing" in order to perform any action skillfully; this would require a model of "picking" among "various interpretations" of one's *own* explanation in order to have an "intention" at all. The logical problem that this poses is very much akin to the idea of explaining our ability to follow the order to "*imagine* a red patch" by appeal to a(n existing) mental image of redness in our minds. Something about the picture is incorrect. As Charles Taylor understands it,

> The reciprocity [between rule and event] is what the intellectualist theory leaves out. In fact, what it shows is that the "rule" lies essentially *in* the practice. The rule is what is animating the practice at any given time, and not some formulation behind it, inscribed in our thoughts or our brains or our genes, or whatever. (Taylor, 1993, p. 178)

Fogelin's view does not go as far as Taylor's in reifying the (hypothetical) distinction between a rule and an event. As he says of the example in §208,

> Here the person doing the teaching possesses certain skills and abilities. She can give examples of uniformities and nonuniformities. She can employ the concept in a variety of contexts. In her teaching, she is trying to imbue her student with these same skills and abilities. She is not holding anything back. She is not in possession of a secret key that she is trying to pass on to her student that, when successfully transmitted, will successfully complete the training. (Fogelin, 2009, pp. 37–38)

Teaching someone to use words by means of "examples and exercises," which Wittgenstein suggests communicates no "less to him than I know myself," points to the *use* of words as the bottom-level locus of a given rule. The rationalist view necessitates a picture of a rule on which the rule must exist independently, somewhere outside of a given practice; the rule is, on that view, the necessary and transcendent condition that makes any instance of the practice possible. But the fact that the teacher and the learner *alike* in Wittgenstein's example have nothing more to go on than the practice—that in teaching by exercises and examples one communicates the *whole* of one's knowledge of that practice—shows that the foundation that a rule in fact is "lies essentially *in* the practice." If, as in the AI examples from the previous chapter, a given skill can be approximated in representational form and therefore *made* to exist outside the practice, this codification of skills does not in fact succeed in reproducing the skillfulness of the human practice from which it was derived; it does not do the very thing it was invoked to do.

It is crucial to note that, while Fogelin emphasizes the utility of Wittgenstein's training in accounting for the entire inculcation of a given skill or practice, this ought not to imply that undertaking anything at all that might aspire to the name of "training" will have the desired outcome (though only, of course, something worthy of the name of "training" would). Wittgenstein's examples themselves often feature the requesting and providing of reasons, justifications, and rationale—and often in the context of misunderstandings, the felt need for clarification, expressions of the wish for further guidance—to the consequences of which Cavell is particularly attuned. The foregoing paragraphs are sufficient to show that the rule to be followed cannot be conceived as contained *in* any explanation, whether this explanation is imagined as given to oneself, internally, or whether it is imagined as provided to the learner in order to guide his or her practice, but this is not to say that in giving explanations, nothing meaningful or relevant occurs at all.

The fact that explanations are thus insufficient—in themselves, that is—means that in instructing anyone else in a practice, there is no guarantee whatsoever that the pupil will acquire the skill. Ultimately, if one proves unable or unwilling to follow another's example in performing a given exercise, nothing else—and particularly no explanation or justification—can stand in for the example. If the necessary reliance upon examples and exercises can account for how we learn skillful practices, in other words, this necessary reliance can also account for how and why we fail. §217 of the *Investigations* considers just such a case: "If I have exhausted the justifications I have reached bedrock, and my spade is turned. Then I am inclined to say [to an interlocutor]: 'This is simply what I do.'" Cavell's take on this scene of educative failure is particularly dramatic:

> Our ability to communicate with him depends upon his "natural understanding", his "natural reaction", to our directions and our gestures. It depends upon our mutual attunement in judgments. It is astonishing how far this takes us in understanding one another, but it has its limits; and these are not merely, one may say, the limits of

> knowledge but the limits of experience. And when these limits are reached, when our attunements are dissonant, I cannot get below them to firmer ground. The power I felt in my breath as my words flew to their effect now vanishes into thin air. For not only does he not receive me, because his natural reactions are not mine; but my own understanding is found to go no further than my own natural reactions bear it. I am thrown back upon myself; I as it were turn my palms outward, as if to exhibit the kind of creature I am, and declare my ground occupied, only mine, ceding yours. (Cavell, 1979, p. 115)

Cavell's figuration of this scene of instruction brings out the consequences of having nothing more than the practice to go on, namely, the constant threat of being "thrown back upon" oneself, a standing threat that he elsewhere expresses by saying that "at any time I may find myself isolated" (Cavell, 1990, p. 100).

The invocation of isolation in Cavell's interpretation, which follows from a reading of "this is simply what I do" as an expression of helplessness in the face of the limits of one's practical knowledge, one that manifests itself in a turning-outward of the palms, emphasizing that this is simply what *I* do, casts the supplying of explanations or justifications in the inculcation of practices merely as a means of guiding or eliciting the practical behavior of others, rather than *providing* these others with an imagined causal condition or final justification for performing any given skill in such and such a way.

The possibility of discovering one's isolation from others in an inability either to exhibit a given practice as others would or to successfully guide another in the performance of this given practice emphasizes the fact that such practices and such skills must be *public*, that is, publicly shared: if such skills and practices can be neither contained nor conveyed in terms of atomized behaviors, propositional knowledge, or rules and maxims—if they in fact are taught and learning in examples and exercises—then they are always learned *from* others, and this does not (cannot) mean that individual subjectivities have equal access to some transcendent codified representation of a rule.

Glendinning puts it perhaps best: "A central feature of Wittgenstein's account of that behavior which one can call 'following a rule' is, therefore, the way in which *a relation to the behavior of others*, and hence a structural *publicness*, is *a priori* implicated by it" (Glendinning, 1998, p. 103). In the notion that any meaningful practice, including teaching, is a shared phenomenon, such that following rules amounts to a "relation to the behavior of others," Glendinning's "structural publicness," implicit in "a relation to the behavior of others," gestures toward the *regularity* implicit in such rule-following activities, that is, as Cavell terms it, "the astonishing fact of the astonishing extent to which we *do* agree in judgment" (Cavell, 1979, p. 31). As Cavell puts it in another place,

> That on the whole we do [agree] is a matter of our sharing routes of interest and feeling, modes of response, senses of humor and of significance and of fulfillment, of what is outrageous, of what is similar to what else, what a rebuke, what forgiveness, of when an utterance is an assertion, when an appeal, when an explanation—all the whirl of organism Wittgenstein calls "forms of life". (Cavell, 1962, p. 52)

Fogelin understands the matter similarly—and he militates against a persistent misinterpretation of what it might mean to agree (publicly) in "form of life": "In rule-following, we join a consensus in *action*—a consensus grounded in the kind of training that we, as humans, *can* successfully undergo and the kind of training that we actually *do* undergo in the community in which we are reared" (Fogelin, 2009, p. 28). A "consensus in *action*" is meant to oppose the notion that one must *come* to consensus on any given occasion, that is, *decide* to give one's consent.

Heidegger, according to Dreyfus, maintains a similar view of the alternative to a rationalist picture on which (public) rule-following would depend upon something like shared access to a transcendent rulebook:

> Heidegger's basic point is that the background familiarity that underlies all coping and all intentional states is not a plurality of subjective belief systems including mutual beliefs about each others' beliefs, but rather an agreement in ways in of actin g and judging. . . . Such agreement is not conscious thematic agreement but is prior to and presupposed by the intentionalistic sort of agreement arrived at between subjects. (Dreyfus, 1991, p. 144)

In simultaneously emphasizing both the fact that the inculcation of skillful practices cannot be achieved through the giving or following of rules as conceived on a rationalist model—what Dreyfus might call an "intentionalistic sort of" rule-giving and rule-following—and the fact that we nevertheless do teach and learn such practices, both Wittgenstein and Heidegger stress the notion that the type of "agreement in form of life" presupposed by the ability to perform and recognize varying levels of skillfulness in a meaningful endeavor *cannot* itself be formalized. To the extent that this sort of "referential whole" can be formalized, it loses its ability to *be* "the essential foundation for everyday circumspective interpretation" (Heidegger, MacQuarrie, & Robinson, 1962, p. 191). In Dreyfus's words, paraphrasing Heidegger: "To do its job of letting things show up as interpretable, the referential whole must remain in the *background*" (Dreyfus, 1991, p. 198).

It is on this point that the Shulman and Lemov projects reveal their problems. Lemov's is perhaps the less serious in this regard, since the 49 techniques so clearly presuppose something like agreement in form of life, even if they are presented as standing alone. It is not, then, in the attempt to declare such and such a technique to be *generally* good practice that Lemov goes awry; it is in adopting a view of skillful practice upon which the fact that any technique is *generally* good either (a) justifies its application in any given setting or (b) provides sufficient guidance for its correct implementation. Once those abilities are revealed to be illusory, the particular type of behaviorism Lemov espouses loses its appeal. Dreyfus puts the distinction well in discussing Wittgenstein's alleged behaviorism:

> This can be viewed as a sort of behaviorism . . . as long as one remembers that the behavior in question is not meaningless physical movements of some object, but the directed, significant, concernful comportment of human beings going about their business in a meaningful social world. (Dreyfus, 1991, p. 147)

Shulman and Ball's approach to teacher training, meanwhile—not simply their assumptions about the ontology of skillful teaching practice, but their recommendations for improving the *professionalization* of teacher training—takes the knowledge that teachers display in excellent practice as a form of "tacit knowledge," but erroneously understand this as only *incidentally* tacit, rather than non-formalizable in principle. When Ball suggests that the improvement of teacher training programs will involve "creating language with which to talk about work that experts often perform tacitly" (Ball & Forzani, 2009, p. 504), she begs the very question that such work is amenable to language at all. On her view, there must be a transcendent structure of knowledge undergirding the regularity of excellent teachers' excellent practices, and if this knowledge structure has been only implicit to this point, it nevertheless can be *made* explicit. Furthermore, she plainly assumes that *having* this language will shore up or fill gaps in existing training protocols.

Recalling Fogelin's reading of Wittgenstein—and Wittgenstein's example of the color chart—one sees not only that no such knowledge structure *need* be formalized in the way Ball imagines necessary, but also that even if it were amenable to formalization, it would not be enough. As Fogelin says, "even if training did produce some such mental intermediary, it would not provide a justification of the student's performance. Appeals to it would simply raise the paradox of interpretation anew" (Fogelin, 2009, p. 36).

Shulman, for his part, seeks a similar regulation or standardization in teacher training programs: the "let a thousand flowers bloom" approach, as he terms it, visible in the variation among various programs, is a threat to very existence of teacher training as such, as the title of his talk, "Teacher Education Does Not Exist," attests (Shulman, 2005). The key to salvaging the field, for Shulman, involves zeroing in on the "small set of 'signature pedagogies' that characterize all teacher education" (Shulman, 2005, p. 7), as though whatever were common to all teacher education programs must contain the core essence of the endeavor, while all divergences were mere window dressing.

Wittgenstein's work in the *Blue Book* shows that a view of essence as expressible in terms of features shared in common cannot perform the work that essence is thought to entail. The work of Cavell, Dreyfus, and Fogelin show that such a view of essence is patently unnecessary, as well. In Cavell's words:

> To summarize what has been said about this: In "learning language" you learn not merely what the names of things are, but what a name is; not merely what the form of expression is for expressing a wish, but what expressing a wish is; not merely what the word for "father" is, but what a father is; not merely what the word for "love" is, but what love is. In learning language, you do not merely learn the pronunciation of sounds, and their grammatical orders, but the "forms of life" which make those sounds the words they are, do what they do—e.g., name, call, point, express a wish or affection, indicate a choice or an aversion, etc. . . . Instead, then, of saying either that we *tell* beginners what words mean, or that we *teach* them what objects are, I will say: We initiate them, into the relevant forms of life held in language and gathered around the objects and persons of our world. (Cavell, 1979, pp. 177–178)

The "initiation" that Cavell pictures here may require any among a variety of explanations, rationales, examples, exercises, and so on; and which explanation, demonstration, etc. will be required in any given situation will be based upon two things: an initiate's response to training thus far (*PI* §145: "The effect of any further explanation depends on his reaction.") and the shared "form of life" that can be neither formalized nor represented. Far from conceiving of the task as one of discovering an essential core of "signature pedagogies," derived from what is common across all teacher training programs, Cavell's work reminds one that training a new or underperforming teacher is always and inescapably personal: "'Teaching' here would mean something like 'showing them what we say and do', and 'accepting what they say and do as what we say and do', etc., *and this will be more than we know, or can say*" (Cavell, 1979, p. 178, emphasis added).

In succinctly detailing the impossibility of framing our knowing-*how* in the form of knowing-*that* that the rationalist assumption requires, Dreyfus invokes both Heidegger's "understanding of Being" and Wittgenstein's spade hitting bedrock:

> To explain our actions and our rules [to others, to an initiate], we must eventually fall back upon our everyday practices and simply say, "this is what one does" or "that's what it is to be a human being." Thus in the last analysis all intelligibility and all intelligent behavior must

hark back to our sense of what we *are*, which is, necessarily, on pain of regress, something we can never explicitly *know*. (H. L. Dreyfus & Dreyfus, 1986, p. 81)

The very nature of the chicken-and-egg problem involved in what Taylor calls the "reciprocity" of something like the articulable rule and the visible practice, which Cahill also calls the "conceptual interdependence of our understanding" (Cahill, 2011, p. 116), precludes the possibility of spelling out either one completely and separately, since each always depends upon the other. This is the sense in which, per Dreyfus, "we can never explicitly *know*" the background. "Our sense of what we are," upon which our skilled or intelligent everyday behavior ultimately possible, cannot be captured in propositional form (cf. Heidegger & Hofstadter, 1971, p. 64). Rather, our intelligent behavior, our ability to follow rules at all, is a matter of a navigating particular situations according to their similarities with other situations and in accordance with their relevance to particular axes of care and concern, which are embedded in and arise out the presupposed whole articulated in our shared everyday practices.

4.3 THE SHARED BACKGROUND, SITUATIONAL RELEVANCE, AND MRS. GRADY

The fact of Kristof's appeal to Mrs. Grady in a *New York Times* column raises problems for the understanding of skillful behavior implicit in the "best practices" view of teaching to which Duncan and Lemov subscribe, and also for Shulman's knowledge-based "wisdom of practice" account. Specifically, the rationalist assumption cannot account for (a) the emergence of a novel response to a given set of circumstances, or (b) a shared or recognized sense of the correctness or appropriateness of any such novel response, both of which are required to explain the dual facts of the excellence that Mrs. Grady displayed and also Kristof's ability to assume the shared understanding of teacher excellence in such a way that Mrs. Grady's example would serve his purpose. Where the rationalist assumption fails in regard to these standards, the ideas of the thinkers considered in this section fare considerably better.

With respect to (a), the rationalist assumption puts out of play the possibility of something wholly unpredictable, since relevance is a matter of prior determination—say, by means of student achievement data—and since potential actions or responses are themselves always specifiable and correlatable with the relevant outcomes aprioristically. Working on the assumption that encouraging children to steal would not appear on any list of specifiable potential teacher actions, Mrs. Grady's response to witnessing Olly Neal's pilfering a book ought not to have been possible as an expression of excellent practice.

However, when examined from a more Heideggerian perspective, perhaps—from the perspective of an ongoing situation comprised of a totality of involvements and structured by the dynamics of care or concern, in which Mrs. Grady's past experiences precede her into the future—Heidegger's *"vorhaben"* (Heidegger et al., 1962, p. 191)—Mrs. Grady's decision not only to allow a child to steal, but also to actively encourage repeated theft, makes sense. Thus, involved practical *concern*, by structuring relevance, enables excellence in new forms, something for which the rationalist assumption cannot account. Or as Dreyfus puts it: "If one is a master of a cultural practice, one can sometimes do what has not so far counted as appropriate and have it recognized in retrospect as having been just the right thing to do" (Dreyfus, 1992, p. xxiv).

In the Introduction I pointed out the implausibility of Mrs. Grady's excellence showing up on the metrics by which Race to the Top proposes to make such excellence visible; in Chapters 2–4, I have described the ways in which a "best practices" or "teacher knowledge" view would prove inadequate to reproducing it. At this point, then, I raise the *fact* of the visibility of Mrs. Grady's excellence in retrospect, without the need for the metrics that Duncan proposes and without the justificatory support of generalizable behaviors.

I argue here that the fact of the visibility of her skillfulness presupposes the sharing of forms of life that Wittgenstein suggests underlie our practical rule-following in general, and in doing so I hint in the direction of Chapters 6–9, which will take up the question of *evaluating* teacher quality more explicitly. But to more directly preview the following section, I wish to stress the dramatic distinction between a *retrospective* account of her practice and the conditions of its emergence in the present of 1957, without an actual happy ending to ease the existential uncertainty of Mrs. Grady's decision.

To the first point, that is, the *fact* of the exemplary role of Mrs. Grady's practice in the absence of all the metrical and observational criteria proposed, I wish simply to suggest that its appearance *as* excellence demonstrates something important about "the astonishing fact of the astonishing extent to which we *do* agree in judgment," as Cavell has it. In the context of the narrative, we are invited to see Mrs. Grady as a teacher who did not let the fact of Neal's difficulty prevent her from believing in him. Nor did her negative experiences with Neal interfere with her recognizing not only his potential but also the conditions which made the realization of that potential so difficult. With her previous experiences with and of Neal going before her, Mrs. Grady's innovative and novel response to witnessing Neal steal a book is on full display in the article, as well that response's excellence. That Kristof's piece can do what it does—hold up an example of excellent practice in the full expectation that it will serve as it is meant to serve—indicates and presupposes the very shared-ness of the shared forms of life in which great teaching shows up as such. His assumption that the example will have the intended effect *at all* evidences this fact. The fact of its recognition recalls the Dreyfusian point about sub-worlds, as opposed to the micro-worlds of AI:

> In our everyday life we are, indeed, involved in various "sub-worlds" such as the world of the theater, of business, or of mathematics, but each of these is a "mode" of our shared everyday world. That is, sub-worlds are not related like isolable physical systems to larger systems they *compose*; rather they are local elaborations of a whole which they *presuppose*. (Dreyfus, 1992, p. 14)

Considering Wittgenstein and Cavell's discussions of forms of life as the ground-level practical involvements, I contend that these practical manifestations of agreement in form of life are precisely the Dreyfusian "whole" presupposed by the particular sub-worlds of "the theater, of business, of mathematics." And of teaching. That teaching might be seen as a *local* elaboration of this presupposed *whole* accounts for Kristof's ability to assume his audience's recognition of Mrs. Grady's excellence: the *whole* of the forms of life in which we agree includes an ordinary sense of teaching, on the basis of which the shared recognition of the excellence of Mrs. Grady's example is possible in the first place.[2]

It is worth noting, too, that Neal's story is precisely the *ordinary* sense of good teaching to which Duncan so often points: here we have a teacher going beyond the requirements of her own job (for she was not his teacher at the time) in the interest of "chang[ing] the course of a student's life" (Duncan, 2009d). The going-beyond involved cannot be accounted for according to pressure to meet benchmarks or objectives because in an official sense she was not *responsible* for teaching Olly Neal at all. Duncan thus has it right when he says that "Teaching ... is not just a job or even an adventure—it's a calling" (Duncan, 2009b). Answering a call here gestures toward the "whole" presupposed by the particular sub-world of teaching. Mrs. Grady's actions can be accounted for, then, in terms of understanding herself *as* a teacher within a larger "totality of involvements" in which "teaching" has its particular resonance.

In fact, in thinking once more of the presupposed whole, her particular choices in that particular situation would defy such general visibility if not for the criterion of "chang[ing] the course of a student's life." In other words, while agreement in forms of life associated with the "whole" enable the *general* public to see Mrs. Grady's example as excellent from a 2012 perspective, and while such a holistic sense of the "concernful comportment" that teaching aspires to would also have been necessary to see it in 1957, such a holistic view would not therefore have been *sufficient* to communicate her quality to a national audience, as no such *life change* had then occurred.

Put differently, the holistic sense of things that enabled Mrs. Grady to act skillfully in that situation required intimate familiarity with the particular domain, one might say. That Kristof can refer to it in 2012 has to do with our agreement in forms of life on the basis of which we have an ordinary sense of good teaching, one of the exposed criteria of which has to do with effecting a transformation in students' lives. But one can assume that Mrs. Grady's practice was excellent before its effects were visible—as in the example of Duncan's mother, too. That Mrs. Grady could act skillfully in precisely the way she did back in 1957, yet without that action seeming to provide any extractable rules or generalizable behaviors—*universal* justifiers—points to an understanding of "skillful" or "excellent" in terms of responsiveness to a local situation.

4.4 REDUX

Here it will be helpful to return to some promises I made in Chapter 1. In that Chapter, I raised and immediately deferred several issues for consideration, mainly related to the claims made by advocates of value-added measures of teacher quality that apparent insufficiencies of such metrics ought not to be overstated. Such attention to the "technical" flaws in value-added measures, these advocates imply, cover up the significant progress that these metrics represent. In light of the foregoing discussions of AI and practical forms of life as it relates to teaching, it seems fitting to raise those issues once more.

Glazerman, et al., in the Brookings Institution report, assert that their methods of determining teacher quality are not as frail as their critics insist. In defending their work, they offer the three claims below. In Chapter 1, I addressed claim (a); here, I wish to reconsider claim (b):

> We have previously issued a report that describes some of the imperfections in value-added measures while documenting that: a) they provide one of the best presently available signals of the future ability of teachers to raise student test scores; b) the technical issues surrounding the use of value-added measures arise in one form or another with respect to any evaluation of complex human behavior; and c) value-added measures are on par with performance measures in other fields in terms of their predictive validity. (Glazerman et al., 2011)

The "technical issues" they refer to, I suggest at this point, are hardly technical at all. They are, rather, what Cahill has called the "intractable difficulties" that arise from the fact that "none of our actual proceedings can meet the requirements for correctness that we imagine [the detached picture] imposes on us" (Cahill, 2011, p. 116). In other words, the lack of fit involved in attempts to measure ordinary-sense teacher quality is not, as Glazerman and his colleagues have it, some inherent property of the complexity of "complex human behavior" itself; it is instead *produced* by misunderstanding the nature and source of the complexity involved.

The ordinary concept of good teaching, as we have seen, has its roots in agreement in form of life, it is simply not available from a detached or purely objective perspective, the stance that the statistical parsing of student achievement data requires. Once more, such a statement is not to imply that *nothing* is available from such a perspective; that would be akin to a claim that words in a language cannot be defined, as dictionaries regularly do. Instead, it is to claim that *what* shows up according to such a detached view leaves out something *essential* to "knowing" English, for example, or "knowing" good teaching; it is to claim that in both the case of language in particular and "complex human behavior" in general, the detached view misses the (engaged, practical) whole that the view itself presupposes.

The danger in misunderstanding the lack of fit between value-added measures of teacher quality and the ordinary sense of good teaching is suggested by AI's manifold problems. That such methods of measuring quality can work *at all* is certainly a feat, analogous to SHRDLU's micro-world success in a domain that is highly specific, structured, and finite. But making such methods work *well and in general* might require, as Dreyfus suggests, an entirely different set of assumptions altogether. It is by no means clear that a modicum of measurement success in a technically-delimited domain indicates that, in the realm of "complex human behavior," one is even on the right track to capturing the whole picture, much less that the distance between present fallibility and future perfection is both relatively small and merely technical. This assumption, no less than in AI, is nevertheless itself all-pervasive. The NCTQ report cited in Chapter 1 makes it plain: "Student growth and value-added methodologies are still emerging. However, examining student achievement as a metric for assessing teacher effectiveness, even if measurement is imperfect, represents a big step forward" (NCTQ, 2011). Such a conclusion is badly undercut by the foregoing considerations of this Chapter. It is certainly a step, but not a step *forward* in any meaningful sense, insofar as the possibility of *arriving* at the goal of knowing teacher quality is precluded by relying on the very methodology that represents the initial step.

I will develop the following argument more fully in Chapters 6–9, but I wish to preview it here: since the detached view blinds us in some important ways to the heart of what we wish to study or evaluate, we are only able to access that which we wish to study or evaluate by means of an *engaged* or *involved* perspective. Earlier I alluded to the intertwined problems of Mrs. Grady recognizing the proper course of action vis-à-vis Olly Neal and some third party recognizing Mrs. Grady's excellence in the present tense of 1957. The sight involved in each instance, I have suggested, is afforded by means of both an understanding of teaching as a local elaboration of a presupposed whole, which is not at all the same as the having of a technical definition thereof, and an involved familiarity with the local conditions of teaching practice. The combination of Mrs. Grady's visible excellence and that excellence's invisibility according to any metrics currently under discussion invites one to raise again Strong's discussion of human judges' ability to predict teacher quality from Chapter 1:

> In every case, judges achieved relatively high levels of agreement but were absolutely inaccurate, leading us to question whether educators can identify effective teachers when they see them. This in turn has motivated us to undertake development of an observational measure that can predict teacher effectiveness. (Strong, Gargani, & Hacifazlioğlu, 2011)

Strong's claims highlight another danger of relying too heavily upon value-added methodologies for the disclosure of teacher quality. In addition to the "fallacy of the successful first step," as Dreyfus will call it, Strong's work also reveals that the sense of taking a *first* step can vanish at a certain point, as well. The judges to whom Strong gestures "achieved high levels of agreement but were absolutely inaccurate." The inaccuracy of their human judgments stands in contrast to the *uncontested accuracy* of value-added measures of teacher effectiveness. The technical sense of good teaching, here, is no longer a means of *moving one toward* an ordinary sense; it has become the only sense worth talking about. It is no longer a *first* step; it is the *final* step.

The suggestion I raise now, and the one I will focus upon in Chapters 6–9, is that the judges' agreement in Strong's example might point to precisely the conceptual gap that classroom observations ought to fill between a technical and an ordinary sense of good teaching. The human observers, Strong's judges, have access to a holistic understanding of teaching that is systematically denied to the detached perspective required by value-added methodologies. That human observers fail to predict who will or will not prove most "effective" in terms of raising test scores is no great argument against human judgment: that sort of prediction of rigid outcome measures is precisely a domain for which detached information processing is designed, and in which algorithmic methods are indeed superior. Were raising test scores actually the *final* step, such a method would also prove sufficient.

However, Duncan's rhetoric, echoed by the NCTQ, has it the other way around: such measures are supposed to represent a step *toward* what we finally want: the ability to say something meaningful to the involved "stakeholders" about the wholesale quality of this or that teacher. In no way are such technical measures intended as the final word, and thus they cannot justifiably usurp such a position.

To return my focus, at this point, to the *development* of skillful practice, rather than its visibility or evaluation, Shulman's example of "Nancy," one might note, also gestures in this direction of local, grounded responsiveness: "Nancy's pattern of instruction, her style of teaching, is not uniform or predictable in some simple sense. She *flexibly responds* to the difficulty and character of the subject matter, the capacities of the students (which can change even over the span of a single course), and her educational purposes" (Shulman, 1987). I have shown that such responsiveness, in contrast to Shulman's view, cannot be accounted for in terms of the rationalist assumption about underlying forms of "teacher knowledge." Yet the flexible responsiveness involved certainly characterizes the practice of both of the examples at work here. It follows that *developing* such responsiveness will require more than the inculcation of further or better rules and techniques. A view of developing skillful practice in the direction of such flexible responsiveness comprises the next chapter of this work.

NOTES

1. I'm adopting Cavell's terminology here (Cavell, 1962)—in the literature, the dialogic form of the *Investigations* had, for a time, described the arguing voices as "Wittgenstein" and an "Interlocutor"; Cavell's "Voice of temptation" and "Voice of correctness" is meant to dodge the assumption that either of the voices obviously *does* or *does not* belong to Wittgenstein himself. If one voice were certainly Wittgenstein and the other were not, then the dialogue would be merely a creative way of advancing philosophical theses, which Wittgenstein claims not to do. Also, it would downplay the power of skeptical temptation itself, the sense in which Wittgenstein (or anyone) might feel honestly compelled by the rationalist picture.
2. It also accounts for the actual professionalism of the teaching profession: that teaching (like all other professions) is a local elaboration of a presupposed whole means that anyone sharing the particular form of life under discussion could *in principle* become a teacher. That teaching is a *local* elaboration of the whole means that not everyone *does*, that there is something *more*—namely training or initiation—that actual teachers have and laypeople lack. Shulman and Ball's work in the late 2000s takes it that whatever professional teachers have and laypeople lack must be something like an occult knowledge, the having of which would *completely* differentiate teachers from non-teachers. I take it that this is meant to militate against the familiar put-down that just anyone can teach, with its implication that there's nothing special about teaching. Shulman and Ball's response is exactly backward, to my mind. They look at the medical profession, which they take to be self-evidently specialized, and model their teacher training on the specialized knowledge that doctors have. I would simply point out that just anyone can be a doctor, too, that the medical profession is equally in-principle public as teaching.

REFERENCES

Ball, D. L., & Forzani, F. M. (2009). The Work of Teaching and the Challenge for Teacher Education. *Journal of Teacher Education*, 60(5), 497–511. doi:10.1177/0022487109348479

Cavell, S. (1962). The Availability of Wittgenstein's Later Philosophy. *The Philosophical Review*, 71(1), 67–93. Retrieved from http://www.jstor.org/stable/2183682

Cavell, S. (1979). *The Claim of Reason*. New York: Oxford University Press.

Cavell, S. (1990). *Conditions Handsome and Unhandsome*. Chicago: University of Chicago Press.
Cavell, S. (1996). Knowing and Acknowledging. In S. Mulhall (Ed.), *The Cavell Reader*. Malden, MA: Wiley-Blackwell.
Dreyfus, H. L. (1991). *Being-in-the-world: A commentary on Heidegger's Being and Time, Division I* (p. xiv, 370 p.). Cambridge, Mass.: MIT Press.
Dreyfus, H. L. (1992). *What Computers Still Can't Do: a Critique of Artificial Reason*. Cambridge, MA: M.I.T. Press.
Dreyfus, H. L., & Dreyfus, S. (1986). *Mind Over Machine: The Power of Human Intuition and Expertise in the Era of the Computer*. New York: Free Press.
Duncan, A. (2009a). Robust Data Gives Us the Roadmap to Reform. (U.S. Department of Education.). Retrieved from http://www2.ed.gov/news/speeches/2009/06/06082009.html
Duncan, A. (2009b). Teacher Preparation: Reforming the Uncertain Profession. (U.S. Department of Education). Retrieved from http://www.ed.gov/news/speeches/teacher-preparation-reforming-uncertain-profession
Fogelin, R. J. (2009). *Taking Wittgenstein at His Word: A Textual Study* (Vol. 2009, p. 200). Princeton University Press. Retrieved from http://books.google.com/books?id=6I9oetOUdQ8C&pgis=1
Glazerman, S., Goldhaber, D., Loeb, S., Raudenbush, S., Staiger, D., Whitehurst, G. J., . . . Quality, B. C. T. G. on T. (2011). *Passing Muster: Evaluating Teacher Evaluation Systems*. Washington D.C.: Brookings Institute. . Retrieved from http://www.brookings.edu/reports/2011/0426_evaluating_teachers.aspx
Glendinning, S. (1998). *On Being with Others*. New York: Routledge.
Heidegger, M. (1977). The Question Concerning Technology. In D. Krell (Ed.), *Basic Writings*. New York: HarperCollins.
Heidegger, M., & Hofstadter, A. (1971). What Are Poets For? In *Poetry, Language, Thought* (pp. 135–137). New York: Harper & Row.
Heidegger, M., & Hofstadter, A. (1982). *The Basic Problems of Phenomenology*. (J. M. Edie, Ed.). Bloomington,: Indiana University Press.
Heidegger, M., MacQuarrie, J., & Robinson, E. (1962). *Being and Time*. New York: Harper & Row.
Lenat, D. (2008). The Voice of the Turtle: Whatever Happened to AI? *AI Magazine*, 29(2), 11–23.
McDowell, J. (1981). Non-Cognitivism and Rule-Following. In S. H. Holtzman (Ed.), *Wittgenstein: To Follow a Rule*. New York and London: Routledge.
Mulhall, S. (1998). *Stanley Cavell: Philosophy's Recounting of the Ordinary* (p. 351). Oxford University Press. Retrieved from http://books.google.com/books?id=Qs193MPr3u4C&pgis=1
NCTQ. (2011). *State of the States: Trends and Early Lessons on Teacher Evaluation and Effectiveness Policies*. Report published by National Council on Teacher Quality, Washington D.C.
Ravitch, D. (2010). *The Death and Life of the Great American School System*. New York: Basic Books.
Ravitch, D. (2013). *Reign of Error: The Hoax of the Privatization Movement and the Danger to America's Public Schools*. New York: Knopf.
Rothstein, R. (2008). *Grading Education*. New York: Teachers College Press.
Shulman, L. (1987). Knowledge and Teaching: Foundations of the New Reform. *Educational Researcher*, 15(2), 4–14.
Shulman, L. (2005). Teacher Education Does Not Exist. *Stanford Educator*.
Stern, D. (1995). *Wittgenstein on Mind and Language*. New York: Oxford University Press.
Strong, M., Gargani, J., & Hacifazlioğlu, Ö. (2011). Do We Know a Successful Teacher When We See One? Experiments in the Identification

of Effective Teachers. *Journal of Teacher Education*, 62(4), 367–382. doi:10.1177/0022487110390221

Taylor, C. (1993). To Follow a Rule. In E. Lipuma, M. Postone, & C. J. Calhoun (Eds.), *Bourdieu: Critical Perspectives*. Chicago: University of Chicago Press.

Wittgenstein, L. (1969). *Preliminary studies for the "Philosophical Investigations", Generally Known as the Blue and Brown Books* (2nd ed., p. xv, p. 192). Oxford,: Blackwell.

Wittgenstein, L. (1983). *Remarks on the Foundations of Mathematics*. Cambridge: MIT Press.

Wittgenstein, L., Anscombe, G. E. M., & Hacker, P. M. S. (2009). *Philosophical Investigations* (4th ed.). Malden, MA: Wiley-Blackwell.

5 A Phenomenological Account of Skill Development

The sort of practical sight that characterizes and makes possible the flexible responsiveness of excellent, or, in Dreyfus's term, "expert"[1] practitioners is neither reducible to nor comprised of abstract rules or behavior. Such sight also cannot be articulated in the form of propositional knowledge without regress, as we have seen,. That these assertions hold is suggested by the failure of AI to generate the skillful behavior on the basis of attempts to formalize the commonsense "knowledge" that provides for the intelligibility and possibility of excellent practical behavior. In opposition to this view, Heidegger and Wittgenstein—and their heirs and interpreters, Taylor, Cahill, Dreyfus, Glendinning and Cavell among them—suggest that both the common-ness and knowledge characteristics of commonsense "knowledge" amount to shared public practices, agreement in forms of life, and thus, because rooted in practical dealings in a shared and structurally public world, also cannot be represented in the propositional form that the rationalist assumption would require.

Nevertheless, the phenomenological description of skill development I offer below—which is Dreyfus's through and through, and which he presents in a vast number of publications over the years (H. Dreyfus & Dreyfus, 1992; H. L. Dreyfus & Dreyfus, 1986, 2005; H. L. Dreyfus, 1988, 2005)—suggests that the sort of involvement with relevance and similarity that affords the excellent practice visible across many different domains is an ordinary feature of life with skills in general. Developing such skillfullness intentionally, particularly in the realm of teaching and learning, requires (a) the recognition that the flexible responsiveness that characterizes the teaching practice of those we hold up as paradigm cases is neither produced nor reproducible according to rationalist requirements, and (b) that as a consequence there must be a specific place maintained for the developing teacher to *have* responsibility for the outcome of situations in which the outcome *matters* to them.

In regard to part (b), I may appear simply to describe the practice of "student teaching," already requisite in nearly every state for certification. But the experience of student teaching varies widely in quality, and this variance is more dependent on specific cooperating teachers than upon the teacher-training programs involved. Some cooperating teachers have been known to vanish from the classroom entirely; others, to remain to observe the developing teacher; still others, to resist relinquishing control in any meaningful way, intervening swiftly when the developing teacher appears to struggle. As such, the mere existence of a requirement for one or more semesters of student teaching does not amount to a requirement for the sort of emotionally engaged coping with situations for which one feels directly responsible.

Shulman also notes the problematic nature of such vagaries in the student teaching experience (Shulman, 2005, p. 7), but his response to the problematic variability is to standardize the experiences themselves around a core or signature set of practices. But this is neither necessary nor sufficient as a response, as we have seen. Rather, the (existential) experience of *caring* about the successful outcome of a lesson for which the developing teacher assumes responsibility is, as I will make clear, crucial to bridging the gap between a degree of skillfulness associated with beginners and a degree of skillfulness associated with professionals.

I have been highly critical of Arne Duncan and his policies throughout, and so I welcome the opportunity to point out this particular item on which his rhetoric laudably takes up the practical aspects of teacher development in a particularly productive way. He singles out as an example of a model teacher-education program a small college in Kansas:

> At Emporia State University in Emporia, Kansas, home of the National Teachers Hall of Fame, the Teachers College is the crown jewel of the school. Roughly 80 percent of students are supervised by full-time education faculty instead of adjuncts—and all elementary education professors are in the public schools every day. Senior year is a 100 percent field-based program in Emporia's public schools, where student teachers do everything from assisting with grading to sitting in on parent-teacher conferences. (Duncan, 2009b)

When Duncan cites other programs, he tends to emphasize the way they use data to track their graduates. With Emporia State, the criteria he cites have to do with the instructors' practical experience and with the practical experience the school requires of their developing teachers. However, the kind of combination of "responsibility" in a situation that "matters" to a developing teacher remains absent from his description of Emporia State's program: "assisting with grading" and "sitting in on parent-teacher conferences" is not coextensive with being responsible for assigning grades or conducting parent-teacher conferences. This is not to imply that Emporia's program is in any way unsatisfactory; it is to imply that Duncan's view of where the developmental value of practical experience lies remains insufficient.

The two most crucial elements of Dreyfus's phenomenological description of skill development are the concession to deliberate rule-following along the lines of the rationalist assumption as a starting condition, and the *necessity* of moving beyond such behavior at a certain point. The means by which this moving-beyond occurs concerns emotional involvement with an outcome and the assumption of responsibility for it. Since his account claims a Wittgensteinian-Heideggerian basis, the role of past experiences in going before a practitioner and establishing relevance beforehand constitutes the (nonformalizable) practical *sight* that examples of skillful practice seem to share in common. Rule-following on the rationalist assumption, one must note, characterizes the early stages of skillful development precisely because it offers a limited approximation of what internalized, engaged experience provides to an excellent practitioner. It is therefore intended as an insufficient, *ersatz* form of experience itself. According to the description Dreyfus offers, one must eventually begin doing something different from consciously following rules in order to improve in the direction of the excellence for which one strives.

In a move that recalls the distinction I drew in Chapter 1 between the technical and the ordinary senses of good teaching, Dreyfus is careful to assert that his model of skill development

> focus[es] upon the most common type of problem area, sometimes called "unstructured." Such areas contain a potentially unlimited number of possibly relevant facts and features, and the way those elements interrelate and determine other events is unclear. Management, nursing, economic forecasting, *teaching* [emphasis added], and all social interactions fall into that very large class. Examples of 'structured areas' of decision-making, on the other hand, are mathematical manipulations, puzzles, and, in the real world, delivery truck routing and petroleum blending. Here the goal and what information is relevant is clear, the effects of decisions are known, and verifiable solutions can be reasoned out. (H. L. Dreyfus & Dreyfus, 1986, p. 20)

The appeal to data that we have seen in Duncan's many speeches has generally to do with the importance of *knowing* quality in teaching; student achievement data seems to provide this means by proxy. But it has the decidedly less salutary effect of unwarrantedly transforming teaching into a "structured" problem area, in which "the goal," if not always "what information is relevant," remains certainly clear. But Mrs. Grady's example reminds one that teaching is always an "unstructured" domain, where a sense of a holistic situation and the relevance of the various facts involved remain inherently uncertain and undefined. Doing the right thing for Olly Neal required, as we have seen, that Mrs. Grady treat the situation in an unstructured fashion; that her view of the situation and her response to it seem to make logical sense in retrospect is the result of the structuring effects of hindsight, not the inherently "structured" nature of the problem area itself. Dreyfus's account of skill development is germane here precisely to the degree that the ordinary sense of good teaching is conceptually different from the technical sense, and that the ordinary sense is the goal of our teacher development efforts. Chapter 1 demonstrates that both of these conditions are the case.

In addition to the problems with knowing teacher quality according to seeking out behaviors or asking after rules, as discussed in Chapter 1, problems crop up for Race to the Top's view of teaching practice, as well. Since research and policy alike tend to view practical skill on the rationalist model, and since observation systems like those of Delaware and Tennessee actively incentivize adherence to such a model, Race to the Top's policies run the risk of positively stifling the development of precisely the great teachers who serve as its own justifying paradigm cases.

5.1 THE STAGES OF SKILL DEVELOPMENT

Dreyfus's view of skill development runs directly counter to the rationalist view of what generalizing from specifics amounts to: on the rationalist account, generalization proceeds from particular cases to the abstract rules or essential characteristics that these cases all share in common. As Dreyfus says,

> We must be prepared to abandon the traditional view that a beginner starts with specific cases and, as he becomes more proficient, abstracts and interiorizes more and more sophisticated rules. It might turn out that skill acquisition moves in just the opposite direction: from abstract rules to particular cases. (H. L. Dreyfus, 1988, p. 102)

What *practical* "generalization" means, on the Dreyfusian assumption, would register as something like an expansion of the domain—the number of particular future and unforeseeable cases—which would be navigable by one's rule-following behavior, but such rule-following, being bound up with "interiorized" past experiences, would amount to the responsive application of "ten thousand special cases" (H. L. Dreyfus & Dreyfus, 2005). The "abstract rules," meanwhile, upon which beginners will rely, will come from the practices of recognizably excellent teachers, and as such, Shulman's research project that seeks out "the wisdom of practice" reveals itself to be not only useful but necessary to teacher development. The argument throughout has been, once more, not that Shulman's approach is useless, but rather that what one has when one has the codified "wisdom of practice" is not in any sense sufficient to its reproduction.

Rather, as one moves through the five stages of Novice, Advanced Beginner, Competence, Proficiency, and Expert, one relies more and more on experience in both establishing relevance and performing actions and less and less on the rules upon which Novices, lacking experience, *must* depend. A consideration of these stages will bear out the importance of the most crucial aspect here: emotional involvement in the undertaking and responsibility for its outcome, both of which aspects are discouraged by the rationalist model of rule following and both of which are simply necessary to the Wittgensteinian-Heideggerian view of practical skill.

Dreyfus's stages of skill acquisition concern primarily the areas that skilled humans seem to navigate with greater aplomb than has so far been demonstrated in AI: the grasping of a holistic situation such that relevance stands out without requiring explicit aprioristic specification, and the ability to "flexibly respond" in such situations, to recall Shulman's characterization of Nancy. The five stages are predominantly distinguished from one another along the lines of both the way a person *grasps* the situation and the way the person responds.

Novice

Dreyfus's Novice stage of skill development is characterized by "learning to recognize the objective facts and features relevant to the skill," as well as "rules for determining actions based upon those facts and features" (H. L. Dreyfus & Dreyfus, 1986, p. 21). Such learning to recognize stems from an "instructor decomposing the task environment into features that the student can recognize without the benefit of experience" (H. L. Dreyfus, 1988, p. 102). For his examples, Dreyfus tends to use skill domains like chess and driving. With respect to driving, the Novice stage would include the consideration of the car's speed in absolute terms, for example, and rules based upon it. "Shift into third at 20 mph" provides an example of the way in which the Novice receives instruction—the relevant information is limited to speed, and speed is characterized as an "objective fact." No information about traffic conditions, anticipated stops or turns, hilly terrain, or other such factors that influence more experienced drivers arise for consideration here. In fact, Dreyfus points out elsewhere that following such abstract rules and facts often leads to poor performance, for precisely this reason. Notes Dreyfus, "A car stalls if one shifts too soon on a hill or when the car is heavily loaded" (H. L. Dreyfus & Dreyfus, 2005, p. 782). For the Novice, lacking the experience necessary to discriminate in any other way, the situation is defined in terms of a narrow range of "context-free" facts, and action is based upon inflexible rules.

Advanced Beginner

With "considerable experience coping with real situations," the Novice begins to perceive situations as similar to past situations where such similarity is not defined according to the similarities of any particular features. This idea recalls Wittgenstein's notion of "family resemblances," and it is one of the difficulties with which AI struggles. Dreyfus says elsewhere that "Everything is similar to everything else in an indefinitely large number of ways. Why should we suppose that any two items should be compared?" (H. L. Dreyfus, 1992, p. xxvi). The reason that we should suppose that any two items should be compared here, invoking Cavell and Wittgenstein, goes back to agreement in form of life, the basis of conceptuality as such, which defies attempts to reproduce such similarity-recognition *merely* in terms of abstract or formalizable features.

Although the Advanced Beginner develops the ability to recognize what Dreyfus calls "situational elements"—as opposed to "context-free features"—through a holistic, experience-driven discriminability, he or she must still consciously apply the abstract rules that such a situation calls for. For some examples of "situational elements," Dreyfus provides (a) a driver recognizing the way an engine sounds when a shift is required (H. L. Dreyfus & Dreyfus, 1986, p. 21); and (b) a chess player recognizing "aspects of positions [such] as a weakened king's side or a strong pawn structure, despite the lack of precise and situation-free definitions" (H. L. Dreyfus & Dreyfus, 2005, p. 783). Though such situational recognition appears at the Advanced Beginner stage, the performer must still rely on particular rules or maxims to navigate the perceived situation: "Attack a weakened king's side" (H. L. Dreyfus, 1988, p. 103)or "Shift up when the motor sounds like it's racing and down when it sounds like it's straining" (H. L. Dreyfus & Dreyfus, 2005, p. 783).

The recognition that characterizes this stage seems not to rely upon context-free features, but Dreyfus characterizes the type of rule-following that the Advanced Beginner displays as based on a "detached, analytic frame of mind" (ibid). The greater experience provides what Polyani refers to as "the good practical knowledge of the art" (Polyani, 1962), in light of which rules or maxims make sense in the first place; but the gaining of experience with applying rules and maxims alone does not suffice, on Dreyfus's account, for the kind of flexible responsiveness that characterizes genuinely excellent getting-around in various domains. It can only account for the increasingly correct application of abstract maxims and rules, as in the rationalist assumption.

Competence

At this middle stage of skill development, the means of even "situational-element" recognition and maxim-application—detached rule-following according to the rationalist assumption—reaches its limit. It will be important to notice two things: in the first place, this is merely the third of five identifiable stages of skill development, and yet the whole conceptual framework of Race to the Top in accordance with which Duncan, Lemov, and Shulman propose to develop teachers and to which Kane, Staiger, Rockoff and others propose to evaluate them holds perfect detached rule-following to represent the pinnacle of excellent practice. In the second place, the very detachment according to which good teaching is imagined to proceed and render itself for evaluation represents the crux of the problem that a competent practitioner encounters. Dreyfus proposes that the detachment of the performer inhibits the kind of skillfulness genuinely excellent teachers exhibit; Nancy's flexibility lies not merely in seeing the "situational elements" involved with particular acuity, but also in responding with similar alacrity. The responsiveness here requires what Dreyfus terms "involvement" (H. L. Dreyfus & Dreyfus, 1986, p. 27, 2005, p. 785).

The sort of involvement that Dreyfus has in mind emerges from a particular kind of breakdown in the detached rule-following process. Specifically, Dreyfus notes that as a developing teacher, for example, becomes more and more experienced, "the number of recognizable context-free and situational elements present in a real-world circumstance becomes overwhelming. A sense of what is important is missing" (H. L. Dreyfus & Dreyfus, 1986, p. 23). Dreyfus clearly heralds the "relevance" problem here, to which problem Simon and Newell offered "heuristic rules" as a means of "cut[ting] down the search space" (H. L. Dreyfus, 1992, p. xxii) and thus limiting the number of facts that could appear for consideration.

Heuristics in AI failed to work, and they resemble very closely Shulman's concept of "strategic knowledge," particularly in their being offered as a solution to an "overwhelming" situation in which too many facts and rules seem to be at play. These heuristics failed in the sense that whatever advantages they offered in terms of the *speed* of the response were not mirrored in the *quality* of the response: by identifying a given situation according to a perspective based on inflexible and detached means, say, probability calculations, heuristics did arrive at a response action more quickly, but in eliminating possible understandings of a situation through the employment of detached and situationally insensitive means, the programs following heuristics found themselves sometimes offering the *correct* response to a *misidentified* situation, or in other words, *failing* to produce the most appropriate response.[2] Dreyfus's move from "detachment" to "involvement" provides a means of accounting for the fact that excellent teachers tend to respond both quickly *and* correctly to a wide range of situations—their responsiveness is *flexible*.

Dreyfus characterizes the competent performer thusly:

> In general, a competent performer with a goal in mind sees a situation as a set of facts. The importance of the facts may depend on the presence of other facts. He has learned that when a situation has a particular constellation of those elements a certain conclusion should be drawn, decision made, or expectation investigated. (H. L. Dreyfus & Dreyfus, 1986, p. 24)

Competent performers continue to see situations as sets of facts; but the situational facts that must arise for consideration are *produced* by the performer's having "a goal in mind." But very broad and general goals—even those applicable to a technical sense of good teaching such as "lift reading scores," to say nothing of the "transform students' lives" goal of the ordinary sense—provide too little guidance in particular situations. Even imagining such goals (erroneously) as composites of smaller, simpler goals (something like "benchmarks") is of no help here.

What is at stake, even on this view, is precisely *which* "benchmark" ought to allow the relevance to stand out. As Dreyfus puts it:

> Naturally, to avoid mistakes, the competent performer seeks rules and reasoning procedures to decide which plan or perspective to adopt. But such rules are not as easy to come by as are the rules and maxims given beginners in manuals and lectures. Indeed, in any skill domain the performer encounters a vast number of situations differing from each other in subtle ways. There are, in fact, more situations than can be named or precisely defined, so no one can prepare for the learner a list of types of possible situations and what to do or look for in each. Students, therefore, must decide for themselves in each situation what plan or perspective to adopt without being sure that it will turn out to be appropriate. (H. L. Dreyfus & Dreyfus, 2005, p. 784)

While the experience of deciding remains a *rationalist* one here, the *awareness* of the inherent uncertainty produces the involvement necessary to further development, as Dreyfus notes: "While [the performer] both understands and decides in a *detached* manner, he finds himself intensely *involved* in what occurs thereafter" (H. L. Dreyfus & Dreyfus, 1986, p. 26). The conscious decision-making, the awareness of an insufficiency on grounds by which to discriminate, and yet the *need* to make a choice in order to act at all is what Dreyfus calls the "combination of nonobjectivity and necessity [that] introduces an important new type of relationship between the performer and his environment" (ibid.).

This involvement, then, amounts to a recognition on the part of the performer that the success or failure of the application of rules and maxims upon which his or her action will now proceed is directly dependent upon *his or her choice of perspective* according to which such maxims or rules are solicited in the first place. Since this choice of perspective cannot itself be produced according to abstract features and rules, the quality of the choice belongs ineluctably to the performer rather than the rules. That distinction, as Dreyfus notes, sets the practice of the competence-stage performer apart from the practice of performers in earlier stages:

> Prior to this stage, if the rules don't work, the performer, rather than feeling remorse for his or her mistakes, can rationalize that he or she hadn't been given adequate rules. But, since at this stage, the result depends on the learner's choice of perspective, the learner feels responsible for his or her choice. (H. L. Dreyfus & Dreyfus, 2005, p. 784)

The responsibility for the choice of perspective and the resulting involvement in its consequences have profound effects on the learner's ability to develop further, according to Dreyfus's account. Since Dreyfus's understanding anchors itself on Heidegger's thought, in which being-in-the-world inherently involves a futural "thrown project," structured by what Bourdieu calls "the active presence of the past" (Bourdieu, 1980, p. 54), responsibility and involvement play an intensifying role with respect to memory formation.[3] Says Dreyfus: "An outcome that is clearly successful is deeply satisfying and leaves a vivid memory of the plan chosen and of the situation as seen from the perspective of the plan. Disasters, likewise, are not easily forgotten" (H. L. Dreyfus & Dreyfus, 1986, p. 26). The way the *choice of perspective* itself constitutes the past that goes "before us, organizing the way the next events show up for us" (H. L. Dreyfus & Dreyfus, 1986, p. 88) encourages the repetition of successful perspective-choices in similar situations and discourages the repetition of unsuccessful ones, where situations and perspectives alike have the character of holistic, nonrepresentational paradigms.

Such *personal* responsibility and involvement remain absent from the rationalist or detached view of decision-making, even with regard to the choice of perspective, and because of that, Dreyfus claims that further skill development on the rationalist view reaches its limit here. In examining now the fourth and fifth stages of skill development, I wish to specifically offer some salient contrasts between Dreyfus's view and the rationalist one, on the specific issue of the role that Duncan ascribes to student achievement data with respect to teaching.

Proficiency

Earlier I claimed that Dreyfus's model seeks to account for skill development beyond the point at which the rationalist view seems to founder: Dreyfus is interested in the ability to grasp a holistic situation such that the relevance stands out immediately, and the ability to "flexibly respond" to relevant situational features as a matter of course. In moving to the Proficiency stage from mere Competence, Dreyfus holds that the proficiency involved amounts to precisely the ability to grasp a situation and its relevance immediately. Where the rationalist view seems to bog down on this point, as AI's failures to find heuristics capable of replicating skillful human practice suggest, the immediate grasping of a situation and its relevance at once results from *involved* experience with making existentially uncertain choices of perspectives in situations where the practitioner bears responsibility for the choice. The ability to "spontaneously see the point and important aspects of the current situation" (H. L. Dreyfus & Dreyfus, 2005, p. 787) I will call—and have called—a particular kind of seeing—say, insight.[4] Theodore Kisiel, transcribing Heidegger's interpretation of Aristotle's *Nicomachean Ethics 6,* has Heidegger saying:

> The uncovering of principles must be without speech. Here, it is simply a matter of "bringing ourselves before the matter itself," traversing the way that leads directly to it. Thus, the resolute choice of my concrete situation of action, which takes into account the various circumstances entering into the situation, abruptly terminates such an accounting and culminates in a simple "oversight" which takes charge of, and acts on, the situation in the "blink of an eye" (Augenblick), in the instant of insight. (Kisiel, 1993, p. 286)

Dreyfus's descriptions of the instantaneous and "spontaneous" grasping of the situation are strikingly similar:

> Because of the performer's perspective, certain features of the situation will stand out as salient and others will recede into the background and be ignored. As events modify the salient features, plans, and expectations, and even the relative salience of features will gradually change. No detached choice or deliberation occurs. It just happens, apparently because the proficient performer has experienced similar situations in the past and so associates with present situations plans that worked in the past and anticipates outcomes that previously occurred. (H. L. Dreyfus & Dreyfus, 2005, p. 787)

However, if Dreyfus's account of the "just-happening" involved in grasping a situation and its relevance at once directly recalls Heidegger's, the distinction from Heidegger's account quoted above lies in the *action* portion of the Proficiency stage. Where Heidegger describes an "oversight that takes charge of, and acts upon, the situation 'in the blink of an eye,'" Dreyfus reserves that sort of action for the final stage. In Proficiency, on Dreyfus's view, the *insight* afforded by experience with involved perspective-choosing in situations for whose outcomes performers were responsible simply plays the role that heuristics were designed to play with respect to establishing relevance. The insight required for relevance merely enables the fluid and correct functioning of detached decision-making with regard to a particular avenue for action: "The proficient performer, while intuitively organizing and understanding his task, will still find himself thinking analytically about what to do" (H. L. Dreyfus & Dreyfus, 1986, p. 29).

To note one important point that will arise again in Chapters 6–9, the sort of insight attributed to proficient practitioners has an *immediate* character: the situation as it is, including relevant features, stands out immediately. I take Arne Duncan to be claiming something similar when he talks about immediately knowing the quality of a school: "We know what success looks like. I see it the minute I enter a school" (Duncan, 2009c). Dreyfus's model of skill development and the discussions of Wittgenstein and Heidegger in the previous chapter both suggest that knowing what success looks like, such that its recognition is immediate, does not necessarily entail the possibility of spelling out this "looking-like" in any sort of articulable proposition.

Expertise

In the phase of Expertise, Dreyfus adds the action to the insight, as suggested in the Heidegger passage above: "The proficient performer, immersed in the world of skillful activity, sees what needs to be done, but decides how to do it. The expert not only sees what needs to be achieved; thanks to a vast repertoire of situational discriminations, he or she also sees immediately how to achieve the goal" (H. L. Dreyfus & Dreyfus, 2005, p. 787). The sense in which Dreyfus can claim, as he does elsewhere, that such excellent practice can be called "skillful coping" has to do with the *transparency* of the situation and its relevance. Drawing upon the practical situations in which most people are most familiar and quite skilled, Dreyfus says, "We usually don't make conscious deliberations when we walk, talk, drive, or carry on most social activities. An expert's skill has become so much a part of him that he need be no more aware of it than he is of his own body" (H. L. Dreyfus & Dreyfus, 1986, p. 30).

In short, at this level of skill, one finally comes upon Nancy's "flexible responsiveness," where correctly responding to most situations is simply a matter of course, something that (in general) demands less cognitive effort than the Novice's rule-following. The Novice's rule-following is that of inflexible logical necessity: once presented with a given set of rules and conditions, the Novice "no longer [has] any choice," as Wittgenstein says. Nancy's skillful coping reveals a different kind of following a rule in which one does "not choose—[she] follow[s] it blindly" (*PI* §218–219), and yet for all this, her practice is something that, in terms of specific behaviors, resists "rigid" predictability in any "simple sense."

In the particular case of teachers, to suggest that at this stage that excellent practice usually *just happens* is to imply neither that great teachers do not think at all, nor even that they never deliberate or consciously reason their way to appropriate actions. It is rather to suggest that these conscious mental deliberations are limited to unusual or particularly problematic situations. When Dreyfus characterizes the competent performer as "overwhelmed," the overwhelming nature of competent practice has to do with an inability to do anything *other* than reason consciously about both the correct perspective according to which to grasp the situation and the action that ought to result, given the relevant features exposed by the chosen situation. That by the Expertise phase, most aspects of teaching do not require the same level of conscious engagement only helps the expert allocate such conscious reasoning to the situations that genuinely require it.

Here once more we encounter the two different senses of following a rule that I discussed in the previous chapter. According to the rationalist view, the rules exist anyway, independent of practices; following a rule amounts to "engaging mental wheels with the already-existing rails," as McDowell puts it. On the other view, the sense of conscious *effort* drops out of McDowell's formulation. To be skillfully engaged in practical dealings is already to have engaged oneself in following rules, and not so deterministically as Wittgenstein's "rules laid to infinity" locution would suggest. The Dreyfusian, Wittgensteinian, and Heideggerian considerations in this chapter have helped to demonstrate that such a rules-as-rails view remains insufficient to account for the regularity or recognizability of our actual rule-following practices. On the rationalist view, the sort of flexible responsiveness of the type that characterizes Dreyfus's final stage of skill development proves impossible—situational relevance and situational similarity each presuppose the other, and thus the transcendent logical conditions that a rule is supposed to *be* cannot establish any traction with regard to *particular* teacher choices or behaviors.

In the Dreyfusian model, no conscious deliberation appears to be involved at all in skillful responsiveness, which to the rationalist (among others), would also seem to exclude the demonstration of "flexible responsiveness" as an instance of following a rule. Such a condemnation, though, assumes precisely the transcendently-anchored picture of rules required by the rationalist view. Following a rule, however, might amount to no more than doing similar things in similar situations, whose similarity is a matter of family resemblance with a basis in agreement in forms of life, and this is not at all to claim that no *thinking* is involved in such rule-following. As Wittgenstein says, "One follows the rule mechanically. Hence one compares it to a mechanism. 'Mechanical'—that means: without thinking. But *entirely* without thinking? Without *reflecting*" (Wittgenstein, 1983, VIII, 61). In distinguishing between reflection in particular and thinking in general, Wittgenstein gestures in the direction that Dreyfus would recognize as a division between knowledge-that and knowledge-how, where the former both implies and requires "detachment" or "disengagement" and the latter implies and requires the opposite. Doing, on an involved basis in which one's being is implicated, *is also* thinking; it is judgment and action at once, indivisibly.

5.2 ARNE DUNCAN AND ACHIEVEMENT DATA: A REPRISE

In light of the previous paragraphs, I ought to return to one of the salutary aspects of using student achievement data that Duncan cites. In the speech directly addressing the role of data with respect to teachers, Duncan says, "They want to know exactly what they need to do to teach and how to teach. *It makes their job easier and ultimately much more rewarding.* They aren't guessing or talking in generalities anymore" (Duncan, 2009a, emphasis added).

In considering Dreyfus's description of skill development, one can see that "easier" teaching takes at least two forms. At the point of Competence, developing teachers (and policies meant to address teacher development) arrive at a crossroads: either the problems that confront teachers will be taken as "structured" or "unstructured." The examples of Nancy and Mrs. Grady that continue to arise, as well as Duncan's own propensity to reify an ordinary sense of good teaching, suggest that the sort of realm that we expect teaching to address is indeed "unstructured."

Coping with unstructured problem areas requires the existential choice of perspective in which the teacher bears responsibility for that choice and for the outcome as well. The way that Duncan proposes to use student achievement data, however, precisely converts the realm teaching addresses into a "structured" one, along the lines of a puzzle or a mathematical manipulation. The teacher's goal, here, in light of which situations have their relevance, requires no insight and no choice; it is simply determined beforehand. Therefore, the data that Duncan wishes to use *will indeed* make the teachers' jobs easier, but only through transforming the sort of teaching that we ostensibly want into the technical version, one characterized by the "preponderant criterion" of lifting test scores. With the implication that every practical situation ought to be grasped in terms of its relation to that criterion, such that relevance never changes, teachers can never undergo the types of conditions that develop the flexibility in either vision or responsiveness necessary to the ordinary sense of great teaching. All of this would be unproblematic if we *knew* that raising test scores sufficed as the goal at which teaching aims; but as Duncan's own words and the examples he cites indicate, we know exactly the opposite.

The fact that the projects of Lemov and Shulman, which share the rationalist assumption of Duncan's Race to the Top, prove essential to the development of great teachers in an ordinary sense is too easily confused with a view that the rationalist model also remains implicitly present in the *excellent practices* of skillful and experienced teachers. Returning to Lemov's art analogy for a moment, one can surely see the sense of his attribution to Michaelangelo of "foundational skills": "You learn to strike a chisel with a mallet. You refine the skill with time, learning at what angle to strike and how hard to drive the chisel." His picture of familiarizing oneself with the tools and media of an artistic craft focuses on the piecemeal aspects thereof: angles and forces. If this is to imply that the *David* would have been impossible without this type of attention to foundational growth in Michaelangelo's youth, Lemov's argument presents no problems. If this is to imply, however, as I understand it, that skillful activity involved in the production of the *David* actually consisted of the *application* of these foundational skills *as* piecemeal actions, then this argument will not serve.

In terms of sufficiency and necessity, with the problems of AI and the considerations of involvement and the role of experience in mind, I might put the issue like this: "foundational skills," in Lemov's terms, or the sort of "teacher knowledge" that Shulman, Ball, and Hill all seek in their research, both of which amount to the "best practices" approach to educational reform touted by Duncan and many others, remain *necessary* to developing excellent ordinary-sense teachers; such an approach is also *sufficient* to the actual production of relatively competent practice. But they are neither necessary *nor* sufficient conditions for the ordinary sense of excellent teaching in practice; and in fact, in order for teachers to develop their skillful practice beyond mediocrity, such approaches must be eventually set aside.

In this way, teaching and many other skills resemble bike-riding, an analogy that Dreyfus also invokes on several occasions. Training wheels are often necessary to the development of the skill: with training wheels on, even a novice bike-rider can approximate competence insofar as the rider stays aloft, as it were. But bike-riding as a skill is more than remaining upright, and in order to develop the sense of balance required for proficiency, the training wheels must come off. In just this sense, that proficient bike-riders do not use training wheels, the conditions necessary to the development of the skill do not remain necessary to its proficient practice, though the training wheels suffice to produce competent riding no matter the experience level of the rider. (It may be important to note that in no case would we consider anyone riding with training wheels a "competent bike rider"—the very fact of the training wheels constitutes the salient criterion to the contrary.)

An important aspect of this analogy is that the step from never having ridden a bike before to riding with training wheels is substantially smaller than the step from riding with training wheels to riding well in their absence. Dreyfus helps one to see, also, that moving from, say, never having held a chisel in one's hands before to a limited ability to chisel does not lead in any linear fashion to the production of the *David*. Adapting a criticism from Maya Bar-Hillel, not only is the step from not being able to do anything *at all* to being able to do it a *little bit* so much smaller than the step from being able to do it a *little bit* to being able to do it *well*, but making that second leap is no mere technical extension of the first step.

What Duncan imagines being replicated when innovations are "taken to scale" is the reproduction of doing something *well*. But by transporting the innovations in terms of formalized rules and behavioral facts, educators transport only the conditions for doing it *a little bit*. This does not suggest that scaling-up educational successes is impossible; it does suggest, however, that merely communicating "best practices" will not, in itself, suffice. Dreyfus allows us to see that making the second leap necessarily involves developing an "entirely different relation" to the skillful activity itself: it requires engagement or involvement, and cannot be achieved through the detached or disengaged means that suffice for mere competence and are in fact necessary to beginners.

Despite their shortcomings in terms of a full account of teacher practice, as I have noted, Lemov and Shulman's methods both produce actual, measurable results: instilling behaviors, techniques, best practices, and abstract knowledge in newcomers to the domain proves effective to a certain point.

The correlation that Hill and Ball demonstrate between their construct of MKT and student math achievement evinces this fact. But the fact that one has traveled some distance *away* from incompetence ought not to be confused with having made meaningful progress *toward* excellence. Stuart Dreyfus puts it colorfully in quipping at one point that such a confusion is like a man climbing a tree and claiming progress toward the moon: true, perhaps, but profoundly misleading.

It must be noted, too, that the above criticisms bear upon Duncan's Race to the Top project precisely insofar as the *examples* upon which he draws in order to rally popular support are invariably examples of ordinary-sense great teaching. That he chooses such examples suggests that his audience—the public, broadly conceived—craves excellent teachers, and also that Duncan recognizes this desire in his audience. The distinction between technical and ordinary rises again at this final point because Duncan effectively pledges ordinary-sense excellence through technical means, and the problems with the rationalist assumption undergirding the "best practices" approach reveal the implausibility of this project.

Were his stated goal *not* the widespread development of excellent teachers, but instead, say, the *aggregate* "improvement" of the teaching corps overall, as visible in central-tendency data, this technical approach might suffice. Despite his rhetoric about excellent teaching, there is certainly evidence that this is in fact the aim of Race to the Top. Lifting measures of central tendency can be achieved, after all, in two ways: either by increasing the number and quality of teachers *above* mean "effectiveness" or by decreasing the number of teachers *below* the mean, through a process of improvement or weeding-out.

My intent in raising Dreyfus's model of skill development is to demonstrate, if "Competence" represents the mean, (a) that these two approaches are crucially different from one another and (b) that the methods involved in *decreasing* the number of sub-par teachers, if applied to the teaching profession as a whole without regard to the role of internalized, involved, and non-formalized experience in moving from mediocrity to excellence, will have the additional and unintended consequence of *hindering* teacher development above the mean.

Kristof's understanding of the Chetty article cited in the Introduction illustrates how easily these two different things are conflated: "This latest study . . . not only underscores the importance of education but also illuminates how we might improve schools. An essential answer: more good teachers. Or, to put it another way, fewer bad teachers" (Kristof, 2012). The latter formulation is not "another way" to "put it"—the "it" is different, and pursuing a "fewer bad teachers" agenda via the policies of Race to the Top will in fact *stifle* the "more good teachers" agenda to which it is imagined to be equivalent. According to a *technical* view—available in measures of central tendency offered in terms of student achievement data—"more good teachers" and "fewer bad teachers" appear identical. They are not.

Ultimately, Race to the Top's proposals in the realm of teacher training and evaluation will indeed, as Duncan promises, have the effect of making "their jobs easier"—but the policies will accomplish this feat not by engendering the skillfulness required to navigate the unstructured realm of teaching and learning, but instead through eradicating by fiat all unstructured characteristics and thereby also preventing the development of the very skillfulness embodied in his many examples.

Duncan presents himself in his many speeches as performing the grim but necessary duty of demanding *more* from teachers and their training programs; he is in fact demanding *less*. The pact his rhetoric makes with the public suggests a "more good teachers" approach; his policies, though, are aimed at a "fewer bad teachers" solution. The statistical identity of these two agendas belies their profound differences. A "more good teachers" effort includes the necessity of conscious deliberation in the development of flexible responsiveness; a "fewer bad teachers" approach, by virtue of misunderstanding the relation between deliberate reasoning and skillful practice, *actively stymies* the development of flexible responsiveness at all.

In this respect, Dreyfus's caution about the misguided fears of AI, with its attendant rationalist assumptions, resounds powerfully: "Our risk is not the advent of superintelligent computers, but of subintelligent human beings" (H. L. Dreyfus, 1992, p. 280).

NOTES

1. Although Dreyfus uses this term pervasively, it is one of the points upon which his critics harp, and precisely for the reasons that they point out, as well as for the reason that "expertise" has a problematic history in the education literature as well (Welker, 1991), I wish to avoid it as much as possible. My goal is excellent skillful practice, not the creation of "experts" as others imagine Dreyfus to mean.
2. A wonderful, if anecdotal, example: a friend of mine recently posted the following status on Facebook: "Dear iPhone autocorrect: I *never* mean 'Holy Shot.'"
3. Again, as this is a phenomenological description, Dreyfus draws only on the reader's acknowledgment of the descriptions for justification, rather than any neuroscientifically robust account of memory.
4. In *Mind Over Machine*, Dreyfus labels what the proficient performer has acquired "intuition," which he explicitly equates with "know-how" (H. L. Dreyfus & Dreyfus, 1986, pp. 28–29). He notably does not include either of those terms in later publications. Know-how, I think, is too easily confused with propositional knowledge and "intuition" too often associated with both a *mysticism* and a *mentalism* that Dreyfus is at pains to avoid. I don't know why he didn't go with either "sight" or "insight" himself, given that term's Aristotelian-Heideggerian legacy.

REFERENCES

Bourdieu, P. (1980). *The Logic of Practice*. Stanford: Stanford University Press.

Dreyfus, H., & Dreyfus, S. (1992). What Artificial Experts Can and Cannot Do. *AI & Society*, 6(1), 18–26.
Dreyfus, H. L. (1988). The socratic and platonic basis of cognitivism. *AI & Society*, 2(2), 99–112. doi:10.1007/bf01891374
Dreyfus, H. L. (1992). *What Computers Still Can't Do: a Critique of Artificial Reason*. Cambridge, MA: M.I.T. Press.
Dreyfus, H. L. (2005). Overcoming the Myth of the Mental: How Philosophers Can Profit from the Phenomenology of Everyday Expertise. *Proceedings and Addresses of the American Philosophical Association*, 79(2), 47–65 CR-Copyright © 2005 American Philoso. Retrieved from http://www.jstor.org/stable/30046213
Dreyfus, H. L., & Dreyfus, S. (1986). *Mind Over Machine: The Power of Human Intuition and Expertise in the Era of the Computer*. New York: Free Press.
Dreyfus, H. L., & Dreyfus, S. (2005). Peripheral Vision: Expertise in Real World Contexts. *Organization Studies*, 26(1), 776.
Duncan, A. (2009a). Robust Data Gives Us the Roadmap to Reform. U.S. Department of Education. Retrieved from http://www2.ed.gov/news/speeches/2009/06/06082009.html
Duncan, A. (2009b). Teacher Preparation: Reforming the Uncertain Profession. U.S. Department of Education. Retrieved from http://www.ed.gov/news/speeches/teacher-preparation-reforming-uncertain-profession
Duncan, A. (2009c). Turning Around the Bottom Five Percent. U.S. Department of Education. Retrieved from http://www.ed.gov/news/speeches/turning-around-bottom-five-percent
Kisiel, T. (1993). *The Genesis of Heidegger's Being and Time*. Berkeley: University of California Press.
Kristof, N. (2012). How Mrs. Grady Transformed Olly Neal. *New York Times*, p. SR13. New York.
Polyani, M. (1962). Tacit Knowing: Its Bearing on Some Problems of Philosophy. *Reviews of Modern Physics*, 34(4), 601–616.
Shulman, L. (2005). Teacher Education Does Not Exist. *Stanford Educator*, 7.
Welker, R. (1991). Expertise and the Teacher as Expert: Rethinking a Questionable Metaphor. *American Educational Research Journal*, 28(1), 19–35. Retrieved from http://www.jstor.org/stable/1162877
Wittgenstein, L. (1983). *Remarks on the Foundations of Mathematics*. Cambridge: MIT Press.

6 Achievement Data and Matters of Inference in Teacher Evaluation

Having addressed the insufficiencies of focusing upon student achievement data in terms of both *knowing* and *doing* the excellent teaching toward which Duncan ostensibly labors, as conceived according to the freezing of relevance required by the rationalist assumption, it will follow in self-evident fashion that using student achievement data in order to ground or justify claims about teacher quality will likewise prove insufficient. This chapter will revisit and recollect the arguments around the use of student achievement data in teacher evaluations with an eye specifically to the role of justification in such evaluative purposes.

In dealing with issues around reporting on—or *telling*—teacher quality, broader questions arise, primarily pertaining to, as I hinted above, the intertwined topics of the measurement of human endeavors and the justification of evaluative claims. This chapter addresses the multiple kinds of data and evaluative claims at work in Duncan's discourse, and it explores the kinds of justification that are both possible and requisite for each. A guiding suspicion of mine as I embark upon this chapter—and in putting it into words, it seems almost too obvious to bear mentioning—is that different forms of measurement, even of ostensibly the same thing, are bound up with different human purposes, and therefore unique to certain uses and not necessarily generalizable or transferrable.

This suspicion stands counterpoised to what I see as Race to the Top's view of the connection between data, measurement, and evaluation: that the sort of data, measurement, and evaluation necessary to distinguish for the Secretary of Education the top 10 percent of California's teachers from the bottom 10 percent ought also and unproblematically to function at a microcosmic level as well, as in communicating something meaningful to a given set of parents about the relative quality of their child's teacher. Such a claim would amount to (and be a species of), I propose, a sort of universalized, formalized view of education as such, in which (a) what the various parties to the educational endeavor desire will always (or should always) be exactly the same, (b) the means for its achievement or effecting will likewise (because causally necessary) be uniform, and (c) the form and content of its expression will further always conform to a single axis or standard.

Achievement Data and Matters of Inference in Teacher Evaluation 143

In Chapter 1, I briefly touched upon this issue in suggesting that Duncan's use of the locution "no one can tell you" which California teachers are in which group in order to signify a quite general epistemological weakness in teacher evaluation protocols. In this chapter, I hope to better express the impulse behind my earlier objection: that the need to be answered by distinguishing the best 30,000 teachers in California from the worst is simply incoherent from any perspective *except* that of the state or federal government, and that there is no reason to assume that the means of answering a state or federal need will also or equally suffice to answer a school-specific, community, or parental need. In brief, the epistemological lack to which teacher-quality measures grounded in student achievement data are meant to respond is not nearly so general as it might seem.

As Chapter 1 in particular has revealed, however, Duncan himself, as well as many others, often finds himself appealing to differing and incommensurable criteria in the discussion of teacher quality. That two differing concepts of teacher quality pervade the discourse has been established, as has the fact that Race to the Top and state policies have insufficient awareness of that fact. The questions confronting us in this chapter are: what is involved in recognizing teacher quality, and what types of evidence and justification are required in order to communicate that quality to others?

6.1 THE FRAILTY OF ORDINARY-SENSE EVALUATIVE CLAIMS

In the Introduction, with broad reference to Race to the Top generally, I asked: "If these means remain insufficient to demonstrate or secure the conceptual recognition of good teaching we wish to reward, *on what basis* is good teaching so immediately visible in Mrs. Grady's story? If not communicable in terms of specific practices or measurable outcomes, how else could our ordinary concept of "good teaching" become visible?"

Speaking broadly, this section marks an attempt in the direction of answering questions around the relative usability of both the immediate visibility of teacher quality to which Duncan occasionally alludes and the version available in terms of student achievement data. In other words, this section explores the basis upon which such immediate visibility finds its foundation and its relation to the basis of teacher value-added in particular and student achievement data in general.

Attending first to instances in which student achievement data plays no role in his own claims about educational quality, I return to two types of statements that Duncan makes. The first type amounts to a claim of educational quality's immediate visibility in the present.

> We know what success looks like. I see it the moment I enter a school. It's clean, orderly, the staff is positive and welcoming, and the kids and the classroom are the focus. I see award-winning school work on

the walls. I see discipline and enthusiasm in the children. I see parents engaged and teachers collaborating on instruction. (Duncan, 2009d)

While I have cited this passage earlier in this project, I wish to highlight at this juncture the fact that Duncan's claim to the immediate visibility of "success" is accompanied by an appeal to the criteria according to which this success emerges. These criteria include the presence of "award-winning school work on the walls," "discipline and enthusiasm in the children," engaged parents and collaborating teachers. Duncan offers these factors as a *description* of "what success looks like." Notably, Duncan offers this description of "what success looks like" in the present tense: the school to which he refers is succeeding right now, in and according to the very characteristics that he highlights in his description.

The second type of statement in which Duncan recognizes educational quality without recourse to student achievement data has to do with present-tense *adult* success. In other words, the teacher quality that these statements recognize lies far in the past, and is expressed as a putative causal condition of present adult achievement. In earlier chapters, I aligned these statements, as well as his claim pertaining to immediate visibility discussed above, with the ordinary sense of good teaching, and I belabored the Secretary's tendency to exhort his audience to recall excellent teachers from their own lives.

In this space, however, I wish to return to his comments about the people in his neighborhood, and his mother's effect on them, in particular, with the intent of drawing out the way in which the quality of teaching long gone, so to speak, comes to visibility only years later, in terms of the successes of the then-children in their adulthood endeavors. In elucidating the importance of good teaching, Duncan points to the present adult success of his own local cohort, and he offers a narrative about the education of this group, an educative endeavor to which he attributes, in causal fashion, the success he describes. In describing this success, he says that,

> from the group of friends I grew up studying with and playing ball with, from one street corner at 46th and Greenwood, emerged literally a brain surgeon, a Hollywood movie star, one of my top administrators at the Chicago Public Schools, and one of IBM's international corporate leaders. (Duncan, 2009a)

He explains the remarkable concentration of successful adults in terms of the quality of the educational endeavors—defined broadly, here, rather than confined to teachers at particular grade levels—of the adults overseeing their childhood experiences:

> How did this happen? Because these children, despite tremendous poverty, despite staggering neighborhood violence, despite challenges at

Achievement Data and Matters of Inference in Teacher Evaluation 145

home, had my mother and others in their lives who gave them real opportunities, real support and guidance over the years, and had the highest expectations for them. (Duncan, 2009a)

The presence of a certain kind of adult in the lives of these children—those who "gave them real opportunities, real support and guidance over the years, and had the highest expectations for them"—is offered here as an explanation of *how* the noteworthy success of this group was possible. In this scenario, the claims regarding the quality of the educative experiences in question receive their justification from the indisputable present-tense fact that Duncan's peer group has achieved remarkable (professional) success. The specific nature of the causal conditions for this success involve a syndrome of attitudes, behaviors, and actions that Duncan lumps together in terms of providing "real opportunities, real support and guidance over the years," and the holding of the "highest expectations."

The criteria that render visible the excellence of the education that Duncan received thus rest in two sites: the current success of his cohort (as well as the statistical improbability of such a concentration of success) and Duncan's own autobiographical attribution of this success to the sort of educative adult attention lavished upon this cohort in the past. Olly Neal's story bears the marks of this species of appeal, as well: a person's striking success is attributed—an attribution accompanied by more or less vivid details—to educative experiences in the past.

The two types of criterial appeals discussed above share an expectation of sufficiency in the absence of the kind of student achievement data envisioned in Race to the Top policies. Neither type of appeal requires support from any other source; they themselves, they alone, make visible the quality of the teaching with which they deal. Both types of appeal are also, perhaps obviously, grounded in observable, present-tense phenomena. In the first case, the phenomena that count as relevant to the revelation of teacher quality are (immediately) visible *in* schools: Duncan focuses on aspects of the building itself (cleanliness, orderliness), aspects of the students (enthusiastic, disciplined), aspects of the teachers and administrators (positive, welcoming, collaborative, kids-first disposition), and aspects of parental relations (engaged).

In the second case, the phenomena that count as relevant are, one might say, restricted to the axis of the student. The primary phenomenon in the second instance is the now-successful *former* student. The success of this former student frames the specific description of the teaching to which the former student attributes his or her present level of achievement. Thus, when Duncan recalls his mother and the other adults that shaped the lives of his cohort, his citation of the "real opportunities, real support and guidance," and "highest expectations" that these educators provided to their young charges, these become the names of the causes of the adult success that Duncan's audience witnesses in the empirical fact of this man in a suit and tie declaiming on American education policy. An audience, whether it is Kristof himself or Kristof's eventual readership or Duncan's listeners, takes the former student's perspective on his or her education and biography as authoritative, as worthy of trust.

In examining the two types of criterial appeals that require no student achievement data as Race to the Top conceives of it, one can already make an important distinction in terms of the nature of the visibility of the teacher quality under investigation. In the first instance, the quality of the education in question is taken to be *immediately perceptible* to a given observer; as such, the means of making this quality apparent to a wider public rely upon a description of the observed features—the school building, the attitudes and behaviors of students, staff, teachers, and administrators. The assumption is that through the process of describing what one sees, one captures and shares not only the empirical facts, as it were, but also the quality of the education itself, the value component.

In the second instance, the quality of the education in question is taken to be, one might say, more *mediately* visible, visible only indirectly, only in light of the former student's present success, and only in terms of the educational experience's presumed causal capacities. In this case, the former student's (or, as in the case of the Kristof article, a second-degree advocate's) autobiographical attribution of causation to the qualities of some teacher, group of teachers, parent, or school provides the means of making educational quality apparent to an audience.

In describing the character of one's own education, one might also be said to make something like teacher quality immediately visible; the "more mediate" label merely reflects the fact that, in subtle contrast with a third-person describer, an embodiment or physically present signifier of success *grounds* the value component of the description of teacher practice in this case. The former student's current success, combined with the autobiographical attribution of its causation to a given facet of the former student's education, renders the quality of that education visible to the public.

Duncan's and Neal's autobiographical ascription of their adult success to the much earlier interventions of teachers highlights another axis—what Wittgenstein would call a grammatical axis—of the concept of teacher quality. The concept of good teaching, now, is revealed not only in terms of its distinctive *practices or features*, as teacher evaluation protocols urged by Race to the Top describe it, but in terms of its specific life effects. Criteria for good teaching thus extend beyond the teacher and the acts of teaching themselves, and take an external valence in the (future) characteristics of students. Adult success appears as one of the concepts that Duncan and Neal, among others, relate to the concept of good teaching. These criteria serve to bring out and demarcate the logical or conceptual space that "good teaching" occupies in our lives.

Various *measures* of, and ways of measuring, teacher effectiveness become salient issues at this point. Agreeing that teachers ought to have

Achievement Data and Matters of Inference in Teacher Evaluation 147

positive effects settles very little. How one establishes the link between particular teachers and particular instances of students' adult success, however—what *counts* as success, and how such success might be apportioned among a student's manifold educative interactions with adults—creates a new problem. Immediately identifying good teaching, as Duncan does in the first example considered in this section, remains perhaps insufficiently tethered to any (other) indication of that teaching's *effects* on students, except obliquely. Pointing to present adult success and attributing it to teaching in the past, even to specific interventions, on the other hand, given the number and pervasiveness of educational experiences with teachers, coaches, tutors, counselors and so on, seems to lack the perspicuity necessary to comment on a teacher's *general* ability.

It may be necessary also to highlight the *temporal* insufficiencies of each of these forms of appeal in addressing the felt need to say something meaningful about the quality of teachers currently at work in the classroom, in light of which insufficiencies student achievement data is to make its entrée. The latter case—that of Duncan's citation of his mother and Neal's of Mrs. Grady—addresses the quality of teachers long-since retired, and so comes vastly too late to be of use in assisting with tenure, retention, or compensation decisions in the present. What it lacks in terms of timeliness, however, it makes up for in terms of the felt authority of its evaluative capacity: if the goal of education, ultimately, is the development of successful adults, what more powerful evidence could there be than the very embodiment of successful adulthood pointing to his or her favorite teacher as the driving force behind his or her success?

The opposite is the case for the "moment-I-enter-a-school" judgment. While capable of sizing up teachers right now, it feels too hasty, too irregular or unregulated, too haphazard. Occurring in the middle of the story, as it were, say at third grade, one cannot know how these children's narratives end, and the observer's judgment lacks the same claim to certainty, or the same purchase on our trust. In the case of observational descriptions of a teacher's quality, one finds oneself in the uncomfortable position of *merely* taking the observer at his or her word.

In other words, and by way of expansion, even if a present-tense evaluator feels confident in declaring this or that teacher "excellent," and even if that evaluator's description of the teaching garners agreement or acceptance from the relevant parties such that (some) other people also laud the excellence of the teaching in question, such claims treat future student outcomes as irrelevant. These value claims make no attempt, in fact, to relate explicitly to future conditions or outcomes at all.

For this reason, such claims cannot cope with any questions that emerge from an assumption that a child's eventual adulthood (broadly speaking) is produced by and in accordance with the relative quality of the child's education. Such questions would take the form of, "But how do you know that it's *working*?"—by which the questioner implies that a lesson ought to have this or that (visible, measurable, futural) effect, and that the evaluator's claim appears not to attend to any sort of "working" that the questioner would recognize. In fact, this is precisely the case. The evaluator would point to the obvious "working" of the visible quality of the good teaching; but the questioner would see *no relevant criteria* of a given lesson's "working." The request for a modicum of certainty about the futural aspects of good teaching would go unanswered precisely because of something like (but not exactly) disagreement in criteria.

The backwards-looking view available in the personal testimony of Duncan and Olly Neal, for all its untimeliness, appears to take care of both of the above concerns: the quality of teaching is immediately visible, one might hazard, in Neal's descriptive narrative of Mrs. Grady's intervention, but its claim to truth or certainty is buttressed by Neal's adult social position, by the career success he attributes to his own education. Despite, however, such warrant behind the claim to certainty upon which Mrs. Grady's quality becomes visible, further consideration reveals that even in Neal's case, problems with dispelling uncertainty remain.

However weak the immediate-visibility case's claim to some sort of certainty or worthiness of trust might appear with respect to its counterpart in the backwards-looking successful-adult judgment, I wish to point out the skeptical problems faced by the autobiographical claims as well, the upshot of which is that one finds himself no less uncomfortably dependent upon another's word in the backwards-looking successful-adult case.

In the first place, a given high school math teacher in an urban or suburban district will teach 120–150 students per year, assuming five sections of 24–30 students with no single-semester electives or enrollment changes. The type of claim that Duncan and Neal assert is the perspective of a single student in a single year. If a teacher's charge is the development of successful adults, plural, then even the *accurate* autobiographical claim of any single student cannot secure the kind of certainty that one feels tempted to attribute to those of Duncan and Neal. Was Mrs. Grady an excellent teacher *in general*? Neal's own experience with Mrs. Grady is insufficient to address the question. Either the narrative would have to make evident that Mrs. Grady's intervention—the practical sight that allowed her to see Neal in the correct light—was somehow characteristic of her, such that similar effects on other students were likely (which the autobiographical nature of the claim precludes), or we find ourselves once again in the discomfiting position of either *assuming* such generalization or rejecting the standing of Neal's claim, neither of which one feels particularly warranted in doing.

Even were such generalization possible, however, Neal's claim about Mrs. Grady's quality remains dependent on a granting of its accuracy. We must hold, to use the other example of this type of claim, that Arne Duncan is *correct* in crediting his mother and other adults with the success he embodies. This amounts to discounting, for example, the interventions of luck, or freaks of fortune, or networking skills, or any other factor, whim,

Achievement Data and Matters of Inference in Teacher Evaluation 149

decision, or circumstance that carries a 12-year-old boy from his middle-school years to the office of the Secretary of Education. Surely Duncan has not partitioned out the effects of all possible covariates in order to make his claim. Nothing beyond his word, his own sense of things, compels one to accept as accurate the claim that his mother and others like her can be considered responsible for the success he describes.

Lastly, what counts as a "successful adult" is a matter of agreement in form of life, and thus subject to all manner of definitional slipperiness that I described in Chapter 4. That becoming a Hollywood actor, a corporate leader, and a major political figure can all count as instances of "success" is not produced by the sharing of any one characteristic in common. One might, for instance, try to claim that all three forms of success share alike the essential characteristic of high income. But one would not call major cocaine smugglers emblematic of the adult success toward which education strives. "Success" itself, as a goal of the educational enterprise, remains itself bound up in the nonformalizable understanding embedded in shared form of life.

The immediate-visibility case, meanwhile, suffers from an intractable inability to dispel uncertainty about the *future outcomes* of the educational endeavor presently at hand because claims to the immediate visibility of teacher quality do not wait upon or predict the future outcomes of the education in question. If it is assumed that excellent teaching in this sense will have visible, positive effects farther down the road, the value of good teaching is not taken to depend upon the emergence of those effects. Thus, claims to the immediate visibility of teacher quality cannot address skepticism about the future with anything that would satisfy the demands of a skeptical interlocutor.

But the backwards-looking autobiographical perspective is also beset by its own limitations in terms of establishing certainty. Not only does one have to accept a single autobiographical narrative as expressing something *general* about a given teacher in the absence of other evidence, and not only does one have to accept the causal conclusion of the autobiographer's (self)-analysis, but in order for the claim to have purchase at all, one must also share the sense that the autobiographer does indeed embody something worth educating toward. None of these acceptances is compelled by logical or natural law, any more than the observer's claims about immediately-visible educational quality can be taken as predictions of future performance with any basis in causal or logical necessity. *Both* types of claims remain strikingly frail when a certain kind of skeptical weight is brought to bear upon them.

The confluence of criteria at work in these two types of claims points, I suggest, to the ineluctable complexity of the educative endeavor as a whole, a complexity that Duncan also acknowledges in his various statements about not wishing to "reduce the complex, nuanced work of teaching" to any single measure. Ways in which we *ordinarily* speak of good teaching—in terms of witness, one might say, either as a third-person observer or an autobiographical confessor—seem perfectly adequate to the situations in which they are offered; and yet also *inadequate* when faced with what is essentially a request for something like complete generality with regard to ascribing to this or that teacher the value of "good." ("She might have been a good teacher during that day, but is she a good teacher *overall*? She might have been a good teacher for that student, but is she a good teacher *overall*?" Or the converse: "She might be a good teacher overall, but is she a good teacher for *that student?*")

The purpose that evaluative claims are meant to serve seems, if not *determinate* of a claim's form, then certainly important to consider. Duncan's "we know what success looks like" list of criterial features is offered primarily as a statement about good teaching's prevalence, its everydayness, and insofar as his audience agrees with him, the statement works in this capacity. However, as it is disconnected from the other criterial areas that bear upon the concept of good teaching, particularly with regard to eventual effects on students, one feels it inadequate to the task of evaluating teaching *as a whole*: it simply omits a portion of the field of criteria that reveals to us what we take the concept of "good teaching" to entail.

This is also the case with the autobiographical account: as Kristof offers the Olly Neal story as a means of dramatizing the importance of good teaching, the first-hand account suffices beautifully. When one wonders whether this unique experience generalizes to Mrs. Grady's effect on other students, however, or whether Olly Neal is correct to discount the influences of, for example, his later college professors or professional mentors, the criteria elicited according to Kristof's narration of the story cannot be summoned as an answer. Both forms of what I earlier called ordinary-sense views of teacher quality, despite their sufficiency to the contexts in which they appear, seem to be wanting when one attempts to apply their criteria *generally*, as in the project of defining good teaching.

6.2 THE OBJECTIVITY AND GENERALITY OF STUDENT ACHIEVEMENT DATA

The analysis of achievement data promises to solve the problems inherent in both types of ordinary appeals cited above. In his many speeches touching upon or directly dealing with the use of data, Duncan treats the availability of longitudinal data as offering something profoundly *new* to the education profession. We have seen that both of the criterial appeals discussed above require a certain acceptance or agreement on the part of those to whom educational quality is reported, that is, a certain sharing of forms of life is simply assumed. Achievement data enters in response to the inadequacies of each type of ordinary appeal.

Achievement Data and Matters of Inference in Teacher Evaluation 151

The felt limitations in each of these kinds of appeal are readily voiced: whatever else they lack (in Duncan and Neal's appeals to their upbringings, for example, the autobiographical claim founded upon present adult success can only tell us about the quality of teachers long since retired), they leave substantial room for doubt, as the explicit reliance upon agreement makes clear. It is neither by logical nor by natural law that one is compelled to accept the claims rendered in these two forms; more than this, the proliferation of levels of agreement required in each case seems to defy the very possibility thereof. Perhaps Cavell puts it best with his simple truism that "we *cannot* have agreed beforehand to all that would be necessary" (Cavell, 1979, p. 31).

Duncan's valorization of student achievement data responds to precisely this slipperiness. In other words, Duncan's proposals surrounding student achievement data are predicated upon the ability of such data to eliminate the uncertainty of "the uncertain profession," as the very title of one of his speeches suggests (Duncan, 2009c). The previous chapters of this book, which seek to highlight the conceptual problem engendered in the attempt to address an ordinary sense of good teaching through resolutely technical means, might be taken as one sort of objection to data so conceived: whatever certainty such data offer cannot get any purchase on the ordinary terrain that generated the need for certainty in the first place. That represents one kind of failure at the overcoming of uncertainty that the use of student achievement data sets out to accomplish.

In this and the following chapters, however, I wish to draw out not the *differences* between Duncan's use of an ordinary sense of good teaching and its technical sense, but rather the *similarities* that they share, specifically around the kinds of uncertainty that pervade the uses of each. If the use of data generates a new kind of conceptual uncertainty through putting an ordinary sense of teaching out of reach, I will argue that it also fails to solve *on its own terms* the kind of uncertainty to which it claims to address itself, the sort implied in Duncan's and Neal's narratives of adult-level success. Data's claim to represent something *new*, something that we have *at long last*, falls flat.

I have previously criticized the use of student achievement data both in terms of its ability to distinguish good teachers from poor teachers without recourse to human judgment, and also in terms of its ability to account for and reproduce the practical examples of excellent practice that scholars and politicians cite in indicating the need for such measures. If my focus here seems to hew closely to the critical aim of Chapter 1, that fact indicates the conceptual interactions inherent in the activities of knowing and telling a given thing—counting something as something, one might say, and recounting it to another. What one takes as necessary to the (justifiable) reporting upon the quality of a given teacher is inherently bound up with what one takes as necessary to the knowing of that quality. At the same time, what one takes as necessary to the (justifiable) knowing of teacher quality has to do with an ability to reveal that quality to someone else.

In Chapter 1, I used the difference between the ordinary and the technical concept of teacher quality to make the claim that appeals to student achievement data could not satisfactorily secure the type of knowledge of teaching happening *right now* that Race to the Top wishes to provide. But student achievement data still makes a demonstrable claim to secure *something* involved in life and learning that we as a polity value, even if it is not the ordinary sense of good teaching. Crucial to the sense of securing this something is data's relative ability to quite literally predict the future. The use of student achievement data thus seems well-positioned to overcome *both* of the problems raised in Duncan's citation to the immediate availability of success and Neal's post-hoc reflection of Mrs. Grady's educational interventions.

Put succinctly, just like Duncan's we-know-what-success-looks-like argument, the use of achievement data to generate measures of teacher value-added also promises present-tense visibility of teacher quality. Offsetting the conceptual slippage inherent in "reducing" the complex or nuanced work of teaching, or assuaging one's anxiety about it, is the crucial second promise that data makes: to make justifiable inferences about students' *future* outcomes from a present-tense perspective. This promise underlines the value of Neal's type of backwards-looking narrative: a measure of certainty about adult success performs a justificatory role with respect to claims about educational quality. But *unlike* Neal's narrative, the use of student achievement data seems to dispatch the worries associated both with the particularity of the autobiographical perspective and also with the attribution of causation.

Significant correlations between data-derived measures of teacher quality and certain measures of future student outcomes provide sufficient grounds to justify claims that teacher value-added tells us something worthwhile and meaningful about the quality of teachers, even if that justification is not taken to rest upon something as solid as causation. Additionally, because teacher value-added is calculated using aggregate data, the claim to a given teacher's quality takes into account the experiences of *all* students enrolled in that teacher's classes, thus disarming the threat presented by relying on the narrative of a single, albeit successful, adult as representative of wider student experiences.

To lay out the matter clearly: the use of teacher value-added, grounded in and derived from student achievement data, makes its claim to *superiority* with respect to the ordinary measures discussed above on the grounds that (a) it enables inferences about the relation between current teachers and future outcomes in a way that is denied in ordinary evaluative means and (b) its objectivity and generality avoid the pitfalls or the definitional slipperiness that arises with respect to relying upon something as nebulous, uncertain, and mutable as "agreement in form of life."

The contention throughout this and later chapters amounts to the following: claim (b) is straightforwardly false; and claim (a) is, one might say, misleading. It is *accurate* to suggest that the use of data enables one to make

Achievement Data and Matters of Inference in Teacher Evaluation 153

inferences about the future in a form previously unavailable to us. It is, however, unclear that this new form is different in *kind* from what has heretofore served for educational evaluation, given the falseness of claim (b). If claim (b) is indeed false, then claim (a) amounts to no more than the laughable suggestion that in previous eras a teacher's likely effect on students' eventual adulthood never factored into ordinary judgments about his or her quality. Moreover, given once more the falsity of claim (b), it is unclear why one should regard the use of student achievement data for judgments of quality as deserving of priority—much less an exclusive claim—in teacher evaluation.

When Duncan and Obama address the need for student achievement data, in fact, they refer to precisely these grounds for preferring them as a basis for claims about teacher quality: the certainty such measures provide about teaching both with respect to the *present* and to the *future*. However, in considering Duncan's thoughts on the use of data once more, one sees myriad problems in terms of claims (a) and (b) bound up together.

Taking the most starry-eyed of Duncan's statements about data's possibilities reveals both the temptations and the pitfalls associated with turning to putatively objective measures of teacher quality. Two temporal axes of certainty show themselves in the following quotation, and I will deal with them separately.

> We can one day do a better job of understanding what makes great teachers tick, why they succeed, why they stay in the classroom and how others can be like them. Hopefully, we can track good programs to higher test scores to higher graduation rates. Hopefully, one day we can look a child in the eye at the age of eight or nine or 10 and say, "You are on track to be accepted and to succeed in a competitive university and, if you keep working hard, you will absolutely get there." (Duncan, 2009b)

Duncan wishes to *do* things with data, that is, to take justifiable present action on the basis of data. For Duncan, the use of student achievement data would allow him to do the following present-tense things: (1) understand what makes great teachers tick, which is also bound up in understanding "why they succeed," (2) know what makes them stay in the classroom and "how others can be like them," and (3) draw a correlative or causal line from "good programs" (of teacher education, presumably) to "higher test scores" and on to "higher graduation rates."

The grasp on certainty that data offers to the educational endeavor then makes possible new kinds of knowledge claims and new forms of reporting on the quality of several aspects of the teaching endeavor. These knowledge claims and any reporting thereof obviously require a kind of grip on reality—the certainty undergirding them is only useful provided that the knowledge or judgment secured speaks to what one might call on-the-ground conditions—and there is substantial reason to doubt that the type of knowledge-claims that data can be used to insure, as it were, do indeed reflect or respond to the phenomena they mean to address, which speaks against both claims (a) and (b), as the claims remain, at this point, intertwined.

Take, for example, Duncan's citation of data's helpfulness in a project meant to "understand what makes teachers tick" as well as "how others can be like them." Data, on this view, reveal something about teachers that a given administrator or researcher can first isolate as correlated with excellent teaching and then transmit or transport to another teacher—in order to allow other teachers "to be more like them." We have already seen the profound difficulties with this assumption in previous chapters: while test scores can make evident something about student learning and, in a limited sense, about teacher quality—an unproblematic concession—*what* data is taken to reveal is something that stands behind the practice of excellent teachers, something that, to recall Shulman, "permits" a given teacher to teach as he or she does. The previous chapters have demonstrated that it is entirely unclear, and in fact extremely doubtful, that *anything at all* stands behind teacher practice in the way that both the "best practices" and the "teacher knowledge" approach assume.

Despite the rationalist assumption's failures to account for or reproduce skilled human behavior, which, as we have likewise seen, has to do with the same "agreements in forms of life" and "shared understandings of being" that threaten the certainty of ordinary-sense claims to teacher quality, study after study demonstrates correlations between this or that abstract characteristic of a teacher's practice—behavior or knowledge—and growth in student test scores (Glazerman et al., 2011; Kane & Staiger, 2008; Kane, Taylor, Tyler, & Wooten, 2011; Lemov, 2010; Rivkin, Hanushek, & Kain, 2005). In addition to the ontological difficulties for "best practices" that earlier chapters have explored, this also has profound epistemological implications for claims to certainty based upon putative knowledge regarding such characteristics.

The "best practices" case provides the most promising means of seeing the limitations that Duncan's appeal to data overlooks. Basing value or knowledge claims upon the information yielded by the use of student achievement data promises a kind of actionable certainty that eludes both the autobiographical narrative of a former student and the immediate sense of a third-party observer. The elusiveness of certainty in the latter two cases, while having also to do with the issue of temporality—an inability to speak to the future and the present, respectively—comes down to a reliance on agreement rather than something "natural" or "objective." Data, in contrast, is supposed to offer something that will *not* boil down to such insubstantial or contingent agreement—that is the basis of the certainty it promises, the essence of claim (b). But the *gathering* of the data on "best practices," as well as the satisfactory implementation of any such practice, both presuppose this same agreement in form of life.

Achievement Data and Matters of Inference in Teacher Evaluation 155

Correlations require two variables. In the case of seeking out "best practices," one variable is always growth in student test scores: the dependent variable. The other is the particular "practice" under investigation, for example, recalling the Lemov discussion from earlier chapters, the breaking down of instructions into "simple" rather than "complex" skills: this is the independent variable. A researcher then compares the test-score growth of the students of teachers who perform those behaviors regularly with those who do not. If the mean difference between the two groups' test scores rises to statistical significance, the extra gains of the former group is then attributed to the intervention, to the instructors' use of the practice itself.

But *just what* does the practice consist in here? Assuming that a given researcher observes real, live teachers ordinarily teaching in many different classrooms, to many different students, how is that researcher to identify the practice of "breaking down instructions into simple rather than complex steps"? The teachers under investigation will not be giving precisely the same instructions (the same words concerning the same tasks) to their many different students. According to what, then, can a researcher count two different sets of words, offered in the interest of directing student activity, as *similar enough* to represent two instances of "breaking down instructions into simple rather than complex skills" in the way that the notion of a practice as an object would require?

Perhaps one acknowledges that telling students to "design a policy brief" will not provide the students sufficient clarity to succeed in the task (but perhaps it will; that depends on prior learning, the course content itself, many factors to which the observer may not be privy at all). But what is to count as *adequately* simplifying the task? "Take out your pencils, then design a policy brief" is of no more help, though one has broken down the task in a sort of rudimentary fashion. At the other end of the spectrum, one might imagine a teacher instructing students to prepare to write an essay in these terms: "Use your eyes to locate your backpack; unzip your backpack; find a pencil; take it out of your backpack; place it on your desk; remove a sheet of paper; recall the events of your summer vacation; choose one of these memories that you think you would like to write about; think of a title . . . " and so on. There are, doubtless, ways of giving directions that are *too* complex for the students at hand, and there are also ways of giving directions that are *too* simple.

That which enables and authorizes a researcher or observer to classify two different manifestations of two different teachers' practices as both examples of "breaking down instructions into simple rather than complex skills," a singular "practice," is not available in behavioristic or context-free form. Instructions, as the most recent example demonstrates, can be *endlessly* atomized; and *all* instructions can, in reverse fashion, be revealed as simplifications of some more complex skill. Some teachers give directions at the *right* level, the *appropriate* level, for their students and others remain too vague. That right-ness, one might say, is established or perceived as a matter of situational fit, rather than by means of comparison to some external or formalizable or empirical standard that transcends classroom contexts. The researcher will categorize two different teachers in two different classrooms as direction-givers who break instructions down into manageable pieces. But that these two hypothetical teachers can be said to have *done* a given thing, to have demonstrated a particular practice, is irreducible to abstract characteristics. There is no bright definitional line circumscribing any "best practice" of direction-giving.

Another way of making this point is to assert that where to *begin* decomposing instructions and where to *stop* decomposing cannot be expressed in formalizable terms. Nor can it (accurately) be seen according to explicit features. What enables the researcher to classify two different sets of practical words and behaviors under one category is itself grounded no more (and no less) solidly than in forms of life. If the use of student achievement data seems to tell us something more certain about "what works" than the ordinary discourses, this greater claim to certainty is predicated upon student achievement data's working with learning and teacher practices as clear, distinct, and solid ontological objects; the above discussion, however, reveals that any ontological solidity in the practices that these studies consider is in fact *produced by* a kind of agreement, by the intervention of human judgment. In point of fact, the ontological foundation of best practices as revealed in student achievement data remains no more solid than that of any practice described in third-party or autobiographical claims.

The previous chapters have dealt with the problems of attempting to recreate *performance* in a given domain based on the rationalist assumption shared by the above example. In attempting to generalize something practical that one researcher has successfully accomplished in formal terms, the reliance upon agreement in background practices or forms of life simply multiplies exponentially. In no sense does this process lessen such reliance on shared understandings of being or agreement in forms of life. If studies correlating a given practice with student achievement have merit, that merit cannot claim the degree of objectivity to which the claimants aspire; thus, the straightforward falsity of claim (b) from above.

Chapter 1 addressed the limitations of the concept of "student achievement" visible in terms of test scores with which teaching practices are correlated, upon which students' futures are rendered predictable, and according to which teacher quality might be judged. The above examples are meant to reveal the shaky ontological status of "teacher practices" that make up the other side of the correlative relationship. The correlations that justify knowledge and judgment claims about teacher practice, including those undergirding "best practices" approaches, therefore establish a measurable degree of certainty (and uncertainty), but the link they establish is a bond between two profoundly *unstable* ontological objects. The ability of data to provide any more certainty about "what makes good teachers tick" and "how others can be like them" thereby loses its grip upon us.

Achievement Data and Matters of Inference in Teacher Evaluation 157

The failure of the rationalist assumption as embodied in Artificial Intelligence projects implies that teachers *may not have at all* anything as secure or isolable or formalizable as a set of repeatable "practices" standing behind their actual teaching to which one might attribute their success. The considerations above imply that what researchers *call* "teacher practices" are not isolable objects of pure empirical investigation: the commonalities among successful teachers are recognizable as such only on the basis of Wittgensteinian agreement. While correlations between teacher practices and test growth purport to offer an objective, stable alternative to the felt inadequacies of something like the recourse to agreement necessitated in appeals to immediate visibility, these correlations *also* come down to the same notion of the shared-ness of shared understandings of being. Student achievement data, then, cannot deliver on the promise of certainty it holds out with respect to knowing and judging teacher quality in the present tense.

With the foregoing discussion in mind, the National Council on Teacher Quality's report on state evaluation procedures bears revisiting. The report notes the importance of classroom observation, and makes particular suggestions as to how these might by implemented:

> A strong observation rubric should focus almost exclusively on teacher practices and student behaviors that can be observed in the classroom. While other criteria are not without merit, they may call for too much subjectivity and guesswork on the part of the evaluator. (NCTQ, 2011)

In Chapter 1, once more, I emphasized the fact that classroom observations so conceived cannot—and, despite implicit claims to the contrary, make no attempt to—address the ordinary sense of good teaching. The claim in this chapter is quite different. Here the claim is that, if "too much subjectivity and guesswork on the part of the evaluator" is a problem that observation rubrics are meant to overcome, they do not succeed. The very idea that a given teacher practice could be *sufficiently* described so as to render the intervention of "subjectivity" or "guesswork" on the part of the observer unnecessary, superfluous, or even minimal proves impossible. Since *what counts* as the demonstration of this or that practice cannot itself be completely described in behavioral or abstract terms, that which allows, permits or enables a given evaluator to check *just this* box when a given teacher performs a given action or utters a given phrase has to do with the evaluator's shared sense of the classroom environment, the teacher's purposes, and a notion of what "teaching" and "learning" look like. Even Tennessee's 116-point evaluation rubric stops short of the fullness of description that a subjectivity-free observation of "teacher practices and student behaviors" would require.

In terms of its ability to establish communicable certainty about teacher quality in the present tense, student achievement data ultimately offers us nothing *superior* to Duncan's the-moment-I-enter-a-school judgment. Both are matters of agreement in forms of life. It does offer a different *expression* or *register* of teacher quality, and that itself has value, a point that will return in a later section, but since Duncan's claims on its behalf take the form of "cracking the code," as opposed to "guessing" (Duncan, 2009b), this exploration suggests that no *such* distinction is warranted.

6.3 ACHIEVEMENT DATA AND THE PREDICTION OF ADULT OUTCOMES

The second half of Duncan's plans for the employment of student achievement data—a project that he presumably sees as lying somewhere over the horizon, but made visible by recent advances in the ability to parse test scores—speaks directly to achievement data's ability to predict future student success. This predictive ability ought to be considered in light of Duncan's insistence about honesty and responsibility in reporting on educational quality. In his speech to the Institute of Education Sciences, he says: "We must tell the truth and we must tell it clearly" and also, "When states lower standards, they are lying to children and they are lying to parents. Those standards don't prepare our students for the world of college or the world of work" (Duncan, 2009b).

Through (1) the use of student achievement data in *setting* (qualitative) standards, based on some alignment with college acceptance and/or graduation rates, and then by (2) *generating* data for particular, current students—by measuring students against those standards and analyzing the particular data that result—we will at last find ourselves in a position to "stop lying" and to "tell the truth" with regard to the quality of our children's education. The upshot appears in Duncan's prophecy: "one day we can look a child in the eye at the age of eight or nine or 10 and say, 'You are on track to be accepted and to succeed in a competitive university and, if you keep working hard, you will absolutely get there'" (Duncan, 2009b). At last, as in Duncan's vision, we will be able to look a third-grader "in the eye" and say *both* that the child is "on track to be accepted and to succeed in a competitive university" and that if he or she "keep[s] working hard," the child "will absolutely get there." This section seeks to assess the firmness of the ground on which Duncan's faith in the promise of data to cope with uncertainty about the future stands.

Bearing Duncan's futural goal in mind—the ability to say something in the present to an eight-year-old about their future *with a high degree of certainty*—it seems highly unlikely that the use of test-score analysis could, in principle, achieve this desired end. Two elements in particular frustrate the attempts at securing futural certainty beyond those available to ordinary means. The first element is the well-documented—as previously discussed in Chapter 1—notion of validity in measurement instruments that generate the data. The second element is a species of

Achievement Data and Matters of Inference in Teacher Evaluation 159

the chicken-and-egg problem that objective analyses of language encounter, and that Lenat, Derrida, and Glendinning address in Chapters 2–5. Attempting to solve or address the validity issue immediately raises the chicken-and-egg problem, as I will show.

The first problematic element confronting the use of student achievement has to do with disagreements within the data itself; such discrepancies indicate a certain validity issue. Student achievement data is produced by assessments that, in the words of psychometrician Daniel Koretz, "are only limited measures of the latent construct of interest, which is some measure of student proficiency. . . . They become meaningful only to the extent that one is justified in generalizing from the score to the latent construct of interest" (Koretz, 2002, pp. 754–755). It is this *justification* of generalizations from limited conceptions of a given domain that comprises the second problematic element of using data in the way Duncan wishes to use it. In terms of the validity issue at hand, Duncan's own citations to various measures of student achievement seem to contradict one another, which raises significant doubt about which assessment, if any, is measuring "the latent construct of interest" *accurately.*

In his speech on the importance of using student achievement data in order to make truthful or honest claims about a student's learning, Duncan makes the following separate claims, the first pointing to high-stakes state-level exam results and the second pointing to a no-stakes national-level test:

> Now, we know the news isn't all bad, of course. We also know that children of all age groups across the country have improved their performance in reading and that younger students are posting strong gains in math (Duncan, 2009b).

> The results from the long–term NAEP show that we have a lot of work left to do, particularly in raising the achievement of our students at the secondary school level, whose test scores have barely moved over the past three decades (Duncan, 2009b).

These claims come moments apart in the speech itself; each purports to *know* something about "what's happening" in American schools; yet they offer contradictory views on the matter. According to state-level exams, the news isn't "all bad": "children *of all age groups across the country* have improved their performance in reading" (emphasis added). According to the NAEP assessment, meanwhile, the scores of students at the "secondary school level . . . have barely moved over the past three decades." Both statements cannot be true. Different assessments seem to result in different conclusions pertaining to the "latent construct of interest," as Koretz calls it. Since both assessment instruments purport to measure the same constructs, some other means will be necessary to put this disagreement to rest; appeals to these same measures cannot settle the matter.

In order for student achievement data to perform the futural task that Duncan sets for it—predicting adult outcomes on the basis of student skill levels in given domains—the assessment protocols that generate this data must accurately measure the construct that they claim to measure: proficiency in certain skill domains. Koretz puts it a slightly different way in the same article:

> Thus, if gains are meaningful, they should generalize from the specific test to other indicators of mastery of the domain in question. Because an exhaustive measure of most domains is impractical, one cannot test the degree of generalization from operational tests to the ideal, complete test. One can, however, examine the degree to which gains on a specific test generalize to other tests and to nontest measures of performance in the domain in question (Koretz, 2002, p. 757).

Koretz points specifically to two means of grounding justifications of generalizations from test scores. One requires that results on a given test match up with the results of other assessment instruments that purport to measure the same construct. Duncan's statements regarding state-level exams—which he takes as telling the truth about current levels of student achievement above—indicate that correlating the results of different assessments is not sufficient in this matter. The other method that Koretz points to involves employing "nontest measures of performance in the domain in question."

Duncan is ignorant of neither problem. To address the first issue, he is explicit on the problem of test-to-test correlation:

> When we match NAEP (National Assessment of Educational Progress, also known as the Nation's Report Card) scores and state tests, we see the difference. Some states, like Massachusetts, compare very well. Unfortunately, the disparities between most state tests and NAEP results are staggeringly large (Duncan, 2009b).

He attributes the "disparities" to the "race to the bottom" impulse to which I alluded earlier, which amounts to an accusation that states really are "lying to children"—not only about how they're doing, but more fundamentally about what reading *is*. If states were simply honest about what "proficiency" means, Duncan implies, then all states would demonstrate the correlation with NAEP that Massachusetts does.

It is important to acknowledge, firstly, that differences in the cut scores that define proficiency across state exams during the NCLB era *do* exist; they *do* contribute significantly (even if not exclusively) to the massive disparity between NAEP results and those of state-level assessments; and such stark disparity in the criteria of proficiency *do* amount to differences in the concept of " reading proficiency" itself. Duncan is not incorrect on any of

Achievement Data and Matters of Inference in Teacher Evaluation 161

these points, and it is no mischaracterization or exaggeration to label such deliberate malfeasance with respect to criteria a type of "lying."

Koretz, however, points also to the additional intervening factors of measurement error and score inflation, the latter of which is the result of what is commonly known as "teaching to the test": a phenomenon in which a given test score rises as the result of test-specific coaching without any comparable rise in one's proficiency in the "latent construct of interest." Score inflation has demonstrably pervaded data-driven reporting of on educational quality in the past, even under less highly-incentivized accountability regimes (Cannell, 1988; Linn, Graue, & Sanders, 1990; Shepard, 1990), and so it is hardly obvious that simply being "honest" about the real nature of proficiency would *suffice* to solve the validity problem that the use of data to make judgments about educational quality presents. The fact that it is possible and in fact relatively easy to move the *indicator* of student achievement without meaningfully improving skillfulness in the "latent construct of interest" presents a further issue, not unlike the case of a child holding the thermometer to the heater while his mother's back is turned.

Bearing in mind that the NAEP exam entails no sanctions for failure, while the stakes attached to state exams continue to rise, it is perhaps reasonable to suspect that one might just as well attribute some portion of the discrepancies between the data from NAEP and from state-level exams to the effects of score inflation (not to say outright cheating, which, as the recent scandals in Washington, D.C. and Atlanta schools suffice to show, also occurs). In recalling that the states of Delaware and Tennessee, among others, explicitly require that student achievement data represent a significant portion of a teacher's evaluation—upon the basis of which Duncan wishes to empower LEAs to make personnel, tenure, and compensation decisions—the *incentive* for teachers to engage in the practices of score inflation has never been higher.

Meanwhile, attempting to peg certain levels of achievement on math and reading assessments to real-world or nontest measures of educational success represents the second problematic element of Duncan's project. Put simply, it is at this point entirely unclear how one might confirm the validity of student achievement data on a large scale by means of *nontest* measures in the domain at all.[1] It is further unclear that there are any large-scale nontest measures *in the domain* at all, that is, that there are national-level, nontest indicators of reading skills *specifically* with which any given reading assessment might be correlated to establish or gauge the validity of the assessments. For a limited example, one might attempt to correlate reading scores with English/Language Arts grades. But the number of confounding variables at work in this relation renders such an attempt futile. Since the giving of specific grades would depend *not only* upon the student's reading skill but also rate of homework return, performance on quizzes, and myriad other student habits, behaviors, and proclivities, such a grade cannot reasonably proxy for reading skill alone.

Koretz's point concerning validity specifically requires that one compare measurement outcomes to "nontest measures *in the domain in question.*" State exams, at the moment, assess reading, mathematics, and science. Why high school graduation rates, for example, should count as a nontest measure of any of those domains in particular (or of all of them together) requires an explanation that is simply not forthcoming from educational reformers. There appears to be an assumption at work here, according to which it is possible to generalize from "limited measures" of specific academic skill domains to the vastly wider domain of educational quality writ large. But the measures to which Duncan appeals—graduation rates, etc.—in order to buttress his validity claims with respect to the student achievement data's relation to "proficiency" are insufficient to secure that sort of validity. What "proficiency" *means*—which ought to be heard broadly, as referring to both its implications for signaling something about success in the future and also to its conceptual sense in the present—remains in need of an anchor, one that Duncan's "college and career readiness" is meant to provide.

Duncan's emphasis in insisting that we stop "lying to children" rests on the notion that we are (in the present) deceiving them about what their so-called proficiency will allow them to *do* (in the future). The college-and-career readiness criterion bears significant weight in this regard: his rhetorical tactic involves tying proficiency to the *outcomes* it is assumed to entail. Establishing the truth about proficiency represents the first step in establishing the concrete criteria according to which students ought to be measured so as to assess their relative fit with a trajectory to "be accepted to and succeed in a competitive college," to continue to use Duncan's example.

What "proficiency" in math and reading means, then, pertains directly to the eventual ability to gain admission to and succeed in college. But this is not a *discovery* about the concept of proficiency in math and reading; it is a *requirement*, something we simply assert or believe *must* be the case. "Education" in the K-12 world is supposed to prepare one for college and career, for opportunity and participation in adult society; that much is unproblematic. Framing the relation from the opposite side, however—considering relative degree of adult success to be the effect of (or causally attributable to) "education"—is more troublesome.

Success or failure in terms of "college and career" may be linked to any among multitudinous intervening factors: alcoholism, mental illness, incarceration, connections and favors, sheer chance, etc., and it is not clear that any of these are directly connected to one's *school* experience. Further, even if adult success as embodied in the "college and career" criterion were directly related to one's school experience, it does not follow that assessments of reading and math skill levels adequately proxy for this overall experience of schooling. And yet, in using various indicators of "college and career" success to generate the cut scores on math and reading assessments that will qualify one as "proficient" or not, these are precisely the assumptions in operation. This is the sense in which proficiency's entailment of college and career success is a requirement rather than a discovery.

On the basis of these assumptions about the nature of the relation between math and reading skillfulness as measured by state and national assessments, one might easily gather and compile test data from the past and compare various levels of achievement with the types of adult outcomes of the (former) students who were tested: this will generate the actuarial probabilities of a given student's achieving college-level success and higher career earnings at some point in the future. In fact, this is just the approach adopted by the Chetty research that generated so much discussion in early 2012 and that President Obama cited in his 2012 State of the Union Address.

The academic task of this research is to see whether differences in teacher quality as represented in teacher value-added are connected to differences in adult outcomes. The specific student achievement data under investigation consists in a nigh-overwhelming number of data points: "The school-district data include approximately 18 million test scores. Test scores are available for English language arts and math for students in grades 3–8 from the spring of 1989 to 2009" (Chetty, Friedman, & Rockoff, 2012, p. 60). Adult outcomes, meanwhile, are expressed like so:

> Our data on students' adult outcomes include earnings, college attendance, college quality (measured by the earnings of previous graduates of the same college), neighborhood quality (measured by the percentage of college graduates in their zip code), teenage birth rates for females (measured by claiming a dependent born when the woman was still a teenager), and retirement savings (measured by contributions to 401[k] plans) (Chetty et al., 2012, p. 60).

The appeal of linking real-world adult outcomes to specific levels of student achievement on math and reading assessments lies in its putative ability to ameliorate certain skeptical worries around existing ways of determining or revealing teacher quality. Duncan's comments on our "basically broken" system of teacher evaluation suggest that repairing it will require that we first link student achievement to adult outcomes and then link a given teacher's quality to his or her relative effect upon student achievement aggregately.

In pointing out that the link between reading and math proficiency and adult outcomes is required rather than discovered, I suggest one sense in which these skeptical worries cannot be overcome in the way Duncan imagines possible: it remains open to doubt whether addressing math and reading scores is actually equivalent to addressing "college and career readiness." It may instead be something akin to attempting to reduce a fever by wrapping the thermometer in a cold towel. The intrinsic link between the indicator and the outcome remains in doubt.

But the Chetty project in particular opens other aspects of the discussion, other ways in which the use of such measures cannot foreclose upon the skeptical worries such that these measures are inherently preferable to the modes of evaluation they are meant to replace.

There is a sort of temporal insufficiency at work, in the first place. In order to render any definition of "proficiency" available in the present, one has to tie it to something empirically available *in* the present; student test scores generated yearly answer that call. But the available method of establishing a connection between student achievement and the outcomes that Duncan has in mind involves using achievement data *from the past* and connecting it to *present* adult outcomes. What will count as a proxy measure of "proficiency" will then be established in accordance with measures of achievement that have *in the past* proven sufficient to secure the outcomes that Duncan takes to be entailed in the concept of proficiency.

Since Duncan's striking example of the benefits of using achievement data involves looking a young child in the eyes and saying something *with certainty* ("you will absolutely get there") about his or her progress toward acceptance to and success in a competitive college, one might offer two points with respect to the insufficiency of correlating past student achievement with present adult success (as indicated partially by college enrollment and quality) and taking those as offering secure and scientific warrant for making inferences about the future.

In the first place, the criteria for admittance to college is an unpredictable and moving target. In addition to the most obvious fact that federal policies, particularly in the area of equity and non-discrimination, (a) affect such criteria and (b) have a habit of changing over time, sometimes dramatically, sometimes even to the point of establishing criteria *where there were no criteria before*, colleges and universities themselves experience serious fluctuations in, for example, the number and quality of their applicants, their acceptance rates, and the achievement measures of those that it accepts. In the spring of 2012, the University of Pennsylvania, surely among the "competitive colleges" to which Duncan alludes, announced that it had accepted 12.3 percent of its applicants for the coming semester (Lee, 2012). The same article notes that in 1991, one of the years from which Chetty, et al. pull their data in order to construct teacher value-added, the same university admitted 47 percent of its applicants. Another wide-ranging study documents the same increase in selectivity across the entire range of higher education, and, significantly, also depicts a marked rise in college entrance exam scores associated with students accepted to "competitive" colleges (Bound, Hershbein, & Long, 2009). It seems clear that application number and quality—and with these the criterial benchmarks suiting any given student for admission—have changed a great deal over the 20 years that Chetty's data spans.

Further, it remains far from clear that the *value* of acceptance to and success in college—as expressed in the socioeconomic data Chetty employs—remains constant over time. A recent study of the effects of the

Great Recession on the job prospects of Americans who graduated college between 2006 and 2010 identifies significant differences in pre- and post-recession figures in terms of unemployment and underemployment (Godofsky, Zukin, Horn, & University, 2011). Considering the "career" portion of the college-and-career readiness indicates that the connection between college graduation and other indicators of adult outcomes, such as income and employment figures, fluctuates in its own right, as well.

Both of the above objections boil down to the following claim: the unpredictable changes in college admission *in general* (which the Bound article implies is linked to the shifting place of a "college education" in the American form of life) and in the labor market for college graduates are merely two of the unreckonable number of contextual features that make up the *ceteris paribus* conditions that would need to remain stable in order for the correlations to be meaningful as justificatory of the sort of decisive actions Duncan wishes to take. It is difficult to see why one ought to assume that achievement levels on math and reading assessments that have *previously* been associated with desirable adult outcomes would seamlessly continue to serve to secure those outcomes in the future.

In addition to this temporal problem with overcoming uncertainty, there is a further issue that involves, once more, agreement in form of life and the notion of the non-formalizable. In order to generate a correlation between a certain range of achievement scores and a successful "adult outcome," the large and vague idea of a "successful adult outcome" must be explicitly defined in quantitative terms. Chetty's study does just that: the researchers expect that *what a successful adult consists in* will be captured in terms of earnings, college attendance, college quality, neighborhood quality, teenage birth rates, and saving for retirement.

Without objecting to any of these as criteria of successful American adults, I wish to point out the function of the parenthetical "measured by" disclaimers in the list of criteria they explored. While it is also the case that the list of indicators itself includes an implicit ellipsis—the list above is not supposed to be, one hopes, the sum total of all characteristics of successful adults—the "measured by" caveats indicate that each individual characteristic opens up on its own list of potential "measured by" conditions.

It is worth pondering how the data (and thus the concept) pertaining to "neighborhood quality" would change, for example, if it were calculated according to the number of restaurants within walking distance instead of the percentage of college graduates inhabiting it, or by the average level of job satisfaction, or by the average home price, or any other characteristic. Neighborhood boundaries, it might also be noted, are defined in the study by zip code boundaries. Perhaps this is, in some metropolitan areas, something close to a reasonable approximation. But I think many would balk at the uncritical acceptance of the designation of Northfield, Minnesota, and all of its environs (zip code 55057), containing thousands of acres of land, two colleges, three area codes, and a population in excess of 20,000 people, as a single "neighborhood."

The truth-telling about proficiency upon which standards will be based, and thus according to which students will be assessed and test scores generated, claims to ground itself on facts about the conditions for adult success as well as facts about the nature of adult success itself: for Duncan's purposes, these are the nontest factors involved in securing the validity of measures of proficiency. Duncan extolls the role of data analysts in exposing "the research and the facts," in moving beyond "ideological statements and the surface conclusions and find[ing] out what is really happening for our children in our classrooms" (Duncan, 2009b). But it remains far from obvious that any of these facts at all escape a reliance upon radically incomplete approximations and fallible indicators of the concepts that matter.

As Wittgenstein notes at one point, "the ground keeps on giving us the illusory image of greater depth, and when we seek to reach this, we keep on finding ourselves on the old level" (Wittgenstein, 1983, VI, 31). Duncan hopes that data will prove capable of diving below what he calls "ideology" to the "facts," but closer examination of the data's derivation reveals something akin to a continued reliance on "ideology," insofar as the link between education and adult success is required rather than discovered, and insofar as the definition of adulthood success (in Chetty's study, anyway) clearly and obviously reflects a very particular (certainly ideological) view of a successful adult. Further, even if Chetty himself were to concede the incompleteness of his "neighborhood quality" measure, for example, it is entirely unclear how one might go about *completing* it, since the factors that contribute to what we mean when we talk about neighborhood quality, as Dreyfus suggests, cannot themselves "capture, but rather presuppose, our shared background practices" (Dreyfus, 1991, p. 75). For reasons, then, of both the necessary *futurity* of the actual non-test measures that will reveal the quality of teaching, and of the necessity of using proxy measures or signifiers of a certain type of "adult outcomes," the "college and career readiness" criterion simply never touches the ground.

This notion strikes at the heart of the primary claim to superiority that Duncan makes on the behalf of student achievement data. The advantage that the use of student achievement data with regard to teacher quality promises has to do with a superior ability to evade problems of uncertainty and doubt that render the other forms of discourse on good teaching insufficiently trustworthy. As we have seen, while Duncan feels comfortable attesting to the criteria of "what success looks like," such claims to immediate visibility are only authorized by virtue of something like common sense or agreements in form of life, and thus they feel somewhat inadequate when brought to bear in a justificatory capacity upon personnel, tenure, and compensation decisions.

The autobiographical and narrative accounts of good teaching made by both Neal and Duncan have greater warrant, it appears: the autobiographers are themselves successful adults and their first-hand accounts underscore the connection between the teaching of an adult in their past and their current success. However, such accounts, pertaining to teachers long since retired from the classroom, are of no use at all in the present. Still further, accepting the linkage between the teacher's practice and the example of adult success also requires a measure of trust in the perspective of another. Finally, were this not sufficient reason to doubt, such acceptance depends upon agreement in the sense of "success" that the narrator embodies.

Duncan's discourse in the lead-up to Race to the Top offers the availability of longitudinal student achievement data as an answer to these myriad problems, a way of eliminating the uncertainty that has heretofore seemed to preclude effective means of evaluating teachers. However, the extensive analysis in this chapter reveals the use of student achievement data to exhibit the *same* insufficiencies, the *same* flaws, as the other forms of discourse that appear in Duncan's rhetoric.

The data supposed to ground the "facts" of the relation between "proficiency" and "successful" adult outcomes fall prey to all of the problems with the narrative autobiography: the correlations established between past student test scores and present measures of adult success are (a) of extremely limited use in predicting *future* correlations, given the wide vagaries of chance and fortune, the ever-shifting ground of social and technological change, and so on (I focused merely upon the implications of changing criteria for college admission and the changing monetary value of a college degree, but obviously possible axes of change proliferate radically), and (b) dependent upon a given researcher scientist's "ideology" with regards to the components of adult success that he or she finds relevant (or available in the necessarily quantifiable terms) and consequently "accounts for," statistically speaking.

Most importantly, however, like both the immediate visibility claims offered by an independent observer and the autobiographical narrative of a currently-successful adult, accepting a judgment of teacher quality derived from student achievement data *also* requires the kind of unstable agreement in the concepts of success and proficiency,[2] for example, to which the use of achievement data is supposed to offer a remedy. Though student achievement data interposes an interim layer between its declarative results and the explicit reliance upon agreement in forms of life, an interim layer which can seem, at first blush, as solid as natural science, this interim layer of measures of adult success and student proficiency itself rests upon nothing more solid than the sharing of the background practices on which our senses of these concepts are grounded.

6.4 ACHIEVEMENT DATA AND THE PROBLEM OF CONCEPTUAL CHANGE

The Utopia heralded by the availability of student achievement data is pictured as a situation in which, as Duncan says, "we can look a child in the eye at the age of eight or nine or 10 and say, 'You are on track to be accepted and to succeed in a competitive university and, if you keep working hard, you will absolutely get there'" (Duncan, 2009b).

In an odd coincidence, in 1988, when I was nine years old, my own third-grade teacher knelt down by my desk and made exactly the kind of absolute claim about the future that Duncan imagines in his own scenario. I have a clear memory of this incident. She looked me right in the eye and told me (not in these exact words) that my future success depended, in part, upon improving my penmanship. She in fact said, "In high school, all of your teachers will require your essays to be done in neat cursive. They will take away points for sloppiness." That part *is* a direct quote.

By the time I entered high school in 1993, of course, my teachers required that I submit all of my essays in typewritten form. The school had a computer lab on the second floor, and a good proportion of my cohort had personal computers and printers in their homes. By the time I entered college in 1997, some of my professors insisted that I submit papers by email; by the time I entered graduate school in 2003, the university used dedicated educational software that included secure means of submitting files electronically. Over the course of a single decade, the process of academic writing and its submission moved from a world of dot-matrix printers to one of electronic file transfer.

Penmanship is hardly the only aspect of the skill and concept of writing to fall into irrelevance, if one can call it that. It is no longer as necessary as it once was to outline or to generate multiple distinct drafts as part of the writing process: erasing typos, reconstructing arguments, and moving entire paragraphs from one place to another no longer require the investment of time or energy that they once did. Over the course of fifteen years, the educational world—to say nothing of most workplaces—simply ceased to accept handwritten works as finished writing products; the process of writing itself has changed. In my academic life, from elementary school to the present, I have never once submitted any sort of written assignment in cursive. My own penmanship remains, at best, questionable.

Applying Duncan's standard of truth-telling, the obvious conclusion to draw from my experience is that my third-grade teacher *lied* to me about what success in high school and college would require. Duncan touts student achievement data as a *remedy* to this problem, as something that would provide teachers (or parents, or administrators—anyone with access to the data) with the knowledge necessary to "be honest" and "stop lying to children." In the above example, however, one confronts the weakness of the available student data relative to its appointed task of predicting the skills, aptitudes, and proficiency levels in each that successful adulthood will require, even in the short term. Student achievement data simply cannot solve *this* problem of knowledge. My third-grade teacher was doubtless relying upon common sense and twenty-plus years of experience in the classroom in order to guide her pupil to attend to some of the conditions upon which scholastic success would depend. She was incorrect: whatever successes and failures I have experienced, academically, have been entirely irrespective of my penmanship. But student achievement data simply could do no better in her situation.

It is also especially worth noting that she was *not* incorrect in suggesting that *writing* would prove crucial to academic success. She looked at my third-grade writing and judged it to lack proficiency: whatever the quality of my sentence structure, my writing was at points, apparently, at least difficult to read, thanks to my poor penmanship. Penmanship was *part of* the skill of writing; it was explicitly one of the factors upon which one's work was graded, along with grammar and style.

Thanks to the re-emergence of writing as part of state-level assessment protocols, however, students once again have to generate timed writing pieces by hand. Tennessee's scoring rubric, according to which students' writing proficiency is rated,[3] discriminates among levels of proficiency in terms of rhetorical organization, supporting evidence, sentence variety, "facility in the use of language," and the number of errors in usage, grammar, and sentence structure. "Illegibility" does indeed arise on the rubric, but only as a means of *entirely disqualifying* an essay from evaluation itself; in this capacity, it is listed as a criterion among "blank or refusal," "off-topic," and "written predominantly in another language." In order to rise to a grader's attention at all, an essay's illegibility has to render it akin to a blank sheet of paper or something in another language. Handwriting no longer spans a value spectrum from "extremely poor" to "excellent." It is no longer among the qualities of writing *to be evaluated*; it is a now a background condition *for the evaluation of writing* itself. Penmanship either makes the essay's reading possible, or else it does not. It no longer admits of variation beyond that minimal standard. The word "cursive" does not appear at all.

In drawing out the differences in the requirements for writing visible among what my third-grade teacher told me in 1988, what my high school required in 1993, what my undergraduate institution demanded in 1998, what my graduate school made possible in 2003, and what the state of Tennessee takes as demonstrative of writing's proficiency in the present, one sees something like an evolution of the *concept* of writing itself. This conceptual fluidity makes itself visible by means of the changing criteria according to which writing's quality is judged, criteria directly tied to the sense of what writing, as a skill domain, *is*. Technological developments in word processing and network connectivity, I suggest, have led to a separation between the skill of "writing" itself and the skill of "letter- and word-formation" by means of physically inscribing a mark onto one surface or another. Even in timed-writing situations that *require* such mark-making skill, that skill is only taken to apply to the concept of "writing" as a necessary condition, not itself something subject to evaluation.

Student achievement data, as a provider of *uniquely* justifiable warrant with regard to the future—and therefore as a credible basis on which to evaluate student progress and teacher quality in the present—founders on precisely this sort of conceptual, and therefore criterial, change. "Reading," "writing," and "mathematics" have claims to something like permanence in American academics as skill domains related to successful adulthood, however one defines the latter. But none of these skills are themselves *conceptually* stable over time, even over the short period of a single student's academic life. Neither is this phenomenon limited to the domain of writing. To continue to use Tennessee as an example, the state's reading standards for grades 6–12 currently include the skills of "previewing and reviewing print *and non-print* texts" (emphasis added) and "understanding visual representations" (*Reading in the Content Area*, 2012), neither of which skill one can imagine necessary apart from a world of prevalent digital media. What we take reading, writing, and even mathematics to *consist in* changes along with our worlds at large.

Student achievement data as represented in test scores, as we have seen in Chapter 1, requires an *explicit definition* of a given skill in order to generate a measure of a given student's proficiency in that skill area. But the generation of an explicit definition requires the freezing of relevance, a problem that I discussed in earlier chapters with regard to the failures of Artificial Intelligence and a "best practices" approach to teacher development. The problem with the freezing of relevance in the area of measuring student achievement has directly to do with the *manifest fact* that relevance even in such seemingly stable domains as reading, writing, and mathematics remains fluid. What was taken as *relevant* to evaluating the skill of writing in 1989 (the first year of Chetty's longitudinal data) had become in fact *irrelevant* to such evaluation by 2009 (the last year of Chetty's data). Statistical methods of smoothing out differences in tests over time cannot cope with this type of variation; *the domain* has changed.

The requirement for an explicit definition of proficiency in a given skill domain at a particular point in time significantly limits the predictive utility of student achievement data: my third-grade teacher may have been wrong in believing that cursive was necessary to my academic success, but in this capacity achievement data could not have offered a corrective. Duncan's notion of an integrated data system that will enable a person to honestly tell a third-grader whether or not he or she is on track for success at a competitive university cannot provide the degree of certainty about the future with which he associates the concepts of "truth" and "lying."

I would not feel comfortable claiming that my third-grade teacher lied to me in telling me that I needed to work on my handwriting in order to succeed at the high school level; I would, however, freely say that she was wrong. The distinction might be expressed in terms of her (perceived) ability to predict the future. All of her past experience in the classroom with students probably similar to me led her to the incorrect conclusion about the relevant writing skills to which I should attend. Duncan's claim about the possibilities afforded by this newfound wealth of student achievement data is that future conditions will be at last predictable, next to which standard, of course, one might really *be* in a position to deceive or not. The fact of conceptual change over time, however, belies such utopian claims. Using student achievement data fails to solve the problems that crop up when relying upon fallible human judgment.

I noted in an earlier section that I wished to focus upon the *similarities* shared between the forms of data-driven teacher evaluation that Duncan's Race to the Top initiatives propose and the ones that such methods are intended to supplant. This chapter has sought to highlight the degree to which *what* one takes as indicative of educational achievement and good teaching has ineluctably to do with Wittgensteinian (or grammatical) criteria, as Cavell calls them, which is to say the *use* of the concept in everyday life, the concept's relation to other concepts. The implication of a causal relation between particular teacher quality (either in terms of particular behaviors or according to contribution to score growth in a particular domain) and particular future student outcomes (in any of the terms of Chetty's research, for example) falls apart on the encounter with temporal criterial change.

While one might make the argument that the future will not be *so* radically different from the past as to dampen the case for taking former correlations to be roughly indicative of future ones, three objections arise to this line of thought. In the first place, the future as a whole does not have to shift a great deal in order to radically destabilize all sorts of concepts[4]—one does not, for example, have to imagine that the concept of adult outcomes will in the future be *unrelated* to income in order to concede that the particular skills necessary to achieve high incomes in a socially exemplary way will change, a shift that will certainly reorder—unpredictably—the relevance and place of each skill, disposition, and talent in the practical cosmos.

Secondly, and relatedly, even conceding the unlikeliness of a radically different world, the use of former correlations as stand-ins for the future straightforwardly discounts the possibility of anything new arising at all—this, I take it, is similar to my earlier argument against adopting a "best practices" approach to teacher development. Strictly defining skill domains and concepts in the present (or based on the past) unwarrantedly restricts recognition of actual quality in the future as the conditions for the demonstration of such quality invariably arise.

In the third and final place, one perhaps ought to concede the merits of using student achievement data in measures of teacher quality based on precisely the claim that former correlations will likely be roughly similar to future ones. But having conceded this fact, it is difficult to see the warrant for Duncan's *prioritizing* of these measures to the exclusion of all others, his assumption that with the availability of student achievement data we have solved a great mystery and stand on the threshold of knowledge. If a ragged basis for rough estimation (albeit a highly technical and mathematically demanding basis) is, in the end, what the use of student achievement data offers, then it is welcome, it would seem, to join the existing chorus of evaluation protocols, as this is what they offer, too. But achievement data seems to merit no *special* place therein.

Duncan suggests, and scholars echo him in this, that the use of student achievement data puts us in the position to say something relatively certain about teacher quality, something objective that perhaps approaches truth, and that, in this respect, it is a *new* development—progress, one might say. The use of student achievement data offers a *general* view of a teacher's impact on students, which autobiographical narratives cannot; and it holds out the promise of predicting the future in terms of adult outcomes, which third-person observations dare not. But its generality cannot speak to the experience of any singular student, which other methods can do; its notion of what a teacher's "impact" might consist in remains much more restricted than the concept available to existing methods, as the Mrs. Grady narrative shows; and its ability to see the future remains frustratingly—merely—human in its scope. That it offers something that other methodologies cannot means that it ought to speak up; that its limitations are real means that it ought to raise its hand like everyone else.

NOTES

1. This is an important caveat: The problem Duncan seeks to address is operative at the state and federal level, of which he treats the local as a species, I think. It would seem to be relatively easy for a given teacher, at the end of a given year, to assess the validity of the reading data for his or her class based on a great deal of personal experience with the students' lived abilities to read. But when adopting the long-distance gaze of the state or federal official constrained by the absence of personal, daily contact with the data points, as it were, one must seek out other *measurement instruments* that would pertain to the same skill domain. But the federal or state official is hamstrung by the fact that, as far as nontest demonstrations of proficiency in *just that* skill domain go, there simply aren't any. If one *must* ultimately ground a question of validity in nontest measures, people at the state and federal level are simply *in the dark*.
2. I've been wondering throughout this section whether or not I'll ever get around to pointing out explicitly the dramatic gap opened up between what Duncan appears to attribute to "proficiency"—which, since it entails so much in the way of holistic future consequences, cannot properly be said to be limited to *a single* skill domain at all—and the concept of "proficiency" as Koretz and psychometricians generally use the term. Proficiency in the latter sense would simply be proficiency at *reading*, for example, which would hardly seem to entail overall *academic* success: high GPA, participation in extracurricular activities, lucid reasoning, and so on. It is easy to imagine a very good reader who is not a particularly good student. In any case, the point is that Duncan's use of "proficiency" itself is extremely problematic, but I leave that for another researcher.
3. Tennessee's is an iteration of the six-trait writing rubric, which is common to most state assessments: thus these criteria generalize beyond Tennessee's particular example.

4. The sneakily hilarious recent film remake of *21 Jump Street* provides an unexpected example. Only five years removed from high school, the former prom king returns as an undercover cop to discover (correctly, as it is in real life) that everything he knows about what it takes to "succeed" socially in high school has changed. The place of violence in masculine homosocial relationships, the role of political knowledge in social situations . . . all of it leads Channing Tatum's character to feel suddenly that he cannot find his feet in this school, this place that for all the world is *just* like the school he ruled five years prior. That these scenes function as comedic at all speaks to the recognizability of the depicted phenomena.

REFERENCES

Bound, J., Hershbein, B., & Long, B. T. (2009). Playing the Admissions Game: Student Reactions to Increasing College Competition. *The Journal of Economic Perspectives*, 23(4), 119–146. Retrieved from http://www.jstor.org/stable/27740558

Cannell, J. J. (1988). Nationally Normed Elementary Achievement Testing in America's Public Schools: How All 50 States Are Above the National Average. *Educational Measurement: Issues and Practice*, 7(2), 5–9. doi:10.1111/j.1745-3992.1988.tb00424.x

Cavell, S. (1979). *The Claim of Reason*. New York: Oxford University Press.

Chetty, R., Friedman, J. N., & Rockoff, J. E. (2012). Great Teaching: Measuring Its Effects on Students' Future Earnings. *Education Next*, 12(3), 58–64.

Dreyfus, H. L. (1991). *Being-in-the-world: a commentary on Heidegger's Being and Time, Division I* (p. xiv, 370 p.). Cambridge, Mass.: MIT Press.

Duncan, A. (2009a). Partners in Reform. (Education, Ed.). Retrieved from http://www2.ed.gov/news/speeches/2009/07/07022009.html

Duncan, A. (2009b). Robust Data Gives Us the Roadmap to Reform. U.S. Department of Education. Retrieved from http://www2.ed.gov/news/speeches/2009/06/06082009.html

Duncan, A. (2009c). Teacher Preparation: Reforming the Uncertain Profession. U.S. Department of Education. Retrieved from http://www.ed.gov/news/speeches/teacher-preparation-reforming-uncertain-profession

Duncan, A. (2009d). Turning Around the Bottom Five Percent. U.S. Department of Education. Retrieved from http://www.ed.gov/news/speeches/turning-around-bottom-five-percent

Glazerman, S., Goldhaber, D., Loeb, S., Raudenbush, S., Staiger, D., Whitehurst, G. J., . . . Quality, B. C. T. G. on T. (2011). *Passing Muster: Evaluating Teacher Evaluation Systems*. Washington D.C. Brookings Institutie. Retrieved from http://www.brookings.edu/reports/2011/0426_evaluating_teachers.aspx

Godofsky, J., Zukin, C., Horn, C. Van, & University, R. (2011). *Unfulfilled Expectations: Recent College Graduates Struggle in a Troubled Economy*. John J. Heldrich Center for Workforce Development.

Kane, T. J., & Staiger, D. O. (2008). Estimating Teacher Impacts on Student Achievement. *NBER Working Paper No. 14607*.

Kane, T. J., Taylor, E. S., Tyler, J. H., & Wooten, A. L. (2011). Identifying Effective Classroom Practices Using Student Achievement Data. *Journal of Human Resources*, 46(3), 587–613.

Koretz, D. M. (2002). Limitations in the Use of Achievement Tests as Measures of Educators' Productivity. *The Journal of Human Resources*, 37(4), 752–777. Retrieved from http://www.jstor.org/stable/3069616

Lee, L. (2012). Admit Rate Holds Steady at 12.3 Percent. *Daily Pennsylvanian*. Philadelphia, PA. Retrived from http://www.thedp.com/article/2012/03/admit_rate_holds_steady_at_12.3_percent

Lemov, D. (2010). *Teach Like a Champion*. San Fancisco: John Wiley & Sons.

Linn, R. L., Graue, M. E., & Sanders, N. M. (1990). Comparing State and District Test Results to National Norms: The Validity of Claims That "Everyone Is Above Average." *Educational Measurement: Issues and Practice*, 9(3), 5–14. doi:10.1111/j.1745-3992.1990.tb00372.x

NCTQ. (2011). *State of the States: Trends and Early Lessons on Teacher Evaluation and Effectiveness Policies*. Washington D.C.: National Council on Teacher Quality.

Rivkin, S. G., Hanushek, E. A., & Kain, J. F. (2005). Teachers, Schools, and Academic Achievement. *Econometrica*, 73(2), 417–458. doi:10.1111/j.1468-0262.2005.00584.x

Shepard, L. A. (1990). Inflated Test Score Gains: Is the Problem Old Norms or Teaching the Test? *Educational Measurement: Issues and Practice*, 9(3), 15–22. doi:10.1111/j.1745-3992.1990.tb00374.x

Wittgenstein, L. (1983). *Remarks on the Foundations of Mathematics*. Cambridge: MIT Press.

7 The Non-Formalizable and Teacher Evaluation

The foregoing chapter, in its attention to the conceptual areas that student achievement data cannot adequately represent or predict, might be taken as an extended exegesis of what Diane Ravitch means when she says that "tests are not scientific instruments, like a thermometer. They are social constructions whose questions and answers are written by fallible human beings" (Ravitch, 2013, p. 264). Ravitch proceeds to underscore the above claim by referencing the work of test-industry veteran Todd Farley; his critique focuses on the "hourly workers who grade standardized tests," the "pressure" they face in rushing to complete their work, and the "arbitrary decisions that determine how they grade student answers" (Ravitch, 2013, p. 264). Her emphasis here lodges a complaint that hinges upon something like Fogelin's "paradox of interpretation": tests cannot be what they purport to be—scientific instruments—because "fallible" human judgments are involved in both their creation and their scoring.

To the extent that reformers such as Duncan interpret the 99 percent statistic as evidence of the failure or weakness of human judgment, then, Ravitch's argument is sufficient to show that no escape from such fallible judgment is actually on offer in testing regimes, either at the development end or the evaluation stage. But her critique of "fallible human beings"—the tone in which it is offered, that is, as though only something based on an *infallible* calculus could count as true measurement, significantly overstates the problem of relying upon human judgment; by taking up Duncan's premise that humanity's fallibility is something that must be overcome or transcended in order to achieve true knowledge of student learning or teacher quality, she risks disqualifying all available forms of evaluation as such. In that, she shares something of the metaphysical picture of measurement with Duncan, one that permits Duncan to argue that in the absence of infallible metrics embodied in "the research and the facts" (Duncan, 2009) there can be no such thing as measurement or knowledge or evaluation at all.[1]

But on the other hand, Ravitch holds up two alternative models of evaluating teachers—models not predicated upon defining teacher quality in terms of growth in student achievement scores: the Peer Assistance and Review program in Maryland and New York City's Performance Standards

Consortium. In documenting the success of these programs, Ravitch points to both the laudable educational outcomes—as indicated in the criteria to which Duncan also points, such as high school graduation rates, etc.—in the New York case and to the number of "low-performing teachers" who were fired for "failure to improve" (Ravitch, 2013, pp. 271–272) in the Maryland example.

Duncan's arguments in the speeches anticipating Race to the Top tie the 99 percent statistic to an epistemological lack in terms of teacher quality, which itself is tied to a further epistemological lack regarding "what works" in teacher practice, or what leads to successful educational outcomes. Ravitch's models show that the 99 percent statistic cannot *simply* be the result of any failure remediable by purely epistemological means, as no epistemological weakness seems to preclude evaluative success in her examples; and she also shows that it is not so necessary to overcome uncertainty in terms of "what works" as the turn to achievement data would suggest. If the previous chapter might be taken as an extended gloss on Ravitch's assertion that "tests are not scientific instruments, like a thermometer," then this chapter, and the one following it, might be understood as an extended gloss on Ravitch's insistence that "accountability should be turned into responsibility" (Ravitch, 2013, p. 273)—what it means, why it is necessary, and how it can be achieved.

7.1 ONTIC AND ONTOLOGICAL MEASUREMENT

The 99 percent statistic, whatever else it is taken to mean, certainly does evidence a failure of responsibility, that is, a refusal to respond to the call or insistence to tell good teachers from bad ones. Race to the Top's solution is to guarantee responsibility by removing it from fallible human hands, whose fallibility, it is imagined, or whose intellectual insufficiency, has made such responsibility impossible. I will argue that this maneuver in fact has the very opposite effect, precluding the possibility of anything like responsibility or responsiveness in reporting on teacher quality. Ravitch's invocation of the two models of evaluation programs above is sufficient to show that the failure of responsibility signified in the 99 percent statistic is not in itself caused by epistemological weaknesses: the weeding out of underperforming teachers, a consequence and criterion of what Duncan has meant by getting serious about improving the teaching profession, proceeds apace in Maryland, and on precisely the basis of human judgment.

But neither is the weeding out of underperforming teachers *simply* achieved by abdicating to student achievement data. Duncan and other reformers have imagined that turning to the unbiased facts, based on student achievement data, would enable principals and districts to cull the teacher corps of its least effective members; and indeed, in states such as Tennessee and Delaware, the significance of the weight given to teacher value-added is meant emphatically to eliminate subjectivity as far as possible. In fact, however, tethering student achievement data to teacher evaluation has not had the dramatic effects that ought to have followed. Once teacher evaluations determinable according to student achievement data were released, Jenny Anderson of the *New York Times* reports that "in Florida, 97 percent of teachers were deemed effective or highly effective in the most recent evaluations. In Tennessee, 98 percent of teachers were judged to be 'at expectations.' In Michigan, 98 percent of teachers were rated effective or better" (Anderson, 2013).

I have quoted Cavell before as praising Wittgenstein for having "discover[ed] the threat or temptation of skepticism in such a way that efforts to solve it continue its work of denial" (Cavell, 1990, p. 23). The turn to achievement data in matters of educational evaluation performs just the "work of denial" pictured above: in denying a space for the human, measures of teacher value-added purport to both objectivity and universal significance, or something like truth. Ravitch's arguments that tests are "social constructions" simply shows that the human is not in fact denied or omitted after all. Anderson's article brings this out differently, by reminding readers that the particular number, the student-growth cut score, by which teachers will be rated "effective" or "highly effective," must still be defined by Ravitch's "fallible human beings," which raises again the specter of NCLB's "race to the bottom": "effectiveness" is the new "proficiency," threatened with conceptual vacuity resulting from the (inherent) manipulability of the definition, a definition that is in part a necessary consequence of the requirement for definition under the technical concept of good teaching.

It was assumed that teacher evaluation protocols reliant upon observations were overly lenient or lacked rigor, and that by bringing achievement data to bear, the evaluation outcomes would be both rigorous and accurate. The opposite has been the case: "'We had three or four teachers that were rated as 'needs improvement' on the observation, but due to changes in the cut scores, they were all bumped up to effective,' Dr. Christopher Small, the principal [of Springwood Elementary], said" (Anderson, 2013). Despite the ability of direct observation to detect teaching of low quality, the "changes in the cut scores" negotiated at the district or state level generate evaluations that inflate the rating of certain teachers. The achievement data is directly implicated in evaluations' failures to tell the truth, as it were.

The above quotation, as well as common sense, suggests that the sort of failure of responsibility embodied in the 99 percent statistic was neither attributable to nor solvable by epistemological means. If teacher evaluations *did not* differentiate among teachers in terms of quality, it is not at all clear that this is because they lacked anything like knowledge or certainty. A newfound reliance on student achievement data represents another and more virulent sort of failure of responsibility precisely because it removes the possibility of responsibility as such: in the view of the locally-situated principal quoted above, the test measures overestimate the quality of certain teachers, but, outside of the reporter who comes asking, there is no one to whom he might raise this objection, no one capable of correcting the error. Except as explicitly defined in terms of a weighted percentage of an evaluative total, the human voice is omitted from the process entirely.

Because reformers imagine that it has been the impurity of human subjectivity or bias that has been responsible for keeping underperforming teachers in the classroom, purifying the process by (supposedly) removing human judgment entirely from the equation has presented itself as the obvious solution. That such purification has not solved the problem is a further indication that the *nature* of the problem has been misidentified. Not only is this purity unachieved, as the "changes in cut scores" make plain, but it is also in principle unachievable, as Chapter 4, in particular, serves to show.

This means, among other things, that the concept of measurement in the realms of teacher quality and student learning alike is, to a certain degree, confused or restricted. The reformers' view of measurement seems limited to the sense of comparing a given object of investigation (say, a tree or a pig or a 40-yard dash or a student's reading ability) to some *absolute* and external measure (say, a meter stick—pegged to a definition of length in terms of the natural property of the speed of light—or the cut-score for proficiency, which is based upon no such universal constant). Robert Crease's wonderful book on the history of measurement, however, describes the millennia-long search for unchanging, naturally-occurring physical constants that one might use to standardize all physical measurement—a system of *absolute* measures—and it concludes with worthwhile thoughts on Race to the Top's implicit view of measurement.

Duncan's particular appeals to student achievement data, that is, as solving an epistemological problem of knowledge or justification, are involved in a project that Crease calls "ontic measurement, after the word applied by philosophers to real independently existing objects or properties," which, as he says, "establishes that one property is greater than or less than another, or it assigns a number to how much of a given property something possesses" (Crease, 2011, p. 269). Duncan's quest to ground the concept of "proficiency" on the criterion of "college and career readiness," a quest echoed in Chetty's research, requires that "college and career readiness" *be* such a "real independently existing . . . property," a property existing independently, that is, of something like agreement in form of life. We have persistently seen, if it were not obvious in itself, that "college and career readiness"—to say nothing of "proficiency" or even "reading and writing"—is no such thing.[2]

But Crease discusses a second type of measurement, as well: "ontological measurement." His describes ontological measurement like so:

> This is the kind of measurement that Plato said is guided by a standard of the "fitting" or the "right.". . . . Ontological measurement

connects us with something trans-human, something *in* which we participate, not something *over* which we command. While in ontic measurement we compare some object to another object exterior to it, in ontological measurement we compare ourselves, or something we have produced, with something in which our being is implicated. (Crease, 2011, p. 269)

In tethering the notion of ontological measurement explicitly to something that he calls the *trans-human*, Crease gestures to the region that Duncan's attempts at bringing student achievement data to bear seem unable to penetrate, and something that further recalls the notion of agreement in form of life, which is also referenced—via Heidegger's terminology—in its connection to "something in which our being is implicated." Race to the Top's teacher evaluation protocols require an explicit standard, explicit definitions of "student learning" and "teacher quality" against which to measure. The ways in which we have seen the process of explicit definition distort the conceptual terrain to which it wishes to speak reveal the serious limitations of ontic measurement in the realm of educational evaluation.

It is nonetheless obvious that one *can* generate ontic measures of teacher quality and student achievement to some extent: constructing standards, norming test instruments, making statistical inferences, and calculating teacher value-added are all evidence of the possibility of using ontic measurement in the domain of education. Even if one perceives the insufficiencies of such ontic measurement, and even if such a perception might express a wish to deny the place or appropriateness of such forms of measurement, one would still want to recognize the real need of which the recourse to student achievement data is an expression. In the same way, given what is surely felt to be an insufficient basis for generality in simply comparing a given teacher to some paradigmatic "example," as ontological measurement would involve, one would also do well to recognize the real need to which ontological measurement speaks, a need wholly unaddressed by means of ontic measurement. The mistake, I am suggesting, may be in taking these two needs to be ultimately assimilable or reducible, one to the other.

At the heart of the issue expressed in Duncan's laudatory view of using student achievement data in the evaluation of teachers lies a certain need for standardization, such that officials at the federal level might compare 4th-grade teachers in Alaska with their counterparts in Connecticut (or, say, the top 30,000 teachers in California to the bottom 30,000). For Race to the Top, such standardization is securable *only* by means of establishing or constructing—not to say discovering—a purportedly ontic property or concept that stands over and outside of the educative endeavor itself, and one against which matters requiring evaluation can be compared: this would be a picture of the property of "teacher effectiveness" as modeled upon a property like mass or distance. A failure of teacher evaluation protocols to seek out and employ some ontic measure of "effectiveness" seems once more to invite, if not necessitate, the sort of failure of responsibility expressed in the New Teacher Project's 99 percent statistic. Addressing the need to get serious about evaluation, on this picture, requires the certainty of an ontic metric whose absence signifies the lack of seriousness requiring amelioration.

Crease, however, speaks of ontological measurement as though it, too, were standardizable on grounds simply *other* than the sort of universal constant to which Duncan aspires. Crease continues in his description of ontological measurement:

> Is this only "metaphorical" measuring? It is comparison against a standard. Placed alongside the fitting or the right example, our actions—and even our *selves*—do not have enough being; there is more to be. . . . Ontological measuring involves no specific property, in a literal-minded respect, for it involves nothing quantitative. Calculate all we please, we will never produce this kind of measurement. No method can lead us to it. (Crease, 2011, p. 270)

It is not at all obvious that teaching and learning are the kinds of things describable, ultimately, in terms of the properties of light or energy; and yet the ontological standard to which we compare ourselves is nevertheless standardized according to, as he calls it, something "trans-human," something not unlike agreement in form of life. He in fact refers explicitly to Heidegger's notion of the "setup" (*Gestell*), by which Heidegger means, as Crease notes, "that the environment in which we measure is not neutral" (Crease, 2011, p. 273). This idea of the "setup" is also what Dreyfus refers to as the presupposed referential whole, and what Wittgenstein refers to in describing the "stage-setting" required to so much as ask for the name of an object.

Chetty and his colleagues, as I have explored, take a number of factors to be indicative of adult outcomes, such as the quality of one's neighborhood and one's fiduciary habits; these are the criteria that they approximate with quantitative measures, such as the percentage of college graduates within a given zip code and one's contributions to a 401(k) plan, respectively. The examples from which Chetty presumably takes or extracts his criteria for success in the first place seem inarguably to be examples of successful American adults, that is, American adults that one would take as exemplary, worthy of emulation. But as I have already explored at length, it simply does not follow that this exemplary nature is decomposable into the features that each example shares in common, even if the measurable proxies of each of these features were flawless. One might recall, at this point, Wittgenstein's assertion that "if a person hasn't yet got the *concepts*, I'll teach him to use the words by means of *examples* and *exercises*. And when I do this, I do not communicate less to him than I know myself" (*PI* §208).

Crease's point in referencing ontological measurement is that the rationalist discomfort—wherein to lack an *inhuman* or ontic measure is to lack the capacity to make meaning from any measure as such—is unwarranted:

what Crease will refer to as the "ontic measurelessness" of ontological measurement does not amount to measurelessness as such, or require denying the existence of a meaningful standard. To acknowledge the axis of the *in*-which that ontological measurement registers, the trans-human normativity, is also to acknowledge and respond to the phenomenological fact that changes in shared background practices or ways of being in the world, in light of which ostensibly stable skill domains are what they are, bring about criterial changes in those skill domains themselves, rendering ontically-aspirational measures derived or constructed at any particular point in historical time obsolete at a certain point, in addition to their inherent flaw of being, by necessity, radically incomplete.

Duncan's view of measurement, wherein he claims a privileged position for the use of student achievement data, requires something external or abstract in order to justify value claims. Just as the rationalist-assumption requirements for teacher practice have proven unable to account for or reproduce skillful behavior in Chapters 2–4, the ability of external or abstract standards and criteria to successfully dispel doubt with respect to the value claims about students and teachers it purports to justify has been rendered dubious at best in the previous chapter.

The arguments against each of these abstract representations of skilled practice and criteria of success boil down to the same form: while it is possible to *produce* serviceable versions of those abstractions (to codify teacher knowledge and best practices, to generate proficiency cut scores based on lived practice and experience), any attempts to reverse the relationship and *generate* skilled practice or *define* skill domains and outcome criteria by means of those abstractions, once codified, fail to respond adequately to ontological-level changes, evolutions in criteria, alterations in the whole of a given shared form of life that each domain and outcome presuppose.

The previous chapter has detailed the ways in which even the ostensibly ontic forms of measuring teachers available by means of the statistical parsing of student achievement data fail to provide the sort of certainty associated with the ontic, upon which Duncan and others rest arguments about these methods' unique access to what he calls "the facts." Thus, the various predictive and justificatory claims that Duncan makes on the behalf of these methods and this data do not stand in contrast to the means of evaluating teachers that have been available to the profession previously: the ontic metrics expressible in terms of student achievement still require a certain intervention in order to express the "teacher effectiveness" connected to future "adult success," and these interventions will of necessity be ontological in nature. In part, Duncan's calls for multiple measures of educational success might be understood as an acquiescence to this fact.

This, the most important conclusion to draw from these considerations, recalls the problems addressed in Chapter 1. A major aspect of the endeavor in the first chapter of this book has to do with uncovering the way that, contrary to Duncan's many citations of the need for "multiple measures" of teacher quality and student achievement, all of the measures that wind up in public policy are either derived from or responsive to state assessments of reading and writing. The multiple measures of educational quality are better characterized as various iterations of the same limited version of quality, one defined purely in terms of student achievement data.

If student achievement data were similar to the speed of light in terms of representing a natural constant—if "student achievement" itself were somehow definable in terms of a natural constant—the utter reliance on the accuracy of this student achievement data would pose no problems. The intervening chapters, however, have drawn out both the ways in which the skill domains of reading, writing, and teaching resist description in such naturalistic terms, and also the ways in which they depend on agreement in forms of life and shared understandings of being for the normativity and recognizability that in fact exists.

It is, then, not the *existence* of student achievement data, the *giving and taking* of standardized tests, which represents the major objection to the teacher evaluation protocols encouraged by Race to the Top. Rather, it is the epistemological and axiological *status* arrogated by policy-makers to such achievement data that calls for an objection.

In devising a teacher evaluation system heavily, even preponderantly, reliant upon measures of teacher quality derived from student achievement data, no state has managed in fact to escape reliance upon the ontological axis of measurement, upon the concerns, biases, and weaknesses of Ravitch's "fallible human beings." But in speaking of student achievement data as unproblematically revelatory of "what works," or "what teachers need to do to teach and how to teach," as Duncan has tended to do, one forecloses upon the ability of any *other* voice to contribute value judgments or to raise objections. The measures themselves may not escape any reliance upon shared forms of life, but in official policy, such reliance is denied, avoided, deflected, or disowned.

7.2 THE CALL FOR THE USE OF ACHIEVEMENT DATA AND ITS IMPLICATIONS

Duncan's assumptions that the use of student achievement data represents a muscular response to certain epistemological weakness by anchoring or justifying claims pertaining to teacher quality invest undue faith in the predictive and reflective powers of ontic measurement in the domain of education generally. Yet it remains the case that Race to the Top's turn to this sort of measurement and the data it produces emerges in response to specific needs. In particular, as I proposed briefly in Chapter 1, the interventions of such data respond to one or more of three felt inadequacies surrounding questions around teacher quality: an anxiety that no one *knows* which teachers demonstrate real quality and which are abject failures; a fear that no one has sufficient grounds to *report* (with consequences) which teachers perform at a high level and which do not; or simply a suspicion that no one *is telling* the good teachers from the poor ones.

Thus far, I have sought to highlight the fact that using student achievement data in order to establish *knowledge* of good teaching cannot meaningfully improve upon existing, even informal, means immediately available to students, colleagues, administrators, or other local observers. The indeterminacy of the eventual world for which one prepares students restricts the validity claims of achievement data on the one hand, while on the other, the reductions of the domain addressed by an ordinary sense of good teaching to the merely technical realm of improving test scores in highly-specific, artificially-formalized academic skill domains diminishes the strength of the student achievement data's grip on the construct it seeks to measure.

With respect to the ability to justify claims about teacher quality and student learning, achievement data faces the same impasses enumerated above and thus cannot secure the basis presumed requisite to any ability to report with accuracy on teacher quality. Where the criteria to which Duncan and Olly Neal appeal in perceiving educational quality either immediately or with authoritative hindsight seem unable to latch onto either the type of relevance to the present day or a claim to broad generalizability, the claims grounded in student achievement data fare no better in addressing these inadequacies, although they fail in the opposite way, or from the opposite direction.

The fact of conceptual and criterial change over time precludes the possibility of accurately defining teacher quality in terms of adult outcomes: we have too little idea what specifically will come together in comprising a "successful adult" and therefore what skills will be necessary to attain that which makes up this concept. Even allowing that reading, writing, and math will almost certainly factor into adult success proves inadequate to the purpose: that which these basic skills require is also susceptible to change along with the worlds in which they will have their purchase.[3] This is not to say, once more, that such measures have *no* value; that would be akin to claiming that the Neal and Duncan autobiographical narratives reveal nothing about the criteria of good teaching. It is rather to say that achievement data cannot overcome the perceived insufficiencies of the sort of evaluation that implicitly undergirds those Duncan and Neal narratives. Yet overcoming those insufficiencies is precisely what seems to recommend the turn to achievement data.

Despite, then, the fact that student achievement data claims to access the "facts" that will enable "honesty" in reporting, it remains unclear that what data-based reporting can offer significantly improves upon any existing means of ascribing quality to a given teacher, including the autobiographical narratives offered by Duncan and Neal. But beyond *knowing* good teaching and *justifying* claims pertaining to it, there remains the third possibility to which the turn to achievement data might be addressed: the suspicion that no one *is telling* good teaching from bad, and that data's intervention will compel such telling.

This third possibility seems at first glance the least likely of the candidates to account for the anxiety that data addresses. But Duncan's words on the matter, which I reproduce below, suggest that the urgency of Race to the Top may require *simply* getting serious about the need to report on teacher quality, irrespective of what particular kind of epistemological failure is taken to underlie the refusal to differentiate among teachers on the basis of quality.

The unspoken and therefore unsupported suggestion of equivalence between using student achievement data as the justificatory and epistemological foundation for claims about teacher quality and something like a general "getting serious" about evaluation requires that we explore the notions of "getting serious" and "courage" at work here. Says Duncan,

> There's so much opportunity for growth and progress in this area. We have the money and we have the technology. The biggest barrier, the only remaining barrier in my mind is whether we have the courage. It takes courage to expose our weaknesses with a truly transparent data system. It takes courage to admit our flaws and take steps to address them. (Duncan, 2009b)

While Duncan associates the opportunity at hand with the availability of (new) money and (new) technology, which will enable a "truly transparent data system," the point of emphasis in these closing remarks pertain to the courage "to admit our flaws and take steps to address them." Given what I have called the "disowning" of the ontological entanglements represented in the need to technically define "effectiveness" and "adult outcomes," it is not clear that an admission of "our flaws"—indeed, that any *self*-exposure—is entailed in reporting teacher quality through the use of achievement data; this is a point that I will raise again later. But whatever else it may represent, the call for the creation of a "transparent data system" certainly amounts to a resolution to tell *something*, to provide a vocal response to the sort of evaluative vacuum signified by Duncan's repeated citation of the 99 percent statistic. The bald-faced absurdity of *that* fact requires a response. *That* fact provides the warrant in light of which data-based reporting is offered in an ameliorative capacity.

Another way of stating the above is to say that Duncan's speeches regarding the role of achievement data in teacher evaluation address a present insufficiency with what Cavell, after Wittgenstein, would call bringing explanations to an end. The 99 percent statistic reveals a failure in this regard, a failure of responsibility, and specifically a failure of the responsibility for satisfactorily putting questions of any given teacher's quality to rest. How to exercise or fulfill this responsibility then becomes precisely the question.

Duncan and the reformers generally take it that achievement data, in transcending a reliance upon the judgment of "fallible human beings," will meet this responsibility for bringing explanations to an end through (at last) achieving a degree of certainty with respect to a teacher's "effectiveness." That achievement data does not in fact put such questions to rest is evidenced in the criterial distinction between the ordinary and technical senses of good teaching, in Ravitch's notes on the necessary role of "fallible human beings" in test construction and evaluation, and the fact that principals' observations (as well as the "judges" in Strong et al.'s study) disagree with the ratings based on measures of teacher value-added. If evaluation protocols pegged to achievement data as a preponderant criterion of quality bring explanations to an end, then, this is not necessarily because the explanations are in any way *satisfactory*; it may be simply because no further questioning is permitted.

The assumption undergirding the recourse to data is, once more, that any such instance of quality's misidentification must be produced by inadequate knowledge of what good teaching *really* is, and that once such knowledge is provided, misrecognition will be more or less impossible. But the results of the investigation so far conducted suggest that there may *be* no single, self-identical *thing* that would be identifiable as "what good teaching really is." If autobiographical narratives such as Neal's and Duncan's can stand on their own—that is, can *satisfy* as pictures of good teaching—and if the criteria that Duncan voices in his "we know what success looks like" locution likewise satisfy, then it is also the case that no such single or self-identical definition of educational quality is *necessary* to its recognition or sharing-in-common, either.

In Chapter 1, I noted that Duncan voices the need for multiple measures precisely to avoid the reduction of the "complex, nuanced" work of teaching to something like a test score. I also noted that the particular multiple measures under development are all themselves defined in terms of student achievement data, such that no genuine multiplicity exists. Something similar is occurring, it appears, in the realm of educational evaluation: the assumption that there must be a bottom to be reached, a kind of ground that will make the apparent multiplicity of senses of good teaching merely apparent, is in fact helping to produce the dissatisfaction with all our existing ways of speaking of educational quality as such. Operating on this assumption means that *only* a measure of teacher quality that subsumes or includes all the other ways of measuring or speaking of educational quality will suffice; until we reach that measure, there is no possibility of satisfaction or of explanations ending at all. But again, the fact that Kristof's recitation of the Olly Neal story *does* satisfy in terms of revealing educational quality demonstrates that this is not the case.

Instead, it may be worthwhile to consider that the relative merit and utility of student achievement data—or any other particular form of publicly evaluating and declaring a judgment of teacher quality—depends profoundly upon who asks for this account and under what circumstances, or for what reasons. It is not at all clear that the educator quality evident in Duncan's autobiographical narrative is merely a subspecies of something that would likewise appear in teacher value-added. The suggestion that "good teaching" is in a strong sense irreducibly *multiple* further acknowledges the possibility that data is in some cases, for all of the limitations highlighted throughout this work, among the most appropriate means of expressing a teacher's quality for evaluative purposes. The suggestion also, however, leaves open the possibility that in some cases and for some purposes student achievement data cannot meaningfully address the needs of those demanding the report.

But buying into this suggestion will obviously require letting go of the assumption that good teaching is indeed singular, that is, measurable ultimately in terms of a single metric; and this is not merely a problem for advocates of conceiving of teaching only in its technical sense, but also for those relying on an ordinary-sense perspective. The assumption to be relinquished is one on which any given person's ability to perceive and declare the quality of a given teacher must be predicated upon an understanding or definition of educational quality that is transcendent and thus in principle universal in its nature, such that if any particular way of perceiving and speaking of teacher quality works in any particular context, then this way of perceiving and speaking of teacher quality ought also to work in any other context, for any other audience, as well, thanks to the transcendent or universal definition of educational quality upon which it is imagined to draw.

This metaphysical assumption, however, is all-pervasive: Duncan's words on getting below the "ideological" nature or "surface conclusions" regarding charter schools provide one example of the strength (and confusions) of this assumption; a parent's letter to the editor of the *New York Times* provides another, one based on a different concept of teacher quality entirely.

Duncan's view of the charter school debate proves enlightening in terms of the assumptions under which he operates with respect to teaching and data, and particularly the assumption of the metaphysical singularity of "good teaching":

> I recently spoke to education writers about the search for truth in education. I challenged them to go beyond the ideological statements and the surface conclusions and find out what is really happening for our children in our classrooms.
>
> It's kind of like the debate around charter schools. Advocates say they outperform traditional schools. Opponents say they don't. The plain facts show that some charter schools do, and some of them don't. But rather than acknowledge the obvious, we devolve into an ideology debate and somehow forget that this is about children and learning. If something helps children, let's do it.

That's where all of you come in with the research and the facts. Education reform is not about sweeping mandates or grand gestures. It's about systematically examining and learning and building on what we're doing right and scrapping what hasn't worked for our children. (Duncan, 2009)

The above most clearly provides a reiteration of Duncan's basic outlook: disagreement about the truth in education is a matter of "ideological statements" and "surface conclusions"; such disagreement, therefore, is to be settled by non-ideological, say, objective, truth—as revealed according to student achievement data. In addressing the Institute of Education Sciences, he says in the second-person, "That's where all of you come in with the research and the facts." These, drawing upon truth rather than ideology, will put the matter to rest.

The matter that "the research and the facts" will settle, however, is unclear. The ideological debate pertains to charter schools and whether or not they "outperform traditional schools." But Duncan says, "the plain facts show that some charter schools do, and some of them don't." The ideological debate gets started, on his view, in the failure to "acknowledge" these plain facts. So where is the call for the "research and the facts"?

Duncan cites "facts" twice in the excerpt quoted above. The first instance refers to the "plain facts" that demonstrate that some charter schools seem to be achieving remarkable success while others are not. These are also the plain facts, "the obvious," that he takes ideologically-motivated antagonists to ignore in their wars of words. The second instance, though, while also referring to facts, seems to refer to facts of an entirely different sort. As an answer to the intractability of the "ideological" debate originating from a disagreement over a denial of "plain facts," he says to his data-analyst audience, "That's where you come in with the research and *the facts*" (emphasis added), which apparently stand in some sort of contrast to the "plain facts" that reveal that some charter schools outperform certain traditional schools and some do not.

Whatever the research and the facts are meant to do in this case, they cannot settle the charter school debate: the *plain* facts that Duncan references show that some charter schools live up to their revolutionary promise while others fail to outperform traditional schools. All that this means is that, according to student achievement metrics, "charter school" is not the decisive variable. Some *thing* that some charter schools do appears to have salutary effects in terms of improving achievement, and some *thing* done by other charter schools is ineffective in this regard. If the "research and the facts" are brought to bear on this case, it will be in the interest of finding out what *thing* works, which will not be a property of charter schools as such. The "research and the facts" will be valuable, that is to say, in terms of discovering something like a "best practice," something to which Duncan alludes in saying, "If something helps children, let's do it." The problems with this way of thinking have been thoroughly explored earlier; suffice it here to say that the singularity of the pronoun in combination with the plural "children" underscores the fact that Duncan takes good teaching to be metaphysically singular—some one thing will help (equally? On average?) all children.

Duncan sees something pertaining to educational quality that stands in contrast to "surface conclusions," something that he calls "facts" amenable to proper "research." But with respect to the charter school debate, the kind of research he has in mind—into the achievement data outcomes of charter schools, that is—is already implicated in the superficiality of the surface conclusions: such research will never be able to reach the bottom that he imagines. There simply is no bottom to the charter school debate; or, put another way, any debate that "the research and the facts" can settle will not center upon charter schools as such.

The point of emphasizing Duncan's use of this example is that, in direct contrast to the way the "plain facts" or "surface conclusions" provide a way of settling the charter school debate—by means of showing that the traditional/charter divide is not the salient issue—the factual results of actual "research" are called upon as a means of settling all debates pertaining to educational quality per se. This is to say both that there *is* a way of settling the charter school debate without further research, and also that the warrant for the sort of "facts" that real research will reveal is predicated upon a metaphysical assumption about the singularity of the conceptual content of "good teaching."

It is perhaps not too much to suggest that Duncan has no idea what sort of "fact" it is that he wishes for, as no facts have ever proven capable of the feats he imagines them to accomplish: allowing him to lay out the *actual* and specific student skills and teacher behaviors that will lead to successful adulthood, and the *actual* and specific growth rates on achievement measures that will secure those outcomes. The improbability of arriving at some singular ground upon which such generally-applicable teacher skills or behaviors will come to rest has been well-established by this point. But the imperturbable assumption that there *is* such a bottom is precisely the begging of the question that short-circuits or precludes robust considerations of the meaning of "multiple measures" in the evaluation of educational quality. The assumption that founds Duncan's quest is that there is something entity-like that helps children, where such helping is both general to all children and revealed in student achievement data. But the likely possibility remains that there is no single thing that helps all children equally: this would be precisely what makes teaching the "complex, nuanced" work that Duncan avers it is.

This assumption, though, is not limited to what one might call the scientific perspective, one based on "the research and the facts": roughly the same assumption undergirds the view of a parent, Carol Penskar, penning a letter regarding teacher evaluation to the *New York Times*.

Teachers' unions, according to your article, argue that "no one has figured out an accurate way to determine" who the best teachers are.

This is ridiculous. My son and daughter each attended 13 years of public school. The parents always knew who the best teachers were. If the parents can figure it out, certainly the education bureaucracy could do the same if it really wanted to? (Penskar, 2010)

Penskar avers that reliable, true knowledge of "who the best teachers were" is plainly open to a locally-situated view, to the perspective of a parent. But in her rhetorical question, Penskar makes it clear that whatever it is that parents know about teacher quality ought to be equally accessible, equally knowable, to "the education bureaucracy."

Indeed, Duncan's recital of his mother's educational work in the context of advocating for better measures of teacher quality rests upon the same assumption: that if teacher quality is visible and knowable *at* all, then it must be visible and knowable, in principle, *to* all. The fact that we know good teaching when we see it, that we recognize examples of good teaching in autobiographical narratives, seems incontrovertibly to imply that there is a *thing*, a universal kind of "good teaching," to which we all, equally, have access. The suggestion throughout has been that whatever reasons a parent (an administrator, a student, a colleague) might provide for ascribing a certain level of quality to a given teacher will not necessarily or simply map onto the "preponderant criterion" of improving student test scores, or vice versa. This is as much as to claim once more that good teaching is meaningfully multiple, which further implies that whatever it will mean to discharge any official and unofficial *responsibility* for evaluating teachers and making salary or personnel decisions based on this evaluation will not be exhausted in arriving, through discovery or dogmatism, at any particular definition or standard of teacher quality.

What Penskar and Duncan both express in their different ways amounts to an insistence that the means of knowing and reporting on teacher quality available to a parent have the same basis and ought to be equally available to a state- or national-level politician and, importantly, vice versa. The assumption is that the knowledge and justificatory grounds had by *each* is had by way of theoretical representation, and thus it ought to be solvable in a general capacity, as a general problem.

But the parental perspective on teacher quality calls to mind the everyday familiarity with background practices that Dreyfus has already brought out. His contention is that a parental ability to tell the good teachers from the bad is entirely unrelated to their having *solved* any common-sense knowledge problem whose solution would then be theoretically available to the "education bureaucracy." Dreyfus argues instead that the parents involved in this on-the-ground evaluation do not have a common-sense knowledge *problem* at all. On his view, the problem involved in formalizing things like "successful adults" and the criteria of "writing" only crops up when one seeks a way to speak about something like educational quality from the perspective of a radical outsider, from an objective prospect..

The obviousness of the quality of her own children's teachers seems to Penskar to indicate that the type of particular and ongoing experience on the basis of which such knowledge *is* obvious ought to make it sufficiently obvious for everyone. But one has then merely a constellation of particular instances without any claim on generality at all. The obviousness of the quality of teachers as it appears according to student achievement data, on the other hand, has large numbers and correlations with adult outcomes behind it. Teacher value-added has the power of the general on its side. But these two means of measurement, the two perspectives from which they operate and the audiences to whom they most directly speak, can disagree with each other. The assumption on *both* sides, the one shared by Penskar and Duncan, is that one of them (the other one) is simply wrong, an example of "ideology" in opposition to "truth." Such an assumption is made possible by the unsupported hypothesis that there is, ultimately, only *one thing* that good teaching is, that when someone knows something about teacher quality, then that person knows something quite general, something universally applicable.

If, on the other hand, as I have sought to bring out throughout this work, the ordinary concept of "good teaching" is inherently bound up with agreement in form of life, then it will be irreducible to any common feature or characteristic; it will rather be a matter of what Wittgenstein calls "family resemblance" or "family likeness":

> We are inclined to think that there must be something in common to all games, say, and that this common property is the justification for applying the general term 'game' to the various games; whereas games form a *family* of members of which have family likenesses. Some of them have the same nose, others the same eyebrows and others again the same way of walking; and these likenesses overlap. (*BB*, 17)

The implication here is bifurcated and will, by this point, be familiar: any features that all "good teaching" share in common will not be *essential* to or defining of "good teaching" in any metaphysical way, on the one hand; and on the other hand, no recognition of membership in the family of "good teaching" *requires* recourse to any *single* feature or definition. In the *Investigations*, Wittgenstein says that we "extend" such concepts as "good teaching" by learning or reciting or revealing criteria thereof, "as in spinning a thread we twist fiber upon fiber. And the strength of the thread resides not in the fact that some one fiber runs through its whole length, but in the overlapping of many fibers" (*PI* §67).

This has profound consequences for the project of educational evaluation in general, especially in thinking of Ravitch's turn from conceiving of evaluation as "accountability" to evaluation as "responsibility." It suggests first and foremost that any hope for a determination of teacher quality predicated upon escaping a reliance on the human is fundamentally misguided and supremely likely to end in failure; it suggests further, for this reason, that the project of what Cavell calls bringing explanations to an end will not be achieved by any *deus ex machina*, any intervention of superhuman truth in the matter. This might also be a phenomenological statement: no evaluation of educational quality whatsoever, including those reliant on measures of "teacher effectiveness," has ever yet been achieved in virtue of any superhuman truth.

In thinking once more of the "responsibility" required of educational evaluation, it seems clear that responsibility is precisely what is deflected or disowned in striving for an inhuman definition of good teaching. More precisely, assuming a transcendent or universal sense of good teaching, an abstract sense, according to which any actual instance of teaching might be measured, removes our shared responsibility for that concept (its criteria and its application) and its responsibility and responsiveness to "what shows up as mattering to us," in Cahill's words (Cahill, 2011, p. 141).

This absence of responsibility or responsiveness appears as a literal kind of unresponsiveness, one that manifests itself as either dogmatism or whim. When a teacher is declared "effective" in virtue of his or her value-added measurement, but is found to "need improvement" according to an observation, there is indeed a way of settling this disagreement, but it is only by a predetermined algorithm that quantitatively ascribes a certain weight to each type of measurement. That is, the algorithm is itself universally applied. In no particular case would an observer have to—or be able to—give reasons for checking such and such a box on the observation rubric as part of an argument *against* ultimately rating a teacher "effective."

Determining whether the observation or the test data will weigh more heavily is a matter of *human* decision-making, negotiated among the district and the union and the state; but once the weights are determined, they function as though they are inhuman, and this is a far cry from a satisfying state of affairs. The Florida principal, for instance, cites the discrepancy between the results of the observation and the algorithmic output as making evident a problem with "the cut scores." The algorithm has generated an evaluative result, but this result is taken as a kind of failure, and glaringly, precisely because the supposed virtue of the algorithm lies in its inhuman functioning, there is no possibility of responsiveness to this failure in this case. The cut scores in Florida may change in the future, but there is no appeal to be made in this teacher's case; indeed, there is no one to appeal to. The judgment rendered by the weighted system is to that extent dogmatic.

The Strong study provides an example of whim. "In every case, judges achieved relatively high levels of agreement but were absolutely inaccurate, leading us to question whether educators can identify effective teachers when they see them" (Strong, Gargani, & Hacifazlioğlu, 2011). The "judges" in this example agreed with each other but disagreed with the measures, leading Strong and his colleagues to conclude that the judges (not the measures) were "inaccurate." The stalemate here, in which Strong has to choose which of the two bases of judgment he will accept as the standard of accuracy to which the other will be compared (or contrasted), highlights the fact that this appears to be, to recall Dreyfus's phenomenology of skill development once more, something like an ungrounded choice of perspective. The standard of accuracy itself is in question.

Strong's conclusion could just as well have been that measures of teacher value-added were self-consistent but completely inaccurate, as they diverged from the judges' agreement with respect to the quality of the teachers they evaluated. We are stuck, it seems, in a position where neither value judgments about teacher quality generated from a highly general perspective nor those generated from a highly particular perspective have adequate claim to universal acceptance, something that will suffice to both the purposes of a Secretary of Education who will never meet most of the teachers whose quality he needs to know and also to the purposes of a given third-grader's parent who is intensely concerned with the quality of one particular teacher. It remains unclear that such a thing exists. Once more, this ought to imply that the process of evaluating teachers according to quality does not, cannot, and should not be modeled upon the comparison of something ontic with a natural constant. The conceptual breadth of "good teaching" requires and in fact rests on something more human; human responsiveness will be intrinsic to any notion of responsibility in the evaluation of teachers.

Duncan proposes the use of student achievement data as a means of getting beneath the "surface conclusions" of "ideological debates." That, he says to the group of analysts, "is where you come in with the research and the facts." But this is a poor construction of the problem, as it seems to deny that we have the requisite knowledge of "the plain facts," a suggestion that Penskar calls, rightly, obviously, "ridiculous." The paradoxical position here is that we seem to have *enough* knowledge and yet seem unable to *do* something important, something that we usually take adequate knowledge to allow us to do, namely, to *say* (broadly, generally, publicly) with some measure of certainty whether this or that teacher is good at what he or she does. That the "plain facts" have not sufficed to preclude disagreement about these judgments is taken to necessitate more or better (or deeper) facts, as evidence that we have yet to reach the bottom.

But it will be important to note that foreclosing on the possibility of disagreement might be substantially different from the task of bringing explanations to an end. Certainly, if the metaphysical and rationalist assumptions were accurate in the domain of teacher quality, then the discovery and articulation of the bottom-level *fact* about what good teaching *is* (what quality education entails, what successful adulthood consists of) would achieve both ends at once, since knowledge of that fact would both prevent disagreement and also *be* the end of all explanations. Those assumptions are not accurate, however, as my arguments throughout have shown. We have seen above, as in the case of Florida's evaluations, that it is possible to preclude disagreement (by failing to provide anyone with whom to disagree) without in fact giving rest to the need for explanation.

That there is no *one thing* that good teaching is not an occasion on which to throw up one's hands and declare defeat. As Crease says, the dissatisfaction with our measures' ability to live up to the "goals we are trying to achieve" with them does not require us to assume that "what we are after lies 'beyond' measuring" (Crease, 2011, p. 275). It rather *increases* the weight of the responsibility that we (humanly) have in something like the evaluation of educational quality. Duncan associates getting serious about educational evaluation with the need for "courage to admit our flaws and take steps to address them," and in this, he is profoundly correct. Turning to achievement data, "the research and the facts," however, accomplishes the opposite: by stipulating rather than discovering the definition of teacher quality in terms of both cut scores and the relative weight of various measures, it renders the process of judgment not only inherently inaccurate, but also fundamentally unresponsive to the expression of legitimate disagreement. It requires no courage, as whatever abstraction of teacher quality is brought to bear as the object of comparison for any particular teacher is itself fully beyond questioning.

The weight of our actual responsibility in evaluating teachers pertains to the absolute need to be *correct* in the absence of any single transcendent *thing* that good teaching is, which will also entail a responsibility to show, to make evident, the correctness of a given judgment. This is the sort of difficulty to which Cavell alludes in pointing to the paradox that "at each step, or level, explanation comes to an end; there is no level to which all explanations come, at which all end" (Cavell, 2013, p. 116). It is also what Wittgenstein means by "difficulty": "The difficulty—I might say—is not that of finding a solution but rather that of recognizing as the solution something that looks as if it were only a preliminary to it. . . . The difficulty here is: to stop" (Wittgenstein, 1967, p. 314). The *sufficiency* of any judgment, the *fact* that it brings explanation to an end, must be both shown (to others) and accepted (by others), and it cannot be given, as though simply asserted, from without.

Joseph Schwab's thinking about teaching and learning helps not only to see why courage might be necessary, but it also offers a means of dissolving the intractable problems that seem to accrue to attempts at knowing and evaluating teaching. In short, Schwab enumerates the ways in which the process of teaching and learning, while certainly more ordinary than high-level astrophysics, nevertheless requires fundamentally different kinds of knowing and doing, and therefore also different preparations for and forms of telling. Seeing teaching and learning as "complex, nuanced work," and yet very differently complex from the paradigm case of complexity that, say, rocket science embodies, is what calls for courage.

NOTES

1. Ravitch goes on, in the chapter just quoted, to point to various studies of the relation of non-cognitive skills to adult success, such as those contained in the work of Henry Levin, James Heckman, and Paul Tough. Her point in raising these is that important factors to be taught and learned in school—like Tough's notion of "grit"—are not accounted for in state assessments. Her arguments against testing come down to invoking the "paradox of interpretation" to undermine the claim to objectivity or truth, and to pointing to non-cognitive skills as a means of highlighting the non-generalizability of test results to the full domain of interest. Both are valuable critiques. Neither quite gets to the heart of the matter.
2. William Johnson's work on the medial form of the bookroll in Roman antiquity brings this out in another way, that is, the extent to which what "reading," in particular, *is* subject to conceptual evolution coextensive with changing background practices shared within any given culture (Johnson, 2013).
3. It will *certainly* be worth noting that the basic claim that I've made here about the relation of the present to the future is not at *all* new with respect to education, although these ideas have primarily been bandied about with respect to curriculum rather than measurement or evaluation (as though those things ought to be separate). Bobbitt's efforts at formulating curriculum based on empirical job analysis—by looking exhaustively to catalogue the specific skills and attitudes necessary to success in the workplace *at present*—turned out (unsurprisingly) not to provide adequate grounds for educating in the direction of the future (Hlebowitsh, 2005). A similar argument is lodged against Shulman's teacher-knowledge project as well, whose title ("Existing Practice Is Not the Template") is simultaneously right (in that existing practice cannot serve adequately to speak to the future) and wrong (in that existing practice provides the *best* examples on which to build) (Evans, 2007).

REFERENCES

Anderson, J. (2013, March 31). Curious Grade for Teachers—Nearly All Pass. *New York Times*, p. A1. Retrieved from http://www.nytimes.com/2013/03/31/education/curious-grade-for-teachers-nearly-all-pass.html?pagewanted=all&_r=0

Cahill, K. (2011). *The Fate of Wonder: Wittgenstein's Critique of Metaphysics and Modernity*. New York: Columbia University Press.

Cavell, S. (1990). *Conditions Handsome and Unhandsome*. Chicago: University of Chicago Press.

Cavell, S. (2013). *This New Yet Unapproachable America: Lectures After Emerson After Wittgenstein* (p. 144). University of Chicago Press. Retrieved from http://books.google.com/books?id=qmWUMQEACAAJ&pgis=1

Crease, R. P. (2011). *World in the Balance*. New York: W. W. Norton & Company.

Duncan, A. (2009). Robust Data Gives Us the Roadmap to Reform. U.S. Department of Education. Retrieved from http://www2.ed.gov/news/speeches/2009/06/06082009.html

Evans, R. (2007). Existing Practice Is Not the Template. *Educational Researcher*, 36(9), 553–559. Retrieved from http://www.jstor.org/stable/30137940

Hlebowitsh, P. S. (2005). Generational Ideas in Curriculum: A Historical Triangulation. *Curriculum Inquiry*, 35(1), 73–87. Retrieved from http://www.jstor.org/stable/3698528

Johnson, W. A. (2013). Bookrolls as Media. In N. K. Hayles & J. Pressman (Eds.), *Comparative Textual Media* (pp. 101–121). Minneapolis: University of Minnesota Press.

Penskar, C. (2010, May 3). LETTERS; Deciding How to Grade the Teachers. *New York Times*. New York.

Ravitch, D. (2013). *Reign of Error: The Hoax of the Privatization Movement and the Danger to America's Public Schools*. New York: Knopf.

Strong, M., Gargani, J., & Hacifazlioğlu, Ö. (2011). Do We Know a Successful Teacher When We See One? Experiments in the Identification of Effective Teachers. *Journal of Teacher Education*, 62(4), 367–382. doi:10.1177/0022487110390221

Wittgenstein, L. (1967). *Zettel*. Berkeley: University of California Press.

8 Schwab's Deliberation and the Responsibilities of Teacher Evaluation

In Chapter 1, I referred to the recent work of Jal Mehta. In bringing Joseph's Schwab's thinking to bear on the issue of teacher evaluations, I am reminded of Mehta's incisive words, which are worth repeating here: "The core of the educational problem is that *we have been trying to solve a problem of professional practice by bureaucratic means*" (Mehta, 2013, p. 270). Putting it in Schwab's own terms, he might say that we have been trying to solve a practical problem by theoretic means. This likewise echoes James Conant's worry that in attempting to get clear about our practices, or say our practical commitments, we can fall victim to the illusion that our understanding of these commitments requires a "reflective detour" (Conant, 1993, p. 206).

Where I objected to Mehta's solution to the problem as he conceives it—on the grounds that his solution misconceives the nature of professional practice—Schwab's work in the realm of professional educational practice may prove adaptable to the practical demands of evaluating teachers in a context in which such evaluations have serious consequences. Schwab's version of "the practical arts" offers something equal to the task of moving from "accountability" to "responsibility," as Ravitch demands, and something therefore equal to what Cavell calls "assuming the burden of finality in the absence of certainty" (Cavell, 1979, p. 31).

It may seem counterintuitive to offer Joseph Schwab's ideas as an ameliorative strain of thought to the present discursive field. Schwab, in the first place, contributed his work in the field of curriculum, rather than evaluation, policy, or measurement. While the curriculum field certainly ought to include such matters, and has a long history of doing so, dating at least to Ralph Tyler, it has become ever more limited in that regard since Schwab's writing. The curriculum field also does not clearly overlap with the exploration of teacher development, and has little to say in the field of psychometrics or educational measurement, except insofar as these are all inherently bound up together. Further, Schwab's writings are more than a generation old by this point: his seminal essays—the practical cycle, as they are known—were published between 1969 and 1983. His former graduate students and intellectual heirs, including giants in the field of education, such as Shulman and Elliot Eisner, are now themselves either mostly retired or passed.

But Schwab's sensitivity to the diurnal concerns of teaching and learning in the context of the public school is precisely what is missing from the policies encouraged by Race to the Top. As such, Schwab seems to speak directly to the impasses that I have traced throughout this work. If one recognizes the relevance of Schwab's thinking at this point, as offering a means of dissolving the problem confronted by the fact of competing claims of differing standpoints, differing reasons for demanding an accounting in the practice of evaluating teachers and pronouncing judgments (as one might awkwardly call it), that will underscore the fact that the *problem* Schwab first identifies and addresses in 1969 has simply been transported from the aegis of curriculum into the realm of teacher development and evaluation. The problem he crystallizes, I argue, remains the problem that undoes Duncan, Penskar, and an army of economists: the failure of the ordinary concept of "good teaching" to bottom out in any metaphysically singular *fact* that might be discoverable according to any one method of analysis.

Schwab's thinking demands the courage that Duncan associates with his own project inasmuch as Schwab requires us to adopt a view of ourselves in which we are neither individually "free to make it up as we go" nor collectively (or individually) privy to some underlying infrastructure of all knowledge. Moving beyond what Cavell will call the "false peace" that follows from either of the above responses to recognizing a reliance upon agreement in form of life will require invoking the trans-human, or turning to one another as legitimate sources of understanding.

If, ultimately, ontological measurement accesses something trans-human, as Crease has it; if our shared grasp of concepts as such come down to agreement in forms of life; if the quality of skillful practice stands out on a background of everyday know-how; then one will do best to seek such lofty things as knowing, doing, and evaluating—at least in the realm of education, in the realm of the human—in direct contact, one might say, with the trans-human, in conversation with other people.

8.1 THE THEORETIC AND THE PRACTICAL

In 1968, Schwab opened the keynote address at the annual meeting of the American Educational Research Association by declaring the curriculum field "moribund." On Schwab's view, the field's morbidity, the story of its arrival in this place, and the potential way out all hinged upon the distinction between his conceptions of the "theoretic" and the "practical." At the opening of this address, he lays out his terms:

> The curriculum field has reached this unhappy state by inveterate and unexamined reliance on theory in an area where theory is partly

> inappropriate in the first place and where the theories extant, even where appropriate, are inadequate to the tasks which the curriculum field sets them. (Schwab, 1969, p. 1)

Schwab goes on to highlight several specific ways in which looking to theory to solve problems in education field fails the curriculum field. In discussing, for example, the shortcomings of a certain revival of Herbartian theories proposing both a theory of mind and a theory of knowledge that merge into a seamless whole, Schwab says,

> A theory of mind and knowledge thus solves by one mighty coup the problem of what to teach, when, and how; and what is fatally theoretic here is not the presence of a theory of mind and a theory of knowledge, though their presence is part of the story, but the dispatch, the sweeping appearance of success, the vast simplicity which grounds this purported solution to the problem of curriculum. (Schwab, 1969, p. 7)

He offers the above example in contradistinction to several other efforts at deriving educative methods from theoretical grounds, most efforts centered around creating objectives according to, for instance, that which is taken as necessary to "live in the modern world" (Schwab, 1969, p. 7). That one, in particular, sounds familiar.

The purpose of quoting Schwab at length here is to draw out the similarities with Dreyfus, in particular, though one also sees the reflection of Glendinning's notion of "phenomenon splitting" at work. Unlike the others, however, Schwab speaks directly to the milieu of educational research.

> These various "things" (individuals, societies, cultures, patterns of enquiry, "structures" of knowledge or of enquiries, apperceptive masses, problem solving), though discriminable as separate subjects of differing modes of enquiry, are nevertheless parts or affectors of one another, or coactors. (Their very separation for purposes of enquiry is what marks the outcomes of such enquiries as "theoretic" and consequently incomplete.) In practice, they constitute one complex, organic agency. Hence, a focus on only one not only ignores the others but vitiates the quality and completeness with which the selected one is viewed. (Schwab, 1969, p. 9)

Schwab points in particular to the ways in which the individual and society mutually influence one another; neither is simply reducible to the other. Roughly speaking, this revelation mirrors the relation that Derrida traces between linguistic events and linguistic systems. Schwab's goal, in fact, aligns closely with the one Glendinning reads in Derrida: to reveal that the traditional ways in which we *study* or *observe* the practical phenomena "in which our being is implicated," as Crease says, actively preclude the resulting knowledge from producing, explaining, or improving our practical skillfulness.

This is to say that the knowledge that we take detached or disengaged study to yield does not suffice—and is not necessary—for the carrying-out of our practical endeavors; it is not, in short, equivalent to the knowledge embodied in our practices themselves. The Dreyfusian critique of AI implies that what we commonly take as *necessary* to intelligence—namely a separate realm of something like pure knowledge on which action is predicated—proves unable to *produce* intelligent behavior: something essential is left out. Derrida's project shows us that what we take as necessary to the use of language—namely knowledge of definitions and grammatical rules—cannot satisfactorily account for language use in practice: something essential is left out.

The insufficiencies on display for Schwab have primarily to do, as he says in a quotation above, with the "dispatch, the sweeping appearance of success," that is, of *each* theoretical viewpoint. As totalizing perspectives, any theory of mind and knowledge constitutes a self-enclosed universe, a total one, and as such each theoretical starting point is structurally immune or deaf to the concerns central to any other theoretical foundation. Schwab points out the incompleteness of each, and then proposes that any atomization of the whole of the what used to be called a life-stream into compartmentalized components—even with the end goal of reassembling them—will lead to a sort of understanding that is *necessarily* incomplete.

My claim regarding Schwab's contribution to the discussion around the policies encouraged by Race to the Top divides into two areas of emphasis: the first is, along the lines detailed above, an emphasis on showing that the formulation of the problems that Race to the Top addresses renders the problems insoluble as such; while the second area of emphasis sketches a means of taking up the problems that the field has heretofore formulated poorly. In dissolving the unsuccessful or insoluble formulations of the problems that curriculum faces, Schwab retains his sense of the need out of which these questions arise, the call for a response. When he proclaims that the theoretic cannot satisfactorily address practical problems, then, this is not to imply that such problems are simply imaginary, or do not require addressing.

Dreyfus's critique of the rationalist assumptions undergirding the pursuits of early AI researchers returns at this point to highlight Schwab's contentions about the "different subject matters" addressed by different theories. Recalling Dreyfus's comments on the construction of micro-worlds from the SHRDLU project, one might see the analogy between the notion of micro-worlds as self-contained atomizations of some sort of larger whole and what Schwab calls the "subsubjects" of the human that "the theoretic" addresses. That which limits the utility of micro-worlds in arriving at actual artificial intelligence bears marked similarities to Schwab's view of the same problem with regard to the use of theory in guiding educational practice.

Given the competing standpoints or "commitments" that each theoretical view assumes, Schwab notes that, "there is no foreseeable hope of a unified theory in the immediate or middle future, nor of a metatheory which will tell us how to put those subsubjects together or order them in a fixed hierarchy of importance to the problems of curriculum" (Schwab, 1969, p. 10), which certainly recalls Dreyfus's comments on the failure of micro-worlds to reach the whole. Such micro-worlds, says Dreyfus, "are not related like isolable physical systems to larger systems they *compose*; rather they are local elaborations of a whole which they *presuppose*" (Dreyfus, 1992, p. 14).

Further echoing or anticipating a Dreyfusian view of skillful coping in which a facts-and-rules approach will eventually overwhelm a given practitioner, Schwab notes of teaching:

> Moments of choice of what to do, how to do it, with whom and at what pace, arise hundreds of times a school day, and arise differently every day and with every group of students. No command or instruction can be so formulated as to control that kind of artistic judgment and behavior, with its demand for frequent, instant choices of ways to meet an ever varying situation. (Schwab, 1983, p. 245)

Schwab is highly sensitive to the non-formalizable nature of skillfully navigating these "moments of choice." Eisner shares Schwab's view of this particular insufficiency of the theoretic, but he expresses Schwab's objections in the specific terms of schooling's differences from a "cybernetic system," which once more invites comparison with Dreyfus's project. Says Eisner:

> In contrast to the "certain" regularity of a positivistic view of planning and teaching, Schwab's work reminded us of what we knew but seemed at the time to have forgotten: that planning of school programs is neither a modified version of an input-throughput-output model nor is it a cybernetic system that will eventually right itself when it goes off course or over-corrects. (Eisner, 1984, p. 202)

Schwab's speech on the shortcomings of the prevailing notion of education's relation to the theoretic, originally offered in the late 60s, thus underscores the fact that the rationalist approach to education has a long-standing and unsuccessful history of its own, a history that the educational field shares with scholarly approaches to many human endeavors.[1]

Where Duncan purports to offer something *new* to the educational field, then, in the form of more and better data, more rigorous assessments and standards, and more advanced statistical techniques, one might note that the earlier failures in thus imposing "theoretic" solutions to the problems of education had little to do with the quality of data or any means of interpreting it. Rather, as Schwab in particular notes, the absence of any "metatheory" for combining the vast "subsubjects" embodied in the educational endeavor renders the rationalist assumption itself, upon which all such data-driven policies rest, fatally incomplete.

The use of methods relying upon the rationalist assumption precludes a priori any hope of speaking to the broad or ordinary concept of educational quality. In revealing and labeling as "theoretic" the rationalist formulation of the "disquieting and disconcerting conditions" that confront the educational endeavor—a formulation that he attributes to inadequate "problemation" (Schwab, 1983, p. 257)—Schwab offers a dissolution of the problem so formulated. On his view, a productive response to the "disquieting and disconcerting conditions" emerging from lived experience will found itself on what he calls "the practical."

The standard to which Schwab holds his "practical" approach to curriculum is exceedingly high. In Schwab's own words:

> It is clear, I submit, that a defensible curriculum or plan of curriculum must be one which somehow takes account of all these subsubjects which pertain to man. It cannot take only one and ignore the others; it cannot even take account of many of them and ignore one. Not only is each of them a constituent and a condition for decent human existence but each interpenetrates the others. (Schwab, 1969, p. 9)

In exploring Schwab's notion of the practical, its ability to respond to the felt need to "somehow [take] account of all these subsubjects which pertain to man" will, I think, provide an important test of the above formulation.

In contrast to his sketch of the theoretic, then, Schwab elucidates his sense of the practical. The fundamental distinction between the practical and the theoretic as he conceives of these terms has not only to do with what I have laid out above—roughly, the inability of the theoretic to account for or to result in appropriate, flexible responses to actual on-the-ground conditions in any particular instance—but also to do with maintaining a focus on the need or call to address particular situations.

Schwab's conception of the "practical" seeks a mode of posing and addressing such disquietudes without requiring our standing-outside of the disquietude's native habitat, so to speak. He is quick to note that the refusal to pull back from the situation ought not to be confused with any disdaining of thinking as such:

> By the "practical" I do not mean the curbstone practicality of the mediocre administrator and the man on the street, for whom the practical means the easily achieved, familiar goals which can be reached by familiar means. I refer, rather, to a complex discipline, relatively unfamiliar to the academic and differing radically from the disciplines of the theoretic. It is the discipline concerned with choice and action, in contrast with the theoretic, which is concerned with knowledge. (Schwab, 1969, pp. 1–2).

If the "practical" requires a type of rigor that will not be expressed in the construction of theory, which, as Duncan's notions of the rigor embodied by student achievement data helps to suggest, continues to function as the preponderant criterion of the very concept of rigor, it will perhaps not be overstating the matter to say that Schwab's version of the practical represents something new and potentially radical with respect to the questions under discussion.

Most radically, Schwab proposes to begin the task of "problemation" with the *particular* rather than the general, as is habitually the case with the "theoretic." Schwab is explicit on this matter: "What we know is not facts *sub specie aeterni*, but facts as parts of a practical problem and as means to its solution" (Schwab, 1959, p. 150). The "choice and action" he has in mind, then, are called for with respect to a sort of Aristotelian "concern" or Heideggerian "towards-which," one that is itself always grounded in particular conditions encountered by particular people. Putting it another way, Schwab avers that "The construction of needed diversities entails attention by planners of curriculum to the *local*" (Schwab, 1983, p. 242). Against a view in which responses or prescriptions or practices are conceived as applicable generally, and are offered as solutions to central tendencies extracted from massive compilations of specific situations as defined in terms of their features, Schwab's "practical" seeks to forego the step back from the immediate instance.

Taking the local as a starting point and offering the "practical" in opposition to the "theoretic" might tempt one to read Schwab as banishing theory from educational problemation and problem-solving altogether. But this is hardly the case. Schwab's discussion of the practical and the theoretic is best conceived as pertaining to *when* and *how* a disquieting situation draws upon a particular realm of the theoretic. Schwab's mistrust of the theoretic is directed precisely at theory's "sweeping appearance of success," which is to say, the sweeping appearance of success visible according to *each* incommensurable theoretical viewpoint. This fact suggests to him, not inappropriately, that each theoretical viewpoint serves to *construct* the problem as well as to solve it—something along the lines of the saying that "when all you've got is a hammer, every problem looks like a nail." Schwab's call to begin with the particular, the local, or the concrete is aimed at defusing this nefarious aspect of reliance upon the theoretic, rather than turning away from theoretical knowledge wholesale.

The correct application of theoretical knowledge, in Schwab, comes by way of what he calls "the arts of the eclectic," which pertain explicitly to overcoming the limitations inherent in employing any single theoretical viewpoint through drawing upon many of them instead. Schwab describes this eclectic response to practical problems like so:

> First, the particularities of each practical problem can be sought in the practical situation itself, the search guided by resources much richer

than any one theory can afford. Second, in each instance of application of a borrowed theory to a practical situation, incongruities can be adjusted by mutual accommodation. Third, restricted subject and limited treatment so characteristic of behavioral theories can be transcended by using more than one such theory. (Schwab, 1971, p. 495)

Taking a particular situation as calling for the application of theoretical knowledge—a disquietude calling for settling—the role of theory is conceived in terms of offering a singular and active *response*, which ought to be understood as distinct from answering a *question* or providing a self-consistent *explanation*.[2]

In suggesting that the search for the problem is to be "guided by resources much richer than any one theory can afford," Schwab seems to allude to something which, as in the test I mentioned above, allows one to "somehow take account of all the subsubjects that pertain to man." The linkage between them points in the direction of agreement in forms of life, shared background practices, the trans-human. It is important to express the sense of this direction now, since Schwab's language can be misconstrued as seeking firmer (formalizable) ground, as perhaps Shulman understands him. Instead, "taking account" of these various subsubjects may turn out to be inseparable from embodying the appropriate response in a given situation.[3]

Such an appropriate response, as Schwab notes, insofar as it requires "mutual accommodation" and "using more than one such theory" seems to imply the necessity of establishing some way of selecting among such theories, a process of enacting the "mutual accommodation" he mentions. This seems to beckon in the direction of the same regress that threatens accounts of skillful practice rooted in the rationalist assumption. In fact, one might take Shulman's "strategic knowledge," which does indeed fall into this regress, as a metaphysical account of that which enables a particular practitioner to successfully navigate such indeterminacy.

Schwab himself avoids such prescription, however, which enables him to slip the regress entailed in providing a theoretical means of deciding among necessarily incomplete theories, much to his credit. He is explicit on this point:

> The methods by which these ends might be achieved have, however, a complication of their own. Although they can be described and exemplified, they cannot be reduced to generally applicable rules. Rather, in each instance of their application, they must be modified and adjusted to the case in hand. Because of this complication, I call them *arts*. (Schwab, 1971, p. 495)

The "eclectic," as Schwab terms the process of selecting portions or aspects of various theoretical positions in order to respond to the disquietude at hand, is not *itself* theoretic in nature, and that fact marks an important break with the various means of addressing educational problems according to the rationalist assumption.

By invoking the notion of an "art," Schwab refers to a region of knowledge or experience that is inextricably tied to *practice,* as well as what Crease might call the "trans-human," or agreement in forms of life.[4] This follows also from Schwab's note that the invocation of "art" is directly motivated by the fact that such "methods . . . can be described and exemplified, [but] they cannot be reduced to generally applicable rules," which more or less directly maps onto Dreyfus's description of proficient and expert performers' reliance upon irreducible, holistic, situational paradigms, as well as onto Wittgenstein's insistence that in teaching someone the meaning of a word, he does so by means of "examples and exercises," and in doing so "does not communicate less than [he] knows [himself]." In describing the "arts of the eclectic," Schwab thus aligns himself with these thinkers in proposing alternatives to a theoretically-grounded view of practical, concrete situations.

The "arts of the eclectic" promise another improvement upon any reliance on the "theoretic" as conceived according to the rationalist assumption upon which Duncan's Race to the Top policies are grounded. In Chapter 6, I explored the temporal limitations that beset the studies that serve to justify the use of teacher value-added, to take that aspect of teacher evaluation as an example. Specifically, I pointed out that because such studies are necessarily based upon *past* academic competencies and, at best, *present* adult outcomes, they have no special power to predict future conditions. Another way of expressing this weakness is to say that the use of such studies to lay out the particular teacher behaviors associated with "successful adult outcomes" for classroom observers freezes the relevance of all the skills involved in teaching, learning, and being a successful adult, which a fortiori renders this use of data a particularly ham-fisted way of dealing with questions of educational quality in the present and the future.

Schwab's notion of the practical arts, however, in refusing to acquiesce to a *single* theoretical viewpoint and in drawing instead upon a *variety* of such theories—as called for by a particular disquietude—leaves open, explicitly, the possibility of accounting for such changing relevance in the act of combining and selecting among theoretical viewpoints:

> What remains as a viable alternative is the unsystematic, uneasy, pragmatic, and uncertain unions and connections which can be effected in an eclectic. And I must add, anticipating our discussion of the practical, that *changing* connections and *differing* orderings at different times of these separate theories, will characterize a sound eclectic. (Schwab, 1969, p. 10)

As the concrete, local situation plays the role of calling for the intervention of theory in the first place, it stands to reason that the ability to respond to shifting relevance embodied in the "*changing* connections and *differing* orderings at different times of these separate theories" would present a contrast with the kind of rigidity in this regard necessitated by the attempt to formulate a universal and abstract means of addressing educational disquietudes. He sums up the matter succinctly: "The problem is to *see* [the various factors]—to take note that each is there and to honor it as possibly relevant to our concerns. This is difficult because we normally see only what we are instructed to look for and we are instructed by theory" (Schwab, 1971, p. 496).

I have noted that Shulman was a student of Schwab's; I take Shulman's search for "the wisdom of practice" as indebted to Schwab's concerns. When Schwab says, as above, that "the problem is to *see*," it is as much as to raise the question of how one may be *brought* to see, may *come* to see, or may *arrive* at seeing a given situation aright—particularly in light of what he calls the "uncertain unions and connections which can be effected in an eclectic," and in light of the need to notice and "honor" features "as possibly relevant to our concerns." The way in which I take Shulman as *mischaracterizing* the thrust of Schwab's problem of seeing, even as he seeks to take it up, brings out a crucial aspect of Schwab's thought, one with particular ramifications for the project of educational evaluation.

For Shulman, the heart of the "professional" lies not only in the excellent performance of a given task, but also in what he calls "knowledge" of "what and why": "The teacher is not only a master of procedure but also of content and rationale, and capable of explaining why something is done" (Shulman, 1986, p. 13). The issue I raised for Shulman earlier is that the picture of a teacher's mastery of rationale is one of *possessing* something—*having* knowledge of "what and why"—which makes any "explaining why something is done" merely the recitation of the correct, masterful (theoretical) rules possessed by the "professional." Reasons why something is done can be judged right or wrong, better or worse, in any given circumstance. But a precondition for such evaluation of one's reasons—it is surely not enough that one simply *have* reasons of whatever quality for taking a given action—involves a shared *sense* of the problem addressed.

What is false or inadequate in the above picture is precisely the way it scants the connection of reason-giving to Schwab's problem of *seeing*: explaining why something is done is revealing not only of a practical process of addressing a given concern, but also *of the nature of the concern itself*. Shulman importantly and insightfully picks up on the weight of the link between the lone teacher facing "moments of choice" in the classroom and the public responsibility for making those choices intelligible to others. What I am calling the falseness in Shulman's picture is the assumption or implication that such intelligibility to others—the shared sense of the *adequacy* of any given set of reasons-why—is given in something metaphysically separate, a region of "knowledge" accessible to both the lone teacher and any (professional?) interlocutor equally. What would demonstrate one's professionalism or rationale-mastery is the ability to recite the *right* reasons, the reasons that constitute one's knowledge of *how* to navigate a given situation.

But Schwab's problem of seeing disrupts the very notion that there *is* a "given situation," that is, that the nature of practical concern to which a teacher responds is *equally obvious* to anyone or everyone else, whether professional educator or parent or layperson. Reason-giving is therefore poorly constructed if it is imagined simply as a transcription of universally-available propositions governing the navigation of practical situations. After all, if the situation *were* simply given, no "professional" practitioner would be asked to give reasons at all, since "why something is done" would be equally obvious to everyone with the same level of "professional" skill. By contrast, reasons are *actually* requested precisely when it is *not* clear (to another) how or whether a given action has appropriately addressed a certain practical problem; this could equally indicate differing opinions on appropriate practical responses to an agreed-upon situation or differing views of the situation itself. Shulman's picture of reason-giving seems unwarrantedly restricted to the former possibility.

It is clear from Schwab's words, however, that "the problem is to *see*" a given situation in light of the relevant features, that is, to zero in on the heart of the matter. That this can be challenged—that others might take different factors to be chiefly relevant—is internal to the problem's *practical* nature: if the problem were theoretical, then the fact that we "see only what we are instructed to look for and we are instructed by theory" would pose no difficulties whatsoever; having the correct theory would be perfectly adequate. But according to Schwab, the opposite is the case. Coming to accept one's view of a problem and the intelligibility of one's response is thus *itself* a practical matter, not one guaranteed or effected by anything theoretic. But if disagreement with one's *view* of the issue is a standing possibility, this also entails the "structural publicness" of one's view, or the standing possibility of another's *coming to share* one's view of the matter. Reason-giving, on this picture of things, would not be the recitation of practical knowledge modeled upon the certainty of a given action's correctness; it would be something akin to the revelation of the practical concerns to which one's actions respond, or in light of which one's actions make sense.

Asking for reasons as pictured above would be a way of lodging a demand on the practitioner for responsibility in making the practitioner and his or her actions intelligible. Giving reasons in response to this demand would then be a way of accepting this responsibility. The notion that no theoretic viewpoint will be sufficient to *generate* relevance means that whatever intelligibility is in fact achieved will not be achieved in virtue of any *theoretic* agreement, the having of any theory in common. Coming to agree on the relevant features and correct actions—or at least seeing the sense in another's practical sight and responsiveness—is a matter of hearing or taking another's reasons as the kind of thing that Richard Eldridge calls "vehicles of reorientation," that is, as potentially elucidating of something not yet or not completely clear:

> [S]uch claims of reason are lodged as reminders and vehicles of reorientation—to and on the behalf of both others and oneself—when the applications of the concepts expressed by these words are somehow both dimly available and yet attenuated or disputed. (Eldridge, 2003, p. 6)

Returning to Shulman's references to the importance of a professional's "knowledge . . . of rationale" embodied in "explaining why something is done" in light of Schwab's words on the problem of seeing reveals another articulation of the insufficiency in Shulman's conception of the "wisdom of practice": an insufficient notion of what calls for reason-giving, and of the purposes that providing reasons serve. Schwab's assertion that "the theoretic" as such is itself inadequate to revealing the (humanly) relevant features of any given problem means that *making sense* of one's actions to another through the giving of reasons will also amount to an invitation to see the problem from one's own perspective. As Cavell notes, there are types of dubiousness expressed in the request for reasons that are "countered not by saying that a fact about the world is otherwise than you supposed, but by showing that your world is otherwise than you see" (Cavell, 1979, p. 180). Schwab's thoughts on the limits of the theoretic and the demands of the practical absolutely require that reason-giving be capable of performing this duty; Shulman's version of practical wisdom does not so clearly leave room for this role.

Selinger and Crease have something like this responsibility to a public intelligibility in mind when they level an attack on Dreyfus's phenomenology of skill development. I do not say that I take their complaint as warranted; I think they exaggerate Dreyfus's commitment to the notion that an expert is immune to criticism or otherwise isolated in virtue of his or her expertise. Nonetheless, the complaint itself reinforces the "structural publicness" of all social practice itself, even at the professional level, a publicness in light of which reason-giving always also amounts to voicing one's stake in a particular *grasp* of a situation, or to announcing one's authority toward it.

> The flaw in [Dreyfus's] assumption that skilled behavior crystallizes out of contextual sensitivity plus experience without contribution from individual or cultural biography can be traced to a failure to take into account the fact that the embodied subject, even when behaving expertly, brings to the situation what has been historically and culturally transmitted to it, and in a way such that the subject can never grasp cognitively all at once. The individual expert performer, as a consequence, does not have a complete purchase on his or her own expert behavior. Therefore, contra Dreyfus, it will always be possible in principle for an expert performer to learn about one's own performance from another, contextually sensitive person—though, again, this is not because the other has managed to obtain an objective position, but

on the contrary, because the other is differently situated. (Selinger & Crease, 2002, p. 262)

If Selinger and Crease note a danger in Dreyfus's view, a danger following from being required to defer to an expert's (singular, limited) view of a given situation, it will be worthwhile to point out that Schwab anticipates the potential issue of relying dogmatically upon any single perspective, even the expert's. Central to the practice of curriculum development for Schwab—and central, likewise, I will propose, to the successful evaluation of teachers—is the notion of "deliberation," a convening of people whose perspectives on the relevant aspects of classroom practice are likely to differ, and a convening in the interest of addressing a need which is—ultimately—local, concrete, and particular.

8.2 DELIBERATION

I suggested in introducing the practical/theoretic distinction that Schwab holds the requirements of the practical to a particularly high standard. Schwab says that an adequate alternative to a theoretic position must "somehow [take] account of all these subsubjects which pertain to man." Schwab's deliberation, then, as one of the "arts of the eclectic," provides an example of a trans-human practice that might succeed in reaching that high bar. Although Schwab conceives of deliberation exclusively in terms of making curricular decisions, the reasons that call for deliberation's intervention hold implications for the evaluation of teachers, as well. Exploring these implications will not require fully spelling out the intricacies of the deliberative process itself (a project to which Schwab himself devotes a significant portion of three full-length papers), or defending deliberation against all possible objections (which I will nonetheless name), or proposing a detailed policy of what one might call deliberative teacher evaluations.

The point, in other words, is to highlight the promising ways in which Schwab's deliberation seems to improve upon the sort of theoretic approach to teacher evaluation one finds in state policies legislated with Race to the Top funding in mind. I propose, in short, to suggest deliberation, along with what Schwab would call an eclectic approach to the evaluation of teachers, as a potential corrective to the rigidity of policies that Duncan incentivizes, which may perhaps suggest the basis for an alternative approach to policy.

Schwab's deliberation, by way of introduction or description, is both and at once a frighteningly large and unwieldy institutional and intellectual reformation, and also a small-scale proposal aimed at locally-achievable ends. Its intimidating scope manifests itself in the conclusion of Schwab's first article on the practical, in which he suggests that deliberation requires "the establishment of new journals, and the education of educators so that they can write for them and read them" (Schwab, 1969,

p. 20). In addition to journals (and the education of educators to contribute to and profit from them), Schwab sees the need for "similar forums" operating in person, composed

> of the teachers, supervisors, and administrators of a school; of the supervisors and administrators of a school system; of representatives of teachers, supervisors, and curriculum makers in subject areas and across subject areas; of the same representatives and specialists in curriculum, psychology, sociology, administration, and the subject-matter fields. (Schwab, 1969, p. 21)

Schwab's deliberation proposes, in effect, a massive restructuring of the educational scene as an antidote to the intellectual apartheid threatened by the tendency to hyper-specialization in higher education. Since the educative enterprise draws upon, or consist in, all of several specialized elements in combination, Schwab's proposal amounts to the creation of a field (in Bourdieu's sense of the term) in which for these various specialties to interact.

The relative feasibility of generating an *institutional* effort to achieve this sort of space on a national level through the formation of new journals, new organizations, and so on remains beyond the scope of my concern. Rather, the feasibility of drawing and relying upon representatives of what Schwab will call, following Aristotle, the "common places" of the school in order to evaluate its work concerns me here. This aspect, one might say, comprises the locally-actionable aspect of deliberation.

Schwab's notion of the "common places" emerges from his attempt to access the *whole* of which each "subsubject" remains merely a part. In his second article in the practical cycle, Schwab describes the means by which one might discover the (overlapping) relations among the central concerns of the enquiries undertaken by otherwise distinct fields. The notion at which Schwab arrives consists in performing a "reflexive enquiry of enquiry" in order to "press past the 'answers' propounded in [a given] paper to the suppressed questions (problems) to which the answers speak" (Schwab, 1971, pp. 513–514). In this way, the practical *concern* ought to emerge as something that requires a response, a response of which the given enquiry is but *one* kind, and not necessarily sufficient. The relative sufficiency is precisely what is evaluated in this process. For him, then, the "common places" seem to represent a marginalized area of educational research, marginal precisely because tangential to the theoretic concerns of this or that particular field.

The invocation of the Aristotelian term, as well as Schwab's vision of "enquiry" as responding to a practical concern, aligns Schwab once more with the philosophers explored in this work, including Dreyfus and Cavell. The way in which Schwab describes, in the early papers of the cycle, the process of arriving at such common places, however—"it is constructed by a certain mode of systematic comparison of principles, premises, methods, and selections used by and in each enquiry" (Schwab, 1971, p. 513)—seems to indicate that this alignment is by no means secure. The reliance, for example, upon a "systematic comparison" of a certain and articulable list of theoretical features, a comparison that will "generate a set of factors to be called 'common places' or 'topica' (Schwab, 1971, p. 513), arouses immediate suspicion.

The "systematic" nature of the exploration, the finite and aprioristically declared list of issues for exploration, and the notion that "common places" in an Aristotelian sense are in principle articulable as "a set of factors" strikes one as markedly similar in *kind* to the forms of enquiry beyond which Schwab's deliberation seeks to go. Put simply, Schwab's discussion of the common places in his second article constructs the common places as something (only?) available to a detached or disengaged perspective, as an epistemological object to be "constructed" or "generated" according to a fixed procedure. Schwab proposes to reach the "practical" by theoretic means, it seems.

Schwab's third article in the cycle, however, casts what he now calls (with no space) the "commonplaces" in a different light. Foregoing the systematic, methodical language of the previous article, he opens his "Translation into Curriculum" paper by referring to the need for deliberation as emerging from the fact that "scholars, as such, are incompetent to translate scholarly materials into curriculum": these scholars "possess one body of disciplines indispensable to the task. They lack four others, equally indispensable" (Schwab, 1973, p. 501). In the first place, one notes that Schwab does not discuss bodies of *knowledge*, but bodies of "disciplines," which speaks to his effort to foreground the way these bodies concern practical *doings*. Where in the previous article, commonplaces were conceived as a "set of factors" generated by a given enquiry, here he notes that they are "concerns, values, and operations, which arise from . . . experience" (Schwab, 1973, p. 501).

In describing these five areas—the subject-matter, the learner, the "milieus" ("milieux" in the earlier article), the teacher, and the curriculum-maker—as diverging along the axes of "concerns, values, and operations," and in insisting that each must learn something from the other's conception of the same, he seeks to move in the direction of the whole presupposed, as Dreyfus would say, by each individual commonplace.

To take the example of "subject matter" as a commonplace, it is by no means clear either that this area is to be conceived as *entirely* distinct from the other commonplaces, nor indeed that it is rigidly bounded by definitions or characteristics, either. Schwab's description of a representative of the subject-matter commonplace brings this out:

> There must be someone familiar with the scholarly materials under treatment and with the discipline from which they come. Suppose the materials under consideration are historical; then a member of the group must be familiar not only with this body of historical material but must also know what it is to be a historian. (Schwab, 1973, p. 502)

Schwab emphasizes, first of all, that the subject matter commonplace is representable as a person, an example, rather than any abstract theory. The representative of his or her particular "discipline" brings two different forms of knowing to bear: a familiarity with "this body of historical material" and also "what it is to be a historian." The latter of these two forms of knowledge is precisely the kind that I have suggested throughout is non-formalizable, the sort that the theoretic cannot touch. A representative of the subject matter, Dreyfus's work implies, *has* a sense of what it is to be a historian, but this sense is, "on pain of regress, something we can never explicitly *know*." A detached or theoretic approach to dealing with matters of schooling would require—indeed, they *do* require, in the present tense, and explicitly rely upon—formalizations of such things as "what it is to be a historian" or "what it is to be a successful adult" in order to measure matters related to education.

In formalizing the essentially non-formalizable, as the previous chapters have argued, the "sense of what we are" that the historian of Schwab's example ineluctably carries with him or her into a given room becomes distorted; or else, worse than this, its resistance to formalization alternatively leads it to be left out of such matters entirely. Schwab's call to convene embodied representatives of the many commonplaces involved in schooling, based precisely upon differences among the "concerns, values and methods" that characterize their respective disciplines, provides a measure of hope that the resulting deliberation might yield something that speaks to the "common" in the commonplace, something that accesses, at long last, the ordinary.

Unlike Chetty's composite construction of indicators of successful adulthood, for example, Schwab's deliberation, occurring in conversation among people, *can* draw upon, test, and make use of the non-formalizable notion of agreement in form of life. Deliberation, consisting of a conversation among representatives of the educational commonplaces, manages to avoid the pitfall Chetty falls into, what Dreyfus calls the requirement for "preanalyzing all situations in terms of a fixed set of possibly relevant primitives," which yields an incomplete and inflexible means of dealing with practical concerns. Through convening people, rather than abstractions, Schwab's deliberation holds out the possibility of bringing both the knowledge of a "body of historical material" and the knowledge of "what it is to be a historian" to bear upon the addressing of a given disquietude.

The language of Schwab's first two pieces in the practical cycle differs substantially from the language in the later two, as I have already suggested. The earlier ones contain the language of dividing subjects into subsubjects, a process which has no obvious endpoint, no regress-stopper; as well as that of prescribing a particular "systematic" means of uncovering the commonplaces, which seems to hint in the direction of timeless universality. The later two pieces speak a more practical language, one might say: he speaks now in terms of "disciplines" rather than subjects or subsubjects; he alludes to characteristic "concerns, values, and methods" rather than "a set of factors" that would denote a given commonplace. While it is possible to object to Schwab's method on a variety of grounds—the National Council on Teacher Quality, for example, would likely find too much "subjectivity or guesswork" in such a process, and it must be noted that Schwab's examples of deliberation would not help Duncan tell the best 30,000 of California's teachers from the worst—I think it mistaken to read the notion of the commonplaces, in particular, as aprioristically fixed elements in the deliberative process.

In other words, one could reasonably object that the existing list of commonplaces is itself incomplete, that Schwab has missed or ignored something crucial, and that this fact undermines the approach. I take issue with such an objection on two grounds: first, there is no indication in Schwab's work that these ought to be the *only* commonplaces that one ought to consider, though there is also no *need* to create more, since his notion of the "milieus" is so expansive. He considers the representative of this commonplace to have "experience of the milieus in which the child's learning will take place and in which its fruits will be brought to bear" (Schwab, 1973, p. 503)—in other words, the local (and likely larger) world. While Schwab notes some of the milieus by name—"the family, the community, the particular groupings of religious, class, ethnic genus"—he also notes that "the relevant milieus are manifold, nesting one within another like Chinese boxes" (Schwab, 1973, p. 503). This certainly does not seem to imply any limit on what may be taken as relevant to the concern at hand.

In the second place, Schwab's most elementary commitment is to the idea of attending to the local concern, the problem at hand, the need requiring a response. Nothing about Schwab's approach seems to preclude the possibility of eliminating or adding commonplaces, should the need arise. In this way, Schwab's deliberation is structurally able to bear the unpredictable issues around shifting or evolving *relevance* in a way that mathematical modeling cannot.

Understanding Schwab's conception of deliberation as an intervention in educational decision-making necessitated by the educative endeavor's resistance to theorizing as such opens a middle way between an unwarranted reliance upon the distorted conceptual terrain inherent to theoretical approaches of the type Race to the Top encourages and the total abdication of any responsibility to tell good teachers from bad that appears in the repeated recitation of the 99 percent statistic.

8.3 RESPONSIVENESS AND JUSTIFICATORY ADEQUACY

This part of the book, beginning most explicitly with Chapter 6, has sought to bring out the ways in which Race to the Top's use of student achievement data amounts to an attempt to subsume the various and meaningfully different projects of and parties to the educational endeavor under a single measure, a single mode of both knowing and telling, which Duncan and others associate with something like the generation of *new* facts, something akin to the discovery of heretofore concealed truth, upon which we can (at last) act with a measure of previously unavailable certainty. The critical thrust of this part of the book has been to demonstrate (a) that these purposes and parties—federal officials and parents, for two instances—remain somewhat distinct from one another with respect specifically to the way in which a given child's education is taken to *matter,* a fact to which Schwab responds with his notion of plural commonplaces, and (b) that the commonality shared among these purposes and parties, while extant, does not relate to these manifold differences in a way that one might characterize as grounding, erasing, subsuming, or overarching. The region of commonality, in other words, cannot render the differences either merely *superficial* or *apparent,* next to which the common or shared would be able to claim the superior status of the real or the primary.

The general outline of Schwab's deliberation, itself an outgrowth of his conception of the practical and the eclectic, differs from the rationalist approach that Duncan adopts in two important ways that render it recommendable to the general purpose of evaluating teachers and reporting on teacher quality.

In the first place, Race to the Top's use of achievement data establishes a priori the primacy of the general in terms of both educative purposes (which are economic in nature, visible in terms of careers and earnings and savings, as the Chetty research has demonstrated) and in terms of an overall evaluative context (which, for student achievement data, is always massively broad: 300,000 California teachers, the discourse of national economic security, international comparisons). The primacy of the general, thus established, allows the knowing of student learning and teacher quality to take place from a radically wide-angled and distant perspective. Diane Ravitch notes specifically the way in which the use of data is taken to supplant any need for familiarity with local context: "With their sophisticated tools and capacity to do multivariate longitudinal analysis, they did not need to enter the classroom, observe teachers, or review student work to know which teachers were the best and which were the worst, which were effective and which were ineffective" (Ravitch, 2010, p. 180).

In contrast, while Schwab includes a place for the "whole polity" under the commonplace of the milieus, his notion of deliberation would bring a representative of that milieu—say, Duncan himself, or more likely an academic or think-tank researcher with expertise in the interpretation of student achievement data—into direct conversation with teachers of the particular students in question, in addition to child psychologists, administrators at the local and state level, children themselves, members of the community, and other representatives of further commonplaces to address the need to say something meaningful about the quality of the particular teachers in a particular school. In other words, this does not deny the appropriateness of responding to national-level concerns; it simply denies that something like the measures of teacher value-added are capable of speaking for themselves, or ought to be simply deferred to as a matter of natural right.

Schwab's view does not, then, stand in direct *opposition* to the teacher-quality policies of Race to the Top. Such opposition would mean that Schwab's deliberation would *only* take into account local conditions and be amenable to a local telling, much in the way that Race to the Top proposes to use broadly general resources—whose relation to the local involves something like the mere statistical approximation of limited and fixed "local conditions"—in order to speak simultaneously and univocally to national and local purposes as though they were in every case identical. Rather, Schwab's deliberation saves a place, explicitly, for the concerns of the general—concerns that find their appropriate response in precisely the use of student achievement data to generate measures of teacher value-added. Part of the deliberative process would involve balancing *this* type of response to the question of teacher evaluation with others, and achieving this balance through interpersonal or intersubjective conversation.

The assumption of the reform movement behind Race to the Top holds student achievement data in such high regard that no such discussion is necessary: in the face of disagreement, student achievement data simply has it right, where local ignorance of one kind or another is responsible for any restiveness or disagreement with its results. In an op-ed advocating for better dissemination of achievement data in reference to (then merely) proposed parent trigger legislation, Peg Tyre laments with respect to school choice or open enrollment policies that "sometimes the parents don't even know that the 'choice' they are making is a bad one." Tyre's solution is standard fare: "parents need unbiased, accessible information about what solid research tells us works best in schools—even if they don't have a computer at home or if English isn't their first language" (Tyre, 2011). In cases where parental judgment as to the quality of their children's education conflicts with "what solid research tells us works best in schools," the parents are simply wrong. It is merely a manifestation of the parents not "even know[ing] that the choice they are making is a bad one."

Disagreement in judgments, for the reformers, indicates ignorance on the part of those who lack the data. Disagreement in judgments, for Schwab, by extreme contrast, expresses the diversity of needs to which education responds; such disagreement expresses the need for deliberation itself (though arriving at consensus is not necessarily its goal). In other words, although this is perhaps a different claim, the standing possibility that parents *can* be incorrect in their judgments calls for *conversation* rather than an attempt at the absolute foreclosure of this possibility via an abdication to "accessible information." Such an abdication would be justified if it were the case that parents could *never* be correct in disagreeing with data's verdicts. The weakness or the clumsiness of the conceptual construction of educational quality behind the data, however, certainly does not warrant this kind of faith, this kind of abdication.

The second area of contrast between Duncan's proposed use of student achievement data and Schwab's concept of deliberation proves to be the most salient, and it follows directly from the above. I have said before, and in fact in many places, that it remains unclear throughout Duncan's many public statements whether the problem he seeks to address by recourse to the use of achievement data is one of *knowing* or one of *telling*, one of epistemological uncertainty or one of felt justificatory inadequacy. Throughout the literature on best practices, one finds that knowing and telling are simply bound up together—the slow spread of "best practices" is taken to be a communication problem, for example. Duncan's statements in the *Daily Show* interview echo this view, as does Tyre's belief that "accessible information" provides a solution to incorrect parental judgment. Once *known*, the *telling* of a thing requires little further effort. Tyre's construction of the matter in terms of "accessible information," in fact, beautifully renders the notion in appropriately passive form. Telling is hardly required at all; the mere publication of the data in a location accessible even to parents who "don't have a computer at home" or for whom "English isn't [the] first language," in Tyre's words, will do the trick.

The centrality of discussion to the deliberative enterprise, as Schwab has it, presents a radical departure from the view behind Race to the Top's policies. On Schwab's view, the right and responsibility to enter into the *telling* of a thing—the declaration of a judgment of teacher quality, for example—is afforded by a certain standing with respect to the educative context in question. The declaration of a judgment is an expression, in fact, of that standing and that responsibility. But precisely this standing, along with its rights and responsibilities, renders one beholden to acknowledge the standings of the other representatives of the further commonplaces. Rendering a judgment within the deliberative process, then, is not itself an act of finality, nor a pronunciation even of a subjective fact; it is rather the staking of claim in the space of conversation, the voicing of a judgment as a means of testing it, of inviting a response.

The most basic idea here partly agrees with Duncan's particular fear of erroneous subjectivity or bias: no practical action in the realm of education, be it curriculum-making or teacher evaluation, can be taken by oneself, all alone; the responsibility is shared; we have to do it together. But Schwab's stance also profoundly disagrees with Duncan's: neither is it the case that someone might create something (algorithmic, robotic, or otherwise) that would then do the work *for* us; the shared responsibility is inalienable; *we* have to do it *together*. Neither recourse to the tyranny of pure subjectivity in judging nor recourse to an inescapably absolute or objective judgment will suffice. Evaluating something connected "with the trans-human," as Crease says, requires trans-human intervention.

On several occasions, I have quoted Cavell as suggesting that the problem of skepticism is such that "efforts to solve it continue its work of denial" (Cavell, 1990, p. 23). Precisely what is denied in Duncan's proposals to remediate the issues evident in the 99 percent statistic by achieving a *new* kind of certainty in the realm of teacher evaluation is the absolute dependency of the ordinary concept of good teaching on the nonformalizable agreements in form of life, which also amounts to a denial of a human responsibility in rendering judgments. Cavell might as well be speaking directly of Race to the Top's recourse to student achievement data when he says,

> My contrary sense [to other early interpreters] was that Wittgenstein was articulating what human assurance amounts to, that it does not stop short of conviction in the world, but that we ourselves become restive with this assurance, and we have the power to undermine ourselves in the name of an, as it were, unachievable or rather illusory rationality. (Cavell, 2010, p. 376)

Throughout this book, I have sought to demonstrate or provide warrant for the idea that the kind of absolute "rationality" that the use of teacher value-added seeks to grasp is indeed "unachievable or rather illusory." Moreover, I have sought to detail the ways in which striving for this illusory sort of rationality in fact amounts to undermining ourselves, precluding us from relying upon what we know, responding to the world as it presents itself. In the new protocols for teacher evaluation, this pattern is particularly apparent.

The most glaring problem with the turn to student achievement data in this area is that it does not adequately solve the problem that called for its intervention in the first place. The fact that the 99 percent statistic can do what it does in Duncan's rhetoric, that is, occasion an exclamation of the form, "That *can't* be right," reveals the problem: the results of teacher evaluations are somehow out of alignment with the (obvious) facts plainly evident to common sense. The turn to student achievement data for the purpose of evaluating teachers attempts to cope with this discrepancy by (a) discovering a universal, ontic metric of teacher quality and (b) comparing classroom teachers to this standard and to one another on the basis of their students' test scores. By creating a *true* measure of teacher quality, then, the use of student achievement data offers to foreclose upon any sort of "That *can't* be right" reaction. In short, it proposes to bring explanations or justifications to an end by discovering the *truth* of the matter, by *making sure* that the judgments are in each case inescapably right.

In addition to the arguments throughout this book that the truth of the matter is in principle resistant to showing up in a form amenable to representation in student achievement data, it is an empirical fact that the employment of student achievement data in teacher evaluations has not in fact prevented on-the-ground human disagreement with the results of the evaluation protocols. The news media routinely cites the failures of data-driven evaluations to align with local judgments, some examples of which I have already quoted. The crowning example, however, is that of Kim Cook, rated unsatisfactory despite her colleagues' having voted her the teacher of the year (Strauss, 2012). The use of student achievement data is supposed to be *simply* correct, to dispel doubts and achieve certainty; if it were capable of doing so, the impersonal nature of its application would present no problems. As it is, any finality of the evaluative judgments is only achieved by fiat: where a teacher like Kim Cook, or indeed any parent or colleague familiar with her work, might wish to lodge an objection based on criteria that teacher value-added has excluded, there is simply no way of raising such issue: there is no one listening for, or prepared to respond to, any such "That *can't* be right" exclamation.

The irony of this consequence is apparent when one recalls the motivating force behind the evaluation protocols championed by Duncan and other reformers: a structural unresponsiveness to a "That *can't* be right" state of affairs. Because teacher evaluations have previously had too little effect upon tenure, compensation, or retention decisions—the fact that constitutes the deafness to, by ignoring the import of, any "That *can't* be right" response—the solution that the Obama administration proposes is to use student achievement data to *get* it right.

But this solution in fact *retains* what I am calling the structural unresponsiveness to any sort of objection to or disagreement with the results of evaluation protocols. What is more, through a commitment to this "unachievable or rather illusory rationality" on the basis of which teacher value-added is derived in the first place, the reliance upon student achievement data as a "preponderant criterion" in teacher evaluation in fact prevents judgments from being accurate at all, that is, with respect to the ordinary sense of good teaching that explicitly motivates school reform initiatives in the first place. To paraphrase something I have said elsewhere, Race to the Top's policies with regard to teacher evaluations respond to the terrifying fact that human beings *can* be wrong, the fact that error is possible, in such a way as to make it *impossible* to be *right*.

NOTES

1. For a much wider perspective on the rationalist lineage in the American intellectual tradition, including especially the shortcomings of "systems analysis" as developed by RAND during the Second World War, see the following, substantially diverse historical monographs: (Levy, 2012; Martini, 2012; Medvetz, 2012; Mehta, 2013).
2. In Wittgenstein's *Nachlass* 219, 81: "That is the fatal thing about the scientific way of thinking (which today possesses the whole world), that it considers every disquietude to be a question and is surprised not to be able to answer it."
3. It may also be important at this early point to militate against an overzealous criticism of Schwab's project on the basis of the obvious utopian impulse behind the urge to "take account of all the subsubjects that pertain to man." Without delving into detail so early, I wish merely to suggest that a consideration of what it may mean to "take account" of all subsubjects may reveal that such a view does not entail the possibility of *having* a sort of panoptic

view of all these subsubjects together. This panoptic perspective, after all, would be awfully similar in ontological status to the "metatheory" that Schwab puts out of play early on. It might rather refer to the practical ability to zero-in on the relevant features of the matter in a manner similar to that which Dreyfus describes.

4. It will be well worth noting, although I do not wish to spend significant time on it, that this conception of an "art" and its requirements is wildly different from Lemov's.

REFERENCES

Cavell, S. (1979). *The Claim of Reason*. New York: Oxford University Press.
Cavell, S. (1990). *Conditions Handsome and Unhandsome*. Chicago: University of Chicago Press.
Cavell, S. (2010). *Little Did I Know: Excerpts from Memory*. Stanford, CA: Stanford University Press.
Conant, J. (1993). Kierkegaard, Wittgenstein and nonsense. In T. Cohen, P. Guyer, H. Putnam, & S. Cavell (Eds.), *Pursuits of Reason* (pp. 195–224). Lubbock: Texas Tech University Press.
Dreyfus, H. L. (1992). *What Computers Still Can't Do: a Critique of Artificial Reason*. Cambridge, MA: M.I.T. Press.
Eisner, E. (1984). No Easy Answers: Joseph Schwab's Contributions to Curriculum. *Curriculum Inquiry*, 14(2), 201–210.
Eldridge, R. (2003). *Stanley Cavell*. Cambridge: Cambridge University Press.
Levy, J. (2012). *Freaks of Fortune: The Emerging World of Capitalism and Risk in America*. Cambridge, MA: Harvard University Press.
Martini, E. (2012). *Agent Orange: History, Science, and the Politics of Uncertainty*. Amherst: University of Massachusetts Press.
Medvetz, T. (2012). *Think Tanks in America*. Chicago: University of Chicago Press.
Mehta, J. (2013). *The Allure of Order*. Oxford: Oxford University Press.
Ravitch, D. (2010). *The Death and Life of the Great American School System*. New York: Basic Books.
Schwab, J. J. (1959). The "Impossible" Role of the Teacher in Progressive Education. *The School Review*, 67(2), 139–159. Retrieved from http://www.jstor.org/stable/1083642
Schwab, J. J. (1969). The Practical: A Language for Curriculum. *The School Review*, 78(1), 1–23 CR—Copyright © 1969 The University of. Retrieved from http://www.jstor.org/stable/1084049
Schwab, J. J. (1971). The Practical: Arts of Eclectic. *The School Review*, 79(4), 493–542 CR—Copyright © 1971 The University. Retrieved from http://www.jstor.org/stable/1084342
Schwab, J. J. (1973). The Practical 3: Translation into Curriculum. *The School Review*, 81(4), 501–522 CR—Copyright © 1973 The University. Retrieved from http://www.jstor.org/stable/1084423
Schwab, J. J. (1983). The Practical 4: Something for Curriculum Professors to Do. *Curriculum Inquiry*, 13(3), 239–265 CR—Copyright © 1983 Ontario Instit. Retrieved from http://www.jstor.org/stable/1179606
Selinger, E. M., & Crease, R. P. (2002). Dreyfus on Expertise: The Limits of Phenomenological Analysis. *Continental Philosophy Review*, 35(3), 245–279. doi:10.1023/a:1022643708111

Shulman, L. (1986). Those Who Understand: Knowledge Growth in Teaching. *Harvard Educational Review, 57*, 1–22.
Strauss, V. (2012). A "Value-Added" Travesty for an Award-Winning Teacher. *Washington Post.* Retrieved February 24, 2014, from http://www.washingtonpost.com/blogs/answer-sheet/wp/2012/12/03/a-value-added-travesty-for-an-award-winning-teacher/
Tyre, P. (2011, September 17). Putting Parents in Charge. *New York Times*, p. SR8.
Wittgenstein, L. (2000). *Wittgenstein's Nachlass: The Bergen Electronic Edition. Text and Facsimile Version.* Oxford: Oxford University Press.

Conclusion
Courage, Conviction, Evaluation

Central to the discussion throughout these recent chapters, surfacing occasionally to demand a response only to find itself deferred or postponed, has been the question of *courage* in relation to the project of evaluating teachers. Duncan proposes that all other elements necessary to the endeavor of reporting on teacher quality are in place, and now:

> The biggest barrier, the only remaining barrier in my mind is whether we have the courage. It takes courage to expose our weaknesses with a truly transparent data system. It takes courage to admit our flaws and take steps to address them. (Duncan, 2009)

The courage to which Duncan refers pertains to transparency, the exposure of weakness, and the admission of flaws. The formulation obviously takes for granted that, in the absence of the resources available thanks to the use of student achievement data, the conceptual content of high-quality teaching and learning has been opaque or unclear: achievement data promises transparency, then, through securing certainty as to what "good teaching" really means and creating a metric against which to compare instances of teaching and teachers. On this picture, an epistemological lack is responsible, at bottom, for the hiddenness or concealment of any flaws engendered by our evaluation practices.

Now that the use of student achievement data enables certainty in this regard, "the only remaining barrier" to rectifying the flawed evaluation systems of the past is "whether we have the courage," the courage, that is, to find ourselves and our education system flawed, to have our flaws named and our weaknesses revealed. Objections to the sovereignty of student achievement data are therefore constructed as manifestations of something like cowardice, a fear of exposure, an unwillingness to address failures.

Quite to the contrary, the arguments against a heavy reliance upon student achievement data and in favor of something more along the lines of Schwab's deliberation follow from a view on which turning to student achievement data as a "preponderant criterion" of teacher quality is an abdication of responsibility both for recognizing examples of good and bad teaching and for entering judgments thereof, judgments that will carry weight in terms of compensation and personnel decisions.

In pointing out the clear incommensurability of the technical sense of good teaching available according to student achievement data and the ordinary sense of good teaching that requires no such statistical representation—the type of good teaching whose existence and recognizability is attested to in the examples of Duncan's mother, Mrs. Grady, Shulman's "Nancy," and the teachers of Carol Penskar's children; and whose ordinariness is revealed in Duncan's and Obama's reliance upon the shared experiences of their audiences for affirmation of statements of the form "We know what success looks like"—I have sought to demonstrate that whatever failure is signified in the New Teacher Project's finding that 99 percent of teachers are all rated the same is not an *epistemological* failure, and thus not a failure correctible by epistemological means, say by providing new facts.

Indeed, revealing that the ordinary sense of good teaching constitutes the need to which Race to the Top and other reform initiatives respond, and revealing that this sense of good teaching is grounded upon a nonformalizable agreement in form of life or shared understanding of being, means among other things that we cannot coherently *doubt* our knowledge of good teaching, our practical ability to recognize instances of excellent, mediocre, or flawed instances thereof. Attempting to construct certainty where there is no genuine possibility of doubt is the skeptic's route to distorting "our fundamental relation to the world" (Mulhall, 1998, p. 106) via an "attempt to convert the human condition, the condition of humanity, into an intellectual difficulty, a riddle" (Cavell, 1979, p. 493).

It is worth considering an idea that I broached earlier: that if the 99 percent statistic represents one sort of denial of a responsibility to tell good teachers from bad teachers, Duncan's proposal of student achievement data simply amounts to a different form of the same denial. Though bolder, one might admit, than absolutely refusing to differentiate among teachers on the axis of quality at all, the construction of abstract and inflexible definitions of both teaching and learning for the purpose of generating ontic measures of "teacher effectiveness" to be applied universally is merely a different inflection of the refusal of responsibility, one whose "sweeping appearance of success" makes recognizing it *as* a refusal of responsibility profoundly difficult.

Ravitch's 2013 work already points to existing examples of alternative approaches to evaluating teachers on an axis of quality when such evaluations will bear consequences. My work has not sought to provide further examples; rather, by examining Joseph Schwab's thoughts on deliberation, and by bringing those into conversation with Cavell's thinking on the application of skeptical procedures generally, it has been my hope to show that the need to which deliberative processes respond must be addressed deliberatively. This need, the need to recite one's reasons and take into account the reasoning of others, cannot in principle be evaded simply by asserting that something like achievement data adequately represents a non-formalizable concept like "good teaching."

In fact, this impossibility is empirically demonstrated, as well, in complaints about the correctness of particular evaluations in Florida, as my earlier example showed. Constructing ontic measures of teacher quality is not equal to the task of bringing explanations to an end. As a metric, teacher value-added and the abstract algorithm according to which it is weighted alongside other measures, is anchored to human concerns in a way that the meter stick is not. Such human concerns express the fact that there is *more* to "good teaching" than what it is available in achievement data, more criteria by which we know and have such a concept.

Cavell's thoughts on the matter sum it up nicely:

> The establishing of criteria makes the process of judging more convenient, more open, less private or arbitrary. One might say: here establishing criteria allows us to *settle* judgments publicly, not exactly by making them certain, but by declaring what the points are at issue in various judgments, and then making them *final* (on a given occasion). That is a practice worth having; human decisions cannot wait upon certainty. But it is therefore one which can be abused. In assuming the burden of finality in the absence of certainty, an authority stakes the virtue of its community: if its judgments are not accepted as scrupulously fair, in its criteria and its application of criteria, the community is shown to that extent not to provide a secure human habitation for its members; it fails to take up the slack between the uncertainty of judgment and the finality of decision. (Cavell, 1979, p. 31)

The teacher evaluation protocols advocated for in Race to the Top express *precisely* the problems to which Cavell offers the "establishing of criteria" as a response, and which the deliberation that Schwab proposes also addresses. The esoteric statistical manipulations that generate teacher value-added, comprehensible only to advanced psychometricians, render the measures themselves effectively "private," the criteria "arbitrary," and the consequent judgments therefore equally private, equally arbitrary.

Schwab's deliberation, the acknowledgement of the need for the multiple commonplaces and the centrality of trans-human conversation among them, embodies the possibilities afforded by an alternative form of telling. The flaws, weaknesses, and incompleteness of each commonplace are voiced, accounted for, and responded to—along with, one must add, the unique and productive view of the multifarious practical situation. The eventual pronouncement of a judgment on teacher quality, the resulting evaluation, would then express a process of "settling judgments," not by means of an *in*human or purportedly objective methodology, but rather by admittedly fallible and incomplete human beings. Perhaps strangely, this ought not to be taken as expressing a shortcoming in terms of human *knowledge*, but as expressing rather something about the knowable *nature* of teaching and learning itself, something I take Wittgenstein to allude to in §208 of the *Investigations:* "The fact that we cannot write down all the digits of π is not a human shortcoming, as mathematicians sometimes think."

In this light, Duncan's reliance on student achievement data, the view on which such data represents something radically new and unquestionably valuable to the prospect of evaluating teachers, represents something like the opposite of courage. As we have seen with the indicators that Chetty's research relies upon, the correlations that justify the use of teacher value-added in the evaluations of teachers rest upon nothing less frail than agreements in criteria, in form of life. But teacher value-added is not taken as an expression of any "uncertainty of judgment"; quite the contrary.

The use of achievement data represents a shunning of responsibility for the "burden of finality": its value is taken to lie in its inhuman objectivity, its ability to *provide* certainty about quality upon which to offer judgments of teachers. Its use indicates precisely a retreat from responsibility to communities and their members; it is a retreat from the trans-human; no one stakes authority or risks exposure in communicating the results of the calculations. For all that, it still fails to *escape* the trans-human, relying, as we have endlessly seen, on the same agreement in forms of life as the methods to which it considers itself superior.

Cavell speaks to this issue, as well:

> The connection between the epistemological and the moral threat to human existence lies in companion ways in which we give over the little moments of perspective and freedom and our disposal—in morality through conformity, stripping ourselves of our partiality; in epistemology through an apparently innate perverseness, stripping ourselves of our shared criteria, opting for false totalities, theories of our lives. (Cavell, 1990, p. 124)

Duncan is quite correct when he insists, first, on the need to get serious about teacher evaluation, and second, on this endeavor's requiring of courage. The 99 percent statistic indicates that, whatever else is taken to be entailed here, distinguishing among teachers in terms of their quality *as* teachers has not been taken as seriously as the obvious variation among teachers demands. That the means of knowing good teaching upon which Duncan's Race to the Top relies prove no less able to escape the vagaries of the trans-human, as demonstrated in both its conceptual limitations in Chapter 1 and its practical limitations in Chapters 2–4, indicates that it cannot serve either as a singular measure itself, nor (what amounts to the same thing) as the ontic ground of the various "multiple" measures. Rather, the criteria expressed in growth in student test scores ought to be brought into *conversation* with other forms of criteria in a public or shared protocol for settling judgments, something Schwab models with his notion of deliberation.

Recalling Strong, et al.'s findings that, despite pervasive agreements among judges, these human judges all disagreed with the verdicts of teacher value-added, one might see the judges as expressing different "concerns, values, and operations," as Schwab would say, rather than *simply* being "inaccurate," as Strong and colleagues have it. Taken this way, each party to this disagreement speaks for and as a mere part of a whole, neither rightfully the occupier of any superior place and each in need of the other's augmentation. Both, one might add, have a *view* of the whole of which they are part (this is entailed in *seeing* themselves as a part of a whole), but these views differ; this is what, in fact, *requires* conversation.

Another way of taking Ravitch's claim that standardized tests "are social constructions whose questions and answers are written by fallible human beings" (Ravitch, 2013, p. 264) would be to aver that these test instruments, no less than the human beings that designed them, express particular interests and concerns, particular systems of value, particular views of what matters most in the educational endeavor. The danger in taking these assessments to be "scientific instruments," as she also has it, is exactly coextensive with the danger in taking human purposes as objects of natural science. Such objective study clearly has a role to play in understanding the human, and one would not wish to banish it from consideration, but such objective study also cannot function as a lone arbiter of truth. Precisely the unclear size of the role that various stakeholders ought to play in evaluating teachers, precisely the number of commonplaces that bear upon the educational endeavor, requires the concepts of courage and responsibility.

Cavell equates the sort of urge underlying the turn to achievement data with the quest for purity in philosophy: "The requirement of purity imposed by philosophy now looks like a wish to leave *me* out, I mean each of us, the self, with its arbitrary needs and unruly desires" (Cavell, 1990, p. 77). This requirement of purity is itself the cause of the distortion I have traced throughout, given the non-formalizable nature of the ordinary concept of good teaching. The need for conversation or deliberation follows directly therefrom: the ordinary concept of good teaching, as something that we cannot fail to know but also cannot successfully or finally formalize, means that "no judge or rule knows better than we, and we have no rules that will decide the issue or that will rule one of us out as incompetent to decide" (Cavell, 1990, p. 114) in matters regarding educational quality.

Cavell's insight is that the possibility of conceptual distortion is a standing threat to the aspirations and conduct of practical human endeavors; it is a further insight of his that attempting to foreclose upon this threat, to defeat it once and for all, say by "discovering" the true fact of what good teaching *really* is, is itself a manifestation of this distortion. I take it that this is roughly what he means when he notes that "Wittgenstein's disappointment with knowledge is not that it fails to be better than it is (for example, immune to skeptical doubt), but rather that it fails to make us better than we are, or provide us with peace" (Cavell, 2005, p. 5), which affirms the intuition that the achievement of peace or rest or satisfaction is not, in any circumstance, a simple effect of epistemic certainty. Employing knowledge in the process of becoming "better than we are" is a matter, for Cavell, of assembling reminders for others, and allowing oneself to be reminded, of values sincerely held but overlooked in the present, or momentarily forgotten. Schwab's deliberation, although originally envisioned as applicable to a process of curriculum-making, lends itself at least equally well to the evaluation of teachers.

Duncan's original call for "courage" in reforming the ways in which teacher quality is made visible and public is explicitly conceived in terms of a willingness to expose "our flaws" (Duncan, 2009). The flaws he speaks of are practical or procedural—student achievement data will reveal what *is not* working, or *where* our educational system is failing. But given the freezing of relevance according to which such achievement data will yield its verdicts, the sort of exposure to judgment that would require genuine courage, genuine responsibility, is ruled out of court: thinking of "our flaws" in terms of forgotten, overlooked, or marginalized values—the ordinary criteria by which we know and have an everyday sense of "good teaching"—any exposure of *these* flaws would require an openness to being reminded of further reasons that education matters, further aspirations that education makes possible. Such a form of exposure, requiring honest courage, would therefore require turning toward others as legitimate sources of understanding in matters of determining the quality of a given teacher or a given educational experience.

Taking it upon oneself to hear reason as well as to provide reasons in a deliberative forum would constitute, I suggest, a way of living up to Ravitch's call to transform accountability into responsibility. Accepting such responsibility in the realm of educational evaluation, through assuming with one's own voice "the burden of finality in the absence of certainty" (Cavell, 1979, p. 31) means also, for each person involved, taking "the power to act on behalf of an attainable world I can actually desire" (Cavell, 2005, p. 33).

In the Introduction, I took Kristof's recitation of Olly Neal's transformative experience with Mrs. Grady as Kristof fairly explicitly intends it to be taken, that is, as an illustration of the warrant or call for the policies encouraged by Race to the Top. Taking Kristof's narrative recounting in this way, I showed that the story's particulars, insofar as reform initiatives would fail to recognize them, do not support such initiatives in the way that Kristof expects them to do.

In raising Kristof's appeal to Mrs. Grady once more at the end of this book, I would like to hear the narrative in a different light, as offering reminders of what we esteem in teaching and in teachers, reminders of what we stand to forget or overlook in turning over the responsibility for accuracy in teacher evaluations to ontic measures of teacher effectiveness. The call for Schwab's deliberation is directly related to Cavell's sense that, as a standing requirement of participation in a democratic society, we are always in principle open to the possibility of learning about ourselves and our values from others. In this sense, Kristof's article reminds us not only that we expect education to have life-changing effects, but also that we value teachers in their capacity to imagine the best for their students, regardless of previous behavior; in their willingness to intervene for the betterment of students not officially enrolled in their classes; in their improvisational ability to sometimes see the particular fit between unconventional means and highly conventional ends in unique or peculiar situations.

To *find* and declare Mrs. Grady an exemplary teacher, someone whose example is worthy of emulation, we must be open to the possibility of being reminded not only that criteria beyond achievement data and even classroom observation can be relevant, but also that rendering a decision or a judgment with respect to educational quality requires in every instance the interaction of these criteria, an "honor[ing]" of such criteria "as possibly relevant to our concerns," as Schwab has said. This, too, is one of Schwab's "arts": there is no abstract method of accurately calculating relevance.

Given, then, that such balancing among possibly relevant criteria, possibly relevant facts, poses a legitimate and inescapable difficulty in the realm of teacher evaluation, Schwab's deliberation provides a model of a forum in which such balancing work might take place. I suggest that one think of Schwab's references to the "commonplaces" in terms of Dreyfus's "sub-worlds," which he has characterized as "local elaborations of a whole which they *presuppose*" (Dreyfus, 1992, p. 14). The concerns and values particular, or particularly apparent, to each of the disparate commonplaces are, on this view, understood as inflections of something held in common, that is, as concerns and values structurally available to representatives of other commonplaces, as well. In this light, Cavell's reading of Emerson's sensitivity to the fact that "our own rejected thoughts . . . come back to us with a certain alienated majesty" (Emerson, 1983, p. 259) might be pictured as a scene within the process of Schwab's deliberation, a scene in which it is possible to reminded by another of something that is nevertheless deeply one's own. Richard Eldridge has something like this in mind when he refers to "claims of reason" as being entered as reminders "to and on the behalf of both others and oneself" (Eldridge, 2003, p. 6), reminders that are called for precisely in situations where "it is our distorted sense of what is important—call this our values—that is distorting our lives" (Cavell, 2005, p. 40).

At the end of the Introduction, I suggested applying "the Mrs. Grady test" to any proposed system for the evaluation of teachers. But to the extent that Kristof's example is plainly recognizable as an example of excellent teaching, the moral of Olly Neal's story is that we require no such litmus test in order to apply the concept of "excellence" (or any other qualitative category) to a particular instance of teaching. Instead of a system, what is required is the sort of courage involved in the actual exposure of flaws or incompleteness, say our partiality. This is the courage to stand behind one's reasons for entering a particular qualitative claim. This is the same courage required to have one's aspirations redirected or fleshed out by the claims of another. This is the courage, in other words, to recognize and receive the "attainable world [one] can actually desire" in another's testimony. The courage involved here is the courage to (take a) stand upon the conviction in the world embodied in our recitations of examples and the aspirations they denote. The truth of what good teaching *really* is lies here, or else nowhere.

REFERENCES

Cavell, S. (1979). *The Claim of Reason*. New York: Oxford University Press.
Cavell, S. (1990). *Conditions Handsome and Unhandsome*. Chicago: University of Chicago Press.
Cavell, S. (2005). *Cities of Words: Pedagogical Letters on a Register of the Moral Life* (p. 458). Cambridge, MA: Harvard University Press.
Dreyfus, H. L. (1992). *What Computers Still Can't Do: A Critique of Artificial Reason*. Cambridge, MA: MIT Press.
Duncan, A. (2009). Robust Data Gives Us the Roadmap to Reform. U.S. Department of Education. Retrieved from http://www2.ed.gov/news/speeches/2009/06/06082009.html
Eldridge, R. (2003). *Stanley Cavell*. Cambridge University Press.
Emerson, R. W. (1983). *Essays and Lectures*Library of America.
Mulhall, S. (1998). *Stanley Cavell: Philosophy's Recounting of the Ordinary*. New York: Oxford University Press.
Ravitch, D. (2013). *Reign of Error: The Hoax of the Privatization Movement and the Danger to America's Public Schools*. New York: Knopf.

Index

A

accountability: reform movement's emphasis on, 2, 37; turning, into responsibility, 176, 191, 196, 225. *See also* Duncan, Arne; "lying"; Race to the Top (RTT) educational policy

achievement data. *See* test scores

achievement gaps: as linked to opportunity gaps, 3; NCLB as exposing, 7–8

action: Duncan's need for, 17, 153; Fogelin on consensus in, 113; Schwab on, as aspect of "the practical," 201–2, 206, 215. *See also* behaviors; doing

advanced beginners, 128–30

AI. *See* Artificial Intelligence

The Allure of Order (Mehta), 2–6, 86

Anderson, Jenny, xix, xx, 47, 177–78

Aristotle, 133, 202, 209–10

art (Lemov on), 95–97, 137–38, 218n4. *See also* "arts of the eclectic"

Artificial Intelligence (AI): aims for, 89, 103; assumptions about teacher education as similar to those about, 59, 84–99, 199–200; failures of, 80, 92–94, 96–98, 101–2, 109, 111, 120, 125, 129, 133, 137, 157, 170, 199; and "family resemblances," 129; fears about, 140; as running on "facts-and-rules" basis, 80, 109, 121, 131. *See also* "micro-worlds"; rationalist assumptions

"arts of the eclectic," 202–5, 208, 213, 226

assessment. *See* data; evaluation (of teaching); tests; test scores (achievement data; "value-added metrics")

B

Ball, Deborah, 60; and Mathematical Knowledge for Teachers, 90, 94, 139; mentalistic views of, 61, 70–71, 100; and Pedagogical Content Project, 5, 71, 81n1, 94; teacher training views of, 114, 122n2, 137

Bar-Hillel, Maya, 138

behaviorism, 80; Lemov's, 63–71, 79, 86, 94–97, 114; Schwab's alternative to, 202–3; Shulman's, 70–77, 86, 94, 96, 126; of teachers' "best practices," defined, 60; Wittgenstein's alleged, 114. *See also* behaviors; "facts and rules" assumptions; rationalist assumptions

behaviors: "best practices" as collection of, that allegedly work, 60, 62–70, 84, 86–87, 100–101, 154, 156, 176, 181–82, 187–88, 215; lack of need for, to justify work of excellent teachers, 117; learning as a set of, 21–22, 29, 39–40, 46, 50–52, 54, 100; rubrics for, in classroom observation, 46–47, 52, 54, 62, 128, 157, 191; search for, that lead toward "ordinary" concept of good teaching, xx, 5, 19, 21–23, 58–59, 69, 72, 86–87, 128, 137–39, 197, 215; standardization of, for student teachers,

126; students' contrary, 63–70; sum of, as less than actual learning, 66–67, 112, 125. *See also* behaviorism; code-cracking metaphor; "facts and rules" assumptions

"best practices" (for teachers): Artificial Intelligence as analogy for, 84–98, 101–2; as collection of behaviors that allegedly work, 60, 62–70, 84, 86–87, 100–101, 154, 156, 176, 181–82, 187–88, 215; defined, 79; Duncan on teacher training as knowing and sharing, 58–59, 90, 94, 98, 138, 215; ordinary good teaching as impossible to reproduce using, 86–87, 94–98, 116–19, 138–39, 154–56, 170–71; origins of, 86; search for, xx, 5, 19, 21–23, 58–59, 69, 72, 86–87, 128, 137–39, 197, 215; sharing of, 79, 94

Blue Book (Wittgenstein), 104, 115

Bourdieu, Pierre, 133, 209

Brill, Steven, xiii–xiv, 42

Brookings Institution reports, 47–49, 54, 119. *See also* Glazerman, S., et al.

Bush, George W. *See* No Child Left Behind (NCLB) educational policy

business world (scaling metaphor in), 20, 78

C

Cahill, Kevin, 85–86, 101, 104, 119–20, 125, 190

California teachers, 23–25, 72, 142–43, 179, 212–13

caring. *See* involvement

causation (educational): assumption of, between good teaching and students' success, xii, 21–22, 45, 47, 52, 142, 144–46, 149, 162, 171; assumption of, between specific teaching behaviors and skillful practice, 73, 77, 84, 112, 153; assumption of, between teacher knowledge and skillful teaching, 84, 94; test scores as replacing, to predict students' future success, 152–53

Cavell, Stanley, 101, 109, 125, 151, 171, 197, 209; on bringing explanations to an end, 184, 191, 193, 196; on educative failure, 111–12; on the human condition, 221; on the moral threat to human existence, 223, 226; on reason-giving, 207; on search for purity in philosophy, 224–25; on shared judgments, 112–13, 117, 130; on skepticism, 17, 28, 38, 68, 122n1, 177, 215–16, 221–22

CBAs (collective bargaining agreements). *See* teachers' unions

certainty. *See* skepticism

certification (for teachers), 19–20, 33–34, 43–44

charter schools: Duncan on, 19, 186–88; reformers' desire to expand, 3, 43. *See also* National Alliance for Public Charter Schools Conference

Chetty, R., et al.: as example of academic discussion of good teaching, xi, xii, xiii; Kristof's summary of, 139; "technical" definition of good teaching used by, xv, xvi, xviii, xix, 4, 223; as tying test scores to students' later economic outcomes, 13, 163–66, 170–71, 180, 211, 213

Chicago (Illinois): Duncan on his mother's teaching in, 29–30, 144–45; Duncan on school turnarounds in, 27; Duncan's pilot performance-pay system in, 35

"chicken-and-egg" language problem, 89, 102–3, 115, 159

CLASS Project, 19, 79

classroom observation. *See* observation (classroom, for teacher evaluation)

code-cracking metaphor (for teaching), 18–19, 22, 61, 85, 110, 158

codified representations (of teacher practice). *See* "facts and rules" assumptions

"cognitivism." *See* rationalist assumptions: in views of skillful human activity

collective bargaining. *See* teachers' unions

colleges and universities: admission policies of, 164–65, 167; students' readiness for careers and, as criterion for evaluating teachers, 9–13, 22, 25, 28–29, 34, 51, 162–66, 178, 194n3; test scores' relation to being admitted to competitive, xi–xiii, xv, 13, 153, 158, 162–68, 170–71, 180, 183–84, 188, 211, 213; value of education in, 164–65, 167
Columbia Teacher's College, 7, 58–59
Common Core standards, 9–10, 17
"common places" (Schwab's use of Aristotelian concept), 209–13, 222, 224–25
"commonsense knowledge problem," 88–89, 91, 102, 125
communication. *See* deliberation; language
compensation. *See* salaries (of teachers)
competence, 128, 130–33, 135–39
"complex skill" (defined), 66
computer science (scaling metaphor in), 20, 78–81. *See also* Artificial Intelligence (AI)
Conant, James, 196
conversation. *See* deliberation; judgment; language
Cook, Kim, 216–17
courage: Duncan's call for, in educational evaluation, 183, 193, 197, 220, 223, 225; of qualitative claims, 226–27; Schwab's approach to, 197, 224
Craig, A., 19, 79
Crease, Robert P., 87, 178–81, 193, 198, 204, 207–8, 215
cursive handwriting, 168–70
"cut scores," 177–78, 181, 191, 193
Cyc, 89, 91

D
The Daily Show (television program), xi, xxi n1, 19, 31, 79, 215
data. *See* test scores
David (Michelangelo), 95, 97, 137–38
"defining down" success, 97–98, 101; heuristic rules as, 131, 133; by Mathematical Knowledge for Teachers approach, 94; in the Natural Language field, 89–90, 96; "relevance freezing" as example of, 98, 170, 204, 225; by RTT's emphasis on test scores to evaluate teachers, 140, 171, 183; Shulman's proposals for, in teacher training, 114–15; by states' definitions of academic proficiency, 7–10, 12–14, 90, 158, 160–62
Delaware, 44, 50, 60, 128, 161, 176–77
deliberation, 193, 208–15, 220–26. *See also* judgment; "trans-human"
Derrida, Jacques, 102–6, 159, 198–99
Descartes, René, 87–88, 109
DeStefano, J., 80, 86, 94
Dictionary of Cultural Literacy (Hirsch), 42–43
direction-giving examples, 63–70, 155–56
discussion. *See* deliberation
"disengaged view." *See* rationalist assumptions
distortion (conceptual, in discussions of teacher quality), xxi, 2, 4, 59, 74, 86, 101, 104, 179, 211–12, 221–26
dogmatism, 177–78, 189, 191, 214, 216–17, 220
doing (defined), 136. *See also* action
doubt. *See* skepticism
Dreyfus, Hubert: on appropriate and inappropriate cultural practices, 117; on commonsense understanding, 88–89, 91, 102, 125; on the fallacy of the successful first step, 78, 121; and the "presupposed whole," 92–93, 113, 118, 120, 166, 180, 200, 210, 226; on the rationalist assumption, 85–93, 108, 113, 189–90; Schwab's similarities to, 198, 204, 209, 218n3; on skill development phenomenology, 125–36, 192, 207–8. *See also* "relevance problem" (Dreyfus's)
Dreyfus, Stuart E., 87, 139
driving example, 129–30, 135
Duncan, Arne, xv; aims of RTT policy of, 6–14, 72, 77, 130, 139–40, 176–77, 213; on charter schools, 19, 186–88; on "courage" in evaluating teachers, 183, 193, 197, 220, 223, 225; *Daily Show* comments by, xi, xxi n1, 19, 31, 79, 215; on "factory model" of

education, 26, 39, 53; hopes of, for test scores, 15–17, 23–26, 28, 40, 53–54, 58, 60–61, 137, 150–68, 170–71, 181–82, 186–90, 200, 202, 215, 220; on immediate visibility of good teachers and schools, 27–34, 38, 42, 86, 134–35, 137, 139, 143–46, 152, 166, 183; mother of, as a teacher, 28–30, 32, 35, 41, 48, 52, 119, 144–49, 151, 166–67, 185, 189, 221; NCTQ's support for reforms of, 42–43, 46, 49–51; scaling metaphor used by, 19–22, 84, 138; skepticism of, as problem his RTT is an effort to solve, 8–9, 12, 14–22, 24–26, 28, 30–38, 45, 51, 64–65, 212–17, 223; on student teaching, 126; on teachers' credentials, 33–34, 43–44; on teachers' unions, 16, 24–26, 39–40, 53; on teacher training, 58–63, 84, 86, 90, 92–94, 98, 116, 137–38; on teaching as a calling, 118; on teaching as complex and nuanced, 12, 16, 26, 34–35, 51–53, 96, 149, 152, 185, 188, 193; on test scores and teacher quality, 14–31, 41, 46–47, 51–52, 60, 85, 101, 117, 121, 140, 142–43, 153, 163–66, 175–76, 181–83, 212–17, 223. *See also* Race to the Top (RTT) educational policy

E

"eclectic arts," 202–5, 208, 213, 226
Economic Policy Institute reports, 40–41, 53
education (in U.S.): accountability movement in, 2, 37; crisis rhetoric in debates about, xiii–xv, 3, 10–11, 32, 52–54, 184; curriculum field in, 196–201, 210; "factory model" of, 26, 39, 53; federal assessment requirements regarding, xviii, xix, 8, 142–43; international education compared to, xiii–xv, 9–13; not specified as a federal power, 8; Obama administration's view of issues in, 6–14; perceived shortcomings of, 1–3, 6–14, 16, 23, 35, 38, 44, 175–78, 182–83, 217, 225; public's view of responsibilities of, xxii n2, 1–2, 4, 10, 22, 149, 162, 226. *See also* Duncan, Arne; federal government; learning; local; Race to the Top (RTT) educational policy; standardized tests; states; students; success; teachers; teaching; test scores
educational reform. *See* accountability; No Child Left Behind (NCLB) educational policy; Race to the Top (RTT) educational policy
effectiveness (quality designation), 14–16, 40–52, 86, 121, 177, 182–84, 221
Eisner, Elliot, 197, 200
Eldridge, Richard, 206–7, 226
Elementary and Secondary Education Act (ESEA), 7–8
ELIZA program, 92
Elmore, R. F., 20–21
Emerson, Ralph Waldo, 226
emotional involvement. *See* involvement
Emporia State University (Kansas), 126
engagement. *See* involvement
enquiry (Schwab on), 209–10
ESEA (Elementary and Secondary Education Act), 7–8. *See also* No Child Left Behind Act (NCLB)
essence, 129, 136, 190. *See also* foundationalism and antifoundationalism
evaluation (of teaching and learning): academic approaches to, xi, xii, xiii, xv, xvi, xviii, xix, 36–38, 42, 52, 62, 74, 84, 210; alternatives to test scores for, 175–76, 192, 197, 208–27; blurring of technical and ordinary senses of teaching in measures used for, xii–xxi, 1–2, 17, 32–34, 37–38, 43, 48, 53, 59, 90, 97, 127–28, 139, 185; conceptual distortion in, xxi, 2, 4, 59, 74, 86, 101, 104, 179, 211–12, 221, 224–26; Duncan's call for courage in, 183, 193, 197, 220, 223, 225; federal requirements for, xviii, xix, 8, 142–43; as having serious consequences, 26, 159, 161, 196, 221; multiple

measures needed for, 31, 35–38, 42, 55n4, 181–82, 185, 188, 214–15, 223; 99% of teachers as having the same, 23–24, 44, 101, 175, 180, 184, 212, 215–16, 221, 223; rationalist assumptions behind test scores for, 22, 86, 94, 98, 119–20, 154, 156, 192–93, 220–27; skepticism about, 14, 22–25, 28, 49–50, 84, 101–2, 158–67, 172, 175–76, 181–85; state policies on, 16, 24–26, 143, 191, 208; students' readiness for careers and college as criterion for, 9–13, 22, 25, 28–29, 34, 51, 162–66, 178, 194n3; of teacher training, 15, 58–81; test scores' limitations in, 14–22, 27–38, 40–41, 49–51, 59, 137, 151–63, 182–90, 205, 213–17, 222; test scores' use for, xvi, xvii, xviii–xix, 3, 12, 14–33, 35–38, 40–41, 43–54, 61–63, 85, 101, 119–22, 127, 142–74, 187, 189, 208, 213–17, 220. *See also* "cut scores"; judgment; measurement(s); observation (classroom); test scores
Evans, R., 194n3
everyday practices, 104, 109, 115–16. *See also* examples and exercises; "form of life" agreement
examples and exercises: as publicly shared, 112–13, 115; Wittgenstein on, as teaching method, 110–13, 115, 180, 204. *See also* "presupposed whole"
"Existing Practice Is Not the Template" (Shulman), 194n3
experts ("skillful coping"), 125, 128, 134–36, 140n1, 200, 204, 207–8. *See also* proficients
explanations (bringing, to an end), 184–85, 191–93, 216, 222

F
"facts and rules" assumptions (codified representations): as animating skillful practice, 110–11; as basis of good teaching, 59, 62–63, 69, 72–80, 84–88, 94, 96–98, 100–102, 104–5, 109, 111, 128; in computer science, 78–81; as insufficient to explain complex skills, 91, 93–94, 112, 125, 138, 200, 203–4. *See also* behaviorism; "best practices"; "defining down" success; flexible responsiveness; holistic situations; non-formalizable; rule-following activities; test scores
"family resemblances" (Wittgenstein on), 129, 136, 190
Farley, Todd, 175
federal government: national tests set by, 8, 159–60; no constitutional mandate for involvement of, in education, 8; state requirements for educational funding from, xix, 1, 7–9, 14, 42, 161, 208; teacher assessment requirements of, xviii, xix, 8, 142–43; teacher quality perspective of, contrasted with local people's view of, 37–38, 121, 172n1, 185, 191–92, 213, 216–17, 224 (*see also* parents). *See also* No Child Left Behind (NCLB) educational policy; Race to the Top (RTT) educational policy
Feigenbaum, E., 91
Ferguson, Ronald, 55n4
flexible responsiveness (of good teachers), 84; rationalist assumptions as unable to account for, 72–73, 76, 80, 116–17, 125, 127–33, 135–36, 140, 200–201; as responsive to practical situations, 118–19, 121–22, 201–8, 226. *See also* "form of life" agreement; holistic situations; judgment; "presupposed whole"
Florida, 44, 191–93, 222
Fogelin, Robert, 111, 113, 115; on "paradox of interpretation," 108, 114, 175, 194n1; on "secret key," 110
Ford Foundation, 20
"form of life" agreement: as non-formalizable, 113–15, 149–50, 152, 165, 178–82, 223; ordinary sense of teaching as bound up with, 117–20, 136, 190, 197, 221–22, 225; Schwab as pointing toward embrace of, 203–4, 206–7, 211–12; as shared

understanding, 68, 113; skill development as part of, 125, 130, 154; and teacher evaluation, 149–50, 152, 156–58, 166. *See also* examples and exercises; judgment; non-formalizable; practical; "presupposed whole"

foundationalism and anti-foundationalism (essence), 76, 95–97, 104–5, 110–11, 113–15, 137–38, 185, 188, 192, 197. *See also* explanations: bringing, to an end; knowledge: transcendent structures of

"foundational skills." *See* behaviors

Frege, Gottlob, 88

G

Glazerman, S., et al., 47–49, 54, 62, 119, 154

Glendinning, Simon, 103, 112, 125, 159, 198

GOFAI, 87, 89. *See also* Artificial Intelligence (AI)

Google, 87

Governors Education Symposium, 7, 9–12

grades: correlating of teacher credentials with, 34, 43; correlating test scores with, 161; inflation of, 161

graduation rates: and "crisis" in U.S. education, xiii, xiv; as measurement of educational success, 12–13, 15, 153, 162, 176, 180

Grady, Mildred (Mrs.): Kristof on, xvi–xxi, 2, 116–19; as model teacher, 41, 116–19, 137, 147–48, 152, 221, 225–26; as test for teacher evaluation methods, xxi, 127, 143, 150, 172, 225–26

Great Recession (2008), 165

Green, Elizabeth: on behaviors that are "adaptable to anyone," 64, 68, 70; on "bite-sized moves," 39, 46, 63, 70, 100; on improving teaching fast and to scale, 20; on teaching as a set of techniques, 22

Grossman, Pam, 60

Guernica (Picasso), 95

H

handwriting, 168–70

Hanushek, E. A., 33, 154

Harvard Elementary School, 27

Heidegger, Martin, 104–5, 127; alternative of, to rationalist assumptions, 113, 117, 129; "being-there/understanding of Being/being in the world" concept of, 93, 108–9, 115, 133, 179; on instantaneous grasping of a situation, 134; on the "setup," 180; on shared public practices, 125; on "towards-which," 202

Hill, Heather, 60; and Mathematical Knowledge for Teachers, 90, 94, 139; mentalistic views of, 61, 71, 100; on teacher training, 137

Hirsch, E. D., Jr., 42–43

Hlebowitsh, Peter S., 194n3

holistic situations (grasping, without rules), 39–40, 93, 118, 121, 127, 129–30, 133. *See also* flexible responsiveness

Hollabaugh, J., 63–64

Horn, C. Van, 165

How to Create a Mind (Kurzweil), 87

I

"ideology," 166–67, 186–87, 190, 192, 224

inequality (economic). *See* poverty

insight, 133–35, 140n4

Institute of Education Sciences, 7, 11–15, 100, 158

Investigations (Wittgenstein). *See Philosophical Investigations* (Wittgenstein)

invisibility. *See* visibility

involvement (caring; concern; emotional involvement; engagement; kindness) (of excellent teachers), 116–17, 125–27, 129, 131–34, 138; Aristotelian view of, 202. *See also* responsibility

J

Johnson, William, 194n2

judgment: behaviorism as excluding teacher, 70; disagreements of, between test scores and classroom observations, 37–38, 214, 216–17, 224; experts' use of, 136; as necessary to include in teacher evaluation, 192, 197, 217, 221–26; in predicting which teachers will have students whose test scores will rise under their tutelage, 121, 156, 170–72; reformers' desire to avoid human, by using test scores, 175–78, 182, 185, 191, 212, 215, 223; Schwab on responsibility associated with, 215–16, 223–24; "strategic," in teachers' practices, 73–76, 107, 131; of test graders, 175, 177, 185; test scores', of teacher quality, 217, 222; "wisdom of practice" as element in teachers', 73–74, 76–77, 84–86, 116, 128, 205, 207. *See also* deliberation; flexible responsiveness; "form of life" agreement; holistic situations

K
Kane, Thomas J., 33, 36–38, 44, 46, 62–63, 86, 130, 154
Kant, Immanuel, 88
Keller, B., 64
Kennedy, John F., xiv
kindness. *See* involvement
KIPP schools, 43
Kisiel, Theodore, 133–34
Klein, Joel, 42
knowledge: about how to do something as consisting of "facts and rules," 59, 62–63, 69, 72–80, 84–88, 94, 96–98, 100–102, 104–5, 109, 111, 128; as being insufficient for carrying out practical endeavors, 199; propagating use of available, 80, 84, 86; propositional, 19, 88–89, 112, 115–16, 125, 135–36, 206; scholars' misunderstanding of relation of, to practice, 101–8, 122, 197–208; "strategic," in teachers' practices, 73–76, 107, 131; of teacher practice, as nonformalizable in principle, 114, 197; teachers', as inadequately constructed, 60–61; teachers as masters of, 71, 74–76, 205–7; transcendent structures of, 77, 84, 86, 90, 97–98, 102–7, 111–14; Wittgenstein's

disappointment with, 225–26. *See also* "arts of the eclectic"; "best practices"; "commonsense knowledge problem"; flexible responsiveness; judgment; Mathematical Knowledge for Teaching (MKT); subject matter
"Knowledge and Teaching" (Shulman), 72
Koretz, Daniel, 159–62
Kristof, Nicholas, xi–xxi, 2, 6, 29–31, 116–19, 139, 146, 150, 185, 225–26
Kurzweil, Ray, 87

L
labor unions. *See* teachers' unions
language (communication; speech; words): as bottom-level locus of a rule, 110–11; "chicken-and-egg" problem concerning, 89, 102–3, 115, 159; Derrida on, 103–5, 198–99; learning, 115; sharing "best practices" as matter of, 94, 138, 215; for teacher training, 114; teaching of, 109–10, 204; using, 103–4. *See also* Natural Language (NL); telling
learning: inadequacies in measuring, 49–50; inconsistencies in conceptions of, 1–2, 58; as more than sum of specifiable behaviors, 66–67, 112, 125; as not guaranteed, 111, 115; restrictions in domain of, 58; as result of "good teaching," xii, 12, 21–22, 43, 45–47, 52, 98, 100, 142, 144–46, 149, 162, 171; as set of behaviors, 21–22, 29, 39–40, 46, 50–52, 54, 100; "technical" *vs.* "ordinary" definitions of, 52, 96; test scores as representing, 58, 62, 98; transmission model of, 18–19, 61, 110. *See also* assessment (of teaching); causation; "defining down" success; knowledge; students; subject matter; success; teaching; test scores
LEAs (local education authorities), 161
Leibniz, Gottfried Wilhelm, 88
Lemov, Doug, 20–22, 39, 74, 80, 90; on art, 95–97, 137–38, 218n4; behaviorism in work of, 61,

63–73, 76–77, 79, 84–87, 92–97, 138; as content with third level of teacher development, 130; as misunderstanding practical skill, 101, 137; teacher training views of, 113–14, 116; and test scores to guide teacher practice, 85, 154–55
Lenat, Doug, 89–91, 96, 102–4, 159
Lewis, Tyson, 75
the local: as elaborations of a whole which they presuppose, 93, 111, 200, 226; ordinary good teaching as visible on the level of the, xviii, xix, xxi, 24, 27–35, 42, 47, 52, 86, 117–20, 125, 143–45, 148–49, 157–58, 166, 177–78, 183, 189, 221; researchers' disregard for, 214–15; as responsible for dealing with teacher compensation, termination, and tenure, 25–26, 161; as a starting point for Schwab's task of "problemation," 202, 204–9, 212–14; *vs.* state and federal government's perceptions of test scores and teacher quality, 172n1, 213, 216–17; teacher evaluations based on, *vs.* on test scores, 37–38, 121, 185, 191–92, 216–17, 224; test scores' uses as a retreat from familiarity with the, 213, 223. *See also* judgment; observation (classroom); parents; students
Loewenberg Ball, Deborah. *See* Ball, Deborah
"lying": integrated data systems as not preventing, 170–71; states' "dumbing down" of academic standards as a form of, 7–10, 12–14, 90, 158, 160–62; by teachers about what success in higher learning would require, 168–70; test scores as implicated in evaluations', 177; test scores as "truthful" solution to, 16–17, 26, 158–60, 162, 166, 172, 177, 187, 213, 216, 224, 227. *See also* "defining down" success; skepticism; trust

M
Martini, Edwin, 5, 217n1

Maryland, 175–76
Mathematical Knowledge for Teaching (MKT), 71, 81n1, 90, 94, 139
mathematics: as a fluid concept, 170; RTT test scores as limited to reading, science, and, xv, xviii, 8, 11–13, 22, 29, 32–33, 50, 52, 58, 137, 162, 182. *See also* Mathematical Knowledge for Teaching
maxims and rules. *See* "facts and rules" assumptions
McDowell, John, 105, 136
McFinn, Colin, 87
measurement(s): efforts to link, to independently existing properties, 178–79; metaphysical picture of, 175; Schwab's offering of multiple, for knowing and telling, 215, 222; single, for knowing and telling, 142, 151, 183–84, 193, 212–15; varieties of, as having different purposes, 142, 146–47, 165–66. *See also* assessment (of teaching); deliberation; observation; ontic measurement; ontological measurement; test scores
Medvetz, Tom, 4–5, 86, 217n1
Mehta, Jal, 2–6, 196, 217n1
memory formation, 133–34
mentalistic views, 63, 70–78, 100, 105–7, 110; of "best practices" in teaching, defined, 60–61. *See also* rationalist assumptions
metaphysical assumption, 175, 186–90, 192–93, 205–6
Michelangelo, 95, 97, 137–38
"micro-worlds," 88, 91–93, 118, 120, 199–200
MKT (Mathematical Knowledge for Teaching), 71, 81n1, 90, 94, 139
Monet, Claude, 95, 97
"Mrs. Grady test." *See* Grady, Mildred
Mulhall, Stephen, 109, 221

N
Nachlass (Wittgenstein), 217n2
NAEP (National Assessment of Educational Progress), 8, 159–61
"Nancy" (excellent English teacher cited by Shulman), 72–73, 80, 101, 104, 121–22, 129, 131, 135, 137, 221

National Alliance for Public Charter Schools Conference, 7, 19, 26–29
National Assessment of Educational Progress (NAEP), 8, 159–61
National Council on Teacher Quality (NCTQ), 42–47, 49–51, 120–21, 157, 212
National Education Association (NEA), 7, 16–17, 20, 25–26, 28–30
A Nation at Risk (Gardner), xiv
Nation's Report Card. *See* NAEP
Natural Language learning (NL), 88–92, 94, 96, 103
NCLB. *See* No Child Left Behind Act
NCTQ. *See* National Council on Teacher Quality
NEA. *See* National Education Association
Neal, Olly, 127, 151–52, 166–67, 183, 185; Kristof's article on, xvi–xxi, 29–31, 116–18, 120, 145–48, 150, 225–26
"neighborhood quality" example, 165–66, 180
Newell, Allen, 88, 131
New Teacher Project: on 99% of teachers having been rated the same, 23–24, 44, 101, 175, 180, 184, 212, 215–16, 221, 223; on teacher hiring policies, 26
New York City, 175–76
New Yorker magazine, xiii–xiv, 42
New York state, 44
New York Times: Anderson's education articles in, xix, xx, 177–78; Kane's interview in, 62; Kristof's education articles in, xi, xii–xxi, 116–19; Penskar's letter to, 186, 188–89, 192
Nicomachean Ethics (Aristotle), 133
NL. *See* Natural Language
No Child Left Behind Act (NCLB), xix; as in fact a "race to the bottom," 8, 160, 177; RTT's similarities with, 7–8, 12; states as "dumbing down" academic standards under, 7–10, 12–14, 160–61
the non-formalizable: adult outcomes as, 149, 165; commonsense understanding as, 91; "form of life" agreement as, 113–15, 149–50, 152, 165, 178–82, 223; knowledge of teacher practice as, in principle, 114, 197; ordinary sense of excellent teaching as, 114, 200, 203–5, 216, 221–22, 225; Schwab's forms of knowledge as, 211. *See also* "form of life" agreement; holistic situations
novices, 128–29, 135

O

Obama, Barack, 7, 153, 163, 217; State of the Union address of (2012), xi, xii, xv–xvi, xix, 13, 31, 163; on teachers' importance, xi, xv-xvi, xviii, xix, xxi, 221; on using students' test scores to measure teacher quality, 153, 217. *See also* Duncan, Arne; Race to the Top (RTT) educational policy
observation (classroom, for teacher evaluation): disagreements between test scores and, 37–38, 177–78, 214, 216–17, 224; as part of RTT guidelines, xix, 35–36, 226; rubrics for, xx–xxi, 46–47, 52, 54, 62, 121, 128, 157, 191; state policies regarding, 42–54, 128, 157; test scores as more objective than, 101, 151, 154, 185, 217; trust associated with, 146–49, 167. *See also* test scores
ontic measurement, 178–83, 185, 190, 216, 221–23, 226
ontological measurement, 178–82, 184, 197
ordinary good teaching: as invisible using RTT metrics, xix, 2, 117, 120–21, 201, 217, 221, 225; quality of, as immediately visible on the local level, xviii, xix, xxi, 26–35, 42, 47, 52, 86, 117–20, 125, 143–45, 148–49, 157–58, 166, 177–78, 183, 189 [vis], 221; as RTT goal, xv–xvi, 53–54, 98, 118, 128, 139, 217, 221; as transcending subject matter, 64, 84, 94
Oregon, 19, 21, 79
Orr High School, 27

P

"paradox of interpretation" (Fogelin on), 108, 114, 175, 194n1
parents: as knowing who the best teachers are, 48–49, 189, 192, 213; trigger legislation for, 214

Pattern-Recognition Theory of Mind, 87
paying attention example, 64–70
Pedagogical Content Knowledge (PCK), 5, 61, 70–77, 81n1
Peer Assistance and Review program, 175–76
penmanship, 168–70
Penskar, Carol, 186, 188–89, 192, 197, 221
performance-based teacher evaluations. *See* evaluation
Performance Standards Consortium, 175–76
Peterson, P. E., 33
Philosophical Investigations (Wittgenstein), 104, 109, 111, 122n1, 190, 223
Picasso, Pablo, 95–96
Plato, 85, 178
Pollock, Jackson, 95
post-hoc explanations (as providing aprioristic guiding functions), 75–77, 96, 100
postmodern literary criticism, 105
poverty, xvi, 3–4, 29
the practical: inability of theory to solve problems that are, 196–208; Schwab's sense of, 201–2, 213
"practices," 62. *See also* behaviorism; knowledge
predictions (of future success), 149, 152–53, 158–72, 204
"presupposed whole": as articulated in shared everyday practices, 111, 116, 118, 120, 200; Dreyfus on, 92–93, 113, 118, 120, 166, 180, 200, 210, 226; and the professionalism of teachers, 122n2
"primitives," 88, 90–92, 94, 103, 211; defined, 92
"problemation" (Schwab on), 201–3
professionals: Mehta on problems associated with, 5; Shulman's description of, 205–7; singling out of teachers for comparison with other, 24; training for teaching, 114, 122n2, 196, 208–9 (*see also* teachers: training of)
"proficiency": and "cut scores," 177–78, 181, 191, 193; discoveries about, *vs.* requirements of, 162–63, 166; Duncan's *vs.* psychometricians' views of, 172n2; teacher "effectiveness" as new word for, 177. *See also* proficients; test scores
proficients, 128, 133–35, 138, 204
psychometrics. *See* measurement(s)
purity (philosophical), 224–25

Q

qualitative measures. *See* deliberation; judgment; observation (classroom); ontological measurement; teaching: ordinary sense of
quantitative measures. *See* ontic measurement; teaching: technical concept of; test scores

R

Race to the Top (RTT) educational policy: as addressing perceived shortcomings in national education system, 1–3, 6–14, 16, 23, 35, 38, 44, 175–78, 182–83, 217, 225; application process for, 6; assessment protocols of, 2, 6, 151, 179, 182, 214–15, 222; assumptions of, 80–81, 84, 91, 93, 128, 137–39, 142, 162–63, 167, 204, 212, 214–15; concept of "teaching" in, 14–22, 60, 139; as content with third level of developing and evaluating teachers, 130, 139; crisis rhetoric around, xiii–xv, 3, 10–11, 32, 52–54, 184; data used in, and purposes toward which they are directed, 18, 48–51, 62, 142, 151, 167, 171, 212; dogmatism associated with, 189, 191, 214, 216–17, 220, 222; as effort to solve a problem of skepticism, 8–9, 14–22, 24–26, 28, 30–38, 45, 51, 64–65, 212–17, 223; as effort to standardize teaching practices, 128–29, 131–32, 137–40, 161, 215–16, 223; as effort to standardize variations in test scores among states, 8–9, 14, 179–80; improving teacher quality as a goal of, 23, 73–74, 86–87, 139–40; as massively broad in scope, 213; NCLB's similarities with, 7–8, 12; NCTQ's support for, 42–51; "ordinary" great teaching as goal of, xv–xvi, 53–54, 98, 118, 128, 139, 217, 221; "ordinary" great teaching as invisible using the metrics preferred by, xix, 2, 117, 120–21, 201, 217, 221, 225; Schwab's approach as alternative to, 197–226; state requirements for funding from, xix, 1, 7–9, 14, 42, 161, 208; student test scores as primary public policy measure of teacher quality under, 181–82, 185, 220–21, 223; technical concept of teaching in, 4, 14–22, 28–30, 32–44, 46–51, 54, 58–59, 96, 98, 177, 183. *See also* assessment; causation; Duncan, Arne; federal government; local; rationalist assumptions; skepticism; states; teachers; teaching; test scores

RAND Corporation, 86–87, 217n1

rationalist assumptions (detached view; disengaged view; intellectualist view): in Artificial Intelligence, 59, 87–93, 98, 102–4, 140, 157; as creating universal general rules from specifics, 128, 162, 189–90, 210–11 (*see also* scaling metaphor); and developing teachers, 126–27, 130–33, 137–38, 181; as discouraging involvement and responsibility, 129, 131–32, 137–39, 215–16, 223; Dreyfus's alternative to, 108, 115–16, 125, 128–36, 199–200; Heidegger's alternative to, 113, 117, 125; history of unsuccessful applications of, to education, 200–201; Mehta on, in U.S., 2, 4–6, 86; on rules as rails, 105, 135–36; Schwab's alternative to, 196–212; separation of mind and world by, 106, 108–9; in teacher quality assessment, 22, 86, 94, 98, 119–20, 154, 156, 192–93, 220–27; as unable to account for flexible responsiveness, 72–73, 76, 80, 116–17, 125, 127–33, 135–36, 140, 200–201; as unachievable and illusory, 216–17, 221, 224–25; as underpinning RTT policies, 128, 204, 213; in views of skillful human activity, 85–86, 100–108, 110–11. *See also* foundationalism and anti-foundationalism; mentalistic views

Ravitch, Diane: on alternative approaches to teacher evaluation, 221; on current educational reform advocates, 2–4, 29, 101, 213; on non-cognitive skills and adult success, 194n1; on schools' duties, xxii n2; on strong education systems and national prosperity, xiv; on tests as social constructs, 175–77, 182, 185, 224; on turning accountability into responsibility, 176, 191, 196, 225

reading: as a fluid concept, 170; RTT test scores as restricted to math, science, and, xv, xviii, 8, 11–13, 22, 29, 32–33, 50, 52, 58, 137, 162, 182

reason-giving, 205–7

Recession of 2008, xiv

reform (educational). *See* accountability; No Child Left Behind (NCLB) educational policy; Race to the Top (RTT) educational policy

regresses (infinite): Dreyfus on, 211; in Lemov's behavioristic assumptions, 68–69; Schwab's avoidance of, 203–4; in Shulman's mentalistic assumptions, 75–76, 107–8; Wittgenstein on, 107–8, 116

regularity (in skillful practices), 104–5, 112–13

Reign of Error (Ravitch), 2–4, 29

"relevance problem" (Dreyfus's): as contrast between humans' and computers' ways of generalizing information, 89–91, 94, 96, 127, 129, 131–36, 205–7, 218n3; freezing of, by using limiting definitions, 98, 170, 204, 225; rationalist assumptions about, 103, 108, 116–17, 125, 133, 135–36, 204; Schwab's

240 *Index*

approach as solution to, 212. *See also* flexible responsiveness
RESPECT initiative (U.S. Department of Education), xi, xii
responsibility: inability to distinguish good teachers from bad seen as failure of, 176–78, 180, 184–93, 212, 221, 223–24; new teachers' need to have, for outcomes, 125–29, 132–34, 137; rationalist assumptions as discouraging involvement and, 129, 131–32, 137–39, 215–16, 223; reason-giving and public, 205–8; Schwab on, of judgment, 215–16, 223–24; test scores' use in teacher evaluations as failure of, 177–78, 189–92, 220–21, 223, 225; turning accountability into, 176, 191, 196, 225. *See also* involvement
retention (of teachers). *See* tenure (of teachers); termination (of teachers)
Rhee, Michelle, 42
rigor (in evaluation), xvii–xx, 9–13, 23–31, 45, 85, 91, 177, 200–202
Ripley, Amanda, 55n4
Rockoff, J. E., 33, 130, 163. *See also* Chetty, R., et al.
Rothstein, Richard, 58, 101
RTT. *See* Race to the Top (RTT) educational policy
rule-following activities: "form of life" agreement as underlying, 117; teachers as shedding, as they gain more experience, 128–36, 138; Wittgenstein on usual practice of, 104, 106–8. *See also* "facts and rules" assumptions; non-formalizable

S

salaries (of teachers): based on the quality of their teaching, 35, 40–42, 147, 221; higher, recommended for better teachers, xiii, xviii, xx; as linked to seniority, 25–26; student test scores linked to, 16, 35, 49, 51, 161, 166, 217; and teacher credentials, 33
scaling metaphor (for teaching): in "best practices" model of teacher training, 62–63, 93–94; Duncan's use of, 19–22, 84, 138; *vs.* "factory model" of education, 39, 53; generalizing issues for, 79, 90–92, 97–98
schools: choice among, 214; Duncan on indicators of good, 27–28, 30, 134, 143–44, 150, 152, 185, 221. *See also* charter schools; students; subject matter; teachers
Schwab, Joseph: deliberation concept of, and teacher evaluation, 193, 208–15, 220–26; on trying to solve a practical problem by theoretic means, 196–208
science: education in, 71; RTT test scores as restricted to reading, math, and, xv, xviii, 8, 11–13, 22, 29, 32–33, 50, 52, 58, 137, 162, 182; scaling up innovations in, 79–80
score inflation, 161
seeing (Schwab on), 205–7, 224. *See also* insight; visibility
Selinger, E. M., 87, 207–8
Sherman Elementary School, 27
SHRDLU program, 91–93, 120, 199
Shulman, Lee, 5, 60, 90, 96, 154; as content with third level of teacher development, 130; mentalistic views of, 61, 70–77, 79–80, 84–87, 92–94, 97, 100, 138; as misunderstanding practical skill, 101; "Nancy" as teacher example used by, 72–73, 80, 101, 104, 121–22, 129, 131, 135, 137, 221; as Schwab's student, 196–97, 205; on "strategic" judgment in teachers' practices, 73–76, 107, 131; on student teaching, 126; on teacher training, 113–16, 122n2, 137; and test scores to guide teacher practice, 85; on "wisdom of practice" as element in teachers' judgment, 73–74, 76–77, 84–86, 116, 128, 205, 207
Simon, Herb, 88, 131
"situational elements," 130–32, 134, 136
skepticism (doubt): about ability to assess teacher quality, 14,

22–25, 28, 49–50, 84, 101–2, 158–67, 172, 175–76, 181–85; about classroom observation as means to assess teacher quality, 37–38, 157, 177; about evaluations of ordinary good teaching, 143–51, 197; about teaching credentials' link to teacher quality, 33–34, 43–44, 221; about test scores' ability to assess student learning, 49–50; about test scores' ability to assess teacher quality, 37, 41–42, 45, 50, 151–58; about what the future holds, 158–59; Cavell on, 17, 28, 38, 68, 122n1, 177, 215–16, 221–22; Mullhall on, 109; Ravitch's, about reform movement's motivations, 3; RTT as Duncan's effort to solve a problem of, 8–9, 12, 14–22, 24–26, 28, 30–38, 45, 51, 64–65, 212–17, 223; test scores' fallibility and manipulability as giving rise to, 12, 14, 50, 161, 164–66; use of test scores to overcome, 151, 154, 185, 217. *See also* "lying"; trust

"skillful coping." *See* concern; emotional involvement; engagement; experts; flexible responsiveness (of good teachers); involvement (caring; kindness) (of excellent teachers); knowledge

Skinner, B. F., 64
Small, Christopher, 177
speech. *See* language
Staiger, Douglas, 33, 130, 154
standardized tests: content of, xv, xviii, 8, 11–13, 22, 29, 32–33, 50, 52, 58, 137, 162, 182; as imperfect, 49; multiple choice, 11–12, 31, 34; as social constructs rather than scientific instruments, 175–77, 182, 185, 224; "teaching to," 161. *See also* NAEP; states: student assessment by; test scores

State of the Union address (2012), xi, xii, xv–xvi, xix, 13, 31, 163
states (U.S.): as adopting of federal educational requirements in order to receive federal money, xix, 1, 7–9, 14, 42, 161, 208; on data and classroom observation, 42–54, 128, 157; as "dumbing down" academic standards, 7–10, 12–14, 90, 158, 160–62; educational policy as prerogative of, 8; as requiring proficiency in conceptually fluid skills, 169–70; RTT's efforts to standardize test scores among, 8–9, 14, 179–80; some, as prohibiting student test scores to be used in teacher evaluations, 16, 24–26; student assessment by, 159–61, 182; student teaching requirements by, 125–26; and teacher assessment, 16, 24–26, 143, 191, 208. *See also specific states*

Stern, David, 108
Stewart, Jon. See *Daily Show* (television program)
strategic knowledge (Shulman's concept), 73–76, 107, 131
Strong, M., 37, 121, 185, 191–92, 224
student achievement data. *See* test scores
students: adults' long-term involvement in lives of, 29–30, 51–52, 144–46, 148–49; alleged economic benefits of good teachers for, xi, xi–xii, xv, xvii, 13, 29, 144–51, 162–66, 170–71, 175–76, 180, 183–84, 188, 204, 211, 213; attendance rates of, 27; "college and career readiness" as new educational criterion for, 9–13, 22, 25, 28–29, 34, 51, 162–66, 178, 194n3; GPA of, and teacher credentials, 34, 43; learning by, not guaranteed, 111, 115; Lemov's approach to non-compliant, 64–69; multiple teachers as responsible for success of, 30, 147; as presumed to be fundamentally identical, 19; successful former, evaluating, 144–46; test scores of, as linked to teacher quality, 14–16, 43–45, 52, 86, 121, 176–77, 179–80, 184, 221; variety of, in any classroom, 69. *See also* grades; graduation rates; learning; Neal, Olly; student teaching; success; teachers; teaching; test scores
student teaching, 125–26

242   Index

subjectivity. *See* judgment
subject matter (of teaching): effective teaching as transcending, 64, 84, 94; efforts to codify "best practices" in teaching of, 60, 97–98, 100, 154; exclusion of much, from test scores, 58; Schwab on, 199, 210–12; of standardized tests, xv, xviii, 8, 11–13, 22, 29, 32–33, 50, 52, 58, 137, 162, 182; teacher as master of, 71, 74–76, 205–7; teacher's knowledge of, as poor predictor of the ability to teach, 71; in the United States, 9–13, 21, 23, 28. *See also* knowledge; mathematics; reading; science
"subsubjects," 199–201, 203, 208–9, 211, 217n3
"sub-worlds," 92–93, 118, 226
success: correlations between good teaching and economic, xi–xii, xvii, 13, 29–30, 144–51, 162–66, 170–71, 175–76, 180, 183–84, 188, 204, 211, 213; criteria of, in adults as debatable, 149, 163–67, 180, 183, 211; Duncan on common agreement on the appearance of, 27–28, 30, 134, 143–44, 150, 152, 185, 221; Duncan's criteria for school, 143–44, 146–47, 152, 157; graduation rates as measurement of educational reform's, 12–13, 15, 153, 162, 176, 180; non-school factors involved in career, 162–63; pegging test scores on reading and math to real-life measures of, 161–67, 183; Ravitch on non-cognitive skills and adult, 194n1; Schwab on appearance of, in simplified theories, 198–99, 202. *See also* "defining down" success
Sweden, 33
systems analysis, 86, 100, 217n1

T
Taylor, Charles, 85, 110, 115, 125
"teacher knowledge approach," 58–81, 154, 181, 193n3
teachers: alleged economic benefits for students of good, xi, xi–xii, xv, xvii, 13, 29, 144–51, 162–66, 170–71, 175–76, 180, 183–84, 188, 204, 211, 213; Chetty et al.'s definition of, xi; "college and career readiness" as new educational criterion for students of, 9–13, 22, 25, 28–29, 34, 51, 162–66, 178, 194n3; effectiveness of, stability of, 39–41, 48–49, 51, 53; "effectiveness" of, 14–16, 40–41, 43–45, 47, 52, 121, 177, 182, 184, 221; "effectiveness" of, defined, 86; experienced *vs.* novice, 59–60, 62, 69, 73, 77, 84, 98, 115, 126–40; flexible responsiveness of excellent, 72–73, 76, 80, 84, 116–19, 121–22, 125, 127, 129–31, 133, 135–36, 140, 200–203, 226; importance of long-term involvement of, in students' lives, 29–30, 51–52, 144–46, 148–49; lack of diversity among, 65; lack of official differentiation among, 14, 23–24, 26, 29–30, 44, 49, 101, 175–77, 180, 184, 212, 215–16, 221, 223; lack of official differentiation among, reasons for, 24; multitude of, as involved in children's learning, 30, 147; quality of, as immediately visible on the local level, xviii, xix, xxi, 24, 26–35, 42, 47, 52, 86, 117–20, 125, 143–45, 148–49, 157–58, 166, 177–78, 183, 189, 221; quality of, said to be biggest influence on student academic growth, 32; regular *vs.* after-school, 55n3; search for "best practices" of, xx, 5, 19, 21–23, 58–59, 86–87, 137–38, 215; seniority rules for, 24–26; sharing of "best practices" by, 79, 94, 138, 215; singling out of, among all professions for comparison, 24; skillful practice of, 5, 18–19, 22, 25, 39–40; skillful practice of, developing, 122, 125–41; skillful practice of, erroneous assumptions about, 59–99; stability of knowledge of, 72–73; training for, xvii, 5,

7, 20, 32–35, 58–81, 85, 90, 93–94, 98, 108–15, 125–41; training for, assessment of, 15, 58–81; training for profession of, 114, 122n2, 196, 208–9. *See also* certification; professionals; salaries; students; student teaching; teachers' unions; teaching; teaching (good); tenure; termination

teachers' unions: cut scores negotiated by, 177; Duncan on, 16, 24–26, 40; and "factory model" of education, 26, 39, 53; and teacher evaluation, 189, 191. *See also* salaries (of teachers); tenure; termination

"Teacher Training Does Not Exist" (Shulman), 114

Teach for America, 19–20, 43

teaching (good): blurring of technical and ordinary senses of, xii–xxi, 1–2, 17, 32–34, 37–38, 43, 48, 53, 59, 90, 97, 127–28, 139, 185; conceptual distortions in discussions of, xxi, 2, 4, 59, 74, 86, 101, 104, 179, 211–12, 221, 224–26; correlations between economic outcomes and, xi–xii, xvii, 13, 29, 144–51, 162–66, 170–71, 175–76, 180, 183–84, 188, 204, 211, 213; credentials' relation to quality of, 33–34, 43–44; Duncan on, as a calling, 118; Duncan on, as complex and nuanced, 12, 16, 26, 34–35, 51–53, 96, 149, 152, 185, 188, 193; Duncan on immediate visibility of good schools and good, 27–34, 38, 42, 86, 134–35, 137, 139, 143–46, 152, 166, 183; as having specific life effects on students, 119, 146, 226; Kristof on, xi–xxi, 2, 6, 29–31, 116–19, 139, 150, 185, 225–26; ordinary sense of, as bound up with "form of life" agreement, 117–20, 136, 190, 197, 221–22, 225; ordinary sense of, as eliminated when focusing on the technical sense, xv–xvi, xviii–xxi, 4, 26–43, 47–51, 53–54, 58–59, 117, 201, 211, 217, 221, 225; ordinary sense of, as impossible to reproduce through "best practices" approach, 86–87, 116–19, 138–39, 154–56, 170–71; ordinary sense of, as non-formalizable, 114, 200, 203–5, 216, 221–22, 225; ordinary sense of, evaluative claims about, 143–51, 166–67, 185; ordinary sense of, qualities of, xviii, 29, 31–35, 51–53, 94, 98, 119, 225–26; as responsive to a local situation, 119–22; search for behaviors that lead toward ordinary sense of, xx, 5, 19, 21–23, 58–59, 69, 72, 86–87, 128, 137–39, 197, 215; as set of behaviors, 21–22, 29, 39–40, 46, 50–52, 54, 100; technical concept of, 4, 28–30, 32–44, 46–51, 54, 58–59, 96, 98, 177, 183; test scores as providing only a "technical" sense of, 28–31, 37–38, 40–44, 46–54, 55n4, 58–59, 116, 119, 137, 139, 151; test scores to assess, xvi, xvii, xviii–xix, 3, 12, 14–33, 35–38, 40–41, 43–54, 61–63, 85, 101, 119–22, 127, 150–58, 187, 189, 208, 213–17, 220; as uniform at a certain level, 95–96; as varied, 185–86, 188–90, 193; Wittgenstein on, 108–15, 125, 129, 135, 180, 190, 204. *See also* assessment; behaviors; "best practices"; causation; flexible responsiveness; holistic situations; learning; observation (classroom); subject matter; teachers; test scores

"teaching to the test," 161

Teach Like a Champion: The 49 Techniques that Put Students on the Path to College (Lemov), 21–22, 63, 67–69, 86, 113–14

telling (ways of, other than through test scores), 29, 222–23. *See also* accountability; evaluation (of teaching)

temporal issues (time): in correlations between students' economic outcomes and the teaching they experienced, xi–xii, xvii, 13, 29, 144–51, 162–66, 170–71,

175–76, 180, 183–84, 188, 204, 211, 213; in judging successful schools in the present-tense, 144–45; in judging teacher quality in hindsight, 127, 144–45, 148–49, 151–52, 154, 167, 183; in measuring of teachers' effectiveness over their careers, 41, 52–53, 117–19, 146–47, 164–65, 167; in predicting success in the future, 149, 152–53, 158–72, 204; and teachers' involvement in students' lives over a long period of time, 29–30, 51–52, 144–46, 148–49. *See also* memory formation; post-hoc explanations; teachers: experienced *vs.* novice

Tennessee: classroom observation rubrics in, 128, 157; and RTT educational policy, xix–xx, 47; as using student test scores to evaluate teacher performance, 44, 161, 176–77; writing test required by, 169–70

tenure (of teachers), xiii–xiv, 42, 147, 166; as disincentivizing analysis of quality teachers, 24; reformers' desire to restructure, 3, 25–26, 40, 217; and students' test scores, 16, 161. *See also* termination (of teachers)

termination (of teachers), 36, 40, 147; fear of, as stifling good teachers, 139–40; using student test scores, 25, 161, 217; using student test scores and classroom observation, 41–42; using student test scores and human judgment, 221. *See also* "cut scores"

tests. *See* "cut scores"; standardized tests; test scores

test scores (achievement data; data; "value-added metrics"): to assess "good teaching," xvi, xvii, xviii–xix, 3, 12, 14–33, 35–38, 40–41, 43–54, 61–63, 85, 101, 119–22, 127, 150–58, 187, 189, 208, 213–17, 220; to assess "good teaching," justifications for, 142–74; cheating scandal involving, 161; classroom observation rubrics linked to, 41–42, 46–47, 51, 54, 128, 157; and Common Core standards, 6–14; Duncan's hopes for uses of, 15–17, 23–26, 28, 40, 53–54, 58, 60–61, 137, 150–68, 170–71, 181–82, 186–90, 200, 202, 215, 220; as examples of crisis in U.S. education, xiii, xiv; fallibility and manipulability of, 12, 14, 50, 161, 164–66, 175–77, 182; from federal-level tests, 159–60; flaws in protocols producing, as merely a technical matter, 17, 48, 119–22; graders of, 175, 177, 185; inflation of, 161; limitations of, in assessing "good teaching" and good schools, 14–22, 27–38, 40–41, 49–51, 59, 137, 151–63, 182–90, 205, 213–17, 222; linking of, to students' career outcomes, xi–xiii, xv, 13, 153, 158, 162–68, 170–71, 180, 183–84, 188, 211, 213; local *vs.* state and federal government's sense of accuracy of, 172n1, 213, 216–17; as "measuring what they claim to measure," 37; MKT's successes with, 71, 81n1, 90, 94; as offering something new to the education profession, 150–51, 153, 170–72, 200, 212–13, 216, 220, 223; as primary public policy measure of teacher quality, 181–82, 185, 220–21, 223; as providing only a "technical" sense of teacher quality, 28–31, 37–38, 40–44, 46–54, 55n4, 58–59, 116, 119, 137, 139, 151; questioning of, as adequate to measure student learning, 50, 58; questions needed for evaluative uses of, 185–86; as restricted to reading, math, and science, xv, xviii, 8, 11–13, 22, 29, 32–33, 50, 52, 58, 137, 162, 182; as revealing what makes teachers tick, 15, 153–54, 156; as revealing "what to do" and "how to teach," 18, 51, 60–62, 84, 98, 100, 136, 182; RTT's effort to standardize variations in, among states, 8–9, 14, 179–80; seen as objective and universal, 175–80, 190, 193; some states as prohibiting use of, in teacher evaluations, 16, 24–26; variety of tests producing, 12–14, 158–62, 171–72. *See also* assessment; "cut scores"; "defining down" success; learning; measurement(s); observation (classroom); standardized tests; teachers; teaching (good)

time. *See* temporal issues

"trans-human," 179–80, 197, 203–4, 208, 215, 222–23

"Translation into Curriculum" (Schwab), 210

transmission model (of teaching), 18–19, 61, 110

trust (and observational descriptions of teacher quality), 14, 146–49, 167. *See also* "lying"; skepticism

truth. *See* "lying"

Tyler, Ralph, 196

Tyre, Peg, 214–15

U

Uncommon Schools, 19–20

U.S.: economic well-being of, allegedly tied to education, xiii, xiv–xv; poverty as major driver of educational inequality in, 3–4; rationalism in, 2, 4–6. *See also* education (in U.S.); U.S. Department of Education

U.S. Constitution, 8

U.S. Department of Education, xi. *See also* Duncan, Arne; Race to the Top (RTT) educational policy

"unstructured" aspects (of teaching). *See* flexible responsiveness

V

"value-added metrics," 37–41. *See also* test scores

"vehicles of reorientation," 207

visibility: lack of, of ordinary good teaching when using RTT metrics, xix, 2, 117, 120–21, 201, 217, 221, 225; of the quality of ordinary good teaching on the local level, xviii, xix, xxi, 24, 26–35, 42, 47, 52, 86, 117–20, 125, 143–45, 148–49, 157–58, 166, 177–78, 183, 189, 221

"*vorhaben*" (Heideggerian term), 117

W

Washington, D. C., 44, 161

What Computers Still Can't Do (Dreyfus), 87–88

"What to Do" technique (Lemov's), 63–70

Winograd, Terry, 92

"wisdom of practice" (Shulman's concept), 73–74, 76–77, 84–86, 116, 128, 205, 207

Wittgenstein, Ludwig, 166, 184, 216; and author's assumptions about word use, 2; author's strategy as based on, 6; on "difficulty," 193; on "family resemblances," 129, 136, 190; on grammatical axis, 146, 171; on his disappointment with knowledge, 224–25; on human shortcomings, 223; Mulhall on, 109; on rule-following in learning, 104, 127; on scientific way of thinking, 217n2; on shared judgments, 130; on "stage-setting," 180; on thinking *vs.* reflecting, 136; on training in teaching and learning, 108–15, 125, 129, 135, 180, 190, 204. *See also* Cavell, Stanley; "form of life" agreement

words. *See* language

writing: as a fluid concept, 169–70. *See also* penmanship

For Product Safety Concerns and Information please contact our EU
representative GPSR@taylorandfrancis.com
Taylor & Francis Verlag GmbH, Kaufingerstraße 24, 80331 München, Germany

www.ingramcontent.com/pod-product-compliance
Lightning Source LLC
Chambersburg PA
CBHW070244230426
43664CB00014B/2404